Robert K. Merton

A Columbia / SSRC Book

Robert K. Merton

*Sociology of Science
and Sociology as Science*

Edited by **Craig Calhoun**

Columbia University Press New York

Columbia University Press
Publishers Since 1893
New York   Chichester, West Sussex
cup.columbia.edu
Copyright © 2010 The Social Science Research Council
Paperback edition, 2017
All rights reserved

Library of Congress Cataloging-in-Publication Data
Robert K. Merton : sociology of science and sociology as science /
edited by Craig Calhoun.
p.   cm.
Includes bibliographical references and index.
"A Columbia / SSRC Book."
ISBN 978-0-231-15112-2 (cloth : alk. paper)—ISBN 978-0-231-15113-9 (pbk. : alk. paper)—
ISBN 978-0-231-52184-0 (e-book)
1. Merton, Robert King, 1910–2003. 2. Sociologists—United States.
3. Sociology—United States. 4. Science—Social aspects. 5. Science—Philosophy.
I. Calhoun, Craig J., 1952– II. Title.

HM477.U6R63 2010
301.092—dc22

2010007240

∞
Columbia University Press books are printed on permanent and durable acid-free paper.
Printed in the United States of America

Cover image: © 1995 Jim Graham/GSI, Courtesy of Harriet Zuckerman

Contents

Preface   vii

Introduction   On Merton's Legacy and Contemporary Sociology   1
Craig Calhoun

One   Reflections on a Common Theme: 32
Establishing the Phenomenon, Adumbration, and Ideal Types
Alejandro Portes

Two   Mechanisms of the Middle Range   54
Charles Tilly

Three   Eliding the Theory/Research and Basic/Applied Divides: 63
Implications of Merton's Middle Range
Robert J. Sampson

Four   The Contributions of Robert K. Merton to Culture Theory   79
Cynthia Fuchs Epstein

Five   Culture and Uncertainty   94
Viviana A. Zelizer

Six   "Paradigm for the Sociology of Science"   113
Thomas F. Gieryn

Seven   A Critical Reconsideration of the Ethos and   140
Autonomy of Science
Aaron L. Panofsky

Eight   Merton, Mannheim, and the Sociology of Knowledge   164
Alan Sica

Nine   The Ethos of Science and the Ethos of Democracy   182
Ragnvald Kalleberg

Ten   Merton's Sociology of Rhetoric   214
Peter Simonson

Eleven   On Sociological Semantics as an   253
Evolving Research Program
Harriet Zuckerman

Twelve   How Merton Sociologizes the History of Ideas   273
Charles Camic

List of Contributors   297

Index   301

Preface

Robert K. Merton was among the most influential sociologists of the twentieth century. He was the primary founder of the sociology of science, one of the clearest of all sociological theorists, and an innovator in empirical research methods. His work continues to be cited and used in the study of social structure, social psychology, deviance, professions, organizations, and culture, as well as perhaps most prominently science.

Yet, for all the fame, Merton's work is not well understood. Different aspects are prominent in different branches of sociology, but integrated perspectives on Merton's work as a whole and its implications for contemporary and future sociology are lacking. The rejection of functionalism as a dominant paradigm in sociology contributed to a tendency to see Merton's work as part of an undifferentiated mass of functionalist theory, somewhat in the shadow of Talcott Parsons's attempts to systematize. Though Merton was indeed a functional analyst, this categorization both misleads generally and obscures many specific contributions not dependent on functionalism or any other paradigm. Indeed, one of the hallmarks of Merton's work was the effort to help theory and empirical advance without tying them to any single, encompassing larger system.

For this and many other reasons, Merton's work is of considerable significance today. It speaks to challenges in both research and theory today—indeed to the challenge of better integrating research and theory and to the role of theory in connecting different fields of empirical research. It speaks to the importance of overcoming the sharp division between allegedly pure and applied sociology. It speaks to the value of a reflexive view of sociology informed by the institutional analysis of science and knowledge. And it offers a host of specific insights for a wide range of analytic concerns.

At the time of his death in 2003, Merton was perhaps the last of an extraordinary generation of sociologists whose work shaped the basic contours of the discipline in the mid-twentieth century. Understanding Merton's work is thus central to understanding the development of the discipline. Yet, the book is not primarily a work of intellectual history. It is an examination of Merton's legacy by active sociological researchers seeking to advance knowledge through renewed engagement with the work of one of sociology's pioneers. It is an effort to engage enduring and emerging intellectual agendas.

It is appropriate that Columbia University hosted the conference where early drafts of the chapters here were presented. Robert Merton taught at Columbia for more than fifty years and was among its major intellectual leaders, not only within sociology but also across the university. We are grateful to Columbia's Institute for Social and Economic Research and Policy for support. We are also grateful to the National Science Foundation, which provided a grant (SES-0411736) to support the conference, and to the Social Science Research Council for additional support, including excellent editorial assistance from Paul Price, Siovahn Walker, and Jessica Polebaum. And we are especially grateful to all those who attended the conference and made intellectual contributions to this volume although they are not authors of chapters.

Contents

In the introduction, the editor offers a brief account of Merton's work, including its development over time, the relationship among its different dimensions, its intellectual context, and its contemporary importance.

The first chapter, by Alejandro Portes, discusses a range of the different concepts that Merton contributed to sociological analysis. He shows how they are integrated in an understanding of scientific innovation, and also how transparently many are incorporated into ongoing sociological analysis without reference to their origins. Care in conceptualization is one of several links between Merton and Max Weber, as Portes emphasizes, connecting Weber's use of ideal types to Merton's understanding of how sociologists establish the phenomena by conceptualizing recurrent patterns across cases.

Charles Tilly develops a related theme in Chapter 2, with attention to Merton's famous argument for theories of the middle range. Tilly identifies this as a precursor to more recent analytic emphasis on the identification of causal mechanisms that can work in many different contexts, distinguishing it from familiar approaches such as reliance on covering laws. It is typical of Tilly that he was the first author to finish his paper, that he was the most concise of all of us, and that his original text needed little revision. Sadly, Chuck Tilly died while this book was in preparation.

In the third chapter, Robert Sampson takes up one of Merton's specific middle-range theories or paradigms, that which analyzes deviance in terms of a disjunction between culturally normative aspirations and structurally available capacities for action. One of the virtues of Merton's approach, Sampson suggests, is the extent to which it integrates theory into empirical research. This means also that successful theories are not always ones that remain unchallenged but often ones that spark new research that may lead to new theories superseding the original.

In the fourth and fifth chapters, Cynthia Fuchs Epstein and Viviana Zelizer have taken up Merton's major contributions to one of the fields of sociological research that grew rapidly after the main period of his career: the sociology of culture. Epstein shows how a variety of Merton's analytic interests inform cultural theory even though they are hardly ever cited in this regard. Merton's contributions to the study of culture come from work addressing many analytic domains from ideology to science to justice. Emphasizing such concepts as "socially expected durations," Epstein suggests reasons why current sociologists would do well to attend to Merton's work and also why categorizing it simply as "functionalist" is misleading. Zelizer also shows this labeling to be a distortion that inhibits recognition of the usefulness of Merton's work. Focusing specifically on the ways in which Merton addressed the challenge of managing uncertainty, a theme of renewed interest today, she shows how his models characteristically emphasize the interaction of five elements: culture, individual intentions, uncertainty, a set of possible outcomes of action, and a social structure.

Chapters 6 and 7 focus on Merton's founding contributions to the sociology of science, though since this interest pervaded Merton's work other chapters also address aspects of it. In Chapter 6, Thomas Gieryn asks what a paradigm for the sociology of science that would be adequate to today's research interests might look like. It would, he suggests, build importantly on Merton (who along with Kuhn introduced the term "paradigm" into the field but who didn't specifically codify one for the sociology of science). It would also incorporate contributions from works challenging Merton's approach. A pivotal challenge for the field lies in integrating institutional analysis—crucially informed by Merton—with other perspectives. In Chapter 7, Aaron Panofsky combines a critical reconsideration of Merton's approach to the autonomy of science, and his emphasis on the ethos of science, with an argument for the continued centrality of Merton's core concerns. He argues for complementing Merton's approach with greater attention to issues of power and struggles for authority. Drawing examples from emergent subfields in genetics, he suggests that science has changed in important ways from what Merton studied, but that an integrated approach to scientific institutions and knowledge production such as Merton sought is, if anything, even more important today.

This raises the question of the relationship between the sociology of science as the study of a specific institutional formation and the more general idea of the sociology of knowledge. In Chapter 8, Alan Sica takes up the question of why Merton did not stay consistently engaged with the field of sociology of knowledge in the form in which Karl Mannheim and other German thinkers had launched it. This was clearly an early interest of Merton, but he came to reject Mannheim's *Wissensoziologie* and to emphasize the more institutionally specific approach to sociology of science. Sica emphasizes a mixture of historical accidents, personal predilections, and sociological reasons. As he evinces regret that the connection between Merton and Mannheim wasn't stronger and more positive, he also suggests opportunities for new sociological work.

In Chapter 9, Ragnvald Kalleberg links Merton's analysis of the ethos of science to a more general concern for normative argumentation and the workings of democratic debate. Merton's classic account of the relationship between science and democracy remains relevant, Kalleberg suggests, but sociological analysis has advanced because of its integration with more recent work on speech acts and discourse. The analysis of ethos needs to be complemented by attention to argumentation. This is not at all foreign to Merton's sociological interests, Peter Simonson argues, for Merton had an enduring concern for rhetoric. This shaped his own writing, but equally he saw it as an important object of sociological attention. Thus, in Chapter 10, Simonson draws on a range of Merton's work to show how Merton developed an implicit sociology of rhetoric that complements his more explicit sociologies of science and specialized knowledge. He relates this to the more literary and philosophical revivals undertaken by Kenneth Burke, Marshall McLuhan, and Richard McKeon and suggests that renewed attention to Merton's work should help occasion a renewal in sociological attention to rhetoric.

Chapter 11, by Harriet Zuckerman, pursues the cognate theme of sociological semantics. She uses Merton's last published book, *The Travels and Adventures of Serendipity: A Study in Sociological Semantics and the Sociology of Science*, as her point of departure. But as this book was published forty years after it was written, it is not surprising that it reveals interests evolving through his career. She shows early Mertonian engagements with the problems that he would later label sociological semantics, and traces the evolution of the research program through *On the Shoulders of Giants* and other work. She also reveals the importance of making sociological semantics more explicit as a research program.

As Zuckerman notes, the conference on Merton's work offered an illustration of the concept of serendipity in the coincidence that both her paper and Charles Camic's paper, now revised as the book's final chapter, emphasize the importance of sociological semantics. They have revealed this to be serendipity, not mere chance—since serendipity refers to chances that prepared minds can seize as opportunity—by going on to collaborate fruitfully on further work in this area. In his chapter, Camic focuses on Merton as a historian of ideas, and specifically the ways in which he is a very sociological historian of ideas. Attention to the role of semantics is a core dimension of this intersection of sociology and the history of ideas. Camic helpfully shows that Merton's famous distinction between the history and systematics of sociological theory should not be taken, as it too often is, to imply that intellectual history is not a properly sociological concern or one that can make contributions to systematic theory.

This is a fitting point with which to end this preface. Engagement with Robert Merton's work at once illuminates a key phase in the history of sociology, renews our grasp of his own key contributions to sociological analysis, and gives impetus and guidance to new sociological research and continued advancement of theory.

Craig Calhoun

Robert K. Merton

Introduction

On Merton's Legacy
and Contemporary Sociology

CRAIG CALHOUN

Robert K. Merton was among the most influential sociologists of the twentieth century. His influence stemmed from intellectual innovation and institutional leadership. It was enhanced by his pellucid prose style, which made his work easy for teachers and research-oriented sociologists to grasp and put to use. It was extended by a combination of modeling and mentoring that inspired and shaped a generation of students who themselves included a range of remarkable leaders.

Context also mattered. As much as anyone, Merton shaped the institutions and style of American sociology during the era of its remarkable postwar expansion. He sought to make the discipline academically respectable but also to make it matter. One of sociology's most remarkable and polymathic intellectuals, he sought to establish the discipline not on the basis of individual genius but on high standards for consistent productivity in the sociological craft.

Along with Talcott Parsons, the noted Harvard sociologist, Merton introduced a new level of explicit theoretical rigor into American sociology. Parsons positioned himself as the importer and synthesizer of crucial European work, and then as the auteur of his own theoretical system ready to stand alongside Weber and Durkheim in a sociological pantheon. Merton, by contrast, made himself the empirical researcher's theorist. He channeled American as well as European forebears into conceptual frameworks, paradigms, and middle-range theories that focused empirical research on explanatory problems beyond the immediate data. At the same time, he probed empirical research for theoretically useful ideas initially left implicit.

Unlike Parsons, Merton was himself an empirical researcher of note. Seeking to understand the influence of religion, economy, and other factors on early modern science, for his dissertation research he coded the biographies of six thousand entries in the *Dictionary of National Biography* by hand (Merton 1938a). Seeking ways to explore opinion formation and response to media, Merton invented the focus group, or as he initially called it, focused group interview (Merton, Fiske, and Kendall 1956). With his long-term friend and collaborator Paul Lazarsfeld, and through the institution of the Bureau of Applied Social Research, he pursued through much of his career what one might think of as a professional practice in applied and problem-oriented research. Bureau research projects sometimes addressed issues the two men cared about as left-liberals, or to use a term more European than American, social democrats.[1] More consistently, the Bureau garnered resources from corporate and foundation sponsors to conduct research that enabled them to explore innovations in theory and methods (and not coincidentally to keep generations of graduate students employed and learning research by practical experience).

Merton's influence on twentieth century sociology derives from his example and passionate advocacy for an integration of theory and research; his emphasis on lucidity in prose, analysis, and most especially in concepts; and his training of an extraordinary group of early graduate students. It derives also from his formulations of explanatory paradigms, as he called them, that deeply shaped, reshaped, or even launched whole fields of research: anomie and deviance, bureaucracy, mass media, and science as a social institution. And it derives from his extraordinary ability to encapsulate whole intellectual agendas in crisp concepts: unanticipated consequences, opportunity structure, self-fulfilling prophecy, role model, and others.

Many of the concepts Merton coined passed into everyday usage. And in a similar way, many of his scholarly contributions passed into the everyday practice and collective history of sociology without any continuing attribution. His influence, thus, is obscured by what he himself labeled "obliteration by incorporation." It is also obscured, however, by the tendency to read his work in fragmentary ways defined by his contributions to what has become a wide range of separate, specialized fields, and by sociology's own weakness in integrating knowledge across its subfields. Merton's contributions are many, but the significance of rereading Merton does not lie in the sum of them. It lies at least as much and perhaps more importantly in reinvigorating connections between theory and research and between different subfields in order to advance sociology in general, as a common enterprise, not a collection of discrete particulars. It is to this that the present volume is especially addressed, a project of history with systematic intent.[2]

Early Career

Robert Merton was born July 4, 1910, and his extraordinary life story evokes both the universalism of science and an American trajectory appropriate to his holiday birthday. Merton's parents were Jewish immigrants from Eastern Europe, and the future R. K. M. was born Meyer R. Schkolnick. The family lived above his father's small dairy products shop in South Philadelphia until it burned down, without insurance, and his father became a carpenter's assistant. Merton's family lacked wealth, but he insisted his childhood did not lack opportunity, and cited such institutions as a very decent public high school and the library donated by Andrew Carnegie in which he first read *Tristram Shandy* and more generally pursued a passionate self-education. Indeed, suggested Merton in 1994, the seemingly deprived South Philadelphia slum in which he grew up provided "a youngster with every sort of capital—social capital, cultural capital, human capital, and, above all, what we may call public capital—that is, with every sort of capital except the personally financial" (Merton 1994a).[3]

The name Robert King Merton evolved out of a teenage career as an amateur magician. Merton took up conjuring partly through taking his sister's boyfriend as a "role model" (to borrow a phrase literally his own).[4] As his own skill improved, he sought a stage name, initially "Merlin." Advised that this was hackneyed, he changed it to Merton. Already devoted to tracing origins, he chose a first name after Robert Houdin, the French magician whose name Harry Houdini (himself originally Erich Weiss) had adapted. And when he won a scholarship to Temple College he was content to let the new name (with its echoes of one of the oldest and greatest colleges at each of Cambridge and Oxford) become permanent. He entered the legal name change at nineteen.

At Temple, a school founded for "the poor boys and girls of Philadelphia" and not yet fully accredited or matured into a university, Merton chanced on a wonderful undergraduate teacher. It was serendipity, he later insisted. The sociologist George E. Simpson took him on as a research assistant in a project on race and the media—"the Philadelphia Negro and the Press"—and introduced him not only to sociology but also to Ralph Bunche and E. Franklin Frazier. Simpson also took Merton to the annual meeting of the American Sociological Society (as the ASA was called in those pre-acronym days), where he met Pitirim Sorokin, founding chair of the Harvard sociology department. He applied to Harvard, even though his teachers told him this was usually beyond the reach of those graduating from Temple. And when he arrived, Sorokin took him on as a research assistant. By Merton's third year they were publishing together—though note that in his second year Merton wrote articles that appeared in *Social Forces* and the *American Journal of Sociology*.[5]

In addition to Sorokin, Merton apprenticed himself to the historian of science George Sarton, not just for his stay at Harvard but for years of epistolary exchanges that Merton loved. It was Sarton who arranged publication of his doctoral dissertation. Merton resembled Sorokin and Sarton in his extraordinarily wide-ranging reading, but as he developed his specific style of sociological analysis other influences were central. He participated in Lawrence J. Henderson's famed Pareto reading group (alongside Talcott Parsons, George C. Homans, Joseph Schumpeter, Crane Brinton, and Elton Mayo). Pareto's idea of "motivating sentiments" was an enduring influence. And he decided late in his graduate student career to sit in on the first theory course offered by the young Talcott Parsons, just back from Europe and working through the ideas that would become *The Structure of Social Action*.[6]

The encounter with Parsons—serendipity again (perhaps)—did not just inform Merton's knowledge of European theory, but deepened his idea of sociology itself. Still, as he wrote later, "although much impressed by Parsons as a master-builder of sociological theory, I found myself departing from his mode of theorizing (as well as his mode of exposition)" (Merton 1994a:4).[7] The laconic parenthesis is telling. Merton is among the clearest and most careful prose stylists in sociology. He edited each essay over and again, even after publication, and left behind added footnotes and revisions both large and small to a host of his writings. It is easy to imagine that he might have been a professional editor had he not been an academic.

Indeed, it is easy to imagine the young Merton turning in any of several directions. His first articles, written as a graduate student and published in 1934–6, addressed the concepts of "Civilization and Culture," "The Course of Arabian Intellectual Development, 700–1300 A.D.," "Fluctuations in the Rate of Industrial Invention," "Science and Military Technique," and "The Unintended Consequences of Purposive Social Action." They appeared in journals of sociology, the history of science, economics, and simply science. As Alan Sica suggests in Chapter 8, Merton's early engagements were deeply informed by German approaches to the sociology of knowledge as well as by recent French sociology and by his own teachers. Merton turned away from this hermeneutic framework, Sica thinks mistakenly, as he did from Sorokin's approach to synthetic history. He was ultimately perhaps more Durkheimian.

Merton wrote his dissertation on *Science, Technology and Society in Seventeenth Century England* (Merton 1938a).[8] This argued a "Merton Thesis" about the influence of Puritanism on early modern science, complementary to that of Max Weber on the relationship between the Protestant ethic and the spirit of capitalism. Narrowly, this was that "Puritanism, and ascetic Protestantism generally, emerges as an emotionally consistent system of beliefs, sentiments and action which played no small part in arousing a sustained interest in science" (Merton 1938a:495). More broadly, Merton argued that social and cultural factors (including religion, economics, and military pursuits) shaped interest in science, scientific problem choice, and the public reception and influence of science. He resisted, however, the relativist conclusion that such external influences so shaped the internal content of science as to undermine its truth-value. But the study broke new ground simply for taking the explanation of the behavior of scientists as an empirical, sociological research problem. In the process, the book helped to invent the sociology of science.

Merton argued that science is misunderstood as the product of individual geniuses able to break free from conventions and norms. Instead, he stressed the "ethos of science," the normative structure specific to the field that encouraged productivity, critical thinking, and the pursuit of continually improved understanding (Merton 1938b, 1942).[9] This was significant not only as part of his historical explanatory project but also as the basis for grasping why science needed relative autonomy in the contemporary era. It offered the basis for a pointed critique of "Nazi science."

To his disappointment, Merton was not hired on as a regular Harvard faculty member. He served a stint as an instructor, then got a good job at Tulane. Neither was a small thing in the midst of the Great Depression. Yet neither was a Harvard professorship, something denied to Merton at least partly because he was a Jew. At Tulane he became a full professor and Chair of the Department of Sociology within a year of his arrival. Then in 1941 he moved to Columbia University. His situation there was propitious. Columbia was entering an era of leadership and intellectual excitement, particularly in the social sciences.[10] But this was not entirely an accident. Columbia distinguished itself among the elite universities of the Ivy League partly by shedding its anti-Semitism earlier and attracting distinguished Jewish faculty members. Location in New York was an added advantage.

The issue of Jewish identity is worth raising as a reminder that Merton, and also immigrants like Paul Lazarsfeld, had reason to feel insecure about their status in the university even as their prestige grew. Merton's name change was not simply whimsical (even if the specific choice of a new name was in part). Nor was it idiosyncratically individual. It was part of the generational experience of Jewish immigrants and their children in the mid-twentieth-century United States. This no doubt attuned Merton to the relationship between social structure and social psychology generally, and to problems of race in particular. In 1940 he joined with the more extravagantly renamed Montague Francis Ashley Montagu to write a stinging rebuttal to an effort to explain crime in biological and partially racial terms (Merton 1939).[11] Montagu was born Israel Ehrenberg. It seems all too likely that the authors would have been received differently without the name changes (Haber 2008).

Still, by the time he was forty Merton was one of America's most influential social scientists and had embarked on a lengthy career at Columbia University. A crucial component of this career was friendship and collegueship with Paul Lazarsfeld. This not only could not have been predicted, but one imagines that their senior colleagues at Columbia would have bet against it. The two men were hired to resolve a conflict between senior leaders of the department. Robert Lynd wanted an empirical researcher; Robert MacIver wanted a theorist. Instead of hiring either at a senior level they hired relatively junior sociologists in each category. The two were wary of each other at first, but Lazarsfeld (slightly the senior) decided to reach out and invite Merton to dinner. In Merton's reminiscence, friendship and collaboration alike were born when Lazarsfeld took him to watch a group interview session that was part of a study of audience response to war propaganda (run for the delightfully named Office of Facts and Figures, predecessor to the Office of War Information). Merton watched with interest then was quick to critique the research approach. The two men fell almost immediately into eager collaboration (at least as they used to tell the story), forgetting dinner and the wives they had left behind. This was the beginning of the trajectory that led Merton to develop the focused group interview (working in part with Patricia Kendall, a graduate assistant who was to become Lazarsfeld's next wife). It was also the beginning of a remarkable collaboration. Ample honors and achievements would follow.

Context

Although Merton published enduringly important work while still a student and junior faculty member in the 1930s, he became truly famous only after World War II. He played a central role in shaping American sociology in an era of enormous expansion that was also an era of decisive professionalization. The field grew not only in numbers but also in public recognition and academic institutionalization. Two generations of remarkable researchers—those like Merton who received doctorates just before the war and those who entered sociology just after—at once established major lines of specialized research and ranged across them in major studies that influenced the field as a whole. Ambitions for the field were great and indeed many remember the period as sociology's golden age. Yet the climax of this golden age came during the crisis of the 1960s. Protests inspired partly by sociological analyses were joined to criticism of older sociologists for accommodating themselves too much to dominant structures of American society.

American universities grew dramatically through the 1950s and '60s, supported by the GI Bill, a growing economy, a population boom, an infusion of immigrant scholars, and a renewed optimism that knowledge could bring progress. Sociology was a relatively new discipline and the era of general expansion in higher education gave it a chance to grow. Indeed, sociology grew very disproportionately as one of the most popular fields for the burgeoning undergraduate population.

Still, the legitimacy of sociology was often in question.[12] Departments of sociology dated only from the 1890s. The field had grown in the early twentieth century with strong extra-academic ties—to Chautauqua, settlement houses, Christian socialism, and labor and reform movements. It had more than its share of radicals. This raised the hackles of more conservative academics, as it would again in the 1960s and '70s. During the 1930s, the ranks of sociologists actually shrank—the ASA lost a quarter of its members. Sociologists had not been central players in Roosevelt's New Deal (like economists and political scientists) and were concerned about bolstering their professional standing. Research in support of the war effort in the 1940s gave sociology renewed momentum (for historical context see Calhoun 2007). Merton himself did some of this research, partly in collaboration with Paul Lazarsfeld, and one project led to his second book, *Mass Persuasion: the Social Psychology of a War Bond Drive* (Merton, Fiske, and Curtis 1946; Merton and Lazarsfeld 1950).

After the War, sociology not only expanded and gained firm institutional bases in universities, but also brought research to bear on many of the major issues that animated public discussions, private anxieties, social conflicts, and government interventions. Foundations and government agencies called on sociologists for "applied" research. Merton was among those who responded. He was a leader in the sociological study of bureaucracy, including studies of business organizations and government agencies (e.g., Merton 1940; Merton and Devereux 1956).[13] He addressed issues of technology and the transformation of work and workplaces (see Merton 1947). He examined the sociology of housing in an era of massive construction in cities and especially suburbs (see Merton et al. 1951a, 1951b;).[14] He conducted influential research on prejudice and racial integration.[15] In the wake of McCarthyism and widespread censorship, he coauthored a defense and analysis of the freedom to read (see Merton, McKeon, and Gellhorn 1957). He analyzed the nature of medical education, and professionalization more generally (see Merton et al. 1957). And he addressed the nature and social significance of mass communication in several studies (Merton, Fiske, and Curtis 1946; Merton 1949).[16]

Merton and other leaders sought both to lay strong foundations for the maturation of the discipline and to defend it against detractors from older, more established fields. To this end they also sought to strengthen its internal quality control and adherence to professional norms. Indeed, Merton presented his major book, *Social Theory and Social Structure*, as an effort to bring theoretical rigor to qualitative analysis (Merton 1968a).[17] Likewise, particularly in partnership with Paul Lazarsfeld, Merton also sought to build institutions to strengthen knowledge production. Columbia was already a major center for graduate education in sociology when Merton arrived in 1941, but with Lazarsfeld and other colleagues he made it the single most influential base for Ph.D. training. Lazarsfeld's Austrian roots, Merton's knowledge of European theory and languages, and Columbia's location in New York made it especially attractive to a number of European immigrants like Lewis Coser and Peter Blau as well as to younger Americans like Alvin Gouldner, Peter Rossi, and James Coleman. Merton and Lazarsfeld built the Bureau for Applied Social Research as a research base, simultaneously gaining financial support from projects undertaken for corporate and foundation sponsors and involving graduate students as apprentices in projects from which they would learn the trade. At an interdisciplinary level, and emphasizing more purely academic work rather than applied research, Merton and Lazarsfeld played central roles in creating the Center for Advanced Study in the Behavioral Sciences in California.[18]

In effect, Merton and others resumed a sort of professionalization campaign that had started in sociology during the 1930s. The *American Sociological Review* was founded in 1936 as the official journal of the American Sociological Association amid a struggle in which the winning faction claimed to be professionalizers while others, more loosely organized but associated broadly with "Chicago-style" sociology, resisted both institutionalization of a new disciplinary hierarchy and a more exclusive emphasis on academic research over activism and public engagement. Merton was involved even as a graduate student, writing "The Unintended Consequences of Purposive Social Action" for the first volume of the *ASR* in 1936. But if Merton was unambiguously a professionalizer, he was nonetheless much more interested in and knowledgeable about earlier

American sociology than his fellow professionalizer and theorist Talcott Parsons. He drew extensively, for example, on W. I. Thomas and others associated with the Chicago School—not least in his use of "the Thomas Theorem" to develop his own idea of the "self-fulfilling prophecy" (Merton 1968b, 1995). He engaged actively in the study of social problems and publication to advance teaching (Merton and Nisbet 1961).[19] He sought to integrate the different branches of sociology, seeking to avoid pitched battles. Already there were tensions between theorists and researchers, qualitative and quantitative researchers, advocates for pure science and for applied research, seekers after academic status and proponents of public engagement. It is instructive that Merton did important work on each side of each of these divisions.

Above all, Merton published journal articles that formulated issues in systematic ways, addressed them by developing concepts and theory that were informed by empirical research but still abstracted from particular cases, and suggested programs for continuing research. "Social Structure and Anomie" appeared in the *ASR* in 1938; "Bureaucratic Structure and Personality" followed in *Social Forces* in 1939 (see Merton 1968c, 1968d). Each became widely influential in the postwar period, partly because Merton included them in *Social Theory and Social Structure*, because his own growing prominence gave them added weight, and because he encouraged Columbia graduate students to follow them up with new work. Each began to be reprinted in anthologies from the late 1940s on. Each helped to define a subfield of sociology and enlisted other sociologists to advance the work each inaugurated. Merton celebrated the ongoing research process in articles and books on the "continuities" in different lines of work (see Merton and Lazarsfeld 1950; Merton 1968e, 1968f). This was different from offering a synthesis of existing theory, as Parsons did with great distinction by publishing *The Structure of Social Action* at about the same time (Parsons [1937] 1961).

Merton's approach made his work influential but also encouraged what he would later term "obliteration by incorporation" (Merton 1968g, 1979).[20] He embraced the idea that good scientific work should contribute to making itself obsolete as science (though it might remain interesting as history). This he signaled by selecting an epigraph from Alfred North Whitehead: "A science which hesitates to forget its founders is lost." As he explained in considering the development of reference group theory,

William James, Charles Horton Cooley, and W. I. Thomas all contributed insights that anticipated the eventual theory. But,

> their conceptions were treated, not as a beginning but as a virtual conclusion, repeatedly quoted and illustrated with new examples of multiple selves, the looking-glass self, responses to the significant gestures of "others" and so on. And because the words of the forefathers became final words, little was built upon their insightful suggestions. They were honored, not in the manner in which men of science do honor to their predecessors, by extending and elaborating their formulations on the basis of cumulatively developed problems and systematic researches bearing on these problems, but in the manner in which littérateurs honor their predecessors, by repeatedly quoting "definitive" passages from the masters' works (Merton and Rossi 1968:332).

Merton saw the process of scientific-knowledge creation as inherently incomplete, and saw premature closure as a problem. This was closely related to another crucial argument of Merton's early work: that science is misunderstood as the product of individual geniuses able to break free from conventions and norms. Instead, he stressed the "ethos of science," the normative structure specific to the field that encouraged productivity, critical thinking, and the pursuit of continually improved understanding (e.g., Merton [1937] 1973, 1973a). He was seldom happy when students left the Mertonian fold in their efforts to push sociology forward, but he recognized that this was how science worked—and analysis of scientific and sociological ambivalence was among his themes (Merton 1976).

In the same spirit, the present book does not remain entirely at the level of celebration. To be sure, its engagement with the work of Robert Merton is partly an effort to strengthen our grasp of the history of the discipline. But it is even more an effort to invigorate sociology today, strengthening connections among subfields and between theory and research so that sociology can keep improving. It is intended to help sociologists take up a range of issues and see how they could be addressed more clearly and productively. This includes examining critically the limits of Merton's formulations or their received interpretations, as for example Robert Sampson (in Chapter 3 below) considers how well Merton's influential theory of deviance squares with contemporary research, and Thomas Gieryn and

Aaron Panofsky consider Merton's sociology of science in light of more recent developments in Chapters 6 and 7.

Influence

Robert Merton was the primary founder of the sociology of science, an enormously influential sociological theorist, and an innovator in empirical research methods. His work continues to be cited and used in the study of social structure, social psychology, deviance, professions, organizations, and culture as well as science. But, though cited frequently, Merton's work is often not read deeply—the citations are part of a ritual of the reproduction of status and legitimacy that Merton himself analyzed (Merton 1973b; Cronin 1984; Small 2004).

On the one hand, there are citations, especially in science studies, that use Merton to identify an older approach to which authors contrast their own claims to be part of the new. Real disagreements did indeed separate Merton from new trends in science studies in the 1970s and '80s, principally about the capacities of social-institutional analysis and about how much respect to accord science as a successful project of knowledge production. But a generation later many writers cite without reading, and seek simply to symbolize their distance from a rejected approach. Commonly, they misrepresent Merton, for example treating his account of the normative order of science as though it were a simplistic (and therefore false and naïve) account of actual scientific practice. And it is not only in science studies that certain of Merton's publications are cited more as icons of a caricatured position than for the substance of their arguments.

On the other hand there are citations that claim Merton for the lineage of Great Thinkers on the shoulders of which a current analyst seeks to stand. While some of these are thoughtful, many are based on little more actual engagement with Merton's texts than the dismissive citations of those who want to distance themselves from him. Several of Merton's contributions have yielded phrases in common usage, but their provenance is often forgotten and their intellectual significance frequently reduced by remembering the catchphrase and not the context in which it was introduced.

Obliteration by incorporation is perhaps the happiest reason Merton's work is not as well known today as his enduring fame and his influence during the postwar era would suggest. Obliteration by incorporation may be bittersweet, but there was no doubt satisfaction in seeing ideas he introduced and fields he helped create both absorb what he had offered and move forward in continued creativity. Merton lived to see his concept of opportunity structure become prominent in new contexts, and to see at least the beginning of the recent vogue for identifying causal "mechanisms" that can function in explanations of disparate phenomena, which of course reproduces important aspects of his notion of middle-range theories (see discussion by Charles Tilly in Chapter 2 below).

But the significance of Merton's work is also obscured for three other reasons, each a bit less happy. First, there was a broad turn against functionalism in the 1960s and 1970s. Though Parsons was a more central target, there was a tendency to see Merton's work as part of an undifferentiated mass of functionalist theory. Merton was indeed a functional analyst, but this categorization both misleads generally and obscures many specific contributions not dependent on functionalism or any other paradigm. Merton also suffered simply from being placed on the "old" side of a generational divide reinforced by both political and theoretical objections. This happened even though Merton had distanced himself from doctrinaire, all-encompassing functionalist synthesis, emphasizing for example that middle-range theories such as role sets could be compatible with Marxism as well as functionalism and other very different theoretical frameworks (Merton 1968h:43). It happened even though he had been much more sympathetic to critical perspectives than many others in sociology's elite—in different ways sponsoring both Alvin Gouldner and C. Wright Mills.[21] And indeed it happened even though Merton denied that social cohesion could be assumed as "normal" and was more attentive to the role of conflict than other leading functionalist theorists.[22] Despite all these ways in which Merton was less extreme in his functionalism, he was in the end still perceived as arguing that overall "the system" worked.

Whatever intellectual reasons may have mattered, younger sociologists also saw Merton as much too identified with a normatively "professional" idea of the sociologist's proper role in an era that they thought demanded activist engagements. Not least, when faced with the intra-university struggles of 1968—as intense at Columbia as anywhere—Merton found himself unable to side with protesting students against the administration (including his friend Jacques Barzun) and it was a moment when there was not much of a liberal middle ground to claim.

The charged political context made rejecting functionalism something of a litmus test that seemed to reveal theoretical sophistication as well as political correctness. What self-respecting graduate student would want to support a theory so thoroughly criticized? Ironically, this was reinforced by Parsons's presentation of functionalism as an all-encompassing system (not to mention his prose). What this obscured was the possibility of recognizing functional analysis (or, as Merton preferred, structural-functional analysis) as one exceptionally useful sociological approach, but only one tool among several.

Merton tried to avoid elevation (or reduction) of a theoretical framework or analytic perspective to an orthodoxy or "ism." This approach fits poorly with the tendency to teach theory as a matter of great systems associated with individual authors. But taking Merton's approach seriously would not mean giving license to empirical researchers to produce analyses devoid of theoretical reflection. On the contrary, it would demand more self-reflective explanatory work, integrating reflection on analytic strategies such as functional analysis, including the critiques of functional analysis, into work that would be simultaneously empirical and theoretical.

This raises the second reason the importance of Merton's work is systematically obscured, the common practice of teaching sociology in three tracks: (1) general theory (often bundled with the history of sociology, and presented as the succession of theoretical orientations more than the cumulative development of explanatory power); (2) methods (focused heavily on techniques of statistical analysis, rather than "methodology" as the understanding of the how different methods work and how the choice of methods influences research); and (3) empirical subfields, each more or less disconnected from each other and from general theory and methods. It was a virtue of Merton's work to combine the three. And the effort to improve their mutual connections should be a goal now.

Indeed, one might interpret Merton's work as an implicit critique of the way in which sociology has separated these domains. Merton saw the project of sociology as a matter of producing increasingly clear accounts of social life that identified general processes and thereby allowed for the study of variation and change and that revealed the connections between different empirical instances and dimensions. As he put it:

Each to his last, and the last of the sociologist is that of lucidly presenting claims to logically interconnected and empirical confirmed propositions about the structure of society and its changes, the behavior of man within that structure and the consequences of that behavior (Merton 1968h:70).

Merton's metaphor is noteworthy: the shoemaker's last invokes an image of sociology as a craft. The sociologist uses tools (theory, methods) to produce a specific sort of object (systematic knowledge of society and social behavior). The production process includes empirical investigations that generate new findings but also, centrally, efforts to interpret the significance of those findings in light of other research, careful conceptualization, and a continual process of integration of sociological knowledge.

Merton does not argue against seeing sociology as a science. On the contrary, the quoted passage follows a discussion of why codification of sociological theory into paradigms is crucial if sociology is to become a science like chemistry, physics, or biology. Nor does he favor a purely empiricist approach. Paradigms have the function of bringing central concepts and their interrelations into simultaneous view. They lessen the likelihood of smuggling hidden assumptions and concepts into theory. They advance cumulation of theoretical interpretation, call attention to gaps, inconsistencies, and other problems, and enable qualitative analysis to attain rigor often associated only with quantification. "Paradigms for sociological analysis are intended to help the sociologist work at his trade" (Merton 1968h:70).[23]

As Alejandro Portes shows in Chapter 1 below, the intellectual work of research starts with establishing the phenomenon under study. Merton recognized this, arguing that effective analysis cannot be a response to data as such without prior conceptualization. Conceptualization itself needs to be thoughtful and based on clear understanding of alternatives and their implications. Significant intellectual labor is involved in the task (though it is too often slighted). Merton built on Max Weber's notion of ideal types and his practice of sociological semantics was intended to improve this process.

Only with the phenomena established and a clear grasp of analytic strategies in mind, Merton suggested, could researchers be effective in generating explanatory models that might reveal generalizable features. Generalization is not a matter of facts that hold true without restrictions of scope, but rather of significant explanatory models that can work in different domains. This is at the heart of his idea of theories of the middle range. Science could advance by developing explanations of particular phenomena, then identifying causal models that could be abstracted from the particular cases, and then studying the extent to which these might operate in other kinds of phenomena. The generalizations might always depend in part on analogies, rather than strict universal identities. But the process would enable analysts to become clearer both about how causal processes worked, and about the commonalities across analytic domains. The strategy anticipates that which has been discussed more recently under the rubric of "mechanisms" (as Tilly notes below). A specific model is transposable into new domains, even where other empirical factors differ. And here is a key way in which research and theory are integrated.

Third, Merton's work is inadequately understood today because it invites a fragmentary reading in which researchers find pieces they can use—or argue with—in their own subfields and pay little attention to the whole. Each fragment is understood mainly as a contribution to a different explanatory problem in a different subfield. Even those who do draw in deeper and more substantial ways on Merton's writings typically draw on a subset identified with a particular line of sociological theory and research. Few of those who draw on Merton's theory of deviance have much awareness of his work in the sociology of science; those who recognize his contributions to the study of bureaucracy may not even know of his work on anomie.

In a certain sense, this is the product of Merton's own approach. He argued for the integration of sociological theory into research. He accepted the development of specialized research fields as necessary to the maturation of the discipline. And he held that broad theoretical synthesis was at once premature and less helpful than the development of theories of the middle range (Merton 1968h, 1968j, 1968k). Merton presented his work largely in discrete essays. Many of these essays introduced an elegant term or phrase to identify the analytic strategy deployed: "unintended consequences," "manifest and latent functions," and indeed "middle-range theories." The phrases served as mnemonic devices but often came to be remembered by themselves with little connection to Merton's original argument. Moreover, each of Merton's essays was crafted as a "whole," not immediately invoking or demanding a larger framework for its understanding.

One might compare the work of Talcott Parsons. Not only did Parsons write mainly in the form of long books. The phrases he introduced generally derived their meaning from labeling a feature of the larger architecture of his theory. "Pattern variables" is not complete in itself; it demands explication, a list. It offers an invitation to expositors, interpreters, and even critics. Merton never wrote an exposition of his overall intellectual perspective codified as a "system of thought," which means that though he was widely known as a theorist, his work is relatively refractory to reading and teaching as "theory."

Enduring Importance

Nonetheless, as Sztompka suggests, "Merton's work constitutes a coherent system of thought, not a scattered set of contributions" (1986).[24] The effort to develop a more integrated perspective on Merton's work is well worthwhile and several of the chapters below are helpful in this regard. But the higher stakes are in developing an integrated perspective on sociology. Here the point is less the integration of Merton's work than the assistance Merton's work offers in thinking about the ways theory, methods, and research can be better integrated.

Merton's understanding of scientific work centers on individual scientists who engage in practical problem-solving activity.[25] They may conduct experiments or gather field observations, but they do so in ways focused by the attempt to resolve intellectual problems (whether these are raised by difficulties using existing knowledge in practice or by efforts to improve knowledge for its own sake). These problems enable them to choose strategic sites for and approaches to research.[26] Their work is guided by broad value commitments (the norms of science) and organized in an institutional structure (which both constrains and rewards), and is in principle cumulative. Merton does not deny that institutional structure may extend to a division of labor that assigns different parts of the overall process to different workers, but neither does he focus on the possibility that this would undermine the craft character of science, including the integration of its different dimensions in the work of individual craft scientists. Merton was himself such a craft scientist and he sought to nurture the same integrated approach in his students.

The development and expansion of sociology as a discipline, however, came with a deficit in integration. While division into subfields might be part of a productive division of labor, this would require a stronger performance than sociology has exhibited in connecting different research domains through theory and mobilizing research to advance theory. Equally, it would require integrating the selection and improvement of research methods more into a common conversation about theory and research strategy. Too often sociological methods are taught as mere technique. Too often researchers simply deploy the techniques they have mastered as hammers for which all research problems are nails. Too often they master only those techniques currently in fashion, rather than taking seriously the strengths and weaknesses of different methods, analyzing their capacities to disclose and their tendencies to obscure.

Parsons of course thought that his functionalist theory could provide the basis not just for connection but also for holistic synthesis. Merton was delicate in criticism of his friend and sometime teacher. He may have distinguished his approach to middle-range theory in part simply to create a space for his own work that would not involve a direct confrontation. But he also worried both that Parsons's attempt at grand synthesis was premature (his main public criticism), and also that its very holism would maximize its autonomous standing as one among other great theories, but inhibit its role as part of a living, continuously improved integration of theory and research. This seems indeed to have happened. To be sure, for twenty years a great deal of sociological research and analysis was presented in Parsonsian—and more generally functionalist—vocabulary. And Parsonsian theory was a central target of those who sought to "shift the paradigm" of sociological analysis in the 1960s and '70s. Merton was swept up in the same maelstrom, and his work more fully eclipsed than Parsons's—partly because it wasn't presented as an integrated theory to be arranged in the series of sociological classics or to be attacked from the vantage point of another integrated theory.

To a considerable extent Parsons synthesized previous theoretical work. His functionalist synthesis could inform research but didn't produce a dynamic interaction of research and theorization. What Merton called for was synthesis of ongoing empirical research, including both its explicit and implicit findings and interpretations of their significance. The synthesis would provide guidance in the development of new research projects and constitute a systematic summary of what was known. It would constitute knowledge not as so many particulars but as a set of models for how one or another feature or dimension of social life worked.

When C. Wright Mills famously mocked the sociology of the 1950s as divided between "abstracted empiricism" and "grand theory," he offered a critique very much in line with Merton's thinking. Mills didn't directly attack Merton, but he infuriated Merton by his disrespectful tone and by taking Merton's friends Lazarsfeld and Parsons as representatives of the two denigrated extremes. Anxious for sociology to gain respect and standing as a science, Merton hardly thought Mills's populist critique productive. But he and Mills shared the sense that the real action was neither in purely theoretical synthesis nor in the accumulation of an ever-larger body of apparently factual information however sophisticated the methods used to construct or present it. Much more than Mills, Merton labored to demonstrate what might lie between the two poles.

Merton's influence—and that of his partnership with Lazarsfeld—was expressed partly through Merton's extraordinary teaching and work as a mentor to young researchers. Impressively, many of these attained distinction both as theorists and researchers. Many worked also with diverse methods; for example, such famous "quantitative" sociologists as Peter Blau and James Coleman did some of their most influential research through qualitative fieldwork.

Among Merton's students were such disparate but important sociologists as Peter Blau, James Coleman, Jonathan and Stephen Cole, Lewis Coser, Rose Coser, Alvin Gouldner, Seymour Martin Lipset, and Alice Rossi (as well as several contributors to this volume including Cynthia Epstein, Viviana Zelizer, and Harriet Zuckerman). In the work of all, even those who took up different paths from Merton's own, one can see not only Merton's specific ideas but also the distinctive style of combining theory and research characteristic of Columbia sociology during his time there. Four features were especially important to this approach:

1. The attempt to be theoretically explicit enough, but also modest enough, to produce theoretical sociology that could be continually improved through application and testing in empirical research (including research assessing practical action and historical experience)
2. The use of theoretical analyses to formulate empirical research agendas and analytically useful concepts that would both open up new insight into their immediate objects and enable systematic comparison and identification of general features in the specific cases
3. The development of new lines of inquiry, and where necessary new methods of research, in order to pursue intellectual problems of major significance (rather than merely repeating or refining existing models or generalizations)

4. The attempt—institutionalized as much through the Bureau of Applied Social Research as through the Department of Sociology—to combine deep scholarship and high scientific standards, with attention to important social problems and the effort to inform practical action

The first two of these are relatively familiar, indeed all but canonical and frequently restated in textbooks, though in fact the relationship between theory and research in sociology is tenuous and problematic. The third is equally important, and more often overlooked. It would please Merton, for example, to see the arguments offered in Chapters 4 and 5 by Cynthia Fuchs Epstein and Viviana A. Zelizer for ways in which his work contributes to tackling sociological problems on which he did not focus.

The fourth point is one on which Merton—and indeed Lazarsfeld—were, I think, ambivalent. Merton did not link his politics directly to his sociology. Yet, Merton did enter into public discussions on themes he thought properly informed by scholarly knowledge, such as censorship. Certainly, Merton did major research on topics of public interest and his sociological work informed practical efforts to address social problems, including not least the Supreme Court's Decision in *Brown vs. the Board of Education.* Yet, Merton and Lazarsfeld kept their "applied" work at the Bureau organized as what I have called a parallel professional practice. Applied research paid for studies that could also advance scientific sociology, though that was not usually the object of those who paid. It was important, then, not to let scientific pursuits be reduced to the level of the specific analyses funders sought.

Merton argued repeatedly that scientific knowledge advanced on the basis of concepts, paradigms, and middle-range theories. These could be developed only in analytic work that depended on abstraction from empirical data and indeed abstraction from the immediate particulars in which social issues appeared in everyday life. As it advanced, sociology offered more and better tools for grasping concrete situations and informing policy. As Merton knew from his earliest research, motivations for science could come from outside science, and ideas originating elsewhere could inform science. But scientific cumulation depended on some level of autonomy for science, from politics and public dispute. Merton worried when C. Wright Mills seemed to breach the boundaries and he worried even more in 1968. His model for what has since been called "public sociology" (by his friend and Columbia colleague Herbert Gans) was based on the socially responsible use of professionally mastered expertise.

Merton was strongly drawn to efforts to structure an integrative approach to sociology, one that would strengthen the field inside universities and in public esteem. By the 1960s—even earlier in some cases, including Mills—others thought that this encouraged too much complicity between sociologists and existing social hierarchies and power structures. Many thought this integrative approach dampened conflicts within the field that could be intellectually productive for it. Many would have preferred more open confrontation with social problems. Struggles over these issues were fought out partly at Columbia University, home to C. Wright Mills and Immanuel Wallerstein as well as Merton and Lazarsfeld, and within the ranks of Merton students, which included Alvin Gouldner. Merton's preference for professionalization—and with it integration, codification, and abstraction from immediate issues—seemed stifling to many, not least in the 1960s.

Indeed, Merton's influence was greatest from the era of World War II to the mid-1960s. He had important students later and he published important work later. But in many ways the context in which he had been most effective was in decline. Paul Lazarsfeld first retired and then died in 1976. Merton settled into the role of senior resident sage at the Russell Sage Foundation, putting his set of editorial stamps to work on the papers of visiting fellows rather than graduate students. He continued to write, both for immediate publication and for files of what promise to be an impressive body of posthumous publications.

Interestingly, during the 1960s Merton also ended his "parallel professional practice" of problem-oriented and applied social research organized through the Bureau. In part he had attained a position where he didn't need the resources applied research brought. In part his interests had shifted to renewed engagement in the sociology of science, and to a mixture of projects in theory and intellectual history that he could pursue in the library rather than in the collective research team. One of these was "sociological semantics," which both Peter Simonson and Harriet Zuckerman address below (in Chapters 10 and 11 respectively). Closely related was the history of ideas that Charles Camic discusses in Chapter 10 and that bore fruit in two remarkable books on the frontiers of literature, history, and sociology: *On the Shoulders of Giants* (Merton 1965) and *The Travels and Adventures of Serendipity* (Merton and Barber 2003).

Merton not only coined but also studied memorable phrases and the patterns of association and evocation in which they were passed on, not least as they informed scholarly reference and the development of reputations. Thus, famously, he traced the phrase, "if I have seen farther it is by standing on the shoulders of giants," through centuries of use. The phrase is most commonly associated with Sir Isaac Newton, though with the widespread success of *On the Shoulders of Giants* Merton must be a very close second. What Merton showed with dazzling erudition and more than a few entertaining digressions was that the aphorism originated with Bernard of Chartres in the twelfth century. This corrected not only those who cited merely Newton but those who credited the phrase to ancient authors, including apparently nonexistent ancient authors, perhaps thinking thereby to accord it greater dignity and impress readers with their Latin references (and here let us not forget the South Philadelphia high school that taught Merton four years of Latin).

Merton's book became famous enough to be known (at least among initiates) by the acronym "OTSOG." This was partly because it was so engagingly written, a scholarly detective story in the form of an extended letter to his friend Bernard Bailyn, a compilation of associations and sometimes improbable connections that invited the allusion to *Tristram Shandy* in the subtitle. But it is also a serious inquiry into the phenomena of scholarly reference and citation, the development of reputations, and the place of science amid humane knowledge.

Merton continued to address the relationship between the first appearances of ideas and the occasions when they begin to have more serious influence, noting how many basic scientific advances were anticipated by "prediscoveries" that failed to change the way scientists thought (Merton 1973c, 1973d). That in turn opened up the question of why this should be, whether in any specific case it was because the "prediscoverer" lacked stature, or because the context wasn't ready, because a crucial connection wasn't made, or because an empirical or practical test wasn't identified. The role of chance connections—serendipity—in scientific breakthroughs became another enduring focus for Merton's boundless curiosity and careful scholarship.

Merton also advocated for "sociological semantics" as a line of research into how verbal formulations influenced substantive sociological thinking. Explored further by Harriet Zuckerman and Charles Camic in Chapters 11 and 12 below, this builds on the still-neglected insight that conceptualizations actually matter in scientific work, and are part of how it advances, not merely more or less felicitous summaries of knowledge already established. A concept like "unanticipated consequences," which Merton introduced in a 1936 article, clarifies a phenomenon, making it "visible" for further study. In this case the concept was taken up by a host of researchers across the range of social and behavioral sciences, and it opened up new directions of empirical research as well as theorizing. Moreover, the clear, revealing conceptualization is as much a methodological tool as an element in theory (more precisely, it is both at once). As Peter Simonson shows in his chapter, this understanding is shaped by Merton's own early explorations in the field of rhetoric. Rhetoric also remained an important influence in Merton's sociology of science, as Ragnvald Kalleberg demonstrates in Chapter 9.

The sociology of science remained the field closest to Merton's heart. He had never entirely abandoned it, but returned to it as his central focus in the 1960s. Thinking it was obvious that science was a social institution of pivotal importance to modern society and that sociology offered crucial resources for its study, he was repeatedly surprised by weak disciplinary interest. This was not merely a personal disappointment for Merton, but, he thought, a danger for the emerging interdisciplinary field of science studies, which needed sociological perspectives. But by a sociological perspective, Merton meant largely an institutional one. And from the 1970s, the sociology of science turned, in large part, away from the study of institutions and toward microsociology of scientific practice. Chapter 6 by Thomas Gieryn situates Merton in the sociology of science, not only historically but also as part of a paradigm for new research.[27]

Many in the field were critical of Merton's emphasis on the norms of science. This seemed to some apologetic and to others idealistic. In any case they pointed to the frequency with which they saw these norms violated. More generally, structural-functionalism was challenged by a variety of perspectives placing greater stress on self-interest and conflict. Merton's work was often cited as emblematic of the now diverted "mainstream," though this was somewhat ironic, since among leading functionalists, he was particularly attentive to dysfunction, historical change, and conflict. Late in his life he worried that the approach of many in science studies was so relativistic and one-sidedly focused on debunking that it made it hard to see the importance of the relative autonomy of science as a social institution.

Conclusion

In short, Merton was one of the towering figures on whose shoulders contemporary sociology rests. He was without question among the most influential sociologists of the twentieth century. He left behind an extraordinary legacy of sociological publications (and unpublished work), of students who carried on various lines of inquiry he helped to launch, and of others he influenced through colleagueship or correspondence.

If Merton's work is less well understood than it should be, this is in fact an opportunity. Revisiting Merton's writings is a source of innumerable insights. Footnotes suggest whole research agendas. Essays still have the capacity to clarify whole fields. Reading Merton is also a reminder of the importance and value of scholarship as such, for even when his arguments are distilled into clear and straightforward prose they reveal foundations in deep and systematic knowledge of previous work (as Alan Sica brings out in Chapter 8).

But even more, there is in reading Merton an opportunity to think anew about how different styles and branches of sociology can better inform each other and strengthen the field as a whole. We can see in Merton's sociology of science not just one more sociological specialty but also one that can help sociology gain capacity for reflection on itself. We should think with Merton about the ways in which theory and research can inform each other, the ways in which middle-range theories can connect empirically disparate subfields, and even the ways in which "applied" research can underwrite scholarly innovation. We needn't always agree with Merton. Even arguments can be productive.

Notes

1. Merton and Lazarsfeld were each politically on the left, particularly in their youth; Lazarsfeld had been an active socialist in Austria. But even in their early Columbia years, their engagements and styles were more professional than political. Robert Lynd, the activist researcher who supported hiring Lazarsfeld partly because he was so impressed with his early study of unemployed workers, repeatedly demanded to know where was his social conscience. Lazarsfeld recalled answering, rather weakly, "Well, that begins after five o'clock" (Smith 1995:150). But the truth was perhaps at least as much that Lazarsfeld's socialist engagements were active in his Vienna milieu

and didn't survive his migration to the United States, though he said he remained a socialist "in my heart." Lazarsfeld also described his social research as "a kind of sublimation of my frustrated political instincts"—a sublimation reinforced by being an immigrant (see Sills 1987). There may have been something of this "sublimation" in Merton's intense professional engagement as well. He was more engaged in social issues than Lazarsfeld, particularly integration. But he channeled most of his engagement through research and efforts to strengthen the discipline of sociology itself, reflecting perhaps both his response to the hostile environment of anti-Semitism and McCarthyism and his conviction that this academic project would matter for public progress. As Smith recounts, Lynd, who had attracted a great deal of attention after the Middletown studies, lost influence and students to Lazarsfeld and Merton precisely because of the stronger professional engagements of the younger men and the greater help they could offer those forging academic careers.

2. By contrast to Merton's famous distinction in "On the History and Systematics of Sociological Theory" (Merton 1967).

3. Composed of his own reflections, the 1994 Charles Horner Haskins Lecture is the most important source for Merton's biography.

4. This was not an altogether amateur or casual undertaking. The boyfriend was Charles H. Hopkins, author of *"Outs": Precautions and Challenges for Ambitious Card Workers*. After Hopkins died in 1948, the Society of American Magicians, Assembly #4, named its annual award in his honor. Merton dedicated *Social Theory and Social Structure* to Hopkins when it was first published the next year.

5. The latter, a pioneering presentation of Durkheim's newly translated *Division of Labor in Society*, was still being reprinted decades later. Sixty years on, Merton recalled the origin of those two first articles. Sorokin had been invited to speak to the Eastern Sociological Conference (a precursor to the Society) on recent French sociology. He couldn't make it and asked Merton to do it in his stead. Not only did the second-year graduate student rise to that challenge, his text was published and also drew the attention of the editor of the *AJS*, Ellsworth Faris, who solicited the second article. Faris himself, as it happened, wrote a dismissive review of Durkheim's book—"nasty, brutish and short" as Merton recalled it—emphasizing the poor empirical source materials from which Durkheim worked. Merton praised the book, trying analytically to bring out its theoretical contributions, but castigated the "infelicitous translation" by one George Simpson, though anxious that it should be clear that this was not the George E. Simpson who had been his undergraduate mentor (See Merton 1994b).

6. Decades on, Merton was at pains to clarify that he went to Harvard to work with Sorokin, having no idea of Parsons's existence: "Parsons had no public identity whatever as a sociologist. He had published just two articles deriving from his dissertation . . . and these had appeared in the *Journal of Political Economy*, a journal it is fair to suppose not much read by undergraduates in sociology bent on deciding where to

do their graduate work.... I do no injustice to Pitirim Sorokin's memory by reporting that although we students came to study with the renowned Sorokin, a subset of us stayed to work with the unknown Parsons." (Merton 1980:69)

7. Though Merton was clearly conscious of Parsons's reputation for dismal prose, which he could gently evoke in the quoted passage, he elsewhere went out of his way to praise the "exceptionally clear, direct, and most un-Teutonic English prose" of Parsons's translation of Weber's *The Protestant Ethic* (Merton 1980:69).

8. For a sampling of the extensive commentary over the years, see Cohen 1990.

9. See discussion by Kalleberg in Chapter 9 below. Later, of course, Merton would address in more detail the social institutions—including reward systems—that supported this ethos.

10. *A History of the Faculty of Political Science, the Bicentennial History of Columbia University,* published by Columbia University Press, 1955.

11. The influential Harvard physical anthropologist Earnest Hooten was the target.

12. Considering the politics of Merton's professionalism from the relative heights of its dominant position in the late 1950s and early 1960s—let alone the struggles of the later 1960s and 1970s—misses the importance of the very different struggles during the 1930s, '40s, and '50s to establish sociology as a leading academic field.

13. Merton's classic "Bureaucratic Structure and Personality" was published in 1940 and reprinted in *Social Theory and Social Structure* (1968d). In addition to a reader in bureaucracy and several other articles, he produced a two-volume report on the use of opinion research and statistics in the AT&T Corporation, *The Role of Social Research in Business Administration,* with E. C. Devereux, Jr (1956).

14. "Social Policy and Social Research on Housing" is the special issue of *The Journal of Social Issues* (1951a) that Merton edited in 1951 with Patricia S. West, Marie Jahoda, and Hanan C. Selvin. This brought into print fragments of a major study by the same authors, *Patterns of Social Life: Explorations in the Sociology of Housing,* which was never formally published and available only in mimeographed form from the Bureau of Applied Social Research. See discussion in Merton 1999. The central intellectual theme of the housing studies was that social structure shapes patterns in social psychological response to factors like racial integration.

15. Merton's studies of integrated housing were cited in the appellant's brief that led to the landmark desegregation ruling, Brown vs. the Board of Education (Merton et al. 1951a, 1951b; Merton 1948a). Merton was a signer of the statement "The Effects of Segregation and the Consequences of Desegregation: A Social Science Statement" that Kenneth Clark drafted as a supplement to legal briefs being sent to the Supreme Court (see Clark 1953). See also Merton 1948b.

16. *Mass Persuasion* (1946) is Merton's most sustained treatment. He also coauthored several studies with Paul Lazarsfeld, including "Patterns of Influence: A Study of Interpersonal Influence and Communications Behavior in a Local Community" (1949).

17. Merton first published this collection in 1949 and it became a shaping influence on postwar sociology. A revised edition was published in 1957 and then the enlarged edition in 1968.

18. The creation of the Center was the source of one of the few enduring quarrels between Merton and Lazarsfeld. Merton played a leading role in the rejection of Lazarsfeld's plan for a hierarchical teaching organization in favor of an institution in which those chosen for membership would be relatively equal and autonomous as they pursued their own projects within an intellectual community.

19. *Contemporary Social Problems* was the anthropology he edited with Robert A. Nisbet through four editions beginning in 1961. Merton was also for many years a consulting editor for Harcourt and in this role an influence on what was arguably the first great textbook of postwar sociology: Leonard Broom and Philip Selznick, *Sociology: A Text with Adapted Readings* (1963).

20. In Merton 1968g, see esp. 27–28 and 35–37.

21. And if Mills and Gouldner both became leading critics of professional American sociology, neither made Merton a target. Merton regarded Gouldner as among his very best students (even if a difficult person). Merton had brought Mills to Columbia and was often his defender, not least in conflicts with Lazarsfeld. Merton did grow exasperated with Mills and was offended by parts of *The Sociological Imagination* (even though he personally was treated gently).

22. In the later regard, he shared much with the anthropologist Max Gluckman; and more generally, Merton's structural-functionalism reflected not only a distancing from Parsons but an embrace of a perspective widespread in social anthropology.

23. As Merton uses the term, "paradigms" are more limited than the broad structures integrating the state of scientific knowledge in a particular era that are analyzed by Thomas S. Kuhn in *The Structure of Scientific Revolutions* (1962). For Merton, paradigms are systematizations of the analyses developed in particular lines of work. For example, he regarded his accounts of deviant social behavior in "Social Structure and Anomie" (1968c) and of "Manifest and Latent Functions" (1968i) each as paradigms.

24. Sztompka's work is perhaps the best starting point for one seeking an integrated perspective on Merton's work. See also Crothers 1987. Two anthologies are also noteworthy though both (like the present volume) are largely focused on specific contributions and their relationships to subfields. See Coser 1975, especially Stinchecombe's chapter (11–34); and Mongardini and Tabboni 1998.

25. It is worth noting that the exemplars in his historical sociology of science come mainly from the age of heroic amateurs, especially the seventeenth century, not the era of science based in universities (or for that matter industrial or government labs). Scientists like Newton and Kepler did engage simultaneously in empirical research, methodological innovation, and theorization. Of course many of their contemporaries were less heroic and less polymathic. Then as now many contributed empirical

observations without clarity as to how to theorize them, though admission to a body like the Royal Society involved less work-discipline than, say, a postdoctoral fellowship in chemistry today.

26. For the notion of "strategic research site," see Merton 1959. Merton's main development of this notion came in "Multiple Discoveries as Strategic Research Site," first published as part of "Resistance to the Systematic Study of Multiple Discoveries in Science" (1963).

27. There is no single authoritative study of Merton's sociology of science. Indeed, Merton himself never attempted this, and the closest substitute is an edited collection of Merton's work on science with a substantial introduction by Norman Storer, *The Sociology of Science*. A special issue of *Social Studies of Science* in 2004 is interesting, but also very incomplete. One of the multiple festschriften honoring Merton focuses helpfully on his studies of science (Gieryn 1980). A recent special issue of the *Journal of Classical Sociology* (2007) offers several engagements with Merton's work.

References

Broom, Leonard, and Philip Selznick. 1963. *Sociology: A Text with Adapted Readings*. New York: Harper & Row.

Calhoun, Craig, ed. 2007. *Sociology in America*. Chicago: University of Chicago Press.

Clark, Kenneth B. 1953. "The Effects of Segregation and the Consequences of Desegregation: A Social Science Statement." *Minnesota Law Review* 37:427–39.

Cohen, I. B. 1990. *Puritanism and the Rise of Modern Science: The Merton Thesis*. New Brunswick: Rutgers University Press.

Coser, Lewis A., ed. 1975. *The Idea of Social Structure: Papers in Honor of Robert K. Merton*. New York: Harcourt Brace Jovanovich.

Cronin, Blaise. 1984. *The Citation Process: The Role and Significance of Citations in Scientific Communication*. London: Taylor Graham.

Crothers, Charles. 1987. *Robert K. Merton*. London: Tavistick.

Gieryn, Thomas F., ed. 1980. *Science and Social Structure: a Festschrift for Robert K. Merton*. New York: New York Academy of Sciences.

Haber, Samuel. 2008. "Robert Merton." In *Encyclopedia of American Jewish History*, ed. Stephen H. Norwood and Eunice G. Pollack, 734–8. New York: ABC/Clio.

Kuhn, Thomas S. 1962. *The Structure of Scientific Revolutions*. Chicago: University of Chicago Press.

Merton, Robert K. 1938a. "Science, Technology, and Society in Seventeenth-Century England." In *OSIRIS: Studies on the History and Philosophy of Science, and on the History of Learning and Culture*, ed. George Sarton, 362–632. Bruges: The St. Catherine Press.

———. [1938b] 1973. "Science and the Social Order." In *The Sociology of Science*, ed. N. Storer, 254–266. Chicago: University of Chicago Press.

———. 1939. "Crime and the Anthropologist." *American Anthropologist* 42:384–408.

———. 1940. "Bureaucratic Structure and Personality." *Social Forces* 18:560–568.

———. 1942. "A Note on Science and Democracy." *Journal of Legal and Political Sociology* 1:115–126.

———. 1947. "The Machine, the Worker, and the Engineer." *Science* 105:79–84.

———. 1948a. "Social Psychology of Housing." In *Current Trends in Social Psychology*, ed. Wayne Dennis, 163–217. Pittsburgh: University of Pittsburgh Press.

———. 1948b. "Discrimination and the American Creed." In *Discrimination and National Welfare*, ed. R.M. MacIver, 99–126. New York: Harper and Brothers.

———. 1949. "Patterns of Influence: A Study of Interpersonal Influence and Communications Behavior in a Local Community." In *Communications in Research, 1948–49*, ed. P. F. Lazarsfeld and F. Stanton, 180–219. New York: Harper and Brothers.

———. 1959. "Problem-finding in Sociology." In *Sociology Today*, ed. R. K. Merton, L. Broom, and L. S. Cottrell, Jr., xxvi–xxix. New York: Basic Books.

———. 1963. "Resistance to the Systematic Study of Multiple Discoveries in Science." *European Journal of Sociology* 4:237–49.

———. 1965. *On the Shoulders of Giants*. New York: Harcourt, Brace and World.

———. 1967. "On the History and Systematics of Sociological Theory." In *On Theoretical Sociology*, ed. R. Merton, 1–37. New York: The Free Press.

———, ed. 1968a. *Social Theory and Social Structure*. New York: Free Press.

———. 1968b. "The Self-Fulfilling Prophecy" In Social Theory and Social Structure, ed. Robert K. Merton, 475–90. New York: Free Press.

———. 1968c. "Social Structure and Anomie." In *Social Theory and Social Structure*, ed. Robert K. Merton, 185–214. New York: Free Press.

———. 1968d. "Bureaucratic Structure and Personality." In *Social Theory and Social Structure*, ed. Robert K. Merton, 249–260. New York: Free Press.

———. 1968e. "Continuities in the Theory of Social Structure and Anomie." In *Social Theory and Social Structure*, ed. Robert K. Merton, 215–48. New York: Free Press.

———. 1968f. "Continuities in the Theory of Reference Groups and Social Structure." In *Social Theory and Social Structure*, ed. Robert K. Merton, 335–440. New York: Free Press.

———. 1968g. "On the History and Systematics of Sociological Theory." In *Social Theory and Social Structure*, ed. Robert K. Merton, 1–38. New York: Free Press.

———. 1968h. "On Sociological Theories of the Middle Range." In *Social Theory and Social Structure*, 39–72. New York: Free Press.

———. 1968i. "Manifest and Latent Functions." In *Social Theory and Social Structure*, ed. Robert K. Merton, 73–138. New York: Free Press.

——. 1968j. "The Bearing of Sociological Theory on Empirical Research." In *Social Theory and Social Structure*, ed. Robert K. Merton, 139–55. New York: Free Press.

——. 1968k. "The Bearing of Empirical Research on Sociological Theory." In *Social Theory and Social Structure*, ed. Robert K. Merton, 156–71. New York: Free Press.

——. 1973a. "The Normative Structure of Science." In *The Sociology of Science*, ed. N. Storer, 267–279. Chicago: University of Chicago Press.

——. 1973b. "The Matthew Effect in Science." In *The Sociology of Science*, ed. N. Storer, 439–59. Chicago: University of Chicago Press.

——. 1973c. "Priorities in Scientific Discovery." In *The Sociology of Science*, ed. N. Storer, 286–324. Chicago: University of Chicago Press.

——. 1973d. "Singletons and Multiples in Science." In *The Sociology of Science*, ed. N. Storer, 343–70. Chicago: University of Chicago Press.

——. 1976. Sociological Ambivalence. New York: Free Press.

——. 1979. "Foreword." In *Citation Indexing: Its Theory and Application in Science, Technology, and the Humanities*, ed. Eugene Garfield. New York: John Wiley and Sons.

——. 1980. "Remembering the Young Talcott Parsons." *The American Sociologist* 15:68–71.

——. 1994a. *A Life of Learning: The 1994 Charles Homer Haskins Lecture*. New York: American Council of Learned Societies.

——. 1994b. "Durkheim's 'Division of Labor in Society': A Sexagenarian Postscript." *Sociological Forum* 9 (1):27–36.

——. 1995. "The Thomas Theorem and the Matthew Effect." *Social Forces* 74 (2): 379–424.

——. 1999. "Opportunity Structure: the Emergence, Diffusion and Differentiation of a Sociological Concept, 1930s–1950s." In *The Legacy of Anomie Theory*, ed. Frieda Adler and William S. Laufer, 3–79. New Brunswick: Transaction Books.

Merton, Robert K., and Elinor Barber. 2003. *The Travels and Adventures of Serendipity*. Princeton: Princeton University Press.

Merton, Robert K., and E. C. Devereux, Jr. 1956. *The Role of Social Science Research in Business Administration*. New York: Bureau of Applied Social Research.

Merton, Robert K., Marjorie Fiske, and Alberta Curtis. 1946. *Mass Persuasion: The Social Psychology of a War Bond Drive*. New York: Harper and Brothers.

Merton, Robert K., Marjorie Fiske, and Patricia L. Kendall. 1956. *The Focused Interview*. New York: The Free Press.

Merton, Robert K., and Paul Lazarsfeld, eds. 1950. *Continuities in Social Research: Studies in the Scope and Method of "The American Soldier."* New York: Free Press.

Merton, Robert K., Richard McKeon, and Walter Gellhorn. 1957. *The Freedom to Read: Perspective and Program*. New York: R. R. Bowker.

Merton, Robert K., and Robert A. Nisbet. 1961. *Contemporary Social Problems*. New York: Harcourt Brace Jovanovich.

Merton, Robert K., George G. Reader, Patricia L. Kendall, editors. 1957. *The Student Physician: Introductory Studies in the Sociology of Medical Education.* Cambridge, MA: Harvard University Press.

Merton, Robert K., and Alice S. Rossi. 1968. "Contributions to the Theory of Reference Group Behavior." In *Social Theory and Social Structure*, ed. Robert K. Merton, 279–334. New York: Free Press.

Merton, Robert K., Patricia S. West, and Marie Jahoda. 1951. "Patterns of Social Life: Explorations in the Sociology of Housing." New York: Columbia University Bureau of Applied Social Research.

Merton, Robert K., Patricia S. West, Marie Jahoda, and Hanan C. Selvin, ed. 1951. "Social Policy and Social Research on Housing." *The Journal of Social Issues* 8 (1 and 2).

Mongardini, Carlo, and Simonetta Tabboni, eds. 1998. *Robert K. Merton and Contemporary Sociology.* New Brunswick: Transaction Publishers.

O'Neill, John, Bryan S. Turner and Simon Susan, ed. 2007. *Journal of Classical Sociology* 7 (2).

Parsons, Talcott. [1937] 1961. *The Structure of Social Action.* Rev. ed. Glencoe: Free Press.

Sills, David. 1987. "Paul F. Lazarsfeld, 1901–1976." *Biographical Memoirs*, Volume 56, 251–282. Washington: National Academy of Sciences.

Small, Henry. 2004. "On the Shoulders of Robert Merton: Towards a Normative Theory of Citation." *Scientometrics* 60 (1):71–79.

Smith, Mark C. 1995. *Social Science in the Crucible.* Durham: Duke University Press.

Stinchecombe, Arthur L. 1975. "Merton's Theory of Social Structure." In *The Idea of Social Structure: Papers in Honor of Robert K. Merton*, ed. Lewis A Coser, 11–34. New York: Harcourt Brace Jovanovich.

Storer, Norman, ed. 1973. *The Sociology of Science.* Chicago: Chicago University Press.

Sztompka, Piotr. 1986. *Robert K. Merton: An Intellectual Profile.* New York: St. Martin's Press.

1

Reflections on a Common Theme

Establishing the Phenomenon, Adumbration, and Ideal Types

ALEJANDRO PORTES

This essay discusses several of the basic concepts that Merton left to posterity, including adumbration, specified ignorance, and the unexpected consequences of purposive action. A common theme and a common style underlie all of them. The theme is the defense of the scientific process and its products. Merton was well aware that scientific innovations, once advanced, acquire the status of a public good. As such, they can be used or misused and even dismissed with the remark that they are not "new." This is the fallacy of adumbration, which he critiqued, with related pitfalls, along his career.

The common style involves the crafting of insights of such clarity that, once in the public domain, they appear obvious. The self-fulfilling prophecy and the typology of action in "Social Structure and Anomie" are examples. This quality allows the dismissal of insights by others who did not discover them and their ready incorporation into public discourse with neglect of their sources. These are also consequences of the status of sociological innovations as public goods.

The thread linking Merton to Weber is clear in their common suspicion of universal laws and grand theories and in the similarity of the theoretical alternatives that they proposed: ideal types, in Weber's case, and theories of the middle range, in Merton's. The affinity goes further, moving along their parallel critical stances toward rationalistic models of society and their common search for the unexpected features arising from allegedly rational purposive action. The Weberian-Mertonian tradition configured a distinct sociological viewpoint resistant to sweeping blueprints and receptive to historically situated investigation, causally delimited explanations, and the surprising complexity of human interaction.

> A basic role of empirical research designed to "establish" the phenomenon is at times downgraded as "mere empiricism." Yet we know that pseudo-facts have a way of inducing pseudo-problems, which cannot be solved because matters are not what they purport to be.... The governing question... "Is it really so?" holds as much for historical particularities as for sociological generalizations. Strongly held theoretical expectations or ideologically induced expectations can lead to perceptions of historical and social "facts" even when they are readily refutable. (Merton 1987:4; quotation marks in original)

This passage comes from one of the last of Robert Merton's writings, "Three Fragments From a Sociologist's Notebook" (1987). One of the fragments admonishes social scientists to "establish the phenomenon" before investigating its character and its causes. Prima facie, the advice appears redundant: how can one study something that does not exist, that is simply a figment? On reflection, however, we come to understand both the pertinence of the advice and its complexity. For "establishing the phenomenon" actually requires two different operations: first, ascertaining the empirical existence of something; second, defining it in sufficiently clear and limited terms that it is usable for theory development and empirical research.

Concerning the first operation, it would seem impossible that time and effort are invested in writing about a phenomenon whose very existence is dubious. In actuality, this happens all the time, and intellectuals, including social scientists, are rather inclined in this direction. Take the concept of "postmodernism." Reams have been written about this condition without anyone demonstrating that it actually exists, that is, that there are persons or groups who go around "disillusioned of the world," rejecting "grand narratives," and resisting anything that smacks of "means-ends" rationality. It sufficed that some French and American intellectuals proclaimed that "we are now living in the postmodern era," for others to take up the call and start embroidering a phenomenon whose reality remains questionable (see, e.g., Jameson 1984; Baudrillard 1988).

The examples could be multiplied. Consider the panoply of concepts associated with Freudian psychoanalysis: the "Id," the "Oedipal complex," the "Thanatos," the theory of repression, the unconscious, etc. Veritable libraries have been written about these and related concepts which eventually were demonstrated to be, when confronted with rigorous empirical evidence, of rather dubious reality. So were shown to be, not incidentally, the benefits of therapeutic treatments based on this theoretical framework (Bachrach 1965; Wolpe and Lazarus 1967). Faced with such experiences, "establishing the phenomenon" becomes a rather appropriate admonition for social scientists, always in search of the latest intellectual novelty.

The second operation is closely related to the first. For if a given phenomenon is defined rigorously, it can be promptly established whether it is real or not. One of the reasons that allowed "postmodernism" to carry on unchallenged in many fields is that is could be anything and any anecdotal evidence could be used to illustrate its existence. Had it been defined tightly, its character may have been shown to be imaginary, a fanciful work of intellectual craftsmanship. Even when the existence of a phenomenon can be unquestionably demonstrated, it is necessary to define it rigorously so as to avoid future confusions and unwarranted conceptual stretches.

Aside from a demonstrable inclination to manufacture realities, intellectuals in general, and social scientists in particular, are equally inclined to appropriate a suddenly popular concept, applying it in multiple ways and, in the process, stretching its meaning beyond recognition. In the contemporary era, several valuable concepts have suffered this fate. Consider "social capital." After its initial and clear definition by Pierre Bourdieu (1979, 1980), the concept has been appropriated and extended in ways that bear little resemblance to the original formulation. In one version (Coleman 1988), it becomes a tool for social control and normative enforcement; in another (Putnam 2000), it becomes "civic spirit," including the ability to "bridge" beyond one's group. Currently, more time and print are spent debating what social capital actually is than investigating the phenomenon according to the original tight definition.

For a second illustration, consider the concept of "institution." Since its resurrection by Nobel Prize winner Douglass North, the concept has taken both development economics and economic sociology by storm, to the point that representatives of both disciplines could declare that "we are all institutionalists now" (Hodgson 2002; Nee 2005; Roland 2004). From past historical research and theory, social scientists know that institutions exist. The problem, at present, is to identify what they actually are and how they differ from other elements of social life. In the enthusiasm for the "institutional turn" (Evans 2004), social scientists have taken the concept along multiple paths, to the point that today it can mean anything—from the norm of reciprocity to property laws, and on to the central bank. In the process, the heuristic value of the concept dissipates, threatening to take it along the path suffered by other initially promising and now semiforgotten insights. "Reference group," "status inconsistency," and "dependency" are just a few of the many concepts that have gone down this sad route.

With these experiences as background, the value of Merton's fragment is evident, but there is another feature of this essay, so far unremarked, which deserves attention. This is precisely the fact that, once said, the point becomes evident. Once Merton declared that, to study a phenomenon, you must first establish it, the argument would strike many as a quasitautology. This is a characteristic feature of Merton's oeuvre: his crafting insights of such transparency and clarity that, once formulated, they would seem obvious to others—almost commonplace. This feature is important not only for Merton's legacy, but for the present and future of sociology as a discipline. The following sections present additional examples and explore their implications.

The Obvious in Merton

Under the title "Social Structure and Anomie," Merton (1968a) developed a crystalline typology famous to our day. The constitutive elements are remarkably simple: first, you take what people want—what Merton calls "culturally defined goals"; then you take the approved ways to achieve these goals—what he calls "legitimate means"; finally, you crisscross them. Presto, you have an exhaustive typology of conformity, innovation, and deviance, whose elements are so self-evident as to be irrefutable. Once the typology reached the public domain, the question "how could it be otherwise?" naturally suggested itself. But neither the basic idea nor its usefulness for decades to come would have been possible without its initial formulation.

Another characteristic of Merton's many theoretical contributions is that they have generated few opponents. There are no "anti-Mertonians" in the same sense that there are "anti-Parsonians" or "anti-Marxists." The reason, I surmise, is that the set of concepts, typologies, and theories that Merton left us uniformly possess this quality of transparency, almost obviousness, once they were brought forward. The "Thomas Theorem," the unanticipated consequences of purposive action, the self-fulfilling prophecy come to mind, as do so many additional examples.

On the other hand, the idea that the processes captured by these concepts are self-evident is an accusation under which the discipline as a whole has long labored. Its most important contributions, beginning with the classics, have been commonly swept aside with the comment of sociology being the painful elaboration of the obvious. This claim is invariably advanced post factum, that is, once the concept or theory has been put forward and explained. It denotes a fundamental weakness of the discipline to our day: its inability to claim as its own or retain some proprietary rights over the scientific and intellectual contributions that it has made for two hundred years. Like effervescent tablets, these insights have been promptly dissolved into the medium of general public consciousness, leaving little behind. "Charisma," "class consciousness," "significant others," "the self-fulfilling prophecy," "social networks," "focus groups" are just some of the terms now diffused into common parlance with nary a word to the discipline that gave rise to them.

Adumbration

Perhaps Merton had something of this in mind when he decided to dedicate a good part of the first chapter of *Social Theory and Social Structure* to the fallacy of adumbration. Adumbration is not the same as the disappearance of scientific insights into everyday discourse, but it represents a parallel form of devaluing them. It is, in other words, a means of dismissing an empirical discovery or a theoretical advance not by saying that it is obvious, but by affirming that it is not new. Merton uses as the masthead of this chapter the trenchant remark by Alfred North Whitehead:

> But to come very near to a true theory and to grasp its precise application, are two very different things. Everything of importance has been said before by somebody who did not discover it. (quoted in Merton 1968b:1)

It is indeed the case, as the Argentine writer Jorge Luis Borges noted in a different context (1962), that writers create their own precursors so that when a novel or poem gains widespread attention, many scholars and critics make it their business to trace parallels and precedents throughout the centuries. The fallacy of adumbration is more insidious because it consists in denying the value of an empirical discovery or conceptual innovation by pointing toward approximations or similarities in the past. This is not difficult to do, but its consequences, like those of the charge of obviousness, can be serious:

> What is more common is that an idea is formulated definitely enough and emphatically enough that it cannot be overlooked by contemporaries, and it then becomes easy to find anticipations or adumbrations of it. (Merton 1968b:16)

The simplicity of the exercise is incommensurate with the intellectual confusion that it can cause, at least in the short run. William James, a frequent victim of adumbration, once noted the "classic stages of a theory's career": it is first attacked as absurd; then, it is admitted to be true, but obvious and insignificant; finally, it is seen to be so important that these adversaries claim that they themselves discovered it." (James 1907:198; quoted in Merton 1968b:22).

This last passage actually combines the charge of obviousness with an extreme form of adumbration, namely the kind where the critic himself claims to have made the original discovery. Merton rallied so strongly against adumbrationism arguably out of two motives: first, because he himself may have been a victim of such practices in his early career; second, and most important, out of a lifelong quest to defend and protect the value of scientific ideas and innovations from misguided detractors. Merton recognized that concepts and scientific discoveries, once formulated, have the character of a public good—anyone can use them or misuse them. That is why they can be dismissed as "obvious" when no one recognized them previously, why they can effervesce into the collective mind with little trace left of their origins, or why they can be simply attributed to someone who did not discover them.

Faced with such multiple perils, scientific and intellectual innovators have little defense. Public denials or reassertions of authorship commonly backfire. The only effective recourse is in an intellectual collectivity educated to recognize these errors. This was the quest to which the first chapter of *Social*

Theory and many other of Merton's later writings were dedicated. In pursuing them, he did not hesitate to note that even his mentors had indulged in some of these errors. Note, for instance, his citation of Sorokin attacking Marx and Engels's dialectical materialism:

> First, from a purely scientific point of view—there is nothing in their theory that was not said by earlier authors; second, what is really original is far from being scientific; third, the only merit of the theory is that it in a somewhat stronger and exaggerated form generalized the ideas given before the time of Marx. (Sorokin 1928:545; quoted in Merton 1968b:26)

Ideal Types and the Middle Range

The defense of the value of scientific ideas in Merton extended beyond the critique of fictitious subjects or the fallacy of adumbration. The next step was noteworthy for its audacity. At the time that he formulated it, sociology was dominated by the ambition of theory-building on a grand scale. As anthropology before it, any sociological theorist worth his salt attempted to construct all-encompassing intellectual edifices in which the words "system," "laws," and "science" were liberally interspersed. Such efforts were numerous and certainly not limited to Marx's "scientific" materialism or Spencer's evolutionism. The German Tonnies, the Frenchman Cuvillier, the Americans Sumner, Cooley, and MacIver, the Russian Sorokin all tried their hand at this enterprise. (Bogardus 1940; Collins 1994)

By the mid-twentieth century, the rising theoretical synthesis in sociology was structural-functionalism and its undisputed creator and spokesman was Talcott Parsons. It took courage to deviate from that orthodoxy. Merton's great merit was to see that such "systems," products of the mind, did not advance science much because they became self-enclosed and self-referential narratives at a high level of abstraction. It is difficult to derive testable propositions from such systems and even more difficult to bring empirical evidence to bear on them. More importantly, they encourage deductive reasoning to the detriment of induction. Those well steeped in the "School" can advance explanations about practically anything without need for empirical inquiry by simply deducing them from general principles and a few anecdotal bits of information. On that basis it was possible for anyone to cook up a presidential address on the origins of the species or the state of modern society in a relatively short period and with the outward appearance of rigor. (Harris 1968:260; Collins 1994:196–197)

Boas had already seen in Anthropology that such systems were not science, but a refined form of charlatanism. Accordingly, he rallied against the Spencerian evolutionary "synthesis," then dominant in his discipline. (Harris 1968; Barrett 1984) Respectful of his mentors, Merton attempted a middle-range approach arguing that concepts and theories at a lower level of abstraction were more useful at the present stage of development of the discipline and a necessary intermediate step for the construction of any general system. He clearly saw that sociology under structural functionalism, like anthropology under Spencerian evolutionism, was going nowhere (Merton 1968c).

With the wisdom of hindsight and in an atmosphere free of the coercive power of grand syntheses, we can confidently see that the "middle range" is all there is. This is no intermediate stage to the arrival of the final synthesis, for the latter will never happen or will simply repeat the errors of the past. Instead, it is at this limited level where theory really pays off, by entering into a dialogue with empirical facts, organizing them and being, in turn, modified by them. Today, sociology has no grand theoretical system; instead, it has a multitude of medium-range theories addressing specific patches of social reality—socioeconomic inequality, organizations, crime, poverty, status attainment, ethnic identities, art and cultural forms, economic behavior, immigration, and many others. It is along these lines that progress is being made, which corresponds perfectly to the Mertonian vision.

This vision had a notable precedent. In his methodological essay *Objectivity in the Social Sciences*, Max Weber had this to say about the attempt to construct grand universal laws:

> Laws are important and valuable in the exact natural sciences, in the measure that those sciences are universally valid. For the knowledge of social phenomenon in their concreteness, the most general laws, because they are most devoid of content, are also the least valuable. The more comprehensive the validity or scope of a term, the more it leads us away from the richness of reality since, in order to include the common elements of its largest possible number of phenomena, it must be as abstract as possible and, hence, devoid of content. (Weber [1904] 1949:80)

Put differently, universal laws (or grand theories) inexorably become vacuously true, applicable to a multitude of things and to none. We can confidently assert that "social change proceeds through a counterpoint of differentiation and integration" or that "society is a system in equilibrium where shocks to one part require counterbalancing adjustment in others" without fear of being proven false. The level of abstraction of such statements protects them from negation, but at the cost, in Weber's own words, of being "devoid of content."

In lieu of universal laws, Weber proposed ideal types:

> An ideal type is formed by the one-sided accentuation of one or more points of view and by the synthesis of a great many diffuse, discrete, more or less present *concrete individual phenomena* . . . .It has the significance of a purely *limiting* concept with which the real situation or action is compared and surveyed for the explication of certain significant components. (Weber [1904] 1949:90, 93; italics in original)

Ideal types are concepts created by the investigator to make sense of certain phenomena. They are not explicit hypotheses, but they implicitly contain the assertion that certain processes or events go together to form a complex whole. Thus, the ideal type "bureaucracy" brings together a series of variables such as meritocratic recruitment and selection, a clear separation between personal and official roles, impersonality, and universalism. (Weber [1922] 1947; Bendix 1962) The investigator rubs the ideal type against specific social realities to ascertain how they compare, reflect, and differ from the ideal construction. This dialogue between the conceptual and the empirical leads to a *clarification* of the structure and dynamics of particular phenomena and also to the modification of the ideal type in response to new features not discovered before. (Weber [1904] 1949; Bendix 1962)

Ideal types and theories of the middle range belong together, the first being an earlier formulation of the same idea in a different intellectual context. Both Weber and Merton assert that such concepts are constructed *inductively* from empirical observation and are then applied to other apparently similar phenomena to clarify them and, in the process, test the concept's validity. The theory's inductive origin and its permeability to new empirical evidence is what make it differ from the universal laws and "grand theories" that both authors criticize.

While Merton had Parsons's system in mind when he wrote his essay, Weber had Marx's. He used the intellectual evolution of scientific materialism to make a second fundamental critique about the pitfalls of all-encompassing intellectual frameworks, that is, their almost inexorable tendency to lose from sight the character of concepts and theories as heuristic devices and to try to substitute them for reality:

> Nothing, however, is more dangerous than the confusion of theory and history . . . . This confusion expresses itself firstly in the belief that the "true" content and the essence of historical reality is portrayed in such theoretical constructs or, secondly, in the use of these constructs as a procrustean bed into which history is to be forced or, thirdly, in the hypostatization of such "ideas" as real forces (Weber [1904] 1949:94; quotation marks in original).

It is only too human for system builders, enamored by their own constructs, to see them as isomorphic with reality. This leads, inevitably, to a deductive mode of reasoning and to the dismissal of contrary evidence. Hence, the absolute need for the middle range. Weber and Merton are of the same mind not only in their keen perception of the character of scientific concepts as mutable heuristic devices, but also in their defense of the value of such concepts, threatened as much by adumbrationism as by reification. I surmise that Merton would heartily endorse this comment:

> all sociologically Marxian "laws" and developmental constructs are . . . ideal types. The eminent, indeed unique *heuristic* significance of those ideal types when they are used for the assessment of reality is known to everyone who has employed Marxian concepts and hypotheses. Similarly, their perniciousness, as soon as they are thought of as empirically valid or as real "effective forces" is likewise known to those who have used them. (Weber [1904] 1949:103; italics and quotation marks in original)

Specified Ignorance

In our value system, knowledge is regarded as good, and a premium is placed on its acquisition. On the contrary, ignorance is a condition to be avoided. There are instances in real life, however, where what is not known can help move things forward. Information is a valuable commodity and keeping it away from others is what enables its possessors to put it to use for profit and self-advancement. When others need to be hired in order to put information to use, it must be compartmentalized so that competition does not proliferate. This is the basic purpose of centralization of knowledge in the top managerial ranks of firms (Edwards 1979; Harrison and Bluestone 1988).

Peasant communities labor quietly and peacefully until the arrival of the media brings with it knowledge of the lifestyles of the developed world, thereby triggering feelings of relative deprivation. This is commonly followed by mass emigration (Stark 1984; Massey, Durand, and Malone 2002). In general, elites benefit from keeping their privileges out of sight of the masses. Generalized knowledge of such privileges triggers invidiousness and may, under the right circumstances, lead to instability and conflict.

Ignorance is not only of benefit to dominant groups bent on preserving their privileges. In other settings, it may also be useful to the less lucky. The Stanford psychologist Claude Steele has demonstrated the existence of "stereotype threat" among minority students, particularly among African-Americans, when knowledge that "others" regard them as inferior may make them perform worse on standard tests than would otherwise be the case (Steele 1997). By contrast, immigrant students, particularly those raised in protective enclaves, commonly do better than average because they are unaware or dismissive of any demonstrations of prejudice directed at them (Zhou and Bankston 1996, 1998; Perez 2001; Portes and Schafer 2007). In this case, ignorance of opinions and attitudes in their immediate environment works to these minority students' advantage.

Instances of the social functions of ignorance could be multiplied, but this would be unnecessary. A helpful catalogue of such cases was compiled, as early as 1949, by sociologists Wilbert Moore and Melvin Tumin. Their essay, bearing a title identical to that of this section, presents an analysis of this general phenomenon as it looked when structural functionalism was the dominant paradigm in American sociology. From that school's overriding concern with social equilibria, ignorance of facts in a number of areas and segments of social life had much to commend itself. (Moore and Tumin 1949).

In science as well, ignorance has its functions. If the goal of science is the acquisition of new knowledge, a first prerequisite is a skeptical stance toward folk or other commonsensical explanations of phenomena. If this is the case in the natural sciences, how much more so in the social sciences where popular accounts of practically every event and trend exist. This is another instance in which the "obvious" is suspect and the scientist's proper stance is a studious ignorance of such accounts in order to approach the phenomenon from a fresh perspective. This was, in fact, the first rule of the sociological method proposed by Durkheim: that social phenomena should be treated objectively, "as things," and without any preconceptions (Durkheim [1893] 1984). While this is rather difficult to accomplish, as Weber noted in his own *Methodology of the Social Sciences,* it is still the case that an approach of deliberate skepticism and resistance to facile explanations is appropriate when investigating phenomena in the social world (Weber [1904] 1949).

The same point has been stressed by a long line of prominent scientists, both natural and social, to the point that the open admission of ignorance has become a value and a mark of scientific distinction. Merton quotes the succinct epigram of Laplace: "What we know is not too much, what we do not know is immense." (Merton 1987:7). Still this generalized admission of ignorance does not take us far. More fruitful is the ignorance that arises from knowledge itself, such that each empirical or theoretical advance leads to new concrete questions. This, Merton called "specified ignorance":

> For the growth of knowledge and understanding within a field of inquiry brings with it the growth of *specifiable and specified ignorance:* a new awareness of what is not yet known or understood and a rationale for its being worth knowing. To the extent that the current theoretical frameworks prove unequal to the task of dealing with some of the newly emergent questions, there develops a composite ... pressure within the discipline for new or revised frameworks. (Merton 1981:v–vi)

Consider, for example, the concept of "informality" or "the informal economy." Once, it was firmly established that a substantial number of waged and self-employed people work, fully or partially, outside the formal legal framework, the next logical questions were how these activities came about and with what consequences. A first, commonsensical interpretation was that people became employed informally because no regular jobs were available to them. Thus, informality was equated with economic marginality and poverty. This initial interpretation was advanced without the benefit of firsthand investigation into the phenomenon (Nun 1969; Tokman 1982).

It was subsequently found that the informally self-employed earned more on average than wage workers in many countries and that their activities were not "marginal" at all because they were connected, in multiple ways, to those in the formal sector (Lomnitz 1977; Portes and Schauffler 1993; Cappecchi 1989). These ways include the provision of goods and services to formal workers and firms, either directly or through multiple chains of subcontracting. These empirical findings led to a reformulated theory where informality was defined as a means to increase flexibility and reduce labor and regulatory costs for corporate actors and large formal enterprises. While informal workers at the bottom could be highly exploited, intermediaries (i.e., informal entrepreneurs) could earn relatively high incomes by organizing this labor force for the ultimate benefit of powerful economic interests (Birbeck 1979; Portes and Sassen-Koob 1987).

The theory also explained why informal activities were found both in the less developed and more developed economies and why they were actually increasing in some First World nations: competitive pressures and the search for flexibility led a number of firms in these countries to close plants and shed protected labor, farming out production of goods and services to subcontractors who tapped, in turn, into the informal labor pool. In this fashion, the labor of sweatshop seamstresses, casual construction workers, garbage collectors and recyclers, piece-rate electronic assemblers, and home workers of all kinds ended up registered as gain in the financial houses of New York and London (Castells and Portes 1989; Sassen 1988).

The same evolution took place concerning the consequences of informality. The initial commonsensical presumption was that it represented a survival mechanism that condemned those so employed to poverty. Subsequent research showed that not only could the informal self-employed do well economically but that, under certain circumstances, entire communities of informal artisans and workers could become prosperous by competing effectively with larger firms in the formal sector. This could happen when levels of bounded solidarity and trust (i.e., social capital according to Bourdieu) were sufficiently high to foster productive collaboration and access to markets and capital that otherwise would not exist. The famous industrial district of Emilia Romagna in central Italy and the origins of the Cuban enclave economy in Miami represent examples of these "informal economies of growth" (Cappechi 1989; Brusco 1982; Portes and Stepick 1993).

I have dwelt on this example at some length because the theoretical evolution of the informal economy provides clear instances of all the pitfalls that Merton's reflection on the course of science identified. Dismissed by some as nonexistent and by others as always existing, the informal economy was ultimately proven to be a real and novel phenomenon. This acceptance led, in turn, to questions about its origins and social and economic effects. For some authors, the answers were obvious and this absence of "specified ignorance" produced erroneous conclusions on both counts. More cautious sociologists and economists, admitting that they did not know the answers, set out to gather additional firsthand evidence on each question. Results of this renewed empirical effort led to quite a few surprises and to the reformulation of the entire theory. This reformulation clarified the actual dynamics of informality and the significant, but concealed, role that it plays in the circles of global capital accumulation.

The Rational and the Unexpected

Despite the failures of the past, attempts to construct grand narratives of society based on a few master principles continue to our day. The latest set of master principles comes from economics and consists of a series of assumptions about rational behavior based on deliberate individualistic calculations of costs and benefits. The project to rebuild both society and sociological theory on rational blueprints has two parts: first, the belief that most social and economic action is explainable through self-centered calculations; second, a means-ends structure where explicit goals are pursued through deliberate purposive selection of means (Becker 1976; Hechter 1987; Coleman 1994).

To proponents of rational action theory, the idea that most of social life is explainable through purposive calculated action seems obvious. The economist who crusaded to extend the cost-benefit paradigm into areas hitherto reserved to the other social sciences made no bones about his convictions:

Indeed I have come to the position that the economic approach is a comprehensive one that is applicable to all human behavior. . . . I do not want to soften the impact of what I'm saying in the interest of increasing its acceptance in the short run. I am saying that the economic approach provides a valuable unified framework for understanding all human behavior. (Becker 1976:8, 14)

Yet, unlike the Mertonian discoveries, this is an instance where the obvious turns out not to be so. Behavioral economics led the charge from the social-psychological angle by noting that the assumption of individualistic maximization turned out to be, in many instances, demonstrably false. In a series of brilliant experiments, psychologists Tverski and Kahneman (1974, 1981) undermined the basis of the rationalistic paradigm at the microlevel of personal choices and face-to-face interactions (Frank 1990). The sociological critique to the "obvious" means-ends paradigm has its modern basis in Merton himself. In an article published in the first issue of the *American Sociological Review*, he not only foresaw the advent of economistic reasoning in sociology, but provided a powerful counterargument (Merton 1936).

As a host of historical and contemporary examples make clear, the best-laid plans are often derailed because they do not and cannot fully take into account the interplay of social forces impinging on their implementation. This occurs both at the individual and collective levels, leading to situations in which the deliberate rational application of means produces consequences that are different or even opposite to those originally anticipated. At the level of collective action, consider the numerous policy catastrophes that the American federal government has inflicted on its own society because of grand plans, supposedly rational. Contemporaneous examples of such catastrophes include immigration, the health system, and the Iraq War, among others.

The rational means-ends structure in U.S. immigration policy consists in attempting to stop the unauthorized flow by beefing up and even militarizing the Southern border. Today, the U.S. Border Patrol is the second largest arms-bearing agency of the federal government, next to the armed forces themselves. The huge expenditure of dollars in this policy has not succeeded in stopping the unauthorized flow, but has succeeded in keeping it bottled up on the American side of the border. Contrary to the prior pattern of cyclical migration, where Mexican workers commuted back and forth across the border, those who, at present, manage to cross into the United States do not return to their countries, given the difficulties of repeating the journey (Massey, Durand, and Malone 2002; Portes 2007). Instead, they bring their families along. As a consequence of this supposedly rational policy, the United States now has in its midst an underground poor and vulnerable population numbering about twelve million (Cornelius 1998; Massey 2007).

The health system of the United States is based ultimately on the rational economic argument that universal access to care would encourage massive "free riding" and, hence, lead to skyrocketing costs. This is known as the "moral hazard" syndrome (Gladwell 2005; Light 1992). To maximize quality of care, the most efficient means is private health insurance because it motivates people to avoid frivolous use of medical facilities lest their premiums go up or they lose coverage. This purposively designed system has led to a situation where more than forty million Americans today lack health insurance, where illness is an ever-present threat among the insured, and where health care in the United States is the most expensive and most unequal in the developed world (Guendelman, Schauffler, and Pearl 2001; Gladwell 2005; Light 1992).

I do not need to belabor the origins and consequences of the Iraq debacle. It is simply the most poignant present example that grand designs elaborated from the heights of power can eventually explode in the faces of their architects because of the intervention of unforeseen actors and forces. Elsewhere, I have sought to extend Merton's core insight by examining the different ways in which social reality can depart from purposive means-ends designs. Results of this analysis are reproduced in Table 1. I will not discuss all the variants here, but note just two of the most important.

The first occurs when the original ends are real but, in the process of pursuing them, they are altered and efforts are turned toward the attainment of new emergent goals. This "change in midcourse" finds its best example in classic sociology in Weber's analysis of the Protestant Ethic. This most famous of his studies is, in essence, an analysis of the social-psychological processes through which the subjective need to achieve certainty of eternal salvation, the *certitudo salutis*, eventually mutated into the ascetic pursuit of gain and capital accumulation in this world (Weber [1930] 1985; Bendix 1962).

The second variant occurs when the original ends are real and they are eventually achieved, not with the foreseen means which fall short, but through an unplanned series of improvisations, adaptations, and just plain luck. Tilly (1996) referred to this alternative—the lucky turn of events—as the "invisible elbow." To the "invisible hand" of Smithian fame, Tilly

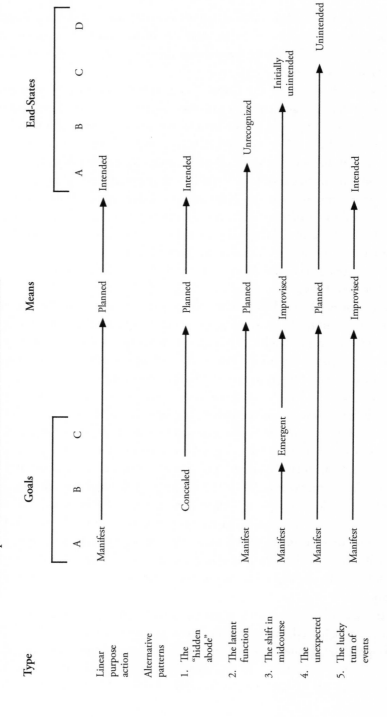

FIGURE 1 Linear Purposive Action and Alternative Behavioral Patterns

Type	Goals			Means	End-States			
	A	B	C		A	B	C	D
Linear purpose action	Manifest			Planned	Intended			
Alternative patterns								
1. The "hidden abode"	Concealed			Planned	Intended			
2. The latent function	Manifest			Planned	Unrecognized			
3. The shift in midcourse	Manifest	Emergent		Improvised	Initially unintended			
4. The unexpected	Manifest			Planned	Unintended			
5. The lucky turn of events	Manifest			Improvised	Intended			

opposes the elbow signifying the multiple improvised and unanticipated ways through which historical ends are actually accomplished. Once they are, the process can be reconstructed *post factum* as a systematic and deliberate enterprise. In reality, there was none such.

Tilly cites the example of Louis XIV and his minister Colbert engaged in, at times, a desperate effort of nation-building, improvising as they went along and using the most various means—legal or not—to browbeat the nobility and the cities, make the clergy fall into line, and extract taxes from a most reluctant populace. Once their decades-long struggle proved successful, the story could be rewritten along the familiar, neat rational lines (Tilly 1996).

All of these are, of course, variations around the original Mertonian theme. From unanticipated consequences to establishing the phenomenon, he bequeathed us a set of intellectual tools, underlined by a skeptical stance toward grand designs and a priori assumptions and aimed at refining and disciplining the pursuit of scientific knowledge. Sociology is still far from absorbing and putting into everyday practice this set of insights and cautions. I surmise that much of the confusion and unnecessary controversies in many subfields of the discipline stem from this failure. It will be in our collective interest to learn and put into practice this priceless legacy.

References

Bachrach, A. J. 1965. "Some Applications of Operant Conditioning to Behavior Therapy." In *The Conditioning Therapies*, ed. J. Wolpe, A. Salter, and J. L. Reyna. New York: Holt, Rinehart, and Winston.

Barrett, Stanley R. 1984. *The Rebirth of Anthropological Theory*. Toronto: University of Toronto Press.

Baudrillard, Jean. 1988. *The Mirror of Production*. St. Louis: Telos Press.

Becker, Gary. 1976. *The Economic Approach to Human Behavior*. Chicago: University of Chicago Press.

Bendix, Reinhard. 1962. *Max Weber: An Intellectual Portrait*. Garden City, NY: Anchor Books.

Birbeck, Christopher. 1979. "Garbage, Industry, and the 'Vultures' of Cali, Colombia." In *Casual Work and Poverty in Third World Cities*, ed. R. Bromley and C. Gerry, 161–183. New York: John Wiley.

Bogardus, Emory S. 1940. *The Development of Social Thought*. New York: Longmans, Green, and Co.

Borges, Jorge Luis. 1962. "Kafka and his Predecessors." In *Labyrinths*, ed. J. L. Borges, 199–201. New York: New Directions Books.

Bourdieu, Pierre. 1979. "Les Trois Etats Du Capital Culturel." *Actes de la Recherche en Sciences Sociales* 30:3–6.

———. 1980. "Le Capital Social: Notes Provisoires." *Actes de la Recherche en Sciences Sociales* 31:2–3.

Brusco, Sebastiano. 1982. "The Emilian Model: Productive Decentralization and Social Integration." *Cambridge Journal of Economics* 6 (2):167–84.

Capecchi, Vittorio. 1989. "The Informal Economy and the Development of Flexible Specialization." In *The Informal Economy: Studies in Advanced and Less Developed Countries*, ed. A. Portes, M. Castells, and L. A. Benton, 189–215. Baltimore, MD: The Johns Hopkins University Press.

Castells, Manuel, and Alejandro Portes. 1989. "World Underneath: The Origins, Dynamics, and Effects of the Informal Economy." In *The Informal Economy: Studies in Advanced and Less Developed Countries*, ed. A. Portes, M. Castells, and L. A. Benton, 11–37. Baltimore, MD: The Johns Hopkins University Press.

Coleman, James S. 1988. "Social Capital in the Creation of Human Capital." *American Journal of Sociology* 94 (Supplement):S95–121.

Coleman, James S. 1994. "A Rational Choice Perspective on Economic Sociology." In *Handbook of Economic Sociology*, ed. N. J. Smelser and R. Swedberg, 166–80. New York: Princeton University Press and Russell Sage Foundation.

Collins, Randall. 1994. *Four Sociological Traditions: Selected Readings*. New York: Oxford University Press.

Cornelius, Wayne A. 1998. "Appearances and Realities: Controlling Illegal Immigration in the United States." In *Temporary Workers or Future Citizens? Japanese and U.S. Migration Policies*, ed. M. Weiner and T. Hanami, 384–427. New York: New York University Press.

Durkheim, Emile. [1893] 1984. *The Division of Labor in Society*. New York: The Free Press.

Edwards, Richard. 1979. *Contested Terrain, the Transformation of the Workplace in the Twentieth Century*. New York: Basic Books.

Evans, Peter. 2004. "The Challenges of the 'Institutional Turn': Interdisciplinary Opportunities in Development Theory." In *The Economic Sociology of Capitalist Institutions*, ed. V. Nee and R. Swedberg. Princeton, NJ: Princeton University Press.

Frank, Robert H. 1990. "Rethinking Rational Choice." In *Beyond the Marketplace: Rethinking Economy and Society*, ed. R. Friedland and A. F. Robertson, pp. 53–87. New York: Aldine de Gruyter.

Gladwell, Malcolm. 2005. "The Moral Hazard Myth." *New Yorker*, August 29:44–49.

Guendelman, Sylvia, Helen H. Schauffler, and M. Pearl. 2001. "Unfriendly Shores: How Immigrant Children Fare in the U.S. System." *Health Affairs* 20 (January-February)

Harris, Marvin. 1968. *The Rise of Anthropological Theory: A History of Theories and Culture*. New York: Thomas Y. Crowell.

Harrison, Bennett, and Barry Bluestone. 1988. *The Great U-Turn: Corporate Restructuring and the Polarization of America*. New York: Basic Books.

Hechter, Michael. 1987. *Principles of Group Solidarity*. Berkeley: University of California Press.

Hodgson, Geoffrey M. 2002. "Institutional Blindness in Modern Economics." In *Advancing Socio-economics: An Institutionalist Perspective*, ed. J. R. Hollingsworth, K. H. Muller, and E. J. Hollingsworth, 147–170. Lanham, MD: Rowan and Littlefield.

James, William. 1907. *Pragmatism: A New Name for Some Old Ways of Thinking*. New York: Longmans, Green.

Jameson, Frederic. 1984. "Post-Modernism or the Cultural Logic of Capitalism." *New Left Review* 146 (July-August):53–93.

Light, Donald W. 1992. "The Practice and Ethnics of Risk-Rated Health Insurance." *Journal of the American Medical Association* 267:2503–07.

Lomnitz, Larissa. 1977. *Networks and Marginality: Life in a Mexican Shantytown*. New York: Academic Press.

Massey, Douglas S. 2007. "Borderline Madness: America's Counterproductive Immigration Policy." In *Debating Immigration*, ed. C. M. Swain, pp. 129–138. New York: Cambridge University Press.

Massey, Douglas S., Jorge Durand, and Nolan J. Malone. 2002. *Beyond Smoke and Mirrors: Mexican Immigration in an Era of Economic Integration*. New York: Russell Sage Foundation.

Merton, Robert K. 1936. "The Unanticipated Consequences of Purposive Social Action." *American Sociological Review* 1:894–904.

——. 1968a. "Social Structure and Anomie." In *Social Theory and Social Structure*, ed. R. K. Merton, 175–214. New York: Free Press.

——. 1968b. "On the History and Systematics of Sociological Theory." In *Social Theory and Social Structure*, 1–38. New York: The Free Press.

——. 1981. "Remarks on Theoretical Pluralism." In *Continuities in Structural Inquiry*, ed. P. M. Blau and R. K. Merton, I–VII. London: Sage.

——. 1987. "Three Fragments from a Sociologist's Notebook: Establishing the Phenomenon, Specified Ignorance, and Strategic Research Materials." *Annual Review of Sociology* 13:1–28.

Moore, Wilbert E., and Melvin M. Tumin. 1949. "Some Social Functions of Ignorance." *American Sociological Review* 14:787–795.

Nee, Victor. 2005. "The New Institutionalisms in Economics and Sociology." In *The Handbook of Economic Sociology*, ed. N. J. Smelser and R. Swedberg, 2nd ed., 49–74. Princeton, NJ: Princeton University Press and Russell Sage Foundation.

Nun, Jose. 1969. "Superpoblacion Relativa, Ejercito Industrial de Reserva y Masa Marginal." *Revista Latinoamericana de Sociologia* 5:178–235.

Perez, Lisandro. 2001. "Growing up Cuban in Miami: Immigration, the Enclave, and New Generations." In *Ethnicities: Children of Immigrants in America*, ed. R. G. Rumbaut and A. Portes, 91–125. Berkeley, CA: University of California Press and Russell Sage Foundation.

Portes, Alejandro. 2007. "The Fence to Nowhere: The Case for a Bilateral Labor Management Program." *The American Prospect* 18 (October):26–29.

Portes, Alejandro, and Saskia Sassen-Koob. 1987. "Making It Underground: Comparative Materials on the Informal Sector in Western Market Economies." *American Journal of Sociology* 93:30–61.

Portes, Alejandro, and Richard Schauffler. 1993. "The Informal Economy in Latin America: Definition, Measurement, and Policies." *Population and Development Review* 19 (1).

Portes, Alejandro, and Steven Shafer. 2007. "Revisiting the Enclave Hypothesis: Miami Twenty-Five Years Later." *Research in the Sociology of Organizations* 25:157–190.

Portes, Alejandro, and Alex Stepick. 1993. *City on the Edge: The Transformation of Miami*. Berkeley: University of California Press.

Putnam, Robert D. 2000. *Bowling Alone: The Collapse and Revival of American Community*. New York: Simon and Schuster.

Roland, Gerard. 2004. "Understanding Institutional Change: Fast-moving and Slow-moving Institutions." *Studies in Comparative International Development* 38 (Winter):109–131.

Sassen, Saskia. 1988. *The Mobility of Labor and Capital: A Study in International Investment and Labor Flow*. New York: Cambridge University Press.

Sorokin, Pitirim. 1928. *Contemporary Sociological Theories*. New York: Harper.

Stark, Oded. 1991. *The Migration of Labour*. Cambridge, UK: Basil Blackwell.

———. 1984. "Migration Decision Making." *Journal of Development Economics*, 14:251–59.

Steele, Claude. 1997. "A Threat in the Air: How Stereotypes Shape the Intellectual Identities and Performance of Women and African Americans." *American Psychologist* 52:613–29.

Tilly, Charles. 1996. "Invisible Elbow." *Sociological Forum* 11:589–601.

Tokman, Victor. 1982. "Unequal Development and the Absorption of Labour: Latin America 1950–1980." *CEPAL Review* 17:121–33.

Tverski, Amos, and Daniel Kahneman. 1974. "Judgment under Uncertainty: Heuristics and Biases." *Science* 185:1124–1131.

——. 1981. "The Framing of Decisions and the Psychology of Choice." *Science* 211:453–458.

Weber, Max. [1904] 1949. *The Methodology of the Social Sciences.* Trans. E. A. Shils and H. A. Finch. New York: The Free Press.

——. [1922] 1947. "Social Stratification and Class Structure." In *The Theory of Social and Economic Organization,* ed. T. Parsons, pp. 424–29. New York: Free Press.

——. [1930] 1985. *The Protestant Ethic and the Spirit of Capitalism.* Trans. Talcott Parsons. London: Unwin.

Wolpe, J., and A. A. Lazarus. 1967. *Behavior Therapy Techniques: a Guide to the Treatment of Neuroses.* New York: Pergamon Press.

Zhou, Min, and Carl N. Bankston III. 1996. "Social Capital and the Adaptation of the Second Generation: The Case of Vietnamese Youth in New Orleans." In *The New Second Generation,* ed. A. Portes, 197–220. New York: Russell Sage.

——. 1998. *Growing up American: How Vietnamese Immigrants Adapt to Life in the United States.* New York: Russell Sage Foundation.

2

Mechanisms of the Middle Range

CHARLES TILLY

Along with *esprit d'escalier* and *Schadenfreude*, Robert Merton found the loanword *chutzpah* "especially congenial" (Merton 2004:251). So do I. But so far I have never had the *chutzpah* to write so ostentatiously learned and self-referential an essay as Merton's vigorously visionary afterword to the Barber and Merton book on serendipity, finally written and published in English more than forty years after the main text's consignment to the unpublished treasury of Merton works in 1958.

Having already published a review of *Serendipity* (Tilly 2005a), I have no intention of repeating my *recensione* here. Instead, I want to point out that Merton's analysis of serendipity performs two feats of great importance to social-scientific description and explanation. First, it identifies serendipity not just as an intriguing concept but as a causal mechanism in that middle range Merton famously recommended. Second, it makes the distinction between serendipity seen as an individual disposition and as an event that occurs in what he called "serendipitous sociocognitive microenvironments." Merton rejects the first view as unwarranted psychological reductionism (Merton 2004:257–258). Instead, he portrays serendipity as a mechanism in which environment and cognition interact to produce an unexpected and significant discovery.

Although the unpublished Merton treasury may yet yield an essay on social mechanisms, the term "mechanism" does not figure centrally in Merton's published methodological writings.[1] I claim that the recent revival of interest in mechanistic explanations within the social sciences advances the program Merton was already advocating half a century ago: developing theoretically sophisticated accounts of social processes somewhere between the stratosphere of global abstraction and the underground of thick description. I also claim that the mechanistic middle range opens social science to history much more readily than do competing approaches to explanation of social processes. I claim, finally, that beyond epistemology and ontology, mechanistic explanations offer a distinctive, superior grasp of how social processes actually work.

Epistemologies and ontologies provide the (often invisible) philosophical grounding of social analysis. Epistemologies and ontologies limit what sorts of explanations are logically possible—a holist can't appeal to individual motivations as her ultimate causes—but they do not dictate logics of explanation by themselves. Social scientists and historians have experimented with a number of different competing logics for the explanation of social processes. They include:

1. Proposal of covering laws for complex structures and processes; explanation here consists of subjecting robust empirical generalizations to higher-and-higher-level generalizations, the most general of all standing as laws

2. Specification of necessary and sufficient conditions for concrete instances of the same complex structures and processes

3. Variable analyses in which statistical analysis shows the extent which one or more predictor variables (often called "independent variables") account statistically for variation in an outcome variable (often called the "dependent variable")

4. Location of structures and processes within larger systems they supposedly serve or express, for example through the claim that element X exists because it serves function Y within system Z

5. Stage models in which placement within an invariant sequence accounts for the episode at hand, for example the stages of revolution or of economic growth

6. Identification of individual or group dispositions just before the point of action as causes of that action—propensity or disposition accounts

7. Reduction of complex episodes, or certain features of those episodes, to their component mechanisms and processes

A full accounting of the last half century's social science and history includes all seven logics on the list.

Most of these explanatory modes, however, exclude history as a significant shaper of social processes. Covering law, necessary-sufficient condition, and system accounts generally resist history as they deny the influence of particular times and places. Stage models do incorporate time, but they usually run roughshod over the actual complexities of historical social processes. Propensity accounts respond to history ambivalently, since in the version represented by rational choice they depend on transhistorical rules of decision making, while in the versions represented by cultural and phenomenological reductionism they treat history as infinitely particular.

Mechanism-process accounts, in contrast, positively welcome history, because their explanatory program couples a search for mechanisms of very general scope with arguments that initial conditions, sequences, and combinations of mechanisms concatenate into processes having explicable but variable overall outcomes. Mechanism-process accounts reject covering-law regularities for large structures such as international systems and for vast sequences such as democratization. Instead, they lend themselves to "local theory" in which the explanatory mechanisms and processes operate quite broadly, but combine locally as a function of initial conditions and adjacent processes to produce distinctive trajectories and outcomes (McAdam, Tarrow, and Tilly 2001; Tilly 2001).

Mechanisms compound into processes: combinations and sequences of mechanisms that produce some specified outcome at a larger scale than any single mechanism. Within contentious politics, analysts commonly invoke such processes as escalation, framing, identity shift, and scale shift (Tilly and Tarrow 2006). But they rarely identify the component mechanisms, much less their combinations and sequences. Nevertheless, in social science as a whole, a substantial intellectual movement has formed to adopt mechanism- and process-based explanations as complements to variable-based explanations, or even as substitutes for them.

As is always the case in new movements, competing definitions and practical proposals for the analysis of mechanisms and processes have proliferated wildly (Bunge 1997, 1998, 2004; Campbell 2005; Cherkaoui 2005; Elster 1999; George and Bennett 2005; Goodin and Tilly 2006; Hedström

2005; Hedström and Swedberg 1998; Little 1991, 1998; McAdam 2003; Norkus 2005; Pickel 2006; Stern et al. 2002; Stinchcombe 2005; Tarrow 2004; Tilly 2000, 2001, 2004). No conceptual, theoretical, or methodological consensus has so far emerged.

Instead of proliferating catalogs of mechanisms, Merton himself commonly identified one or two mechanisms at a time, but explored their operations with reflective care and multiple examples. When it came to discussing inequality, for example, he approached it from two different ends. His famous essay "The Self-Fulfilling Prophecy" specified one small bundle of mechanisms by which in-groups help create the apparent inferiority they attribute to members of out-groups. In "Social Structure and Anomie" and "Continuities in the Theory of Social Structure and Anomie," Merton identified mechanisms that help produce the apparently deleterious *consequences* of inequality. Both sets of mechanisms depend on the capacity of people in higher-ranking categories to impose constraints on people in lower-ranking categories.

"The specious validity of the self-fulfilling prophecy," according to Merton, "perpetuates a reign of error" (Merton 1949:423). Since he was about to analyze ethnic and racial conflict in the United States, I imagine Merton chuckling at his play on the Reign of Terror. In any case, the central mechanism in his pernicious prophecy consists of justifying exclusion from advantages on the basis of inferior or undesirable attributes, and thus reproducing the ostensible evidence of those inferior or undesirable attributes. That mechanism bears second-cousin kinship to the central mechanism in "Social Structure and Anomie," where:

> It is only when a system of cultural values extols, virtually above all else, certain *common* success-goals *for the population at large* while the social structure rigorously restricts or completely closes access to approved modes of reaching those goals *for a considerable part of the same population,* that deviant behavior ensues on a large scale (Merton 1949:146; emphasis in original).

Although the specter of "a system of cultural values" as a social agent makes me very uneasy, it doesn't take much imagination to convert Merton's insights into an agent-centered argument concerning the process by which powerful and privileged groups perpetuate their power and privilege.

My own mechanism-centered analyses of categorical inequality proceed in a similar spirit. To give it a full, cumbersome label, we might call my

line of argument an "interactive resource control theory of material inequality generation." Here is how the argument runs:

Material inequality results from unequal control over value-producing
resources (for example, some wildcatters strike oil, while others drill
dry wells).

Paired and unequal categories such as male-female or white-black consist of asymmetrical relations across a socially recognized (and usually incomplete) boundary between interpersonal networks. Such
categorical pairs recur in a wide variety of situations, with the usual
effect being unequal exclusion of each network from resources controlled by the other (for example, in U.S. urban ghettos, immigrant
merchants often make their livings by selling mainly to black people,
but never integrate into the black community).

An inequality-generating mechanism we may call *exploitation* occurs
when persons who control a resource enlist the effort of others in the
production of value by means of that resource but exclude the others
from the full value added by their effort (for example, before 1848,
citizens of several Swiss cantons drew substantial revenues in rents
and taxes from non-citizen residents of adjacent tributary territories
who produced agricultural and craft goods under control of the cantons' landlords and merchants).

Another inequality-generating mechanism we may call *opportunity
hoarding* consists of confining disposition of a value-producing resource to members of an in-group (for example, Southeast Asian
spice merchants from a particular ethnic-religious category dominate the distribution and sale of their product).

Two further mechanisms reinforce the effects of exploitation and opportunity hoarding: emulation and adaptation. *Emulation* occurs
when those who control an inequality-generating set of social relations import categorical distinctions (e.g., by gender or caste) that
bring with them readily available practices and meanings (for example, early-twentieth-century operators of South African gold and
diamond mines build the distinction between "Europeans" and "Na-
tives" directly into the workforce, with white workers enjoying su-
pervisory positions and enormously higher pay).

Adaptation involves subordinates' adjustment of their daily routines (e.g.,
their meetings with friends) so that they actually depend on the social

arrangements generating inequality (for example, factory workers meet their production quotas through speedups and collaboration in order to create time for sociable leisure with their workmates, but by that very effort commit themselves to management-imposed quotas)

Both exploitation and opportunity hoarding generally incorporate paired and unequal categories at boundaries between greater and lesser beneficiaries of value added by effort committed to controlled resources (for example, the distinction between professionals and non-professionals—registered nurses and aides, scientists and laboratory assistants, optometrists and optical clerks, architects and architectural drawers, et cetera—often marks just such boundaries).

Local categorical distinctions gain strength and operate at lower cost when matched with widely available paired, unequal categories so that their boundaries coincide (for example, hiring women as workers and men as bosses reinforces organizational hierarchy with gender hierarchy).

Over a wide range of circumstances, mobility across boundaries does not in itself change the production of inequality, but alters who benefits from inequality (for example, so long as college degrees remain essential for engineering jobs, acquisition of those degrees by immigrants reinforces the exclusion of non-degree holders, even among immigrants).

Inequalities produced in these ways become more durable and effective to the extent that recipients of the surplus generated by exploitation or opportunity hoarding commit a portion of that surplus to reproducing boundaries separating themselves from excluded categories of the population, and unequal relations across those boundaries (for example, landlords devote some of their available wage-labor to building fences and chasing off squatters).

Those are the theory's bare bones (for more sustained treatments, see Tilly 1998, 2005). Taken in these terms, it provides no direct explanations for individual-by-individual variation in success and failure or for change and variation in the overall distribution of a country's wealth and income. Yet the theory has direct implications for Merton's recurrent concern: exclusion. It centers on exclusion (complete or partial) from benefits generated by control of resources. Both exploitation and opportunity hoarding exclude members of subordinate categories from benefits. If the argument is correct, that exclusion usually produces categorical boundaries between ins and outs.

I confess that only in writing this chapter did I notice the Mertonian tones of my decade-old argument. Call it serendipity. I claim nevertheless that the argument falls into Merton's preferred middle range, and does so with a mechanism-process specification he probably would have found congenial.

These days, bright new energy is flowing into mechanism-process explanations of social processes, including the generation of inequality. Douglas Massey's sweeping synthesis of changes in American patterns of inequality since 1900 not only focuses its explanations specifically on categorical mechanisms but begins by quoting Barbara Reskin's ASA presidential address with its stirring call for mechanistic explanations (Massey 2007:xv). With less stress on inequality and more stress on organizational processes, Ronald Burt has built a whole research program around the mechanisms of brokerage and closure (Burt 2005). Although Massey does not cite Robert Merton, Burt does so extensively. The revival of interest in mechanisms of the middle range tells us that Merton's inspiration continues to work its magic, with or without chutzpah.

Note

1. Functional analysis in sociology, as in other disciplines like physiology and psychology, calls for a "concrete and detailed" account of the mechanisms that operate to perform a designated function. This refers not to psychological but to social mechanisms (e.g., role segmentation, insulation of institutional demands, hierarchic ordering of values, social division of labor, ritual and ceremonial enactments, etc.) (Merton 1949:52).

References

Bunge, Mario. 1997. "Mechanism and Explanation." *Philosophy of the Social Sciences* 27:410–465.

——. 1998. *Social Science under Debate: A Philosophical Perspective.* Toronto: University of Toronto Press.

——. 2004. "How Does It Work? The Search for Explanatory Mechanisms." *Philosophy of the Social Sciences* 34:182–210.

Burt, Ronald S. 2005. *Brokerage and Closure: An Introduction to Social Capital.* Oxford: Oxford University Press.

Campbell, John L. 2005. "Where Do We Stand? Common Mechanisms in Organizations and Social Movements Research." In *Social Movements and Organization Theory,* ed. Gerald F. Davis, Doug McAdam, W. Richard Scott, and Mayer N. Zald. Cambridge: Cambridge University Press.

Cherkaoui, Mohamed. 2005. *Invisible Codes: Essays on Generative Mechanisms.* Oxford: Bardwell Press.

Elster, Jon. 1999. *Alchemies of the Mind: Rationality and the Emotions.* Cambridge: Cambridge University Press.

George, Alexander L., and Andrew Bennett. 2005. *Case Studies and Theory Development in the Social Sciences.* Cambridge: MIT Press.

Goodin, Robert, and Charles Tilly, eds. 2006. *The Oxford Handbook of Contextual Political Analysis.* Oxford: Oxford University Press.

Hedström, Peter. 2005. *Dissecting the Social. On the Principles of Analytical Sociology.* Cambridge: Cambridge University Press.

Hedström, Peter, and Richard Swedberg, eds. 1998. *Social Mechanisms: An Analytical Approach to Social Theory.* Cambridge: Cambridge University Press.

Little, Daniel. 1991. *Varieties of Social Explanation: An Introduction to the Philosophy of Social Science.* Boulder: Westview.

——. 1998. *On the Philosophy of the Social Sciences: Microfoundations, Method, and Causation.* New Brunswick: Transaction.

Massey, Douglas S. 2007. *Categorically Unequal: The American Stratification System.* New York: Russell Sage Foundation.

McAdam, Doug. 2003. "Beyond Structural Analysis: Toward a More Dynamic Understanding of Social Movements" In *Social Movements and Networks: Relational Approaches to Collective Action,* ed. Mario Diani & Doug McAdam. Oxford: Oxford University Press.

McAdam, Doug, Sidney Tarrow, and Charles Tilly. 2001. *Dynamics of Contention.* Cambridge: Cambridge University Press.

Merton, Robert K. 1949. *Social Theory and Social Structure. Revised and Enlarged Edition.* New York: Free Press of Glencoe.

——. 2004. "Afterword: Autobiographic Reflections on *The Travels and Adventures of Serendipity.*" In *The Travels and Adventures of Serendipity: A Study in Sociological Semantics and the Sociology of Science,* ed. Robert K. Merton and Elinor Barber. Princeton: Princeton University Press.

Norkus, Zenonas. 2005. "Mechanisms as Miracle Makers? The Rise and Inconsistencies of the 'Mechanismic Approach' in Social Science and History." *History and Theory* 44:348–372.

Pickel, Andreas. 2006. *The Problem of Order in the Global Age: Systems and Mechanisms.* London: Palgrave Macmillan.

Stern, Paul C., Thomas Dietz, Nives Dolšak, Elinor Ostrom, and Susan Stonich. 2002. "Knowledge and Questions After 15 Years of Research." In *The Drama of the Commons*, ed. Elinor Ostrom, Thomas Dietz, Nives Dolšak, Paul C. Stern, Susan Stonich, and Elke U. Weber. Washington DC: National Academy Press.

Stinchcombe, Arthur L. 2005. *The Logic of Social Research*. Chicago: University of Chicago Press.

Tarrow, Sidney. 2004. "Bridging the Quantitative-Qualitative Divide." In *Rethinking Social Inquiry. Diverse Tools, Shared Standards*, ed. Henry E. Brady & David Collier. Lanham, Maryland: Rowman & Littlefield.

Tilly, Charles. 1998. *Durable Inequality*. Berkeley: University of California Press.

——. 2000. "Processes and Mechanisms of Democratization," *Sociological Theory* 18:1–16.

——. 2001. "Mechanisms in Political Processes," *Annual Review of Political Science* 4:21–41.

——. 2004. "Social Boundary Mechanisms," *Philosophy of the Social Sciences* 34:211–236.

——. 2005a. "Now That You Mention It," *Contemporary Sociology* 34:451–453.

——. 2005b. "Historical Perspectives on Inequality" In *The Blackwell Companion to Social Inequalities*, ed. Mary Romero and Eric Margolis, 15–30. Oxford: Blackwell.

Tilly, Charles, and Sidney Tarrow. 2006. *Contentious Politics*. Boulder: Paradigm Publishers.

3

Eliding the Theory/Research and Basic/Applied Divides

Implications of Merton's Middle Range

ROBERT J. SAMPSON

It is said that one of the most cited articles in sociology is "Social Structure and Anomie," published in 1938 by Robert K. Merton. In it, Merton proposed a theory of crime and deviance that became an instant classic, one still read widely today. His notion of a disjuncture between structures of opportunity and the institutionally prescribed means of obtaining economic goals—one that results in "blocked opportunities"—is widely accepted as an explanation of crime among sociologists. A popular phrase from Merton's classic argument gets at the idea: "A cardinal American virtue, 'ambition,' promotes a cardinal American vice, 'deviant behavior'" (Merton 1957:146). Distortions of the "American Dream" through inequality and relative deprivation, in other words, are thought to induce deviant adaptations of which crime is one.[1]

One of the intellectual hats I wear is "criminologist," so it would be natural for me to reflect in this chapter on Merton's anomie theory of crime—its importance, historical context, lasting impact, and so on, perhaps including influences on my own criminological work. But truth be told, my work has never been directly or substantially influenced by Merton's anomie theory, at least the traditionally criminological components. (Indirect influences will be noted later). Moreover, an argument can be made that Merton's anomie theory of crime has not stood the test of empirical verification. In a telling phrase, Merton (1968a:198) noted that "whatever" the relationship between socioeconomic status and crime, "the greatest pressures toward deviation are exerted upon the lower strata," thereby creating the notion that Merton's is a "strain" theory of crime. But it is exactly the relationship between social class background and crime that has been questioned, with one well-known article in the leading *American Sociological Review* simply titled, "The Myth of Social Class and Criminality" (Tittle, Villimez, and Smith 1978). A number of other critics have likewise claimed that Merton's theory has proven wrong (see Hirschi 1969; Katz 1988; Kornhauser 1978). For example, in Jack Katz's sharp critique of deviance theory in *Seductions of Crime* (Katz 1988), he lambastes strain, relative deprivation, and materialistic accounts of deviance derived from the Mertonian tradition. As Katz pens his direct attack on Merton's legacy in this area: "After a hiatus during much of the Republican 1970s and 1980s, materialist theory—the Mertonian ideas now bolstered by rational-economic models of social action that had become academically attractive in the interim—is again promoting the lack of opportunity … to explain crime," citing, among others, a paper I published on unemployment, family structure, and rates of violence (Sampson 1987). Katz goes on to say, "That this materialist perspective is 20th century sentimentality about crime is indicated by its overwhelming inadequacy for grasping the experiential facts of crime" (1988:314, 358).

With that kind of challenge, I might also be expected to defend myself along with Merton. But I see no need to do so, as the intellectual historical record has already adjudicated the class-crime debate, to my mind.[2] Although some might disagree, overall I think it is fair to say that despite its citation count, Merton's anomie theory of deviance has not proven to be as important as his other contributions to sociological theory. Moreover, so much has been written on anomie theory and crime that there is not much original left to say, if anything. Even Merton himself weighed in with an analysis of his theory of anomie and crime toward the end of his career, a topic he resisted revisiting for many years (see Cullen and Messner 2007; Merton 1995).

Rather than focus on the merits of the anomie theory per se, I wish instead to tackle more general issues that bear on the distinction between theory and method (or theory and research), starting with the related and hoary distinction often made between *basic* and *applied* research. Merton's foray into criminological theory makes for a fitting example of sociological practice that exposes these distinctions, helping in turn to explain sociology's ambivalence to crime. Interrogating these issues also brings into view Merton's contributions that, in an indirect way, continue to influence much criminological and sociological research, especially the current "analytic sociology" movement, which is self-consciously traced to Merton by its proponents (Hedström and Udehn 2009), and the current emphasis on community-level social mechanisms and neighborhood effects that I link in research style to Merton and Lazarsfeld's program.

Sociological Practice and the Study of Crime

At first glance the study of crime is as applied as it gets. Not only does it deal with pragmatic issues, mainstream criminology gets its hands dirty and involves studying people largely on the margins of society such as pimps, prostitutes, drug dealers, gang members, and delinquents. Occupationally, the study of crime also entails the police, social-welfare workers, public defenders, and prosecutors, many of whom occupy positions of low social status in American society and among intellectuals. For a number of reasons, then, the study of crime in early-twentieth-century sociology quickly came to be seen as secondary, as part of "social problems" (to which a journal was later devoted)—and perhaps even worse, as "applied." This term hardened and became pejorative, a stigma of sorts that to this day is widely interpreted to signify secondary status by academic sociologists who are thought to do real sociology instead, such as stratification, theory, or "macro." Criminologists, like demographers, eventually became interdisciplinary in nature and moved away from sociology proper (I set aside whether this intellectual move was a result of "push" or "pull"), forming their own societies and journals. These societies are intellectually alive and vital, perhaps more so than we see reflected in the ideological activism that seems to have taken hold in some sociological societies.[3]

It is surprising in retrospect that the broad and largely abstract questions posed by Durkheim in *Suicide* (Durkheim [1897] 1951) and, later, Merton on deviance eventually came to be seen as applied. Yet, as Merton's insistence on blurring the basic/applied distinction indicated, the hierarchical placement by the discipline of the sociology of applied questions to secondary status is not sustainable on intellectual or scientific grounds. In fact, I would argue that some of the most important and difficult intellectual questions in sociology turn on so-called practical problems. As one of my mentors, Travis Hirschi, once said, what could be considered more fundamental sociologically than questions of social order? In the introduction to *Causes of Delinquency*, Hirschi (1969) noted that some of the best minds in sociology from Durkheim onward had been attracted to the vexing problem of why people violate norms in which they believe, and by implication, why rates of crime and deviance vary from place to place, or why some societies are consistently high in crime. We are fortunate that from Durkheim to the early Chicago Schoolers, to Merton, Sutherland, Goffman, Ohlin, Cohen, Short, and Hirschi (among others) through the present day, a host of independent-minded scholars, perhaps as a form of intellectual deviance, actively rejected the "applied" stigma to focus on hard intellectual questions. Although certainly bearing pragmatic implications, these questions went to the core of sociological theory and, ultimately, redounded to the benefit of the discipline.

Merton's close colleague Paul Lazarsfeld signed up as well to the idea that pragmatic or applied problems should not be shunted aside in favor of something called basic research. The Bureau of Applied Social Research proudly said as much in its name, all the while conducting seminal research on major theoretical issues and attracting some of the best graduate students in the discipline. I am reminded of Jim Coleman's report of his "conversion" experience at Columbia (Coleman 1992) and his work at the Bureau. As he stated in an autobiography written right before his death, the intellectual atmosphere at Columbia in the 1950s was intellectually "electric," as Merton and Lazarsfeld teamed up to address important empirical questions that resonated in society and that were theoretically driven, if also applied. Even today, *Contemporary Social Problems* (Merton and Nisbet 1961) is a good theoretical read, surprisingly so given how much students are trained to think of social problems as little better than social work.

Hence, to say that something is applied does not mean the research surrounding it is somehow *un*-basic. The major sociologists that have contributed to the study of crime over the decades, Merton especially, were motivated by deep intellectual puzzles in their own right, not by narrow policy. Merton was particularly taken with the enigma of why a wealthy society like the United States was nonetheless so crime ridden. This is an interesting and very hard theoretical question, made all the more obvious as crime rates soared during the period of great economic prosperity in the 1960s. The answer to the crime puzzle requires basic research which may or may not have policy relevance. And indeed Merton's answer was policy relevant only in the most abstract sense: change the social structure and its articulation with cultural expectations for success. This is a far cry from policy evaluation research (e.g., does a policy work or not? what are its costs/benefits?) and most certainly is not the same thing as applied research in the narrow sense. Strain theory has been notably ridiculed in some quarters precisely because of its alleged policy irrelevance (or failure), which tied to its focus on unchangeable structural features of society (Wilson 1975).

Even in the hard sciences, the distinctions between applied and basic are increasingly seen as problematic, with applied usually taken to mean the application of scientific discovery by industry which is then marketed to the public (through patents, profits, and the like). To be sure, when doctors stand to gain financially from the sponsors of their research, we must look hard at conflicts of interest. But this is very different as a matter of principle than studying intellectual problems such as crime in society, or stem cells in biology. The promise of stem cell research is far reaching in its potential practical applications, yet researchers work at the very basics of scientific discovery and revolutionary advances in the human genome.

In short, I would argue that sociology's historical ambivalence to the study of crime is rooted in a stereotyped and fundamentally misleading distinction between basic and applied approaches. Even the intellectual heft of Merton's 1938 intervention in the form of "Social Structure and Anomie" was not enough to overcome the institutional and intellectual ambivalence of elite sociologists, which remains to this day but seems to be easing.[4] Merton was far more successful eliding the divide during the mid-century rise of the Columbia School, with its ambitious program of research touching on a wide range of empirical topics.

The Columbia School

Rejection of the basic/applied distinction is closely related to the rejection of the theory/research divide that so characterizes much of sociology and perhaps surprisingly, even criminology.[5] My reading of "On Sociological Theories of the Middle Range" (Merton 1968c) is that it provided an organizing context at Columbia under Merton for the fusion of theory and research in a uniquely productive way. The article starts out with a prescient bang: "Like so many words that are bandied about, the word 'theory' threatens to become meaningless" (Merton 1968c:39). There is evidence to back this claim, and also the claim that many "theorists"—then as today—tend to see their role as sitting high above the data, without standards for the assessment of competing ideas. Merton worked hard to overcome this sociological straightjacket, insisting that theory bears on empirical research just as much as empirical research bears on theory (Merton 1968b; 1968d). The thesis of the middle range was that the two worlds were inextricably intertwined. And unlike the naïve positivism he is sometimes accused of (Steinmetz 2005), Merton argued that empirical research was not passive but played an active role in shaping theory, which in turn was needed to understand facts on the ground, including through the theoretical invocation of unobserved mechanisms (e.g., in his case, the unintended consequences of social action and the self-fulfilling prophecy). This latter point alone disqualifies Merton as an unreconstructed positivist in the traditional sense (Hedström 2005; Hedström and Udehn 2009).

Or consider Peter Blau's reflections on the implications for sociological practice of the interplay between theory and research: "The atmosphere at Columbia in those days ... tended to destroy the preconception, which most of us students initially shared, that a social theorist is not concerned with systematic empirical investigations" (quoted in Merton 1995:20). Or as Jim Coleman reflected:

> There was a brief courtship, in those early days of quantitative data analysis, between survey data and theoretical problems in sociology. This courtship was apparent in Katz and Lazarsfeld's *Personal Influence*, in Lipset's *Union Democracy*, but most strikingly in a study that never fully made its way into print: Merton's "forthcoming housing study." It was only those of us in Merton's classes at the time who, in the comparison between Craftown and Hilltown, saw exhibited the difference that social structure made, saw social theory and social research come together" (quoted in Merton 1995:22). (See also Clark, Modgil, and Modgil 1990:28–29).

This sort of fusion provided fertile grounds for the midcentury "Columbia School" to flourish and produce one the strongest, if not the strongest, set of students in the history of the discipline. People like Jim Coleman,

Daniel Bell, Seymour Martin Lipset, Peter Rossi, Peter Blau, to name just a very few (Merton 1995:18–19). Coming from a firm believer in the Chicago School and someone who is institutionally charged with promoting Harvard's not so shabby record in producing future generations of scholars, this is not faint praise.

Merton's Columbia School also produced an abundance of empirical work under his tutelage, much of which is the subject of other papers in this volume. As Craig Calhoun has noted in a remembrance of Merton (Calhoun 2003), these included empirical, theoretically relevant, and yes, "applied" studies often overlooked, such as integrated housing projects in World War II, which Coleman argued were influential (Merton, West, and Jahoda 1951), a case study of the use of social research by the AT&T Corporation, and research on medical education practices.

Merton's connection to applied methods was further reflected in a project that led to the "focused group interview" (Merton, Fiske, and Kendall 1956). Although there is some disagreement about the coinage of terms, there appears to be a close link between the focused group interview of Merton and what is now taken for granted as an applied methodological tool—"focus groups." Whether by politicians, market researchers, or survey researchers, focus groups are widely used and bear close resemblance to Merton's early methodological approach and publication of a (quite applied) manual for using focused group interviews (Merton, Fiske, and Kendall 1990). Although perhaps mistaken, it is common to cite Merton as the inventor or intellectual father of focus groups (Denzin and Lincoln 1994).

More famously, working with his Columbia colleague Paul Lazarsfeld and students, Merton carried out studies of propaganda and mass communications during World War II and wrote the classic *Mass Persuasion* (Merton 1946). Again, a defining feature of the work was the connection of methods to theoretically inspired sociological goals. Merton and Lazarsfeld made for a very formidable team, producing important work together and influencing each other.

Merton and Lazarsfeld's constructive approach was also central in turning methodological attention to one of the foundational commitments of sociology—to study not just individual persons but "groups, communities, organizations, and other collectives." Then, as now, most sociologists would probably agree that the core subject matter of our discipline pertains to collective phenomena. But it is also true that then, as now, the majority of published research in sociology focused on individuals. In a series of papers, Lazarsfeld in particular specified concrete methodological parameters for relating individual and collective properties. To study "collective" properties is exceedingly complex and there are multiple units of analysis one could discuss. I will therefore be selective and focus briefly on community or neighborhood systems as an example of theoretically motivated research on collective entities. I do this for two reasons. One, the study of community systems occupied not just Lazarsfeld's thinking but even more so one of his and Merton's most influential students, Jim Coleman, who later addressed the micro-macro link that animates many sociologists interested in social mechanisms (Hedström 2005). The second is because the study of collective community properties connects to the Chicago School of Sociology that has shaped my own social inquiry, and to a long-term research tradition in sociology on neighborhood effects.

Contextual Typology and the Study of Collective Processes

Lazarsfeld's basic typology proposed three types of properties that describe collectives: *analytical* properties based on data about each member; *structural* properties based on data about the relations among members; and *global* properties, not based on properties of individual members (Lazarsfeld and Menzel 1961).[6] Examples might include: for analytical, the average neighborhood income of residents; for structural, the network density of friendship ties; and for global, proximity to a factory. Lazarsfeld wrote on the measurement operations involved in the construction of collective measures. His emphasis was not so much statistical but methodological in the sense of theoretically informed research design. Theory and method were, once again, inseparable. From my reading of the literature, Merton and Lazarsfeld were in frequent communication over this very issue, especially during the time Lazarsfeld put together what I consider one of the finest theoretically inspired books on methodology, one I devoured in graduate school—*The Language of Social Research* (Lazarsfeld and Rosenberg 1955).

It turns out, however, that community-level research failed to properly and fully examine collective properties. Coleman noted in *Foundations of Social Theory* (1990) how the proud tradition of community research was led astray in the 1960s with the increasing dominance of survey research. Then, just as Lazarsfeld was publishing his articles on collective properties, the focus in sociology was turning, ironically, even more to individuals, both as units of data collection and targets of theoretical inference.[7] This dominance continues today despite a dramatic resurgence of interest in so-called neighborhood effects. To my mind much of this research is impoverished, firstly because it treats the neighborhood as just one more characteristic to be tagged on to the individual and used to predict individual variations in some behavior (Sampson 2008a). Secondly, and perhaps more important, research that does examine collective measures almost always resorts to analytic properties, in Lazarsfeld and Menzel's (1961) language. In other words, most neighborhood research looks to the aggregate composition of individual members, such as race, class, and family status, neglecting social organization at the level of the community (Sampson, Morenoff, and Gannon-Rowley 2002).

Why, to take a prominent example, is concentrated poverty (which is, after all, the proportion of poor people) correlated so robustly with child and adolescent outcomes such as infant mortality, low birth weight, teenage childbearing, dropping out of high school, child maltreatment, and adolescent delinquency? If neighborhood effects of poverty on these behaviors exist, presumably they are constituted from social interactional or organizational processes that involve collective aspects of community life, such as epidemics, collective socialization, or institutional capacity. Capturing this requires that social scientists theorize and properly measure community-level variations in social mechanisms. What we usually get instead are the compositional characteristics of individuals rather than social-level properties. To be sure, there are good research examples in the sociology of structural and global properties. Structural approaches in network research are alive and well, to take a notable example. Yet applications to urban sociology have been limited, with few studies actually comparing network structures across multiple community contexts. And few studies have examined truly global properties of neighborhoods. Survey research with an emphasis on precise population estimates for individual parameters continues to rule the roost in exactly the way Coleman worried about.

Although Lazarsfeld's vision for the integrative application of analytic, structural, and global properties has been slow to emerge, there is a distinct movement afoot in several corners of social science to take on the challenge. I do not have time to review it here, but suffice it so say that a new generation of research has begun to explore in direct fashion the workings of community-level social processes, such as mutual trust, shared expectations, density of acquaintanceship, reciprocated exchange of information, social control, public order, institutional capacity, and the network connectivity of community leadership. A major challenge for this agenda is to build strategies for direct and reliable measurement of the social mechanisms and collective properties hypothesized to be of theoretical relevance.

In my own attempt to address these issues, I have mounted a concerted methodological effort to enhance the science of the ecological assessment of social environments—what my colleague Stephen Raudenbush and I have labeled "ecometrics" in a paper in the 1999 *Sociological Methodology*. The basic idea is take the measurement of ecological properties and social processes as seriously as we have always taken individual-level differences, as the long history of "psychometrics" shows. One might consider this the second generation of Lazarsfeldian-Mertonian approaches to assessing collective properties and providing a foundation for assessing macrocausal factors. Using systematic social observation (e.g., videos), clustered household surveys, and comparative network studies of community organizations, my goal, and the subject of a book in progress summarizing a decade's worth of work, is to assess the social structure of the city. One might say its approach strives to be Merton, Lazarsfeld, and Coleman meet a contemporary Chicago School.

The larger point is that Merton and Lazarsfeld were on to nothing less than a rethinking of how to do truly sociological research (what Merton termed "structural sociology") on big questions with empirical import. Not mindless empiricism and not abstract theory or theory about other theorists. Merton developed *theory about how the world works*, a phrase I recall Jim Coleman using when we were colleagues at the University of Chicago. I liked that way of putting things from the first time I heard it, as it seems to capture the essence of sociological theory that is not about the intellectual history of ideas, but about empirical social processes. Coleman brooked no patience for theories about theorists (i.e., who really meant what and why) or abstract theory in itself, and I suspect neither did Merton despite his fondness for Parsons.

For me, then, the lesson for urban sociology has been clear: take seriously the study of community-level processes in their own right. Rather than treat the community as an attribute tagged on to individuals, develop a social theory of community and assess empirically the causes and consequences of salient dimensions of community processes (Sampson 2002; 2008b). Considerable groundwork for this goal was laid by Lazarsfeld's analytics, which served as a departure point of sorts for the ongoing collaborative work of the Project on Human Development in Chicago Neighborhoods. Ambitiously stated, it is my hope that this work will allow us to reinvent the classic concept of community study by placing community-level processes on a new theoretical and methodological foundation (see Sampson 2002). In the Merton-Lazarsfeld tradition, method and theory are inextricably linked for the purpose of enhancing sociological inquiry about macro-level processes and, ultimately, social causation.

Conclusion

In closing, I think Merton had things mostly right as he spelled them out in his essay "Theories of the Middle Range." My thesis is that the sort of theorizing that Merton pioneered helped elide, or at least diminish, the pernicious distinctions that still rile the field: theory versus research, basic versus applied, positivist versus nonpositivist, and more.[8] As Merton said, the words "theory" and, even more so, "positivism" have become meaningless, used today mainly as promiscuous verbal weapons. As I see it, the Merton position tried to combine the best of relevant worlds, so that, in his case, "middle" was not a watered down compromise but the scientifically proper way to approach social phenomena. In the language of today, Merton's approach might be called "realism,"[9] although the term "positivism" continues to be invoked in a way that seems meant to denigrate empirical hypothesis testing and so-called normal science. [10]

Lest I be accused of exaggerating, consider the claim that Merton played a key role in translating Parsonian grand theorizing into "methodological positivism," especially "with his highly influential *empiricist-positivist* notion of 'middle range' theory" (Steinmetz 2005:131, emphasis added). Merton as a naïve positivist beholden to mindless empiricism? I demur as do others.[11] Merton's cogent theoretical claims about class and crime might be wrong, as much of the cumulative evidence on strain theory would seem to suggest (Hirschi 1969; Kornhauser 1978), but unlike some of his antiscience critics, at least Merton's claims can be demonstrated through productive theoretical examination linked to systematic empirical research.[12] That is the essence of the middle range, an approach that continues to hold relevance for the analytic study of a wide range of social phenomena.

Notes

1. For an analysis of the influence of "Social Structure and Anomie," see Cole 1975 and Cullen and Messner 2007. A recent rendition of Merton's theory, updated for the contemporary era, is found in Messner and Rosenfeld 1997.

2. Besides, an irony in this debate is that my criminological framework stemmed not from Merton's alleged materialism (i.e., economic strain as a motivation to crime) but a revised theory of macrolevel social control, stemming primarily from the Chicago School's social disorganization tradition (Kornhauser 1978) linked to Wilson's 1987 macrostructural theory of urban restructuring. (I believe Katz is right about many things, but that his error was to infer that materialist causes must have materialist mediating mechanisms, in this case strain.)

3. For example, the American Society of Criminology and the Population Association of America draw thousands of attendees to their annual meetings. Many sociologists of crime and sociologically trained demographers attend these meetings and not those of the American Sociological Association. *Criminology* and *Demography*, the peer-reviewed journals of each field, respectively, are widely thought to publish the best work in their areas and are highly cited.

4. A case in point is the increasing and thriving area of the "sociology of punishment" motivated by the unprecedented increases in mass incarceration since the 1970s (Western 2006). In addition to the Foucauldian turn, theories of punishment and the State connect to classic themes in deviance theory going back to the mid-twentieth century (Garland 2001; Vogel 2006).

5. For an interesting intellectual history within the field of criminology, see Laub 2006.

6. This is not to be confused with what today is often referred to as "analytic sociology," which focuses on action-based theorizing, micro-macro links, and quantitative methods suitable to analyzing social mechanisms and processes, especially the consequences (mostly unintended) of individual actions for macro or emergent phenomena. For a major statement of analytic sociology, see Hedström 2005 and Hedström and Bearman 2009. Overall, I see analytic sociology as a natural extension of Merton's middle-range approach, focusing as it did on social mechanisms (although Merton did not use the language of mechanisms in this way). For a similar reading of Merton on this issue, see Tilly 2007 and Hedström and Udehn 2009 The latter ties analytic sociology directly to what they consider Merton's (admittedly somewhat "fuzzy") concept of middle-range theorizing.

7. Coleman nonetheless criticized Lazarsfeld for overemphasizing the individual as the unit of analysis and the discipline of sociology in the 1950s (and the Columbia School which dominated it) for losing its capacity to "reconstitute—still quantitatively—from individual actions the behavior of the social system composed of those individuals" (Coleman 1992:92). For the rest of his career and culminating in Foundations of Social Theory (Coleman 1990), Coleman was obsessed with the goal of uniting micro-macro processes (Coleman 1994).

8. Another distinction Merton apparently wished to elide was between pure and integrated theories of deviance. For a discussion of this issue, see Cullen and Messner 2007.

9. There are many types of realism, including (among others) scientific, critical, and philosophical. For the purposes of this paper, I need not make an argument about which fits best, although I would guess that Merton, were he alive, would likely agree with a recent elaboration of a middle-ground approach termed "constructive realism" (see Gorski 2004).

10. It is commonplace to hear snide comments made about normal science, but of course even revolutionary advances build from its contributions and evidentiary claims. Also, critics seem to set aside the implications of the fact that by definition, revolutions and radical new insights in science are rare. If we were to insist on only such contributions the journals would be empty for quite some time, perhaps especially so in sociology. While we await the Kuhnian breakthroughs, it is not clear what kind of science is to be preferred over normal.

11. *Pace* Steinmetz, even a fellow historical sociologist seems to agree, recognizing the interpretive interplay between data and theory in Merton's middle range (Gorski 2004:26).

12. Although beyond the scope of this paper, it appears that antiscience sociologists either misunderstand or deliberately disregard how science is performed in practice, offering instead a caricature (e.g., deterministic, narrowly experimental, lack of theorizing about unobserved mechanisms, concerned mainly with prediction, rejection of contingency, rigidly deductive). Evolutionary theory, to use but one example, violates each of these prescriptions but is hardly antiscientific and might be the better model for sociology than a physics straw man (Lieberson and Lynn 2002). It is true that hard scientists sometimes promote a stylized version of positivism for public consumption and perhaps legitimation (authority) purposes, but this is separate from the science itself. I thank Chris Winship for drawing my attention to this latter point and for several helpful conversations about causality. For an insightful middle ground in the "science wars," see Hacking 1999, especially Chapter 3. For a programmatic statement of the "new causality" in the social sciences, see Morgan and Winship 2007, and for the link between analytic sociology's focus on mechanisms and Merton, see Hedström and Udehn 2009.

References

Calhoun, Craig. 2003. "Robert K. Merton Remembered." *Footnotes* 31, no. 3 (March), http://www.asanet.org/footnotes/mar03/indextwo.html.

Clark, Jon, Celia Modgil, and Sohan Modgil, eds. 1990. *Robert Merton: Consensus and Controversy.* Bristol, PA: The Falmer Press, Taylor and Francis, Inc.

Cole, Stephen. 1975. "The Growth of Scientific Knowledge: Theories of Deviance as a Case Study." In *The Idea of Social Structure: Papers in Honor of Robert K. Merton,* ed. L. A. Coser, 175–220. New York: Harcourt Brace Jovanovich.

Coleman, James. 1990. *Foundations of Social Theory.* Cambridge: Harvard University Press.

Coleman, James. 1992. "Columbia in the 1950s." In *Authors of Their Own Lives: Intellectual Autobiographies by Twenty American Sociologists,* ed. B. M. Berger, 75–103. Berkeley: University of California Press.

Coleman, James S. 1994. "A Vision for Sociology." *Society* 32 (1):29–34.

Cullen, Francis T., and Steven F. Messner. 2007. "The Making of Criminology Revisited: An Oral History of Merton's Anomie Paradigm." *Theoretical Criminology* 11:5–37.

Denzin, Norman K., and Yvonna S. Lincoln, eds. 1994. *Handbook of Qualitative Research.* London: Sage.

Durkheim, Emile. [1897] 1951. *Suicide.* New York: The Free Press.

Garland, David. 2001. *The Culture of Control: Crime and Social Order in Contemporary Society.* Chicago: University of Chicago Press.

Gorski, Philip S. 2004. "The Poverty of Deductivism: A Constructive Realist Model of Sociological Explanation." *Sociological Methodology* 34:1–33.

Hacking, Ian. 1999. *The Social Construction of What?* Cambridge: Harvard University Press.

Hedström, Peter. 2005. *Dissecting the Social: On the Principles of Analytical Sociology.* Cambridge: Cambridge University Press.

Hedström, Peter, and Peter Bearman. 2009. "What is Analytic Sociology all About?: An Introductory Essay." In *The Oxford Handbook of Analytical Sociology,* ed. P. Hedström and P. Bearman, 3–24. New York and Oxford: Oxford University Press.

Hedström, Peter, and Lars Udehn. 2009. "Analytical Sociology and Theories of the Middle Range." In *The Oxford Handbook of Analytical Sociology,* ed. P. Hedström and P. Bearman, 25–50. New York and Oxford: Oxford University Press.

Hirschi, Travis. 1969. *Causes of Delinquency.* Berkeley, CA: University of California Press.

Katz, Jack. 1988. *Seductions of Crime: Moral and Sensual Attractions in Doing Evil.* New York: Basic Books.

Kornhauser, Ruth Rosner. 1978. *Social Sources of Delinquency: An Appraisal of Analytic Models.* Chicago: University of Chicago Press.

Laub, John H. 2006. "Edwin H. Sutherland and the Michael-Adler Report: Searching for the Soul of Criminology Seventy Years Later." *Criminology* 44:235–256.

Lazarsfeld, Paul F., and Herbert Menzel. 1961. "On the Relation between Individual and Collective Properties." In *Complex Organizations*, ed. A. Etzioni, 422–440. New York: Holt, Rinehart & Winston.

Lazarsfeld, Paul F., and Morris Rosenberg, eds. 1955. *The Language of Social Research: A Reader in the Methodology of Social Research.* Glencoe, IL: The Free Press.

Lieberson, Stanley, and Freda Lynn. 2002. "Barking up the Wrong Branch: Scientific Alternatives to the Current Model of Sociological Science." *Annual Review of Sociology* 28:1–19.

Merton, Robert K. 1938. "Social Structure and Anomie." *American Sociological Review* 3:672–82.

——. 1946. *Mass Persuasion.* New York: Harper & Brothers.

——. 1957. *Social Theory and Social Structure.* New York: The Free Press.

——. 1968a. "Social Structure and Anomie." In *Social Theory and Social Structure*, 185–214. New York: The Free Press.

——. 1968b. "The Bearing of Sociological Theory on Empirical Research." In *Social Theory and Social Structure*, 139–155. New York: The Free Press.

——. 1968c. "On Sociological Theories of the Middle Range." In *Social Theory and Social Structure*, 39–72. New York: The Free Press.

——. 1968d. "The Bearing of Empirical Research on Sociological Theory." In *Social Theory and Social Structure*, 156–171. New York: The Free Press.

——. 1995. "Opportunity Structure: The Emergence, Diffusion, and Differentiation of a Sociological Concept, 1930s–1950s." In *The Legacy of Anomie Theory: Advances in Criminology Theory*, ed. F. Aldler and W. S. Laufer, 3–78. New Brunswick, NJ: Transaction Publishers.

Merton, Robert K., Marjorie Fiske, and Patricia L. Kendall. 1956. *The Focused Interview.* New York: The Free Press.

Merton, Robert K., Marjorie Fiske, and Patricia L. Kendall. 1990. *The Focused Interview: A Manual of Problems and Procedures.* London: Collier MacMillan.

Merton, Robert K., and Robert A. Nisbet, eds. 1961. *Contemporary Social Problems: An Introduction to the Sociology of Deviant Behavior and Social Disorganization.* New York: Harcourt, Brace & World.

Merton, Robert K., Patricia S. West, and Marie Jahoda. 1951. "Patterns of Social Life: Explorations in the Sociology of Housing." New York: Columbia University Bureau of Applied Social Research.

Messner, Steven, and Richard Rosenfeld. 1997. *Crime and the American Dream.* Belmont, CA: Wadsworth.

Morgan, Stephen, and Christopher Winship. 2007. *Counterfactuals and Causal Inference: Methods and Principles for Social Research*. New York: Cambridge University Press.

Raudenbush, Stephen W., and Robert J. Sampson. 1999. "'Ecometrics': Toward a Science of Assessing Ecological Settings, with Application to the Systematic Social Observation of Neighborhoods." *Sociological Methodology* 29:1–41.

Sampson, Robert J. 1987. "Urban Black Violence: The Effect of Male Joblessness and Family Disruption." *American Journal of Sociology* 93:348–382.

——. 2002. "Transcending Tradition: New Directions in Community Research, Chicago Style." *Criminology* 40:213–230.

——. 2008a. "Moving to Inequality: Neighborhood Effects and Experiments Meet Social Structure." *American Journal of Sociology* 114:189–231.

——. 2008b. "After-School Chicago: Space and the City." *Urban Geography* 29:127–137.

Sampson, Robert J., Jeffrey D. Morenoff, and Thomas Gannon-Rowley. 2002. "Assessing 'Neighborhood Effects': Social Processes and New Directions in Research." *Annual Review of Sociology* 28:443–78.

Steinmetz, George. 2005. "The Epistemological Unconscious of U.S. Sociology and the Transition to Post-Fordism: The Case of Historical Sociology." In *Remaking Modernity*, ed. J. Adams and E. S. Clemens, 109–157: Duke University Press.

Tilly, Charles. 2007. "Mechanisms of the Middle Range." Paper presented at "Robert K. Merton: Sociology of Science and Sociological Explanation." Columbia University, New York, New York (August 9th); Chapter 2 of this volume.

Tittle, Charles R., Wayne Villimez and Douglas R. Smith. 1978. "The Myth of Social Class and Criminality: An Empirical Assessment of the Empirical Evidence." *American Sociological Review* 43:643–656.

Vogel, Mary, ed. 2006. *Crime, Inequality and the State*. London: Routledge.

Western, Bruce. 2006. *Punishment and Inequality in America*. New York: Russell Sage Foundation.

Wilson, James Q. 1975. *Thinking About Crime*. New York: Random House.

Wilson, William Julius. 1987. *The Truly Disadvantaged: The Inner City, the Underclass, and Public Policy*. Chicago: The University of Chicago Press.

4

The Contributions of Robert K. Merton to Culture Theory

CYNTHIA FUCHS EPSTEIN

Far from being exclusively a functional social structuralist as he has been characterized by several generations of academic critics, Robert K. Merton was, ultimately, a theorist of cultural sociology. Unfortunately, Merton is neglected today by serious analysts and theorists of cultural sociology, such as Jeffrey Alexander, Karen Cerulo, Eviatar Zerubavel, and the networks of cultural sociologists around them, and his name is hardly to be found in the references of the most recent textbooks and articles on cultural sociology.[1] Yet many of Merton's key concepts for the analysis of social life centered on the cultural domain, mated with structural variables. In this paper I shall point out how a number of Merton's concepts and theoretical perspectives have contributed to cultural analysis. With a bow to Merton's last work—the 2003 afterword to the work written in 1958 with Elinor Barber, *The Travels and Adventures of Serendipity: A Study in the Sociological Semantics and the Sociology of Science*—I serendipitously (not, alas, systematically) conjure up a number of concepts and perspectives that I believe locate Merton among the seminal sociologists of culture.

Usually, Merton's line of intellectual descent is traced to Durkheim's *Suicide* ([1897] 1951) for its analysis of the power of group affiliation, but it is instructive also to consider the influence of Durkheim's *The Elementary Forms of Religious Life* (1928) and the power of values in his perspective. And of course, Merton was inspired by W. I. Thomas and his famed aphorism, "If men define things as real, they are real in their consequences" (Thomas and Thomas 1912:571–2). Merton's agreement that cultural definitions of reality were powerful may also be traced to Weber's *The Protestant Ethic and the Spirit of Capitalism* (1904–1905), the model for Merton's dissertation on science and the impact of Puritan values on the early members of the Royal Society of London and his later work on the ethos of science. Reference to "The Thomas theorem" reappears in the 1995 article "The Thomas Theorem and the Matthew Effect" in which, with his customary reach into old archives, Merton traces "recognition of the subjective component in human action" to Epictetus's observation that "what disturbs and alarms man are not actions, but opinions and fancies about actions" (382). In this article he notes that George Herbert Mead observed this phenomenon in purely sociological terms, saying that "If a thing is not recognized as true, then it does not function as true in the community" (383). Merton's observations about the ways in which beliefs are transmitted and held by social groups were a function of, and an extension of his interest in, science and scientific communities.[2]

Further, Merton's supreme contribution to generations of his students was, as he put it, the sociological "angle of vision." This lens was that of skepticism—*organized skepticism*, according to his rubric—not a formula or specified process, but a questioning mind, an outlook. Organized skepticism suggests a cultural orientation of disputation—a kind of collective "show me" mentality, which, he claimed, is the necessary cultural foundation for an understanding of how social life works.

Unlike the cultures of other domains of social life (e.g., the Church, in which belief is the foundation, or the family, where convention, religion, and emotion are the modes of orientation), the culture of science and of social science rests, for Merton, on disbelief and a disconnect from affectual ties that together create a sociological "angle of vision." By asking the question "what is?" the scientist learns how to pose problems and questions and then explore them systematically. Of course, Merton was talking about "the rules of the game" for science—agreed-upon rules—and applying them to the social sciences (i.e., sociology), although the discipline has had its internal cultural disputes and its sectarian dissenters as well as its rule breakers.

To put it another way, learning to think like a sociologist, according to Merton, requires going beyond the individual as the unit of analysis, as is the focus of rational-choice theorists or mainstream psychologists today. The sociologist is required to consider the cultural web in which individuals are embedded, the social context that causes them to make certain choices and to act in concert with others because they share or are persuaded by social conventions that lodge them in institutional frameworks, which in turn circumscribe their options.

The "angle of vision" idea took hold in a number of incarnations in Merton's analysis of human behavior. Merton saw how his students learned to think like sociologists and how others, in different occupational settings, learned to think like, and therefore *to be* like, doctors, scientists, or bureaucrats. To think like one of these professionals, one has to have some cultural acumen. This process extends to the ability to make discoveries. When Merton writes of serendipity (Merton and Barber [1958] 2004), for example, he notes that serendipitous discoveries typically are made by those whose value orientations made them open to discovery, referring to Pasteur's maxim that "chance favors the prepared mind" (Merton 2004:259; Epstein 2006). In his analysis of scientific discovery in the afterword to *The Travels and Adventures of Serendipity* (2004), Merton notes with disdain, that of the "cumulating research on 'creativity' encompassing nearly 10,000 scientific and scholarly writings, only 59 were under the heading *cultural factors*" (259). One needs to not only have the right tools and be intellectually endowed and positioned (i.e., social structurally in the right status), but also one has to think within the cultural context as a professional and, at the same time think "outside the box."

In other work (Merton 1957) he notes how not only *thinking* like the incumbent of an official position, in a sense *anticipating* becoming one of them, could change one's behavior and prepare one to enter a world of which he or she was not yet a part. Similarly, failing to think like one of them, or to internalize their culture, made one an exile from their domain. To assume an identity derived from part of a collectivity one aspired to, Merton notes, one has to be a keen observer of its culture, and in anticipation, socialize oneself to take on the manners as well as the intellectual attributes of the desired position. Merton calls this "anticipatory socialization," and it requires that an individual become a kind of anthropologist studying the domain into which he or she is poised to plunge. Merton knew at an intellectual level and also, I suspect, at a personal and emotional level, that merely learning the content of the roles accompanying the statuses one inhabited or aspired to is not enough. One has to convey, through posture, manner, and articulated ideology that one is a proper inhabitant. That is, one has to, as it were, "go native." His own journey from underprivileged youth of immigrant parents to scholar accepted in the sophisticated world of academia was a product not only of his erudition and strong work ethic, but also his ability to become the epitome of a "man of science" and a weaver of images through words and insights into the ways people negotiate their realities. All of these attributions together created the image and stature that played such an important role in his eminence.

His understanding of the role that culture plays is also exemplified in his work on reference group theory. Building on work done by Herbert Hyman, Merton, with Alice Rossi (Merton 1957), notes the ways in which individuals might move beyond their own structural positions and identify with the values and habits of a group to which they do not belong. In this work, Merton takes a different position than Marx, who saw people's detachment from the interests of their group as "false consciousness." Merton does not see class location as so solid a state. For him, reference group theory explained part of the puzzle of mobility. His concept of anticipatory socialization served as a conceptual tool (Swidler 1986) to identify a certain degree of agency in the process of mobility. Thus, if one took as one's reference group a group with higher education than was typical of one's own group, one might be mobilized to become more educated in anticipation of, and preparation for, class mobility.

Names

Other aspects of Merton's reference group analysis and its linkage to mobility are worth noting. For example, he knew the power of a name. Names are, of course, culturally designated (Lieberson, Stanley, and Bell 1992). There are two types of names: those identifying a *particular* person throughout his or her life (e.g., Henry Wadsworth Longfellow) and those that identify the statuses individuals are born with or acquire (e.g., *King* James; *Doctor* Livingston). Names locate a person in society; they have meaning in that they carry symbolically the baggage of lineage and ethnic identity. Different stages are set in the United States (and elsewhere) for the person introduced as a Carnegie, a Rockefeller, or a Kennedy, rather than an O'Malley, a Napolitano, or a Rabinowitz. Here too, Merton's biography is instructive. He changed the name he was given at birth—Meyer Schkolnick (Merton 1994)—to become Robert King Merton, paving the way to his metamorphosis of boy from the working class to a member of the intellectual elite. As Merton recalled in the autobiographical lecture he delivered to the American Council of Learned Societies in 1994, "I was born almost at the bottom of the social structure in the slums of South Philadelphia to working-class Jewish immigrants from Eastern Europe." But, he did acquire "every sort of capital—social capital, cultural capital, human capital" (9) through exposure to the free cultural resources available in his neighborhood. Of course, Merton had physical resources on which to create his new self. He was tall (a valued attribute in this culture) and attractive, and he soon adopted the manner of the perfect professor—pipe in hand, tweed jackets, edited words. It was not irrelevant that his knowledge of border crossings and symbolic capital, (Epstein 1992; Lamont and Fournier 1992) qualities that permitted or restrained the movement of individuals from one social class to another, led to his scholarly contributions to culture theory.

Merton wrote extensively about the names given to *statuses* and social positions—and how they were characterized independently of the individuals holding them. No person need inhabit the status of *doctor*, for example, for us to know how a person holding that status ought to behave and probably would behave. But beyond defining the structural elements contained in defining statuses and their institutionalization, Merton was sensitive to the power of naming in general.

My description of Merton the man by no means suggests that his intellectual power to determine the force of culture in molding people's lives was generated by his biography alone. He learned that social position or class position does not determine *all* by also reflecting on the passages of many of his fellow academics who wished to leave the defining character of their names (and backgrounds) behind in the anti-Semitic climate of their early careers. Many intellectuals of his time moved out of the social environments they grew up in, casting aside the definitions of identity that their birth names conveyed (for example, Leonard Bloom, who became Leonard Broome; Ivan Greenberg, who became Philip Rahv; and Irving Horenstein, who became Irving Howe) as they acquired other forms of social capital to achieve positions of high rank in academic circles.

Opportunity Structure

Merton was well aware of social climates, as he notes in his work on "opportunity structure" (Merton 1957). Had Merton lived to write the more extensive treatise he planned on this subject, I suspect he would have more clearly defined the role of culture in determining the availability of opportunities to individuals. Although there were various iterations of this concept, beginning with the first article he wrote in 1938, culture was not highlighted. It was, rather, embedded in his work. For example, in a collection of works on the theory of anomie in 1994, Merton begins his article noting that "central to the first, 1938 formulation of the SS&A paradigm in print was the sociological idea of a continuing interplay and frequent tension between the cultural structure (the distribution and organization of values, norms and interest—e.g., "the American Dream" and the social structure (the distribution and organization of social positions and statuses, the opportunity structure) (Merton 1994:4). The work on opportunity structure reviewed by Merton in 1994 referred to his paper on "Social Structure and Anomie" as being about the "sociological idea of continuing interplay and frequent tension between the cultural structure (the distribution and organization of values, norms and interests) and the social structure (the distribution and organization of social positions or statuses)" (Merton 1994).

Merton had more theoretical machinery to do this than we see in the work of Bourdieu or Foucault, who focus on the tyrannies of the power structure in making opportunities available selectively, according to class position and class reproduction. Merton was interested in the ways in which individuals could transcend social place by adaptation, using formal and informal mechanisms to move beyond their socially prescribed destinies by being culturally astute.[3]

Role and Status Conflict

Yet, perhaps Merton's own journey made him particularly cognizant of the contingent nature of border crossing from one status category to another. Merton saw that individuals could suffer from ambivalence when they hold roles and statuses with equally demanding norms and values, thus potentially in conflict. They might, he notes, have problems of conscience or stress, facing competing pressures. These are not, as he points out, psychologically oriented issues, but are locked into the social positions people occupy where clashing values perplex people wanting to do the right thing when each right thing crowds out the other. Merton cites Robert Lynd who, in his book *Knowledge for What?* (1939) chronicles the clashing, albeit strongly held, values of Americans. Merton points to, but did not explore, the problems of cultural conflict though he does note its problems for individuals who find themselves forced to compromise one value in order to maximize another. What Merton points to is not that separate cultures may clash (Samuel Huntington's thesis [1996]) but that they may harbor cultural contradictions within themselves. (We see this in people who exceed the social class position of their parents, making them at once subject to the class prejudices of two classes at the same time.) Further, people often encounter another kind of sociological ambivalence when they acquire (or have thrust upon them) a "conflict of interests or of values" in which "the interests and values incorporated in *different* statuses occupied by the same person result in mixed feelings and compromise behavior" (Merton 1976:9).

Sociological Ambivalence

One doesn't see many references to the term "sociological ambivalence" anymore, but it is appropriate to the current debate over what a slew of scholars and feminist activists are calling "work-family balance." Merton would have noted that "balance" is an entirely incorrect term, because the culture of each realm is characterized by the extremely demanding expectations Merton's students Rose Laub Coser and Lewis Coser (1974) wrote about, pointing to these same realms—the family and the workplace—as institutions whose time and affiliation demand total commitment, and hence, are termed "greedy institutions." What is an institution without its accompanying culture of expectations—laden with value judgments— that its members not only do the right thing but *believe* it is the right thing to do? In fact, analyzing doing the right thing is part of what Merton contributed to "justice theory" which adds to the rich analysis done by Guillermina Jasso (2000), connecting Merton's contributions to justice theory through reference group theory.

To return to conflicts in status and role sets, arising when values embedded in the institutions to which they are attached conflict, balance does not fulfill cultural expectations that a person will give their all. No one is happy. (Epstein 1996). My collaborators and I saw a particularly strong example of this in a study of part-time work in the law (Epstein et al. 1999) where lawyers reduced their work hours to achieve balance in their work and family lives only to see their career possibilities diminish. But that is only one example of the phenomenon. All of us see it in the news every day for as when, for example, Iraqi men and women face conflict, not balance, juggling their conflicting roles as officers of the state during the day and as sectarians during the night when they engage in violence against people from different tribes. In his paper (and then book) *Sociological Ambivalence* (1976), Merton also points to the stresses people face, using as an example the case of immigrants who have become oriented toward differing sets of cultural values. Here he links to his theory of anomie (Merton 1938), in which people on the margins—the immigrant who has internalized the American value of success, for example, but who is prevented from attaining it—live out their cultural goals by various normative or abnormal means. As Viviana Zelizer writes in Chapter 5 of this volume, "Merton saw human intentions (which he conceived of as deeply constrained by existing culture) confronting social situations shaped by culture."

Merton notes that one account of social roles is the depictive (1957). These are representational portraits, described in terms so concrete and vivid that the reader would at once recognize them. The sociologist, he writes, stands between the depictive, graphic art of the sociological novelist and the analytic, abstract formulations of the [scientific] sociologist. The "sociographer at work classifies social roles in categories drawn from everyday life" rather than from the abstract formulations of sociological theory (Merton 1976:13).

At this point, he notes the sociology of social roles is on "the plane of sociographer" (13). In posing this distinction, however, Merton is somewhat contradictory. In his fierce commitment to the establishment of a social *science* he contradicts his defining analysis of science as a value system as well as a methodology.

Science and Culture

It is Merton's work on the sociology of science that clearly identifies him as a cultural sociologist. As he wrote in a new introduction to *Science,*

Technology and Society in 2001, his paper "Science and the Social Order" (first published in 1938 and reprinted in all the editions of *Social Theory and Social Structure*) introduced the concept of "the ethos of science." Merton defined the ethos of science as "the emotionally toned complex of rules, prescriptions, mores, beliefs, values and presuppositions which are held to be binding on the scientist." He went on to note that his 1942 paper "The Normative Structure of Science" proposed that "four sets of institutional imperatives—universalism, communism, disinterestness, organized skepticism—comprise the method of modern science." ([1942] 1973:10) Only then, Merton writes, was there a definite recognition that, along with a distinctive and evolving body of knowledge, modern science is also a "social institution" with a distinctive *normative* framework, shared in part with some institutions and in tensioned conflict with others (xiii). The *norm of universalism* was especially important given the time in which he was writing, at the beginning of World War II. In a period when the Nazis in Germany were isolating and condemning scientists who were Jews and condemning their work as "Jewish science," Merton's essay on "Science in the Social Order" (1938) laid out an opposing "democratic" set of norms, which he asserted were necessary to engage in a productive scientific enterprise. Cultural concepts such as "universalism" and "communism" were embedded in the true scientist's value structure, he maintained. Merton's essay specified the norms of universalism—the notion that knowledge should not be judged by a scientist's personal attributes, ethnicity, religion, or social class (and, he said years later, he would now [2001] add sex or gender).

It is curious that Pierre Bourdieu, writing for a festschrift in honor of Merton's eightieth birthday (one of the few essays in which he referred to Merton's work at all), criticizes him for singularly focusing on the normative rules of science: communism, objectivity, originality, and utility (1990). Of course the normative mode interested him. It sets the standard. But Bourdieu did not appreciate how interested Merton was also in the disjuncture between the stated norms: the problem of the clash between values within science and the clash between the norms of science and those of the larger community. For example, in Merton's essay on sociological ambivalence he describes the pressures faced by the scientist who is urged to publish swiftly, to fulfill norms of originality and priority, and at the same time must heed the scientific call to be careful and considered in the announcement of any scientific finding and not rush to publish.

Time

Another sphere in which Merton contributed to culture theory is in the analysis of *time*. First writing on time with Sorokin in 1937 in a paper, "Social Time: A Methodological and Functional Analysis," the joint article drew little attention and Merton himself did not write on the subject again until a lecture in 1982 (published in 1984) on "socially expected durations." Arne Kalleberg and I found this a useful concept in considering research on time sequences in work life (2004), but time theorists have not given to Merton's interesting speculations on the interplay between time norms and social position their due. Time norms were integrated into Merton's analysis of social roles and statuses. Further, integrated within his analysis of *status sequences* (Merton 1957)—the passages individuals make toward the acquisition of statuses that require prior preparation or merely age—are cultural attitudes toward the appropriateness of certain time sequences. Obviously, time norms are arbitrary—created by "status judges" (another Merton term that has somehow been lost), who by power of their office make judgments about how much time is necessary to socialize prospective recruits to their desired "offices" in life (i.e., to make the person internalize the skills, values, and attitudes of a new status). No one in academia can avoid such concepts as "the tenure track"—a period of seven years—the time normatively set in the bylaws of institutions somewhat similar to the less institutionalized "partnership track" in large private law firms which demand seven years or more of performance at the associate level before a lawyer is considered for "elevation" to partner. Similarly, physicians must spend a year as an intern in a hospital before qualifying to become a resident in a specialty. Each specialty requires a particular number of years. When people try to slow the process (taking off time for child bearing, for example), the rules have to be reset and there is often much discussion about the rightness of the change in timing. Judgments about the time periods thought necessary to prepare individuals to acquire certain statuses are usually justified by reference to the need for training, but few individuals can actually support this claim. For example, there has long been dialogue in the legal profession about the possibility of shortening legal training from three years to two (I heard Judge Richard Posner suggest it in a speech some years ago), and in other countries (and in the past in the United States) no formal schooling is required because an apprenticeship to practicing lawyers may be substituted. Merton wrote that "socially expected durations" are applied to many positions in life—all of which are the result of negotiations, although they often are regarded as logical and mandated by physical attributes or experience. Retirement age for example, comes out of a socially expected duration of the number of years a person ought to work before leaving the sphere of paid employment; and the appropriate age of marriage varies from state to state in the United States and there is wide variation throughout the world.

Merton's contributions to this sphere often center on the deviations from socially approved value judgments about time. He was as interested in people who were off track as in those who conformed to time expectations. Yet, Merton's work on the cultural aspects of time is not noted even in a critical paper on Merton's contribution to sociological studies of time in the festschrift for his eightieth birthday by Simonetta Tabboni (1990).

Merton's work on the accumulation of advantage is a clear precursor of Bourdieu's work on habitus (Bourdieu 1984). The 1942 paper alluded to the "accumulation of differential advantages for certain segments of the population that are not [necessarily] bound up with demonstrated differences in capacity" (15). Merton later spelled out his theory in greater detail in a paper "The Matthew Effect" in 1968 and in his further work with Harriet Zuckerman (1971).

Conclusion: The Invisibility of Merton's Contributions to Cultural Theory

These are but first thoughts about the contributions of Robert K. Merton to cultural analysis. How odd that his insights have been so obliterated—perhaps not by incorporation, as he observed about many other contributions of his own and those of others, whose insights become such a part of established wisdom that they no longer are attributed to the person who first thought of them. But perhaps it is not strange at all. It is not uncommon that new generations of scholars wish to appear entirely innovative, an orientation that requires the destruction of their elders to establish a new platform for ideas that can be designated as innovative. I believe such a change, particularly after the student movements of the late 1960s led many students who matured in the 1970s and '80s to turn a collective back on Merton, and thus on his contributions to culture theory. Further, stereotyping him as an unbending "functionalist," a designation he despised, intellectually and personally, redirected their interest to scholars whose theoretical work was regarded as more socially transformative.

Merton also had no patience or taste for intellectual combat. In discussions with him, I learned that generally, he refused to engage in disputes about his work, even when he felt his intentions and meaning were violated[4]. Further, by the time the field of cultural analysis became part of the sociological canon,[5] he had returned to his first love, the sociology of science, engaging a different set of sociologists and philosophers of science than those who had become active in cultural analysis. Those who became prominent in this specialty were of a generation whose mentors did not include Merton's legacies in their syllabi and the references in their own work.[6]

One could cite many more concepts to illustrate Merton's views on culture and its impact on social life. This task might be of interest to historians of sociological thought, and for wordsmiths like Merton whose intellectual curiosity drove him to identify the life path and use of words and concepts. In a way, the academic amnesia about Merton's work in general is self-exemplifying of social processes that Merton himself characterized as "obliteration by incorporation." This is the process by which insights "discovered" and the concepts that describe them become so much of a part of common usage that their authors become lost in time.

Nevertheless, in the forum this volume represents, we can acknowledge how much Merton's insights illuminated the power of culture in the design of human society, years before his sociological descendants thought to turn to the subject.

Notes

This paper was presented at a conference on the work of Robert K. Merton at Columbia University on August 10, 2007. The able research assistance of Jessica Sperling and the editorial hand of Howard Epstein are acknowledged with thanks.

1. I have not done a systematic study, but as I have taught courses in Cultural Sociology and reviewed syllabi on the web, and collections such as Jacobs and Hanrahan's *The Blackwell Companion to the Sociology of Culture* (2005) and Spillman's *Cultural Sociology* (2002), I have found only a few references to Merton's name and no analysis of his work.

2. In particular, note his papers "The Normative Structure of Science" (1942) and, with Harriet Zuckerman, "Patterns of Evaluation in Science" (1971).

3. Or, of course, they might be defeated by cultural barriers.

4. Unless, of course, the topic under attack tickled his sociological fancy. For example, his article "The Thomas Theorem and the Matthew Effect" (1995) was a response to a charge of sexism by R. S. Smith (1995) because he credited the "theorem" to W. I. Thomas alone and not also to his wife, the sociologist Dorothy Swaine Thomas. Merton not only established that Dorothy Swaine Thomas confirmed to him that the idea was indeed W. I. Thomas's but uses the attack as a jumping off point to examine the nonsexist character of the word "scientist" in a subsequent article, "De-Gendering 'Man of Science': The Genesis and Epicene Character of the Word *Scientist*" (1995) in which, among other things, he includes a section on "Cultural Resistance to the New Word" (230).

5. A search of the *Annual Review of Sociology* shows only eleven articles with culture in the title between 1984 and 1993, sixteen between 1994 and 1998, and nineteen between 1999 and 2003. Merton died in 2003.

6. At a recent "miniconference" on cultural sociology, I asked a number of sociologists informally whether they had read Merton's work in their PhD training and found it surprising that some leading figures had not.

References

Bourdieu, Pierre. 1990. "Animadversiones in Mertonem." Trans. Jon Clark. In *Robert K. Merton: Consensus and Controversy*, ed. Jon Clark, Celia Modgil, and Sohan Modgil, 297–301. Bristol, PA: The Falmer Press, Taylor and Francis, Inc.

——. 1994. *Distinction: A Social Critique of the Judgment of Taste*. Trans. Richard Nice. Cambridge, MA. Harvard University Press.

Clark, Jon, Celia Modgil and Sohan Modgil. 1990. *Robert K. Merton: Consensus and Controversy*. Bristol, PA: The Falmer Press, Taylor and Francis, Inc.

Coser, Lewis, and Rose Laub Coser. 1974. "The Housewife and Her Greedy Family." In *Greedy Institutions,* ed. Lewis Coser, 89–102. New York: Free Press.

Durkheim, Emile. [1897] 1951. *Suicide*. Ed. John A. Spaulding and George Simpson. Glencoe, IL: The Free Press.

——. [1912] 1965. *The Elementary Forms of Religious Life*. New York: Free Press.

Epstein, Cynthia Fuchs. 1992. "Tinkerbells and Pinups." In *Cultivating Differences: Symbolic Boundaries and the Making of Inequality*, ed. Michele Lamont and Marcel Fornier, 232–250. Chicago: University of Chicago Press.

——. 1996. "The Protean Woman: Anxiety and Opportunity". In *Trauma and Self,* ed. Charles Strozier and Michael Flynn, 159–173. Lanham, Maryland and London: Rowman and Littlefield Publishers, Inc.

Epstein, Cynthia Fuchs, and Arne Kalleberg, eds. 2004. *Fighting for Time: Shifting Boundaries of Work and Family Life*. New York: The Russell Sage Foundation.

Epstein, Cynthia Fuchs, Carroll Seron, Bonnie Oglensky, and Robert Sauté. 1999. *The Part-Time Paradox: Time Norms, Professional Life, Family and Gender.* New York: Routledge.

Huntington, Samuel. 1996. *The Clash of Civilizations and the Remaking of World Order.* New York: Simon and Schuster.

Jacobs, Mark, and Nancy Hanrahan. 2005. *The Blackwell Companion to the Sociology of Culture.* Malden, MA and Oxford: Blackwell Publishing.

Jasso, Guillermina. 2001. "Some of Robert K. Merton's Contributions to Justice Theory." *Sociological Theory* 18:320–339.

Lamont, Michèle, and Marcel Fournier. 1992. "Introduction." In *Cultivating Differences: Symbolic Boundaries and the making of Inequality,* ed. Michèle Lamont and Marcel Fournier, 1–20. Chicago: University of Chicago Press.

Lieberson, Stanley, and Eleanor O. Bell. 1992. "Children's First Names: An Empirical Study of Social Taste." *American Journal of Sociology* 98:511–554.

Lynd, Robert. 1939. *Knowledge for What?: The Place of Social Science in American Culture.* Princeton: Princeton University Press.

Merton, Robert K. 1938. "Science and the Social Order." *Philosophy of Science* 5:321–37.

——. 1938. "Social Structure and Anomie." *American Sociological Review* 3:672–682.

——. [1942] 1973. "The Normative Structure of Science." In *The Sociology of Science: Theoretical and Empirical Investigations,* ed. Robert K. Merton & N. W. Storer, 267–278. Chicago: The University of Chicago Press.

——. 1957. *Social Theory and Social Structure.* Glencoe: The Free Press.

——. 1968. "The Matthew Effect in Science: the Reward and Communication Systems of Science are Considered." *Science* 199:55–63.

——. 1976. *Sociological Ambivalence and Other Essays.* N.Y.: The Free Press.

——. 1984. "Socially Expected Durations: A Case Study of Concept Formation in Social Structure." In *Conflict and Consensus: Essays in Honor of Lewis A. Coser,* ed. W. Powell and R. Robbins, 262–283. N.Y.: The Free Press.

——. 1994. "A Life of Learning." *American Council of Learned Societies.* The Charles Homer Haskins Lecture for 1994. Occasional Paper No. 25.

——. 1995. "The Thomas Theorem and the Matthew Effect." *Social Forces.* December. 74:379–424.

——. 1997. "De-Gendering 'Man of Science': The Genesis and Epicene Character of the Word *Scientist.*" In *Sociological Visions,* ed. Kai Erikson, 225–253. Lanham, New York, Boulder, Oxford: Rowman and Littlefield.

Merton, Robert K., and Elinor Barber. [1958] 2004. *The Travels and Adventures of Serendipity: A Study in the Sociological Semantics and the Sociology of Science.* Princeton: Princeton University Press.

Merton, Robert K., George Reader, and Patricia Kendall, eds. 1957. *The Student Physician.* Cambridge: Harvard University Press.

Smith, R. S. 1995. "Giving Credit Where Credit Is Due: Dorothy Swaine Thomas and the 'Thomas Theorem.'" *The American Sociologist* 26:9–28.

Sorokin, Pitirim, and Robert K. Merton. 1937. "Social Time: A Methodological and Functional Analysis." *American Journal of Sociology* 42:615–629.

Spillman, Lyn. 2002. *Cultural Sociology.* Malden, MA, and Oxford. Blackwell Publishing.

Swidler, Ann . 1986. "Culture in Action: Symbols and Strategies." *American Sociological Review* 51:273–286.

Tabboni, Simonetta. 1990. "Robert K. Merton's Contribution to Sociological Studies of Time." In *Robert K. Merton: Consensus and Controversy,* ed. Jon Clark, Celia Modgil, and Sohan Modgil, 427–438. Bristol, PA: The Falmer Press, Taylor and Francis, Inc.

Thomas, W. I., and Dorothy Swaine Thomas. 1928. *The Child in America.* New York: Knopf.

Weber, Max. [1904–1905] 1958. *The Protestant Ethic and the Spirit of Capitalism.* Trans. Talcott Parsons. New York: Charles Scribner's Sons.

Zelizer, Viviana A. 2009. "Culture and Uncertainty," Chapter 6 of this volume.

Zuckerman, Harriet, and Robert K. Merton. 1971. "Patterns of Evaluation in Science: Institutionalization, Evaluation Structure and Functions of the Referee System." *Minerva* 9:66–100.

5

Culture and Uncertainty

VIVIANA A. ZELIZER

In the fall of 1971, toward the end of his teaching career and toward the beginning of a new career stressing his work as synthesizer and mentor, Robert K. Merton taught his by then famous course on social structure at Columbia University. Among the students that semester was an uncertain recent immigrant from Argentina, deeply impressed by the presence of one of her field's master theorists.

I can no longer recite the lectures one by one. Yet, from that semester I took a set of problems that have informed my work ever since. In particular, as Alejandro Portes points out, Merton's concept of unanticipated consequences is one of those brilliant notions that only seem obvious once someone else has articulated it. It undermines the common sociological presumption of intended cause and effect. But, more importantly, it opens up the question of how the erratic and often ineffectual actions that you and I carry on every day accumulate into coherent consequential social processes.

That same fall, I found myself intrigued by a tantalizing footnote in the 1936 *American Sociological Review* paper on unanticipated consequences which stated that "the present writer hopes to devote a monograph now in preparation to the history and analysis of this problem." I stopped by Bob Merton's office to ask him where I could find the promised materials. With an amused smile, he told me there was nothing to show, adding that I should consider this a lesson about academics' frequent device of using footnotes to promise future work that they never deliver.

Of course, we now know that he did deliver, brilliantly. Even as we spoke that afternoon, the serendipity manuscript, coauthored with Elinor Barber, had lain hidden in a drawer since 1958. In an autobiographical afterword to an edited volume of papers first presented at a 1987 international conference on "Robert K. Merton and Contemporary Sociology" in Amalfi, Merton cracked open the drawer by declaring:

> For in an early footnote, the author of that *Jugendwerk* had the innocent temerity to announce that a monograph devoted to the "history and analysis" of the central idea of unanticipated consequences and kindred ideas was in progress. And indeed it was. But that footnote may turn out to be the most prolonged and periodically renewed promissory note in the recent history of sociological scholarship. For although the thematics of unanticipated consequences and related ideas have remained an enduring element in my work ever since, that promised full-scale monograph is still in intermittent preparation—a mere half-century later. (Merton 1998:298)

Indeed, Merton pursued the varied problems of uncertain outcomes, chance, luck, discovery, and serendipity throughout his career. In particular, "the unintended consequences of intended actions" remained, he writes in the afterword to *The Travels and Adventures of Serendipity*, "a theoretical fixation of mine" (Merton 2004:234). Twenty years earlier, in an "epistolary foreword" to the collected essays of his former student Louis Schneider, Merton had already noted their shared "lifelong obsession with the phenomena of unanticipated and unintended consequences of social action . . . along with such kindred themes and special cases as manifest and latent functions and dysfunctions, the self-fulfilling and self-defeating prophecy, and the continuing play of irony in social structure and social change" (1984:xlii). For Merton, one of the "fundamental problems of theoretical sociology" consisted in developing a "conceptual scheme that would help us discover the sources and consequences of nonrationalities as well as rationalities" (1984:xli–xlii).

Concentration on the unexpected may have been partly an effort to dis-entangle his version of functional and structural analysis from what Mer-ton described as an "Arcadian sociology in which everything mysteriously works together for good in a society" (Merton 1984:xli). But it was far more than that. With verve and sociological insight, Merton targeted fun-damental existential concerns: our inescapable human fallibility, the alea-tory element in our lives, the humbling limits on managing the unknown, and the place of luck in a seemingly rationalized contemporary existence. His investigations probed incessantly the paradoxical and ironic features of social life in multiple domains, as in his study of coexisting norms and counter-norms in science, medicine, and business organizations, or more broadly, his exploration of sociological ambivalence (Merton 1976). Mer-ton, Donald Levine admiringly observed, "masterfully articulated the iro-nies of social action" (1978:1280; see also Schneider 1975).

To be sure, as Merton himself reminds us in his 1936 essay, he was not the first to address the problem of the unexpected in social life. The long list of illustrious intellectual forebears includes Machiavelli, Adam Smith, Pareto, Max Weber, Marx, Sorokin, and more. Yet, perhaps due to its his-torical associations to "transcendental and ethical considerations," Merton noted, "no systematic, scientific analysis of [the problem] has as yet been effected" (1936:894). He took on that task.

In all of Merton's efforts to construct a sociology of uncertainty, cul-ture figures prominently. Merton the cultural analyst may surprise those who hail him mostly as sociology's master structuralist, the author of the legendary *Social Theory and Social Structure* (for an extended discussion of Merton as a cultural analyst, see Cynthia Epstein's essay in this volume). After all, when he turned sixty-five his friends and students honored him with a 1975 volume on *The Idea of Social Structure*. Yet, despite his reputa-tion as a structuralist, throughout his career Merton thought about en-counters between social structure (seen as the residue of previous human action), culture (seen as shared understandings and their representation in practices), and intentional human action. Describing his obsession with dictionary reading, Merton actually identified himself as a cultural histo-rian (Merton and Barber 2004:140).

This paper focuses on Merton's analyses of uncertainty, looking closely at how culture figured in his approach. In particular, it traces the progres-sion from the 1936 unintended consequences paper to the 1949 version of his 1938 article on social structure and anomie to the 1958 serendipity volume. The paper then turns to some more recent Merton-inspired analyses of relations between uncertainty and culture in economic activity.

Explaining Uncertainty

Examined closely, Merton's recurrent model actually contains five elements: culture, individual intentions, uncertainty, a set of possible outcomes of action, and a social structure. In phenomenon after phenomenon, Merton saw human intentions (which he conceived of as deeply constrained by existing culture) confronting social situations shaped by structure. Unceasing uncertainty concerning the outcomes of various possible actions links the two halves of the model.

Throughout Merton's analysis, moreover, we can identify four distinct yet interlinked phenomena: uncertainty, unanticipated consequences, self-fulfilling prophecy, and serendipity. Although all four flow out of what Merton referred to as his persistent "sociological interest in the generic phenomenon of unintended consequences of intended action," they each take on distinctive orientations (2004:235). While uncertainty represents a contextual environment where the outcomes of action are unpredictable, unanticipated consequences concern the actual unexpected effects of deliberate, purposive action. Self-fulfilling prophecy, meanwhile, refers to actions that do have anticipated effects but for different reasons than those originally intended by actors. Finally, serendipity describes what occurs in the course of deliberate action when an unexpected anomaly opens up a new, unplanned beneficial path. As Merton observes: "the unexpected occurs twice over in the serendipity pattern. An unanticipated observation yields an unanticipated kind of new knowledge" (Merton 2004:236).[1] In each of Merton's four categories of action, culture enters the analysis.

In the 1936 paper on unintended consequences, among the various elements creating unexpected outcomes of purposive social actions Merton includes values: "instances where there is no consideration of further consequences because of the felt necessity of certain action enjoined by certain fundamental values" (1936:903). Here the grip of shared values—a powerful form of culture—distracts people from the full range of possible consequences of their actions, leading paradoxically in some cases to behavior undermining those very values.

Shared cultural goals figure prominently in Merton's 1938 analysis of social structure and anomie. In the 1949 version of that paper (a few years after he reported discovering the word serendipity in the Oxford English Dictionary), Merton added explicit references to uncertainty: the "doctrine of luck" now appeared in the inventory of adaptations to the disjunction between cultural glorification of pecuniary success and constrained opportunities (1949). Citing E. W. Bakke's famous studies of unemployed men, Merton proposed that resorting to luck as an explanation of life's circumstances results from the differential exposure of groups to cultural materials and to structural limits. For example, down and out workers explain their situations as a consequence of bad luck rather than, say, exploitation. Merton also speculated that integration of workers into labor organizations might reduce that form of uncertainty, thus decreasing explanations based on fate or chance (1968:202n26). Notice the rich research agenda contained within Merton's footnoted hypothesis. What other types of structural and cultural sources can we identify for historically variable beliefs in luck and chance? When are people, for instance, more likely to consult fortune-tellers rather than therapists? How does that vary by categorical position, class, gender, ethnicity, age?[2]

In that same essay, Merton famously distinguished between individualistic and socially grounded explanations of adaptations to frustrating conditions. In the process, he critiqued notions of culture as "a kind of blanket covering all members of the society equally." In his typology, Merton pointedly observed, "these responses occur with different frequency within various sub-groups in our society precisely because members of these groups or strata are differentially subject to cultural stimulation and social restraints" (1968:194n12).

Culture likewise figures interestingly in Merton's famous 1948 *Antioch Review* essay "The Self-Fulfilling Prophecy." He moves subtly by describing an imaginary run on the Last National Bank of Millingville. From that story of uncertainty turning foul, he arrives at his definition: "The self-fulfilling prophecy is, in the beginning, a *false* definition of the situation evoking a new behavior which makes the originally false conception come *true*" (Merton 1948:195). Soon we learn that the "originally false conception" that interests him does not stem from individual errors of judgment but from available cultural materials. In Merton's main examples, false conceptions about undesirable attributes of outgroups such as African-Americans and Jews create inequalities that, to the eyes of believers, confirm the undesirable attributes. Those false conceptions are cultural creations.

By the 1950s, these themes took center stage in Merton's thinking. *The Travels and Adventures of Serendipity*, coauthored with Elinor Barber, traces Merton's increasing interest in chance and the unforeseen. By then, he had formalized the concept: "The serendipity pattern refers to the fairly common experience of observing an *unanticipated, anomalous, and strategic* datum which becomes the occasion for developing a new theory or extending an existing theory" (Merton 1968:158). Accordingly, in Merton's model, serendipity has three elements: a datum, an anomaly, and a strategic intellectual location.

Notice that culture is crucial to that definition. People who experience serendipity may, like the princes of Serendip, be more perceptive than their peers. But they are drawing on accumulated culture. In the case of scientific serendipity, obviously, previous scientific work provides the relevant accumulated culture. In his afterword, Merton introduces the term "institutionalized serendipity" to denote "special sociocultural environments" that foster scientific discovery (Merton and Barber 2004:294). In their book, furthermore, Merton and Barber explicitly draw attention to parallels between scientific serendipity and the more general moral problems of reconciling existence with uncertainty and injustice (Merton and Barber 2004:149–57). In a culture that values predictability and rationality, how, they ask, do people justify unexpected good or ill fortune? How do they find meaning "in the general irrational aspects of the world"? (Merton and Barber 2004:150).[3] Following up Merton's 1949 exploration of the belief in luck, they introduce the valuable notion of "structured uncertainty," calling attention to differential social exposure to chance success and chance failure (Merton and Barber 2004:154).

I do not mean, of course, that Merton learned nothing between 1936 and 2004 or that he saw no differences among the situations described in these three writings. I do mean to say that he consistently pursued the interaction of five elements: culture, individual intentions, uncertainty, a set of possible outcomes of action, and a social structure.

Some of the great minds in contemporary social science have found Merton's questions about unintended consequences so compelling that they have gone on to frame their own answers to those questions. Among authors in this very volume, both Alejandro Portes (2000) and Charles Tilly (1996) offer intriguing extensions. Tilly, for instance, proposes the notion of "invisible elbow" to draw attention to the significance of error correction in coping with life's ubiquitous erroneous interactions and unanticipated consequences. Portes's 1999 American Sociological Association's presidential address, "The Hidden Abode: Sociology as Analysis of the Unexpected," highlights the promise and problems created by sociology's affinity for "the dialectic of things, unexpected turns of events, and the rise of alternative countervailing structures" (2000:2–3).[4] More generally, relying on the Social Sciences Citation Index, Eugene Garfield (the Science Citation Index's creator) reported in 2004 that Merton's 1936 UC article had been cited over 240 times (2004a:848; see also Garfield 2004b). The paper remains widely cited, and with even greater frequency.[5]

More recently, a set of intriguing extensions of Merton's reasoning about uncertainty and, especially, self-fulfilling prophecies have appeared and gained considerable influence within recent studies of economic activity. Let us now consider some (unexpected) lessons economic sociologists can draw from Mertonian theory.

Uncertainty, Culture, and Economic Activity

Expounded for the first time over seventy years ago, Merton's crisp principles for analyzing the social organization of uncertainty turn out to have significant implications for the contemporary analysis of economic activity. As Jens Beckert (1996, 2002) has forcefully argued, uncertainty's ubiquity should serve as the rallying concept for economic sociology's distinctive account of economic activity. Rather than bullying *homo economicus*, Beckert contends that sociologists should challenge economists' standard notions of utility maximization and make uncertainty central to this critique. Economic theory, he explains, "cannot maintain the maximizing assumption convincingly in the face of situational structures that are characterized by uncertainty" (Beckert 1996:804). Beckert defines uncertainty as "the character of situations in which agents cannot anticipate the outcome of a decision and cannot assign probabilities to the outcome" (1996:804). "What do we do," Beckert asks rhetorically, "when we cannot know which decision maximizes our utility?" (2002:202). Thus, uncertainty disrupts efficiency explanations that suppose seamless mean-ends rational action. By revealing in systematic ways how and why purposive action yields unexpected outcomes, Merton's analysis deals a powerful blow to rational-action explanations of economic activity.

To be sure, from within the field of economics, behavioral analysts and game theorists have already brilliantly demolished neoclassical assumptions of rationality. Their emphasis, however, remains largely on individual variation or strategic interaction, investigating, for instance, how people evaluate the probability of uncertain events (for landmark studies, see Tversky and Kahneman 1974; Kahneman, Slovic, and Tversky 1982). The challenge for sociology is to further develop systematic and empirical analyses of uncertainty and unanticipated events by focusing on cultural, structural, and relational variation. Why and how does the intersection of rationalizing organizations with shared cultural meanings and social relations produce unanticipated results? How do shared understandings and social interaction shape differential responses to uncertainty? (For important insights, see DiMaggio 2002; Bandelj 2008).

Focusing on the cultural organization of uncertainty, consider three brief extensions of Mertonian principles in the area of economic activity: the first drawn from my own work on life insurance that I began while a student at Columbia (Zelizer 1979); second, from intimate economies; and finally, from the emerging field of performativity studies.

As an aleatory contract, life insurance emerged as a key contemporary tool to cope with economic uncertainty. Aleatory contracts are those "in which at least one party's performance depends on some uncertain event that is beyond the control of the parties involved" (Garner 1999:319). The business of life insurance hinges on the indeterminate timing of their customers' death. From its contentious development in the United States, we can identify four broader questions concerning culture and uncertainty.

First, what we ordinarily anticipate is itself a product of existing culture. My study of life insurance's development in the United States documents a large cultural transformation, the shift from a fatalistic view of mortality to an activist conception of control over disease and death. Furthermore, the same shift moved people from revulsion at setting a price on life toward the active desire to set an adequate monetary compensation for death.

Second, conceptions of uncertainty themselves vary from one cultural setting to another. In the United States, many nineteenth-century religious leaders strongly opposed life insurance because it challenged the credibility of a divinely regulated order. Providence, not economic institutions, was supposed to take care of life's uncertainties. Other segments of the population feared life insurance as an unholy wager on death. Thus a significant division in receptivity held through much of the nineteenth century, until even religious leaders began to think about life insurance as a Christian duty.

Third, the aspects of life thought to be uncertain also vary from one cultural setting to another. In affluent segments of the United States, life insurance came to be a prudent way of assuring the continuity of lineages, whereas in working-class America it centered on the necessity of arranging a decent burial. For the rich, inheritance was uncertain, while for the less rich, dignified death was uncertain.

Finally, possible and acceptable reactions to uncertainty likewise form as a consequence of the cultural setting. Critics initially opposed life insurance as an un-American, speculative approach to reducing uncertainty, inferior to the solid Benjamin Franklin principle of putting pennies into savings banks for rainy days. By the latter part of the nineteenth century, speculative ventures acquired new respectability, making life insurance a popular strategy for the management of uncertainty.

The second application concerns uncertainty in intimate relations. Intimate interactions are inherently uncertain, as they depend heavily on mutual trust. That trust, if violated, not only breaks hearts, but, among many other ill effects, can ruin livelihoods, disrupt social connections, upend lifestyles, and even spoil reputations. Consider, for instance, that intimacy involves the sharing of particularized knowledge and attention that is not widely available to other people. The disclosure of such private information to third parties can be devastating (Zelizer 2005). Most importantly, people involved in long-term intimate relations rely on the continued material and emotional availability and support of their intimates. To be sure, formal legal mechanisms exist to protect against these and other forms of intimacy's uncertainties. But people also develop informal mechanisms for the management of uncertainty in intimate relations.

Economic activity, for instance, can mitigate uncertainty between intimates. My book *The Purchase of Intimacy* (2005) documents the multiple ways in which people use economic transactions to stabilize their intimate relations. Let me briefly illustrate from the forms of intimacy and uncertainty that grow up within long-distance migration streams by focusing on remittance systems. Almost any time substantial numbers of low-wage migrants move in streams from low-wage areas to distant high-wage areas while leaving significant numbers of relatives behind, remittance systems spring up. They do so without any globally available cultural model, the promotion of any worldwide organization, or any legal requirement. Yet they operate in remarkably similar ways across the globe, with migrants at their destinations regularly earmarking major shares of their usually meager wages for transmission to home folks.

Immigrant remittances, however, not only provide crucial survival funds, but often serve to mitigate the uncertainty of immigrants' long-distance relations with kin. Will the intimate relationship survive the distance? Will the obligations be fulfilled? Here is a case in point concerning uncertain relations between grandparents and grandchildren. Interviewing Salvadoran immigrant children in San Francisco, Cecilia Menjívar (2000) heard their longing to reunite with their grandparents. Menjívar reports her conversation with nineteen-year-old Edwin M:

> [He] told me that he misses his grandmother and often worries about her. He wants to get a job so that he can send remittances to her regularly and send her a plane ticket so that she can come to visit.
> So too Carolina and Ileana A. "with their eyes watery . . . expressed the wish to have [their grandparents] close . . . .When they started earning an income, they saved money to send to their grandparents for airfare so that they could come to the United States for a visit." (Menjívar 2000:268n9)

Here we see intimates using available cultural materials—in their case remittance culture—to master uncertainty. Thus, across a wide range of intimate relations, people adopt culturally meaningful economic buffers against the uncertainties inherent in intimacy.

Finally, Merton's insights into unexpected outcomes and, in particular, his notion of the self-fulfilling prophecy have been coopted and modified by a set of mostly European and British scholars working on the sociology of economics, and more specifically on economics' performativity. By performativity they mean the impact of economic theory in shaping actual economic processes in ways that make those processes or their outcomes correspond to the theory. First proposed by Michel Callon, a prominent sociologist of science that became interested in markets, performativity has been gaining increasing prominence and influence. Along with Donald MacKenzie and others, Callon argues that far from merely discovering the laws of the market, the discipline of economics has actually created intellectual tools that shape capitalist economies. As Callon boldly stated in his pioneering 1998 article: "economics, in the broad sense of the term, performs, shapes and formats the economy rather than observing how it functions" (Callon 1998:2).

Callon and his allies call that shaping performation or performativity. For example, in his *An Engine, Not a Camera: How Financial Models Shape Markets* (2006), MacKenzie assesses the extent to which theories developed in financial economics played a crucial part in the expansion of financial markets after 1970. Since theorists of performativity do not claim that economists conspired to produce the result of their discipline's success, they are describing a subtle version of the self-fulfilling prophecy: an initially false conception becomes true by producing remarkable outcomes conforming to that initially false conception. The conception itself qualifies eminently as a cultural creation[6].

As they demonstrate the unanticipated ways in which economic theory shapes actual economies, performativity scholars recognize their intellectual debt to Merton's self-fulfilling prophecy.[7] Moreover, MacKenzie's most powerful case for performativity sets up a compelling intergenerational saga by linking Merton's theory with those of his own son, Nobel-Prize-winning economist Robert C. Merton. In a 2003 paper with Yuval Millo, MacKenzie claims that the Black-Scholes-Merton option-pricing formula (for which Myron S. Scholes and Robert C. Merton received the 1997 Nobel Prize in Economics) had a performative effect on financial markets. He and Millo document, among other things, how at first the model's assumptions were unrealistic, detached from the actual operation of financial markets and from empirical prices. Yet gradually, as they show, "financial markets changed in a way that fitted the model. . . . Pricing models came to shape the very way participants thought and talked about options" (MacKenzie and Millo 2003:137).

This remarkable instance of what MacKenzie calls "Barnesian" performativity—named after sociologist Barry Barnes and which MacKenzie distinguishes from the weaker effects of economics on market construction—echoes directly Merton's self-fulfilling prophecy. Although MacKenzie identifies significant differences between their two concepts, he acknowledges that "'Barnesian performativity' could be read as simply another term for Robert K. Merton's famous notion of the 'self-fulfilling prophecy'" (2006:19).

Moreover, MacKenzie remarks that he might have adopted the term "Mertonian performativity" because Merton "emphasized the feedback between social knowledge and the referents of that knowledge much earlier than Barnes did" (2006:306n35). One of the reasons he did not do so, MacKenzie explains, was because of Merton's son: "the economist Robert C. Merton, plays a central role in my story, and 'Mertonian performativity' might thus be misunderstood as a reference to the economist rather than the sociologist" (2006:306n35).

Both Mertons seem to have relished the unexpected father-son linkage. In a letter dated April 25, 2005, Robert K. Merton (signing as "father of the economist") wrote MacKenzie that "like Bob, I took great pleasure in your linking 'modern finance theory' to the core sociological idea of the self-fulfilling prophecy." A year later, on April 21, 2001, praising a paper by MacKenzie on "Physics and Finance," Merton wrote to him that "all apart from its fine-grained linkage of the feedback component of the self-fulfilling prophecy and Barnes's S-loops. It is, I believe, the very first paper in which Bob and I are co-cited!"[8]

Robert C. Merton went further. Examining various approaches to the design of financial systems, Merton, in a paper coauthored with Zvi Bodie (2005) made explicit reference to parallels and differences between the self-fulfilling prophecy and performativity. In an attempt to synthesize neoclassical, neoinstitutional, and behavioral perspectives into an approach he calls "functional and structural finance," Merton and Bodie reviewed individual-driven and sociologically grounded behavioral distortions of efficient risk allocation and asset pricing. Among the social accounts they include approvingly both the self-fulfilling prophecy and performativity theory. They note that beyond its interpretation of pricing models, performativity could be applied to the evolution of institutional change, suggesting that:

> If a better theory of institutional dynamics starts to become more widely adopted, its predictions about those dynamics will become more accurate as its adoption spreads and more players use it to make decisions about institutional changes (Merton and Bodie 2005:20n45).

Merton son and Bodie, however, also point to a fine, yet crucial difference between performativity and the self-fulfilling prophecy. Performativity posits that widespread belief in a particular economic model, such as the Black-Scholes-Merton option-pricing formula, results in actual pricing practices that conform to that model. Performativity, at least in the short run, can work whether the initial model is accurate or mistaken. The Mertonian self-fulfilling prophecy, meanwhile, applies only when an influential prophecy—such as the option-pricing formula—is invalid. Because it is presumed to be true, the prophecy shapes responses in such a way as to turn the initially false prediction into a reality. In the self-fulfilling social belief, as Robert K. Merton succinctly put it, "confident error generates its own spurious confirmation" (1968:182). Therefore, if the initial prophecy is valid, its adoption does not conform to Merton's conception of a self-fulfilling prophecy.[9]

Focusing on the self-fulfilling prophecy's effects, Robert C. Merton suggests an additional distinction between: "1) a public prophesy [in this case the publishing of an economic model] that 'causes' the economic system to change its behavior so that it conforms to the model more accurately than it did prior to its publication, *and* that change truly improves the functioning of the system, and 2) a public prophesy that 'causes' the system to change its behavior so that it conforms to the prophecy more accurately *and* that change is dysfunctional for the system, the latter being a characteristic of the SFP" (personal communication, dated October 30, 2008, signed "son of the sociologist").

Uncertain Futures

Uncertainty, unanticipated consequences, self-fulfilling prophecies, performed economies: all raise sobering questions concerning the feasibility of constructing superior social arrangements. How can we engage in deliberate social planning or effective policy-making when unpredicted consequences—whether the outcome of beliefs, values, or other triggering mechanisms—relentlessly trump our efforts? Portes offers a thoughtful reflection:

> At the level of policy, awareness of the dialectics of social life does not lead to paralysis . . . but to more cautious forms of intervention. These alternative forms require relentless questioning of the initial blueprints and an examination of the various contingencies at each step of program implementation (2000:14–15).

This means, Portes argues, that in order to avoid failed social interventions, sociologists should stay away from overly ambitious grand social engineering. Instead, they should approach their task as "social craftsmen," carefully analyzing social processes, attentive to their "concealed and unintended manifestations" (2000:15).

To be sure, already in 1936, Merton had pondered the impact of unanticipated consequences on social planning and betterment. In the closing pages of his article, he left us an ambivalent, yet fundamentally optimistic legacy. He called for a systematic study of the limits of purposive social action with the hope of identifying specific conditions that would allow such planning. So too in "The Self-Fulfilling Prophecy," Merton contended that "a deliberate and planned halt can be put to the workings of the self-fulfilling prophecy and the vicious circle in society" (1948:208). The solution lay not in well-meaning but often futile moral sentiments, he tells us, but institutional change. "The self-fulfilling prophecy, whereby fears are translated into reality," Merton declared, "operates only in the absence of deliberate institutional controls" (1948:210). Presciently, following up his "sociological parable" of the Last National Bank of Millingville, he offered the example of the Federal Deposit Insurance Corporation and other Roosevelt-era banking legislation as mechanisms that effectively reduced "panic-motivated runs on banks" (Merton 1948:209).

Performativity scholars offer their own twenty-first-century version of cautious optimism. If the world can be performed, then performances—and markets—can be improved. In the last few lines of his 2006 book, MacKenzie leaves us with a crucial concern. "The notion of performativity," he notes, "prompts the most important question of all: What sort of a world do we want to see performed?" (2006:275).

These concerns transcend mere academic speculation. Consider the 2008 global financial debacle. Certainly, among other factors, neoliberal theory's pervasive, unwavering belief in the efficiency of free markets created a "self-fulfilling" reality. By fostering rampant deregulation, free-market economic doctrine led to financial practices that, in turn, appeared to confirm the initial theory of a "natural" free market. In that sense, free-market theory "performed" a deregulated economy. Indeed, starting in the 1970s and for much of the 1990s and 2000s, politicians and economists were able to design a world of self-regulated markets (see Bourdieu 1998:94–105; Harvey 2005).

In the end, economic reality tore into the neoliberal fantasy. Even its staunchest advocate, Alan Greenspan, former chairman of the Federal Reserve, famously conceded in October 2008 before the House Committee on Oversight and Government Reform that he had "found a flaw" in his free-market ideology. With the breakdown of the housing market, record home foreclosures, and multiplying bankruptcies, economic theory's free-market prophecy transmuted into its counterpart, a frightening case of what MacKenzie labels "counterperformativity" and Merton called a self-defeating or "suicidal" prophecy, "which so alters human behavior from what would have been its course had the prophecy not been made, that it *fails* to be borne out" (1968:477). Far from its scenario of market-driven efficiency, neoliberal ideology led to profound economic disruption, and paradoxically, to momentous governmental intervention.

No doubt Robert Merton would have found a way to establish connections between his own analyses of uncertainty and contemporary extensions of Mertonian principles more elegantly and comprehensively. But surely he would have recognized in these more recent efforts, echoes of great themes that activated his monumental work.

Notes

For generous and wise advice, suggestions, and references, I am grateful to Jens Beckert, Craig Calhoun, Meg Jacobs, Daniel Kahneman, Pierre Kremp, Donald MacKenzie, Robert C. Merton, Alejandro Portes, Edgardo Rotman, Leandro Rotman, Charles Tilly, Harriet Zuckerman, and two anonymous reviewers.

1. I am grateful to Alejandro Portes for pointing out key distinctions in Merton's uncertainty concepts.

2. Merton (1968:203) suggested that lower-class "orientation to chance and risk-taking" combined with frustrated goals might explain that strata's interest in gambling as a form of "innovative" adaptation. For different perspectives on class and gambling, see Light 1977; Garvia 2007. On class, gender, and fatalism, see, for example, Purcell 1982 and Westwood 1984.

3. For a different kind of discussion concerning the moral dimension of unexpected outcomes, see moral philosophers' theory of moral luck, especially Williams and Nagel 1976 and Williams 1982.

4. See also Coser 1969 and Fine's 2005 presidential addresses to the Society for the Study of Social Problems; Boudon 1982; Keller 1975; Hirschman 1991. Hirschman (1967) proposed the "principle of the hiding hand" to describe a common mechanism that conceals from decision makers unforeseen obstacles entailed by any new enterprise. By masking uncertainty, Hirschman contends, the "hiding hand" serves to spur innovation. Thanks to Edward Tenner for this reference.

5. For instance, between 2005 and 2007 we find thirty-nine citations, up from twenty-three in 2002 through 2004. The recent upswing could be due to an increase in the general number of publications. Note, however, that citations count only articles, thereby excluding citations to reprints of Merton's papers in edited collections.

6. MacKenzie, Muniesa, and Sieu, however, warn against associating performativity with a causal account based exclusively on ideas (2007:5). In Callon's account, for instance, beliefs matter but material technologies critically intervene in the construction of economies. For an insightful analysis introducing national variation to show how economic theories constitute different economies, see Fourcade 2009. For historical evidence of what they call the "ideational embeddedness" of markets, see Somers and Block 2005.

7. For further connections between Merton's work and performativity scholars, see Zuckerman, Chapter 11 in this volume.

8. My thanks to Donald MacKenzie for generously sharing with me his correspondence with Robert K. Merton.

9. MacKenzie distances performativity in finance theory from what he calls the self-fulfilling prophecy's "pathological" overtones, by which he means the premise that the initial prophecy had to be false. MacKenzie points to limits in the impact of false theoretical formulas, noting that if an option-pricing formula is incorrect and leads to systematic losses, its dominance will be fleeting. By 2000, Merton seems to have moved in a similar direction. In a letter from April 25, 2000, he wrote to MacKenzie: "We are wholly agreed that self-fulfilling prophecies are far from being necessarily pathological, although the concept has worked to alert us to the mechanisms through which such phenomena as racist beliefs appear to be validated." On differences between performativity and Merton's self-fulfilling prophecy, see MacKenzie 2006:19–20; MacKenzie 2007:77–78; Callon 2007:321–324. For the historical and social limits on economic theory's Barnesian performative impact, see MacKenzie and Millo 2003:138–141.

References

Bandelj, Nina. 2008. *From Communists to Foreign Capitalists: The Social Foundations of Foreign Direct Investment in Postsocialist Europe.* Princeton, N.J.: Princeton University Press.

Beckert, Jens. 1996. "What Is Sociological about Economic Sociology?: Uncertainty and the Embeddedness of Economic Action." *Theory and Society* 25 (6):803–840.

——. 2002. *Beyond the Market: The Social Foundations of Economic Efficiency.* Princeton, N.J.: Princeton University Press.

Bourdieu, Pierre. 1998. *Acts of Resistance: Against the Tyranny of the Market.* New York: New Press.

Boudon, Raymond. 1982. *The Unintended Consequences of Action*. New York: St. Martin's Press.

Callon, Michel. 1998. "Introduction: The Embeddedness of Economic Markets in Economics." In *The Laws of the Markets*, ed. Michel Callon. Oxford: Blackwell.

——. 2007. "What Does It Mean to Say that Economics Is Performative?" In *Do Economists Make Markets?: On the Performativity of Economics*, ed. Donald Mackenzie, Fabian Muniesa, and Lucia Siu, 311–357. Princeton, N.J.: Princeton University Press

Coser, Lewis A. 1969. "Presidential Address: Unanticipated Conservative Consequences of Liberal Theorizing." *Social Problems* 16 (Winter):263–272.

——, ed. 1975. *The Idea of Social Structure: Papers in Honor of Robert K. Merton*. New York: Harcourt Brace Jovanovich.

DiMaggio, Paul. 2002. "Endogenizing 'Animal Spirits': Toward a Sociology of Collective Response to Uncertainty and Risk." In *The New Economic Sociology: Developments in an Emerging Field*, ed. Mauro F. Guillén, Randall Collins, Paula England, and Marshall Meyer, 19–100. New York: Russell Sage Foundation.

Fine, Gary Alan. 2005. "The Chaining of Social Problems: Solutions and Unintended Consequences in the Age of Betrayal." *Social Problems* 53:3–17.

Fourcade, Marion. 2009. *Economists and Societies: Discipline and Profession in the United States, Great Britain, and France, 1890s to 1990s*. Princeton: Princeton University Press.

Garfield, Eugene. 2004a. "The Unintended and Unanticipated Consequences of Robert K. Merton." *Social Studies of Science* 34:845–853.

——. 2004b. "The Intended Consequences of Robert K. Merton." *Scientometrics* 60:51–61.

Garner, Bryan A. 1999. *Black's Law Dictionary*. 7th ed. St.Paul, MN: West.

Garvia, Roberto. 2007. "Syndication, Institutionalization, and Lottery Play." *American Journal of Sociology* 113 (November):603–52.

Harvey, David. 2005. *A Brief History of Neoliberalism*. New York: Oxford University Press.

Hirschman, Albert O. 1967. *Development Projects Observed*. Washington, D.C.: The Brookings Institution.

——. 1991. *The Rhetoric of Reaction: Perversity, Futility, Jeopardy*. Cambridge, MA: Harvard University Press.

Kahneman, Daniel, Paul Slovic, and Amos Tversky, eds. 1982. *Judgment Under Uncertainty: Heuristics and Biases*. New York: Cambridge University Press.

Keller, Suzanne. 1975. "The Planning of Communities." In *The Idea of Social Structure: Papers in Honor of Robert K. Merton*, ed. Lewis A. Coser, 283–299. New York: Harcourt Brace Jovanovich.

Levine, Donald N. 1978. "Review of *Sociological Ambivalence and Other Essays*, by Robert K. Merton." *American Journal of Sociology* 83 (March):1277–80.

Light, Ivan. 1977. "Numbers Gambling Among Blacks: A Financial Institution." *American Sociological Review* 42 (December):892–904.

Menjívar, Cecilia. 2000. *Fragmented Ties: Salvadoran Immigrant Networks in America.* Berkeley: University of California Press.

MacKenzie, Donald. 2006. *An Engine, Not a Camera: How Financial Models Shape Markets.* Cambridge, MA: MIT Press.

———. 2007. "Is Economics Performative?" In *Do Economists Make Markets?: On the Performativity of Economics*, ed. Donald Mackenzie, Fabian Muniesa, and Lucia Siu, 54–86. Princeton: Princeton University Press.

MacKenzie, Donald, and Yuval Millo. 2003. "Constructing a Market, Performing Theory: The Historical Sociology of a Financial Derivatives Exchange." *American Journal of Sociology* 109 (July):107–145.

MacKenzie, Donald, Fabian Muniesa, and Lucia Siu. 2007. "Introduction." In *Do Economists Make Markets?: On the Performativity of Economics*, ed. Donald Mackenzie, Fabian Muniesa, and Lucia Siu, 1–19. Princeton: Princeton University Press.

Merton, Robert C., and Zvi Bodie. 2005. "Design of Financial Systems: Towards a Synthesis of Function and Structure." *Journal of Investment Management* 3:1–23.

Merton, Robert K. 1936. "The Unanticipated Consequences of Purposive Social Action." *American Sociological Review* 1 (December):894–904.

———. 1938. "Social Structure and Anomie." *American Sociological Review* 3: 672–82.

———. 1948 "The Self-Fulfilling Prophecy." *Antioch Review* 8:193–210.

———. 1968. *Social Theory and Social Structure.* Enlarged ed. New York: Free Press.

———. 1976. *Sociological Ambivalence and Other Essays.* New York: Free Press.

———. 1984. "Texts, Contexts and Subtexts: An Epistolary Foreword." In *The Grammar of Social Relations: The Major Essays of Louis Schneider*, ed. Jay Weinstein, ix–xlv. New Brunswick, N.J.: Transaction.

———. 1998. "Unanticipated Consequences and Kindred Sociological Ideas: A Personal Gloss." in *Robert K. Merton & Contemporary Sociology*, ed. Carlo Mongardini and Simonetta Tabboni, 295–318. New Brunswick, N.J.: Transaction Publishers.

———. 2004. "Afterword: Autobiographic Reflections on *The Travels and Adventures of Serendipity*." In *The Travels and Adventures of Serendipity*, ed. Robert K. Merton and Elinor Barber, 230–298. Princeton, N.J.: Princeton University Press.

Merton, Robert K., and Elinor Barber. 2004. *The Travels and Adventures of Serendipity.* Princeton, N.J.: Princeton University Press.

Portes, Alejandro. 2000. "The Hidden Abode: Sociology as Analysis of the Unexpected: 1999 Presidential Address." *American Sociological Review* 65 (February):1–18.

Purcell, Kate. 1982. "Female Manual Workers, Fatalism and the Reinforcement of Inequalities." In *Rethinking Social Inequality*, ed. David Robbins, 43–64. Farnborough: Gower.

Schneider, Louis. 1975. "Irony and Unintended Consequences." In *The Sociological Way of Looking at the World*, 35–58. New York: McGraw-Hill.

Somers, Margaret R., and Fred Block. 2005. "From Poverty to Perversity: Ideas, Markets, and Institutions over 200 Years of Welfare Debate." *American Sociological Review* 70 (April):260–287.

Tversky, Amos, and Daniel Kahneman. 1974. "Judgment under Uncertainty: Heuristics and Biases." *Science*, New Series 185 (September 27):1124–1131.

Tilly, Charles. 1996. "Invisible Elbow." *Sociological Forum* 11 (December):589–601.

Westwood, Sallie. 1984. *All Day, Every Day: Factory and Family in the Making of Women's Lives*. London: Pluto.

Williams, Bernard.1982. *Moral Luck: Philosophical Papers 1973–1980*. Cambridge: Cambridge University Press.

Williams, Bernard A. O., and Thomas Nagel. 1976. "Moral Luck." *Proceedings of the Aristotelian Society, Supplementary Volumes* 50:115–135, 137–151.

Zelizer, Viviana A. Rotman. 1979. *Morals & Markets. The Development of Life Insurance in the United States*. New York: Columbia University Press.

——. 2005. *The Purchase of Intimacy*. Princeton, N.J.: Princeton University Press.

6

"Paradigm for the Sociology of Science"

THOMAS F. GIERYN

My title belongs to Robert K. Merton, although (to my knowledge) he never used the phrase explicitly in print, unless you count the index to his 1973 collection *The Sociology of Science*, where one is sent to fifteen different pages for putative discussions of a "paradigm for the sociology of science." Or, more generously, you count eight decades of countless books and articles in the sociology of science which add up in their immense breadth and depth, brilliance and theoretical consistency, to a paradigm-by-example. Or you grant the father of this specialty something akin to naming rights, so that whatever the sociology of science looks like in Merton's hand becomes paradigmatic. I have searched, and searched again, for an intensely condensed and propaedeutic "paradigm for the sociology of science," like those Merton famously prepared for the sociology of knowledge in 1945, for functional analysis in 1949, and for structural analysis in 1976. Nada.1

The task ahead becomes self-evident: what would a paradigm for the sociology of science look like if imagined *now*, built not only on that sturdy Mertonian foundation but also on the alternative foundation of dissenting works that continue to challenge Merton's project? My goal is not to conjure a paradigm for the sociology of science that Merton would have written had he chosen to do so, say, during the last years of his long life. Rather, I want to use the daunting exercise of inventing my own paradigm as an occasion to think more deeply about the nature of paradigms in science and scholarship, and to raise the possibility that the utility of paradigms changes historically with the dynamic state of knowledge in a field.

In other words, I intend my paradigm to focus on some conceptual ingredients we need to study science sociologically in the twenty-first century. But at the same time, I need to ask whether "paradigms" as Merton once deployed them remain viable as tools for where we are now in the sociology of science. It turns out that my paradigm for the sociology of science will look different in substance and intent than Merton's, and these differences will politely subvert—in a self-negating, ironic way—the very idea of paradigms as Merton saw them.

There are three immediate limitations. First, in extracting Merton's sense of what paradigms consist of and their functions and dysfunctions, I restrict my attention to the three examples just mentioned: sociology of knowledge, functional analysis, and structural analysis. There are other candidates: Merton used the word paradigm in papers on interracial marriage (1941) and racial discrimination (1948), and inter alia, suggests that the typology developed in "Social Structure and Anomie" (1938) might be a paradigm along with the paradigm of the self-fulfilling prophecy (1994). I shall make no use here of the "lesser" Mertonian paradigms. Second, I have precious little to say about the substance of his paradigms. Flatly, I am not interested in Merton's designs for the sociology of knowledge, functional or structural analysis, or the impact of these paradigms on subsequent sociological work. They are exemplars, offering a form and function for me to emulate (if that is possible) in order to fashion a paradigm for the sociology of science. Third, Merton's sense of paradigm has surely taken a back seat to Thomas Kuhn's inescapable usage of same word. I'll leave Kuhn (1970) aside. If Margaret Masterman (1970) could enumerate twenty-one distinct definitions of Kuhn's "paradigm" more than three decades ago, certainly that number has increased tenfold in the years since.

The Stuff of Paradigms

Looking at Merton's three major-league paradigms: What do they consist of? What discursive form do they take? What are their functions and dysfunctions? Are there changes in the paradigms from 1945 to 1949 to 1976? I have made a meta-list of the words that Merton used to describe the contents of a paradigm. Deep breath now, for it is very long:

assumptions (2004:267)
problem sets (2004:267)
problematics (1976:132)
key concepts (2004:267)
generalizable concepts (1996:58)
central concepts (1996:58)
conceptual apparatus (1968:514)
logic of procedures (2004:267)
procedures of inquiry (1996:57)
scheme of analysis (1968:514)
vocabularies (1996:81)
postulates (1996:38)
classification (1968:514))
ideological imputations (1996:81)
inference (1996:81)
substantive findings (1996:57)
inventory of extant findings (1968:514)
types of pertinent evidence (1976:132)
basic propositions (1996:57)
interpretative schemes (1968 73)
provisional agreement (1976:120)

Plainly, we need a paradigm to simplify the contents of paradigms! Paradigms consist of: (a) what we know about the social world, either by empirical observation or logical inference or reasonable premise; (b) how sociologists should study the social world (not Lazarsfeldian "methods" or techniques but the conceptual tools we think with); (c) prototheories that explain in causal fashion why society is the way that it is.

These three elements—what we know, how we can learn more, and why—assume a similar form in the three model paradigms. The paradigm for the sociology of knowledge is a list of five questions and schematic answers; the paradigm for functional analysis is a list of eleven items, concepts, or problems, each punctuated by a Basic Query; the paradigm for structural analysis presents fourteen stipulations. (At this rate, Merton's next paradigm surely would have had 23.6 numbered points.) The three paradigms share several formal attributes: they are enumerated lists of compact (even elliptical) assertions, stated unpretentiously, disciplined by logic, derived from longstanding intellectual lineages, and capable of anticipating tomorrow's sociology. My paradigm for the sociology of science will respect this form, although it will depart from the three models in substance and utility (and, mercifully, it will have fewer than 23.6 numbered points).

It is hardly surprising that a devotee of functional analysis like Merton would inquire into the functions (and dysfunctions) of paradigms. I have distilled those functions down to five: (1) Paradigms *reduce*: they have a "notational" function (1996:58). Immense arrays of ideas are condensed into a "small compass" (1996:58), enabling simultaneous side-by-side comparisons and "cross-tabulations" (1996:59) of concepts, problems, and findings—all at a glance. In a way, paradigms are intended to be like Functional Analysis for Dummies, without the pictures. (2) Paradigms *codify*: they consolidate and logically arrange what we know, enabling selective accumulation and the identification of convergences, continuities, and discontinuities in sociological thought. (3) Paradigms *expose*: they lay bare tacit assumptions and unnoticed lacunae or weaknesses, enabling greater self-awareness and preventing "logically irresponsible" (1996:59) ad hoc theories; (4) Paradigms *guide*: they are "propaedeutic" (1996:57) because they provide schematic and preliminary exemplars or models that enable the undertaking of more advanced sociological research. There is an inescapable normativity to Merton's paradigms: they are intended not just to guide, but to steer. (5) Paradigms *extend*: they are written at a level of abstraction that enables the easy transit and transposability of concepts and theories across disparate substantive domains of sociology. Paradigms generate cognitive power by sensitizing sociologists to unexplored problems that can be examined with the same conceptual logic used in better-understood territories, resulting in the greater generalizability or empirical "reach" of theory.

Of course, paradigms have their Dark Side. Merton saw three dysfunctions: By steering the foci of research in some directions but not others, paradigms may occlude interest in problems worthy of investigation. By announcing explicitly "what is known," paradigms may lead to a premature foreclosure of inquiry. And by imposing themselves hegemonically, paradigms can become scientific straightjackets leading to the stagnation of a field. But these potential dysfunctions have their antidotes. In Merton's view, no paradigm in sociology should ever gain a monopoly on the direction of research—the plurality of paradigms is expected to be permanent. Moreover, his paradigms were always presented as provisional, temporary, available for change and partial in their scope: "a single paradigm proposed as a panacea . . . would constitute a deep crisis with ensuing stasis." (1976:118)

Variations in Merton's Paradigms

The three paradigms from 1945, 1949, and 1976 differ in their tone—and in their ambition. The paradigm for the sociology of knowledge lays out an agenda for a new substantive field of inquiry: what could a sociology of knowledge possibly be? Others had tried earlier to answer that question—Marx, Scheler, Mannheim, Durkheim, and Sorokin—so the point of Merton's first paradigm is to create a map of questions on which to locate each of these precursors, thus exposing their differences and similarities while identifying the gaps where nobody had bothered to look. He takes on the challenge of bounding this new field: "the term 'knowledge' must be interpreted very broadly indeed, since studies in the area have dealt with virtually the entire gamut of cultural productions (ideas, ideologies, juristic and ethical beliefs, philosophy, science, technology)" (1973:7). Sociological interest in knowledge, however defined, arises in identifiable social conditions, where there is *conflict* over norms, values, and attitudes. Merton deftly handles the thorny question of whether the social determination of ideas undermines their validity, and presciently observes that the sociology of knowledge "came into being with the signal hypothesis that even 'truths' were to be held socially accountable, were to be related to the historical society in which they emerged" (1973:11; 1996:207). Later sociologists of scientific knowledge would remove the scare quotes.

The sociology of knowledge is poised to ask five questions: Where is the production of ideas located? What is to be included as "knowledge"? How is knowledge related to the social substrate or "existential conditions"? Why do ideas exist (i.e., what are their functions and dysfunctions)? When are the links between ideas and social conditions made theoretically explicit? There is an unmistakable optimism that the best is yet to come: "the sociology of knowledge is fast outgrowing a prior tendency to confuse provisional hypothesis with unimpeachable dogma; the plenitude of speculative insights which marked its early stages are now being subjected to increasingly rigorous test." The closer coupling of data and generalization, afforded in part by Merton's paradigm, gives hope for "what promises to be a fruitful union" (1973:40).

Four years later, the paradigm for functional analysis shows Merton at his feistiest. There is an unmistakable confidence that *this* theoretical orientation has legs, as evidenced in his stirring first line: "Functional analysis is at once the most promising and possibly the least codified of contemporary orientations to problems of sociological interpretation" (1968:73; 1996:65). There is more than a little policing going on in the second paradigm, as Merton demarcates appropriate from inappropriate definitions of the word "function," while also distinguishing the preferred functional analysis from three "debatable and unnecessary" postulates (1968:79; 1996:71) common to some social anthropologists (functional unity of society, universal functionalism, and indispensability). Moreover, he purifies from functional analysis any inherent ideological implications, suggesting that it "is neutral to the major ideological systems" (1968:96), whether conservative or radical.

The enumerated paradigm itself introduces conceptual distinctions that make up Merton's "hard core of concept, procedure and inference" (1968:104; 1996:81): motives versus functions; functions versus dysfunctions; manifest versus latent functions; equilibrium versus disequilibrium; structure versus function; functional imperatives versus alternatives/equivalents. There is little question that Merton in 1949 had put his money down on functional analysis, and his challenge was to make certain that other sociologists making the same bet pursued their studies in a paradigmatically proper way. He is confident about the promise of this now codified and clarified functional analysis, even if he is slightly less boastful at the end of the essay than at the start: "sociology has one beginning of a systematic and empirically relevant mode of analysis" (1968: 136).

Twenty-seven years later, the paradigm for structural analysis seems to lose a little of 1949's swagger, and a defensiveness creeps in. There are wolves at the door, creating a different intellectual dynamic. The challenge is no longer to lay down a primer so that all functional analysts follow the right rules of procedure. Set against noisy assertions of a "crisis" in sociology (Gouldner 1970), Merton rails against "theoretical monists" (1976:118) and a "total subjectivity in which anything goes" (1976:114). He hesitates to declare that structural analysis is now the most promising of contemporary orientations, although he does admit to a personal preference for it: "Structural analysis has generated a problematics *I find* interesting and a way of thinking about problems *I find* more effective than any other *I know*" (1976:119). Merton backs off into a "pacifist position" (1976:119) of reconciliation, in which his paradigm becomes a tool for spotting "spheres of agreement and of complementarity" (1976:119) among an inevitable plurality of paradigms in sociology.

So, Marx, Durkheim, Levi-Strauss, Chomsky, Parsons, and even Thomas Kuhn become cozy structuralist bedfellows—and the only real crisis in sociology, says Merton, would be a war unto death among the paradigms, based on the pernicious fallacy that victory for one of them would be good for the discipline. The fourteen stipulations (among other things) trace the intellectual history of structuralism *avant la lettre*; center analytic attention on conflict, ambivalence, and change at micro and macro levels; and identify the core process of "the choice between socially structured alternatives" (Stinchcombe 1975:12). In a nutshell, the paradigm for structural analysis seeks a common ground among sociologists of diverse persuasions. It is an olive branch in the form of a catechism of provisional, partial, incomplete stipulations that the warring tribes can find something to agree on.

The differences among Merton's three paradigms suggest that the creation and deployment of such enumerated descriptive protocols may reflect distinctive moments in the life cycle of a scientific or scholarly field. To be sure, the histories of intellectual fields need not follow some fixed or essential sequence of stages, nor do they necessarily evolve at the same pace or move toward the same end state. Nevertheless, it is easy to recognize Merton's 1945 paradigm of the sociology of knowledge as an attempt to *inaugurate* a putatively new field of study out of scattered and not-yet-synthesized works by precursors. His 1949 paradigm for functional analysis *consolidates* a near-hegemonic theoretical orientation with heavy boundary-work (Gieryn 1999) designed to demarcate the proper explanatory strategies and tactics from flawed impostors. Merton's 1976 paradigm for structural analysis measures a discipline now with no theoretical hegemony but rather multiple viable schools of thought slugging it out: his hopeful last paradigm *conciliates* in the pursuit of hitherto unnoticed convergences.

A paradigm for today's sociology of science will measure (and, inescapably, construct) a field that is not quite like any of these three cases.

The sociology of science is too old and established to be inaugurated now by a birthing paradigm; it is without any obvious hegemonic theoretical orientation that could be consolidated and policed; and it is seemingly beset by so many passionate disputes over "domain assumptions" (Gouldner 1970:72) that conciliation appears naive or utopian. Instead, a paradigm for the sociology of science becomes an exercise in postwar reconstruction, a Marshall Plan bringing recovery to a specialty weary from battle.2 Without a dominant theoretical orientation to consolidate and with still too many divergent conceptual schemes to make honest conciliation imaginable, the sociology of science can only hope for a paradigm so *equivocal* that—when compared to Merton's confident and forceful catechisms—it may no longer be a paradigm at all.

Sociology of Science, Paradigmed

Paradigms are historical inventions, shaped by the life cycle circumstances of a scholarly field but at the same time driven by the ambition to make a field into something more, something better. Merton's paradigms offer decisive answers and firm stipulations coming from a voice that had already made up its mind. In contrast, my paradigm for the sociology of science (see Table 6.1) consists of seven antinomies, irreducible and irresolvable contradictions of principle. These paradoxical oppositions have long been battle lines dividing sociologists of science. Neither side has won or will ever claim victory, and it is equally unlikely that advocates for any specific position will ever concede. My paradigm is grounded in the hope that this field could (at least) move on.

Table 6.1
Paradigm for the Sociology of Science

It is (ambivalently) stipulated that

1. Science is social and cognitive
2. Science is cooperative and competitive
3. Science is institutionalized and emergent
4. Scientific objects in the world are real and constructed
5. Science is autonomous and embedded
6. Science is universal and local
7. Scientific knowledge is cumulative and . . . not

A paradigm for the sociology of science will acknowledge that these seven oppositions are permanent, while morphing them from causes of war into sources of creative tensions and innovative provocations. Such a paradigm will avoid any appearance of either choosing sides or resolving differences, because it is precisely this accommodation to irresolvable antinomies that will energize the field and render these seven specific oppositions as something no longer worth fighting over. As a result, new and different battle lines will emerge, and this may be a progress of sorts because the tired and stale oppositions listed in my paradigm have (I think) ceased to inspire. I am suggesting that a resignation to the permanence of these oppositions might have the same positive function for sociology that Merton attributed to its "chronic crisis" in his paradigm for structural analysis: "Paradoxically, then, a sense of crisis can be occasioned by new knowledge, resulting in more exacting demands being made of old knowledge" (1976:112).

It is ironic that my paradigm can make stipulations only ambivalently—a posture crucially absent, I think, from the three paradigms created by the man who wrote the book on *Sociological Ambivalence* (1976). In calling these stipulations "ambivalent," I intend to suggest that the sociology of science today rests productively on "opposing normative tendencies," which is the language Merton used (1976:12) to describe the often incompatible expectations associated with a social role (although, with my list, it is impossible to know which side could be privileged as the "norm" as opposed to the "counter-norm"). Ambivalence is built into the research agenda of this specialty, so that sociologists of science are expected, for example, to treat scientific objects in the world as both real and constructed, and to treat science itself as irreducibly universal and local. The next sociological research on science will acknowledge these paradigmatic contradictions, revel in their ambivalent expectations, transcend these oppositions in the search for different fault lines of contestation, and, most vitally, never try to resolve or adjudicate them.

In a sense, paradigms always come too late: the improvements they seek are already underway by the time they are proposed. So, even though Merton's 1945 paradigm sought to inaugurate a sociology of knowledge, he is able to point to the "growth of publications and . . . the increasing number of doctoral dissertations in the field" (1973:8). Parsons was well on his way toward consolidating functional analysis, and, with the 1951 publication of *The Social System*, might have succeeded even without Merton's paradigm. Structural analysis was already a going concern in 1976 (and possibly in 1876), even if contentious epistemic politics of the day prevented many from seeing the convergences that Merton enumerated. So it is with my paradigm for the sociology of science: it is not difficult to find works that have already accommodated themselves to the competing demands of each of my seven antinomies, and moved on. My job here is not to review in some comprehensive way the latest best work in the sociology of science, but to use the paradigm to identify especially promising lines of inquiry that come into view when nobody is forced to choose between one or the other side of the seven contradictions.

SCIENCE IS SOCIAL AND COGNITIVE

It seems self-evident now that science is *both* people doing things together (social) *and* a body of claims about the world (cognitive). Not so long ago, however, the sociology of science appeared to move along separate tracks: some people studied *scientists* (and the norms and opportunity structures that shape their behavior) and others studied *knowledge* (and the laboratory practices, specimens, instruments, and discourses through which facts and theories are made). Merton's reluctance to make a particular scientific fact or theory into the explicit dependent variable of his analysis created an opening for the sociology of scientific knowledge (SSK), whose enthusiasts were themselves less inclined to search for enduring structures of evaluation, reward, and sanctioning that transcend laboratory walls or disciplinary boundaries. Once upon a time, a sociologist of science was forced to choose whether to examine science as either social or cognitive, with big methodological implications: Mertonians used quantitative co-citation data to understand patterns of influence or status hierarchies, while SSKers conducted laboratory ethnographies to understand how transcendent truth emerges from messy, mundane work at a bench somewhere; SSKers became competent in the fields they watched in order to be able to understand the grounds on which scientists themselves evaluated evidence and explanations, while the content of scientific knowledge and technique remained offstage for Mertonians.

But the tracks had to converge, eventually. These days, sociologists interested in the behavior patterns of scientists and their structural constraints are expected to trace out the implications of their project for the construction of scientific knowledge. Those interested in controversies over scientific facts or theories are expected to trace out the implications of their project for institutional structures and the allocations of rewards. Forced choice has given way to normative ambivalence: even as sociologists of science continue to lay greater emphasis on either behavior patterns and social structures *or* on bench practices and technical discourse, they cannot act as if the other side does not exist. To illustrate: James Moody's (2004) work on networks of scientific collaboration looks superficially like an exemplary study of scientists, just as Harry Collins's (1998) work on physicists' disputes over what counts as legitimate evidence for the existence of gravitational waves looks superficially like canonical SSK. But in fact, neither paper is able to separate the social from the cognitive, scientists from knowledge, structures from practices.

Moody starts his paper: "Recent work in the sociology of knowledge suggests that the sets of ideas one holds to be true is largely a function of the group of people one interacts with and references to authorities recognized by the group" (2004:213). His analysis builds on previous work by Martin (2002) and Friedkin (1998) suggesting that consensus over scientific ideas "depends critically on the underlying shape of the social network" (Moody 2004:215). Moody's empirical analysis in this paper, it must be said, centers on the description and explanation of observed network structures, while the consequences of these structures for scientists' beliefs or ideas remains inferential. Harry Collins finds that physicists at Louisiana State University and at Frascati (Italy) employ different standards and criteria when they decide whether empirical assertions about gravitational waves should be taken as real data or noise—differences that he attributes to distinctive "evidential cultures in their institutional context" (1998:295). That is, judgments about what constitutes credible physical evidence depend on the dense networks of collaborating scientists in evaluating putative evidence for gravitational waves. Collins is cautious: "it would be wrong to draw crude causal connections between the structures and pressures within the respective environments and the scientific choices made by individuals." And yet: "every scientist discussed here . . . would also have to accept the possibility that structural forces might affect their larger judgments in subtle and invisible ways" (1998:336).

Neither Moody nor Collins goes all the way: Moody could collect additional data on his scientists' beliefs (methodological preferences or even their standards for evidential legitimacy), just as Collins could make visible those subtle structural influences by creating Moody-like networks that extend beyond LSU and Frascati. Those imagined studies would surely trigger productive theoretical debates: Moody might opt for the greater significance of social structure (network position) in shaping scientific beliefs and practices, while Collins might give greater weight to culture. But happily, those debates leave in the dust the old battle over whether science is social *or* cognitive.

SCIENCE IS COOPERATIVE AND COMPETITIVE

Perhaps nobody in the sociology of science ever felt compelled to describe science as *either* cooperative *or* competitive. What remains interesting is the fact that two prominent sociologists who otherwise have had little to agree on—Merton and Bourdieu—both announce the paradoxical coupling of these oppositional tendencies as a distinctive feature of science, responsible for whatever success scientists might have. Bourdieu characteristically pulls no punches expressing his distaste for Merton's functional orientation to science (1975), and Merton characteristically returned the favor by ignoring Bourdieu completely, at least in print. In the commentary written into the oral version of his final lectures at the Collège de France, Bourdieu admits that his earlier and undeniably savage attack on Merton was "unfair," and grounded in his ignorance of Merton's early work on the history of science and in his initial misrecognition of the person. The "elegant, refined Wasp" Bourdieu once saw at a meeting turned out to be "a recent Jewish immigrant" whose "exaggerated . . . British elegance" was actually a "disposition toward hypercorrectness" (2004:13). Still, the two giants might have found common ground had they been inclined to examine more patiently what the other had written about the coincidence of cooperation and competition in science.

Tucked away laconically in Merton's classic 1942 analysis of the moral economy of science is this: "There issues a competitive cooperation" (1996:272). Scientists compete for recognition (and ensuing material rewards) by being first: "Those controversies over priority which punctuate the history of modern science are generated by the institutional accent on originality" (1996:272). Without original contributions to the stock of certified knowledge, science dysfunctionally stands still. To be sure, one meaning of "cooperation" refers to Merton's *On the Shoulders of Giants*3 theme: "the essentially cooperative . . . quality of scientific achievement . . . results from the realization that scientific advance involves the collaboration of past and present generations" (1996:273). But there is more: scientists also cooperate in making judgments about which claims get certified as scientific knowledge. Success in the competition for priority, recognition, and reward depends intimately on evaluations of provisional knowledge claims by a scientist's expert and authorized competitors. Shifting from the norm of communalism to the norm of disinterestedness, Merton writes, "Involving as it does the verifiability of results, scientific research is under the exacting scrutiny of fellow experts" (1996:274–5). So, even though "there is competition in the realm of science," "the translation of the norm of disinterestedness into practice is effectively supported by the ultimate accountability of scientists to their compeers" (1996:275). Perhaps Merton chose "compeer" instead of the more common "peer" to signal that science is as much *competitive* as collaborative.

Merton's analysis of the normative regulation of institutionally engendered competition is the cornerstone of his abundant later work on the reward and recognition system of science, and would be unremarkable in this context except for its explicit anticipation of Bourdieu (the apparent rival). In "An Enchanted Vision," his final spar with Merton, Bourdieu characteristically creates a distinction to gain symbolic capital, writing: "Structural-functionalism sees the scientific world as a 'community' which has 'developed' for itself just and legitimate regulatory institutions and where there are no struggles—or at least, no struggles over what is at stake in the struggles" (2004:11). It is not easy to discern exactly what "stake in the struggles" Merton supposedly missed: material rewards (prizes, prestigious jobs), recognition (influence, visibility), priority, cultural authority, credibility, truth, and just about every other kind of Bourdieuian capital have been examined somewhere by Mertonians. Moreover, when Bourdieu gets down to his own "refined" (2004:43) theories about science, distinctions with Merton fade: "The fact that producers tend to have as their clients only their most rigorous and vigorous competitors, the most competent and the most critical, those therefore most *inclined* and most *able* to give their critique full force, is for me the *Archimedean point* on which one can stand to *give a scientific account of scientific reason,* to rescue scientific reason from relativistic reduction and explain how science can constantly progress towards more rationality without having to appeal to some kind of founding miracle" (2004:54). Stripped of its uniquely Bourdieuian vocabulary (fields, dominant agents, habitus, logic, trajectories, and positions), the idea that competitors in science themselves decide who wins is, in the end, just a slight change from Merton. Still, what for Merton is cooperation (collective and skeptical assessments of knowledge claims) becomes for Bourdieu a struggle for dominance and power (that nevertheless yields "progress toward more rationality"). The tussles linger.

SCIENCE IS INSTITUTIONALIZED AND EMERGENT

I never suspected that my constructivist-inspired research on the cultural boundaries of science (Gieryn 1999) could inform this paramount question: how might sociologists best explain the historic rise and global spread of modern science? But after reading recent work in the "world society" variant of neoinstitutional theory (Drori et al. 2003; Schofer 2003, 2004; Schofer and Meyer 2005), I realized that I have a dog in this fight. For them, science is an institution; for me, it is an emergent cultural space— and we seem to be searching in different galaxies for the best explanation of the ubiquity of science.

Happily, there is a little common ground. We are all more interested in cultural representations of science rather than the knowledge-making practices of scientists at the bench, although neoinstitutionalists are inclined to see these representations as stable myths while I see them as highly variable and contingent strategies. Neither of us is inclined to explain the rise and spread of science instrumentally (i.e., more science gives greater control over the vicissitudes of nature) or functionally (i.e., science grows because society needs certified knowledge). We all agree that science has lots of cultural authority and that scientists often serve as the legitimate arbiters of factual claims in a wide variety of settings. However, this epistemic authority is, for them, inherent in the packaged cosmology of a modern, rational, progressive, lawful, and standardized world that science epitomizes, while for me, authority is the outcome of jurisdictional struggles over the professional boundaries of expertise and credibility (Abbott 1988). We all have a principled theoretical interest in cultural classifications and categorizations, which become imposing rules or models for neoinstitutionalists but flexibly deployable rhetorical tools for constructivists like me. We share an empirical curiosity about the intersections of science with policy deliberations, although neoinstitutionalists are more likely to count the rising number (and geographical spread) of national science ministries or scientific societies, while this constructivist interpretatively homes in on episodic debates over who or what is really scientific.

At the heart of our differences is the significance attached to the agentic activities of scientists themselves in securing the rise and spread of science—small for them, much larger for me. The global reach of science results, I think, from sustained efforts by professional scientists to establish, enlarge, monopolize, and defend their cultural authority with boundary-work (Gieryn 1983), that is, situation-specific attempts to demarcate genuine science from impostors with rhetorical attributions to scientists that make them seem preferable for the job at hand. The cultural space for science gets constructed in contextually contingent ways, pliably shaped into those features that rhetorically work best to distinguish real scientists from their rivals as particular circumstances warrant. Boundary-work (and other discursive efforts to represent science on occasions when its utility or credibility is on the line) serves to advance the interests of professional scientists, and their long-running success at these constructions is indicated, in part, by the global expansion of everything scientific.

Neoinstitutionalists shift attention to the states, NGOs, and SMOs who demand and provide resources for scientists because of its legitimating capabilities. That is, science grows because states and other organizations gain legitimacy to the extent that they can base their policy decisions on scientific grounds. So, even impoverished nations establish science ministries and create universities with departments of science because objectivity, rationality, and empiricism form the logic (scheme, regime, frame, script) of modernity—and exactly these qualities define the institution of science. Neoinstitutionalists are skeptical of the theoretical significance of scientists' efforts at professional self-promotion: "Scientists clearly do perpetuate their own necessity to justify their professional standing, to encourage further sponsorship of their activities, and to support their social status. But unless scientists are seen as having extraordinary manipulative power and competence, and unless everyone else is seen as foolishly taken in, this explanation assumes what it sets out to explain." (Drori et al. 2003:27)

I see it differently. Science remains an ambiguous cultural space, and ordinary people remain fuzzy about its limits and potential—until its boundaries and contents get constructed (mainly) by scientists who choose to give science a particular meaning salutary for the professional stakes at risk then and there. Nobody is duped: scientists probably believe that science really is homologous to these episodic and strategic representations, and audiences for their boundary-work assign greater or lesser credibility to science (versus its putative competitors) depending on their own immediate interests, utilities, and practical rationalities. The case for science (as a legitimate source of truth about the world) will forever need to be made, and its contents will forever vary depending upon the contingent circumstances in which representations of this cultural space become the basis for assigning credibility.

Still, after reading these neoinstitutionalist studies of science, I am forced to admit that the boundaries and contents of science do not require explicit discursive construction at every moment. At times, science does indeed become more like an institution: a homogenous logic or script that gets reproduced implicitly all over the globe without much attention to its meaning and not requiring scientists to promote favorable images of themselves. Even constructivists must acknowledge that some discursive representations of science get sufficiently stabilized and sedimented, so that science expands seemingly on autopilot. On the other hand, neo-institutionalists have not ignored scientists' boundary-work: "Curricula and textbooks are tools to shape this public perception" that "science is a privileged kind of knowledge and method" (Drori et al. 2003:147; this chapter was written by Elizabeth H. McEneaney). I am intrigued by their hypothesis (wrong, I think) that "to the extent there is a cultural trend toward the expansion of science, we should see a softening of the claims of distinctiveness made on behalf of scientists" (2003:147). But how could a neoinstitutionalist empirically test this hypothesis without a careful examination of episodes of boundary-work (and other constructions of a cultural space for science)? These days, we both attend to the questions of the other, ambivalently so.

SCIENTIFIC OBJECTS IN THE WORLD ARE REAL AND CONSTRUCTED

To describe something as either real or constructed no longer has any analytic or conceptual utility, even though distinctions between real and constructed as actors' categories remain fundamental for sociological understandings of human cultures and societal change. However the *sociologist* might choose to define real (out-there, autonomous, pristine, material, physical, permanent, inevitable, inviolate, objective), any entity so classified would also have indelible marks of being constructed (made, understood, interpreted, evaluated, altered, represented, used, invested with emotions, subjective). This ancient opposition is especially blurry in the sociology of science, where actor-network theory has replaced the old antinomy with an analytic gradient, so that all sorts of entities (social, natural, ideational, material, discursive, technological) slide back and forth between real and constructed depending upon what actors do to or with them (see Latour 1987, 2004; Callon 1986).

Donald MacKenzie's recent analysis of financial markets (2006) is a superb illustration of why Durkheim's struggle to defend philosophical realism over nominalism is no longer our burden, nor is the opposite. MacKenzie tells us that his book is about financial markets and financial theories (i.e., models). Naively, the markets look real (in the sense that they are the real-world objects of social-scientific inquiry, both external to individual subjectivities and surely capable of constraining behavior), just as models of markets look constructed (shaped by ever-changing theoretical and methodological tastes, and varying between, say, economists and sociologists). MacKenzie complicates these easy assignments of reality and construction, ultimately undoing any conceptual utility in the distinction itself.

The price of bread at a supermarket seems real enough to somebody wanting to make a sandwich: $1.39 per loaf. The laws of markets that culminate in $1.39 also have a reality about them: increasing supply or decreasing demand will reduce price, which is not unlike the reality of the laws of gravity predicting that whatever goes up must come down. Not so fast. MacKenzie joins a chorus of economic sociologists who argue that "markets are not forces of nature, but human creations" (2006:275) dependent upon historical infrastructures of "social, cultural and technical conditions that make them possible" (2006:13). In some very complicated ways, the price of bread is shaped by futures trading in wheat commodities at the Chicago Mercantile Exchange and Board of Trade. To look inside the pits where traders yell the price they will pay for wheat not yet grown dissolves any sense that markets, bread, and wheat are not constructed.

MacKenzie draws on Michel Callon's useful concepts of "disentanglement" and "framing" to describe how markets work, and how markets appear to be real. A trader in the pit just bought "5000 bushels of Chicago No. 2 winter wheat" for an agreed upon price per bushel (cf. Cronon 1991). Consider the infrastructural constructions necessary for that "simple" transaction: units of measure and quality must be standardized and consensually acknowledged (bushel, dollar, "No. 2"); the "probity" of grain inspectors who grade wheat as No. 1 or No. 2 must be assumed; even the architectural design of the pit gives advantages to those traders located higher up (Beunza & Stark 2004). The price of bread is constructed in and through all of these framings, even though $1.39 per loaf seems to disentangle them from your very real sandwich. But MacKenzie is cautiously ambivalent. Markets are artificial, because "they can be seen as prostheses . . . that enable human beings to achieve outcomes that go beyond their individual cognitive grasp" (2006:268). However, there are constraints on our understandings of markets and how they work, and MacKenzie rejects "the crude claim that any arbitrary formula for option prices, if proposed by sufficiently authoritative people, could have 'made itself true' by being adopted." A model to describe derivatives markets (MacKenzie's specific focus) "would soon cease to hold sway if it led those using it systematically to lose money" (2006:20). The constructed character of markets is never so absolute that any representation of them is as good as any other.

On the other hand, financial theories and models do have an unreality about them. The Black-Scholes-Merton (Robert C., the son) Model for pricing options is "deliberately simplified so that economic reasoning about markets or processes can take a precise mathematical form" (2006:6) and is a "hopeless idealization" (2006:9). Whatever reality these obviously constructed, unrealistic models might have does not come from their verisimilitude: "'Truth' did emerge . . . but it inhered in the process as a whole; it was not simply a case of correspondence between the model and an unaltered external reality. . . . The Black-Scholes-Merton model itself became a part of the chain by which its fit to 'reality' was secured" (2006:32–3). Using Barry Barnes's (1988) concept of "performativity," MacKenzie suggests that some financial models and theories became more real as they consequentially changed the infrastructure, practices, and outcomes in derivatives markets, so much so that their "success was not discovery of what was already there" (2006:259). Various mathematical models got built into software used uncritically to price derivatives; they became part of the everyday vocabulary used by everybody to talk about these markets; and, with an authority rooted in economic *science*, the theories distinguished "legitimate" futures trading (2006:252) from mere gambling. In a very real sense, some economic theories about puts and calls enabled the creation of what was, in June 2004, a market of "derivatives contracts totaling $273 trillion" (2006:4).

So, markets cannot be real if "reality is conceived of as existing entirely independently of its theoretical depiction" (2006: 24). Models are real because "the economic theory of derivatives and the 'actual practices' of derivative markets are interwoven too intimately" (2006: 263). Markets and models are real and constructed. Emphatically but provocatively, the concepts that MacKenzie uses to study economics—disentanglement, framing, performativity—are equally useful in sociological studies of physics, chemistry, biology, informatics, and any other science.

SCIENCE IS AUTONOMOUS AND EMBEDDED

Perhaps this stipulation should read: "Science *has been* autonomous and embedded." It could be that science has, during its three- or four-century run, oscillated between autonomy and embeddedness amid changing historical circumstances. Or, perhaps the appearance of science as either autonomous or embedded is generated by the distinctive theoretical or methodological orientations employed by sociologists of science. Is the flow of science back and forth between autonomy and embeddedness a historical reality or theoretical artifact?

Arguments for the emerging autonomy of modern science may be traced back through Parsons's and Durkheim's functional theories of institutional differentiation, picked up famously by Merton in his dissertation on *Science, Technology and Society in Seventeenth Century England* ([1938] 1970). Through the passage of historical time, as societies moved from simple to complex and from traditional to modern, functional theory predicts that core institutions like the economy, polity, family, religion, and science would move away from each other centripetally (in conceptual space) toward a never-complete autonomy. Merton suggests that the institution of science has followed this historical pattern. Once deeply embedded in the religious values and technical interests of seventeenth-century English society, scientists have ever since moved toward institutional autonomy in four respects (Gieryn 1988:584): their role-expectations and actual behavior patterns are increasingly specialized and thus distinct from other social roles; scientists come to have greater control over the evaluation of scientific work and the allocation of rewards and recognition; science is increasingly able to legitimate its activities in a self-referential way, using its own distinct values to justify the worth of its accomplishments rather than relying on the values borrowed from other institutions; scientists come to gain greater control over the direction of the research agenda and the selection of problems for inquiry.

For Merton, science in the seventeenth century was embedded: its values and goals could not easily be disentangled from those of the economy or powerful religious institutions. Puritan values emphasizing diligence, hard work, individualism, utilitarianism, "blessed reason," profitable education, and the glorification of a God who authored such an orderly universe created a culture in which the "scientific" investigation of nature became a valorized pursuit and an honorable career choice. Moreover, the foci of research attention in seventeenth-century England was palpably shaped by a growing economy in the earliest stages of industrialization: natural philosophers of the day chose to investigate practical problems such as how to pump water from coal mines, how to get cannonballs to land closer to their desired targets, and how to navigate the high seas. By the mid-twentieth century, however, the dependence of science on religious values for cultural legitimation and the explicit steering of research agendas by technological or political ambitions had all but vanished. "It is only after a typically prolonged development that social institutions, including the institution of science, acquire a significant degree of autonomy. . . . Science gradually acquired an increasing degree of autonomy, claiming legitimacy as something good in its own right. . . . Once science was established with a degree of functional autonomy, the doctrine of basic scientific knowledge as a value in its own right became an integral part of the creed of scientists" (Merton 1970: x, xxii, xxiii).

And, according to functional theory, the trend toward increasing institutional autonomy should continue in perpetuity. At mid-century, evidence supporting this hypothesis was easy to find: Vannevar Bush's "endless frontier" inaugurated a compact (institutionalized in the National Science Foundation) in which the state provided abundant material resources for pure research to scientists, who would decide themselves what kind of new knowledge, in exchange, would benefit mankind (Zachary 1997). Merton's own research agenda in the sociology of science from the 1950s through the 1970s reflected an assumption that science had ratcheted up considerable institutional autonomy from politics, the economy, and religion. Studies of multiple discoveries, priority disputes, role ambivalence, evaluation and reward systems, and age-structures centered attention on "internal" processes that were explained without the theoretical need to embed scientists in the extrascientific array of political, economic, and cultural forces.

Then something changed, but the jury is still out on whether science itself has now became less autonomous or whether sociologists have recently adopted theoretical models that bring institutional embeddedness to center stage (or both). A recent collection of essays with paradigmatic aspirations of its own (Frickel and Moore 2006) hopes to steer sociological research on science toward empirical questions that embed science in markets, citizens-based social movements, and state regulatory apparatuses. With only a fleeting glance back at the functional theories that had long predicted the opposite, the coeditors confidently write: "the interdependence of science, politics, and economy has become virtually axiomatic in contemporary science studies . . . [and] the politicization, commercialization, and regulation of science carry profound implications for human health, democratic civil society, and environmental well-being" (2006:4, 5). The book includes chapters on: how the embedding of academic biotechnological research in corporate and financial networks has created a "proprietary science" in which the "internalist" evaluation and reward system explored by Merton has given way to hybrid status hierarchies (Owen-Smith 2006); how patient rights groups and other health-care social movements have defined "their embodied experience of illness as a counter-authority to technocratic decision making by engaging directly with scientific knowledge production itself" (Morello-Frosch et al. 2006:246); how recent changes in drug regulatory regimes liberalized rules for the "direct-to-consumer advertising of prescription drugs" and for the approval of new drugs simultaneously, enhanced the power of the pharmaceutical industry, and increased opportunities for consumer groups to intervene in this market (Klawiter 2006:436).

Plainly, science is not just for scientists anymore, if it ever was. But now its embeddedness is different from that of the seventeenth century: then, science needed to embed its activities in the values and interests of other social institutions to give it borrowed legitimacy and direction; these days, science gets borrowed by other institutions seeking to benefit from embedding its technological potency and perceived objectivity in their pursuits.

SCIENCE IS UNIVERSAL AND LOCAL

Even philosophers of science have given up arguing for the universality of science: although Rosenberg says that "laws are by definition true everywhere and always, in the past, in the present, in the future, here and everywhere else in the universe," he then immediately indicates that he is referring to *natural* laws (2005:32). By contrast, *scientific* laws remain our current best guesses about natural laws, explicitly here and now. Once upon a time, some sociologists went even further to proclaim the universality of scientific knowledge: "Philosophers have often speculated that, beyond the bounds of human understanding, there is a kind of universal and impersonal understanding in which individual minds seek to participate by mystical means: well, this kind of understanding exists not in any transcendent world but in this world itself. It exists in the world of science" (Durkheim 1977:340–1). As theoretical commitments to the universality of science waned, a fruitful sociogeography and even architecture of science has recently sprung up, reframing the opposition between universal and local into something other than a forced analytical choice.

Interpretations of scientific ideas vary depending on where they are taken up: they "do not diffuse over a flat cultural plain. Rather, they are encountered in particular places" (Livingstone 2003:113). Darwin's theories, for example, were read in consequentially different ways in Edinburgh, Belfast, Princeton, Charleston, and New Zealand, as distinctive religious or ideological contexts gave evolution different utilities for different projects (Livingtone 2003). In the nineteenth century, the very idea of a "statistical population" varied between England and France, so much so that the discipline of demography and even standards for evaluating certain knowledge took different paths on each side of the Channel (Schweber 2006). Economists' theories of markets assumed different contents in England, France, and the United States (Fourcade-Gourinchas 2009). Finally, biotechnological research and development has taken different directions in Britain, Germany, and the United States as a consequence of distinctive political cultures and histories. Assessments of the risks and benefits of genetically modified organisms, in vitro fertilization, and cloning take place within local "civic epistemologies" that comprise "different assessments of what is acceptable or unacceptable, and different legislative, judicial, and policy instruments for correcting perceived threats" (Jasanoff 2005:30).

Evidence for the persistent locality of all things scientific would seem to annul pretensions of its universality, unless, perhaps, the relationship between local and universal becomes something other than zero-sum. Recent work on the concrete places where science happens—laboratories, field sites, libraries, museums, accelerators—suggests that undeniably local architectural and cultural features of such sites of knowledge-making *facilitate* the global circulation of scientific facts, theories, and applications. "Ironically, place was once thought to pollute the credibility of science—merely local knowledge was parochial and idiosyncratic and thus untrustworthy. Now that the production of scientific knowledge has gone global with a vengeance (the view today is from everywhere), place will reassert its significance as a ratifier of authenticity and trust" (Henke and Gieryn 2008:369). The suggestion is that the global spread of scientific claims is enabled by architecturally and geographically secured cultural assumptions about the trustworthiness and validity-enhancing capabilities of local places where reliable knowledge comes from, sites that have been given a variety of conceptual labels: "truth-spots" (Gieryn 2006); "centers of calculation" (Latour 1987); "placeless places," referring to laboratory-like environments (Kohler 2002); and "serendipitous sociocognitive microenvironments" (Merton and Barber 2004:260).

SCIENTIFIC KNOWLEDGE IS CUMULATIVE AND . . . NOT

I save this one for last, because it returns the discussion to the historicity of paradigms in science (and the conditions of their eclipse). Contrasts between Merton's paradigms and my own paradigm measure generational differences in how science is presumed to work (he was born exactly forty years and four days before me). Merton's paradigms played to the cumulative nature of science (however selectively), mine to the permanently oppositional. Merton's paradigms pursued convergences and continuities, reconciliations and advances, resolutions and adjudications; mine celebrates uncommon ground, paradoxes that will not be resolved, and irreducible contradictory starting points—and ending points. In the paradigm for structural analysis, Merton writes: "the convergence of separate lines of thought can, and in this case does, involve a process of consolidation of concepts, ideas, and propositions that result in more general paradigms" (1976:123). Earlier in the same essay: "The ideal of a unified comprehensive theory is not here in question. Like other ideals of the Pareto type T, this one may be functional, even when not attained, for advancing the state of sociological knowledge" (1976:117–8). I *do* question "unified comprehensive theory" even as an ideal, and I remain skeptical that "convergence" and "consolidation" can (or should) lead to "more general paradigms." Permanent contradictions can themselves energize research in a field, even without the dream of progress toward something unified or comprehensive. My paradigm cannot shoulder the steering and policing functions of Merton's paradigms, for it is weaker, less confident, even hesitant—and in this sense, my use of the paradigm-form to describe where we are now in the sociology of science is ironic and self-subverting. Merton called for a "plurality of paradigms" (1976:148–53); I prefer a (vanishing) paradigm of paradoxical pluralities.

And we are both right.

Notes

1. Cole and Zuckerman (1975) offer a more delimited "paradigm" to enable "examination of the cognitive development of [scientific] specialties and their institutionalization."

2. How easily the language of war fits scholarly life (as in Latour 1987). Battles between Mertonians and post-Mertonians marked the 1970s. Battles *among* the more or less victorious post-Mertonians marked the 1980s. The "Science Wars" marked the 1990s, pitting science studies against philosophers and scientists hoping to rescue science from its apparent deconstruction. This is all too pat, of course, just as the metaphor of war itself hides so much about scholarly and scientific life.

3. As Newton put it, "If I have seen farther, it is by standing on the shoulders of giants." (Merton 1965:1)

References

Abbott, Andrew. 1988. *The System of Professions*. Chicago: University of Chicago Press.

Barnes, Barry. 1988. *The Nature of Power*. Cambridge: Polity

Beunza, Daniel, and David Stark. 2004. "Tools of the Trade: The Socio-Technology of Arbitrage in a Wall Street Trading Room." *Industrial and Corporate Change* 13:369–400.

Bourdieu, Pierre. 1975. "The Specificity of the Scientific Field and the Social Conditions of the Progress of Reason." *Social Science Information* 14:19–47.

——. 2004. *Science of Science and Reflexivity*. Chicago: University of Chicago Press.

Callon, Michel. 1986. "Some Elements of a Sociology of Translation: Domestication of the Scallops and the Fisherman of St. Brieux Bay." In *Power, Action and Belief: A New Sociology of Knowledge?*, ed. John Law, 196–229. London: Routledge and Kegan Paul.

——, ed. 1998. *The Laws of the Markets*. Oxford: Blackwell.

Cole, Jonathan R., and Harriet Zuckerman. 1975. "The Emergence of a Scientific Specialty: The Self-Exemplifying Case of the Sociology of Science." In *The Idea of*

Social Structure: Papers in Honor of Robert K. Merton, ed. Lewis A. Coser, 139–74. New York: Harcourt Brace Jovanovich.

Collins, H. M. 1998. "The Meaning of Data: Open and Closed Evidential Cultures in the Search for Gravitational Waves." *American Journal of Sociology* 104: 293–338.

Cronon, William. 1991. *Nature's Metropolis: Chicago and the Great West*. New York: Norton.

Drori, Gili S., John W. Meyer, Francisco O. Ramirez, and Evan Schofer. 2003. *Science in the Modern World Polity: Institutionalization and Globalization*. Stanford, CA: Stanford University Press.

Durkheim, Emile. 1977. *Evolution of Educational Thought*. London: Routledge and Kegan Paul.

Fourcade, Marion. 2009. *Economists and Societies: Discipline and Profession in the United States, Great Britain, and France, 1890s to 1990s*. Princeton: Princeton University Press.

Frickel, Scott, and Kelly Moore, eds. 2006. *The New Political Sociology of Science*. Madison: University of Wisconsin Press.

Friedkin, Noah E. 1998. *A Structural Theory of Social Influence*. Cambridge: Cambridge University Press.

Gieryn, Thomas F. 1983. "Boundary-Work and the Demarcation of Science from Non-Science: Strains and Interests in Professional Ideologies of Scientists." *American Sociological Review* 48:781–95.

——. 1988. "Distancing Science from Religion in Seventeenth-Century England." *Isis* 79:582–593.

——. 1999. *Cultural Boundaries of Science: Credibility on the Line*. Chicago: University of Chicago Press.

——. 2006. "City as Truth-Spot: Laboratories and Field-sites in Urban Studies." *Social Studies of Science* 36:5–38.

Gouldner, Alvin W. 1970. *The Coming Crisis of Western Sociology*. New York: Basic.

Henke, Christopher R., and Thomas F. Gieryn. 2008. "Sites of Scientific Practice: The Enduring Significance of Place." In *The Handbook of Science and Technology Studies*, 3rd ed., ed. Edward Hackett et al., 353–76. Cambridge: MIT Press.

Jasanoff, Sheila. 2005. *Designs on Nature: Science and Democracy in Europe and in the United States*. Princeton: Princeton University Press.

Klawiter, Maren. 2006. "Regulatory Shifts, Pharmaceutical Scripts, and the New Consumption Junction: Configuring High-Risk Women in an Era of Chemoprevention." In *The New Political Sociology of Science*, ed. Scott Frickel and Kelly Moore, 432–60. Madison: University of Wisconsin Press.

Kohler, Robert E. 2002. *Landscapes and Labscapes: Exploring the Lab-Field Border in Biology*. Chicago: University of Chicago Press.

Kuhn, Thomas S. [1962] 1970. *The Structure of Scientific Revolutions*, 2nd ed. Chicago: University of Chicago Press.

Latour, Bruno. 1987. *Science in Action*. Cambridge: Harvard University Press.

——. 2004. *Politics of Nature*. Cambridge: Harvard University Press.

Livingstone, David N. 2003. *Putting Science in its Place: Geographies of Scientific Knowledge*. Chicago: University of Chicago Press.

MacKenzie, Donald. 2006. *An Engine, Not a Camera: How Financial Models Shape Markets*. Cambridge: MIT Press.

Martin, John-Levi. 2002. "Power, Authority, and the Constraint of Belief Systems." *American Journal of Sociology* 107:861–904.

Masterman, Margaret. 1970. "The Nature of a Paradigm." In *Criticism and the Growth of Knowledge*, ed. Imre Lakatos and Alan Musgrave, 59–89. Cambridge: Cambridge University Press.

Merton, Robert K. [1938] 1970. *Science, Technology and Society in Seventeenth-Century England*. New Jersey: Humanities Press.

——. 1938. "Social Structure and Anomie." *American Sociological Review* 3:672–82.

——. 1941. "Intermarriage and the Social Structure: Fact and Theory." *Psychiatry* 4:361–74.

——. 1948. "Discrimination and the American Creed." In *Discrimination and National Welfare*, ed. Robert M. McIver, 99–126. New York: Harper and Brothers.

——. 1965. *On the Shoulders of Giants: A Shandean Postscript*. New York: Free Press.

——. 1968. *Social Theory and Social Structure*, enlarged ed. New York: Free Press.

——. 1973. *The Sociology of Science*. Chicago: University of Chicago Press.

——. 1976. *Sociological Ambivalence*. New York: Free Press.

——. 1994. "Life of Learning." In *Sociological Visions*, ed. Kai Erikson. New York: Rowman and Littlefield.

——. 1996. *On Social Structure and Science*. Chicago: University of Chicago Press.

Merton, Robert K., and Elinor Barber. 2004. *The Travels and Adventures of Serendipity: A Study in Sociological Semantics and the Sociology of Science*. Princeton: Princeton University Press

Moody, James. 2004. "The Structure of a Social Scientific Collaboration Network: Disciplinary Cohesion from 1963 to 1999." *American Sociological Review* 69: 213–38.

Morello-Frosch, Rachel et al. 2006. "Embodied Health Movements: Responses to a 'Scientized' World." In *The New Political Sociology of Science*, ed. Scott Frickel and Kelly Moore, 244–71. Madison: University of Wisconsin Press.

Owen-Smith, Jason. 2006. "Commercial Imbroglios: Proprietary Science and the Contemporary University." In *The New Political Sociology of Science*, ed. Scott Frickel and Kelly Moore, 63–90. Madison: University of Wisconsin Press.

Parsons, Talcott. 1951. *The Social System*. New York: Free Press.

Rosenberg, Alexander. 2005. *Philosophy of Science: A Contemporary Introduction*. London: Routledge.

Schofer, Evan. 2003. "The Global Institutionalization of Geological Sciences, 1800 to 1990." *American Sociological Review* 68:730–59.

——. 2004. "Cross-national Differences in the Expansion of Science, 1970–1990." *Social Forces* 83:215–48.

Schofer, Evan, and John W. Meyer. 2005. "The Worldwide Expansion of Higher Education in the Twentieth Century." *American Sociological Review* 70:898–920.

Schweber, Libby. 2006. *Disciplining Statistics: Demography and Vital Statistics in France and England, 1830–1885*. Durham, NC: Duke University Press.

Stinchcombe, Arthur L. 1975. "Merton's Theory of Social Structure." In *The Idea of Social Structure: Papers in Honor of Robert K. Merton*, ed. Lewis A. Coser, 11–33. New York: Harcourt Brace Jovanovich.

Zachary, G. Pascal. 1997. *Endless Frontier: Vannevar Bush, Engineer of the American Century*. New York: Free Press.

7

A Critical Reconsideration of the Ethos and Autonomy of Science

AARON L. PANOFSKY

One of Robert K. Merton's most enduring contributions to the sociology of science was his work on the normative structure of science, in particular the idea that there is an analytically identifiable "scientific ethos." This he defined as an "affectively toned complex of values and norms which are held to be binding on the man of science. . . . They are legitimized in terms of institutional values. These imperatives, transmitted by precept and example and reinforced by sanctions are in varying degrees internalized by the scientist, thus fashioning his scientific conscience" (1973:268–9). Analysis of the ethos occupied a sizeable part of the work that Merton and his colleagues conducted on science. In addition to questions specific to science such as the components of the ethos, the degree of scientists' conformity to it, and its relationship to the "advancement" of knowledge (Zuckerman 1988:514–526), Merton's analysis of the normative structure of science was central to the development of concepts such as "sociological ambivalence" (e.g., Merton 1973:383–412) and the control of deviance within professions (e.g., Merton and Gieryn 1982; Zuckerman 1977).

The "scientific ethos," like so many of Merton's concepts and coinages, has become embedded in commonsense for sociologists as well as other observers of science and scientists themselves. However, also like much of Merton's work, today the commonsense invocations are much of what remains. From the 1950s until the 1970s, the ethos of science was at the center of an active and often contentious collective research agenda (Stehr 1978). Toward the end of that period, sociological debates about the scientific ethos became wrapped up in the larger set of disputes in the social study of science that shifted the center of gravity from Merton's institutional approach to the constructivist sociology of scientific knowledge. As epistemological concerns took center stage in these debates, attention to the ethos and other of Merton's core interests in science waned.

The purpose of this paper is to argue for sociologists to return to the topics of the ethos and autonomy of science. As the basis for this return, I develop a critical analytic perspective that seeks to bring together important features of both the Mertonian tradition as well as the constructivist sociology of scientific knowledge to consider important issues that have fallen through the cracks.

The Ethos, Autonomy, and Advancement of Knowledge

At the heart of the matter is the relationship between the ethos of science and scientific autonomy, particularly how different ways of organizing this relationship impact the production of knowledge. That is, Merton and his associates were concerned with identifying the institutionalized features of science that distinguish and separate it from other spheres of social life and that endow it with the capacities to generate reliable knowledge regularly. Merton and his associates saw the relationship between the ethos and autonomy as positive and mutually reinforcing: the freer a scientific community from extrascientific influence, the stronger its institutionalization of the ethos; and the stronger the collective commitment to elements of the scientific ethos, the less vulnerable they would be to extrascientific influences.

At stake in this connection between the scientific ethos and scientific autonomy is the "advancement of knowledge." As Merton writes, "The institutional goal of science is the extension of certified knowledge. . . . The institutional imperatives (mores) derive from the goal and the methods. The entire structure of technical and moral norms implements the final objective" (1973:270). As quotes like these demonstrate, Merton saw the ethos, autonomy, and valid knowledge as intimately intertwined: freer scientific communities who have institutionalized ideals of "pure science" are more likely to produce true knowledge. For the most part Merton justified this claim in negative terms—though it might be thought of more accurately as a notion or sensibility than a claim, per se. Deviations from the ethos or incursions on scientific autonomy corrupt the pursuit of knowledge. For example, Merton wrote that the norm of universalism "militates against all efforts to impose particularistic criteria of validity," (1973:270); that is, this aspect of the ethos helps ensure cognitive objectivity in the evaluation of data and claims. He put this idea more generally by stating the "failure to adhere to this injunction [i.e., the "purity" of science] will encumber research by increasing the possibility of bias and error" (1973:261).[1]

The idea that scientific autonomy and the scientific ethos are mutually reinforcing might seem tautological since the notion of a distinctive institutional culture presumes that science is, indeed, relatively distinct (i.e., autonomous) from "society." But Merton and associates also saw the ethos and autonomy as properties of science's institutional structure that vary over time, between societies, and among scientific communities. For example, Merton wrote of the ethos and autonomy of science as historical achievements (see esp.1970; 1973:228–253, 267–278). He claimed (provisionally) that science would flourish best in democratic societies where the political ethos would be relatively unlikely to come into conflict with the scientific ethos so political powers would be disinclined to challenge science's autonomy (1973:254–278). In 1938, before he had codified the ethos into its now familiar form, Merton wrote that the "function of this sentiment [of scientific purity] is to preserve the autonomy of science. . . . as the pure science sentiment is eliminated, science becomes subject to the direct control of other institutional agencies and its place in society becomes increasingly uncertain" (1973:260). This quote is from Merton's passionate essay on sources of hostility toward science. Written against the backdrop of Nazi anti-intellectualism and corruption of science, it highlights Merton's sense of the fragility of science, and that its status as a bastion of truth against power must not be taken for granted.

Much of the Mertonian sociology of science has sought to measure variations in the ethos's manifestations and how these linked to the organization of scientific communities. For example, many studies have claimed that the scientific ethos (especially communalism and disinterestedness) has less of a hold on scientists working in industrial or applied settings than it does on those working in the relative autonomy of the academy.[2] Others have emphasized that the state of a community's cognitive development can mediate the relationship between the ethos and autonomy:

> It is when . . . a universe of discourse is only slightly developed (as in the Kuhnian "preparadigm" stage in the development of a new discipline or during a "scientific revolution"), or when group loyalties outside the domain of science take over, that violations of the norms become more frequent, leading some to reject the norms entirely. (Storer 1973:xix)

As a field becomes more cognitively institutionalized, that is, its scientific problems and procedures clarified by the community through practice, members become more committed to the scientific ethos and less beholden to extrascientific commitments. Thus while the ethos/autonomy relationship can appear tautological in analytic formulations, Merton and others have studied it empirically and conceived of the elements as varying and contingent.

The connection between the ethos/autonomy and the production of knowledge has been much less pursued as a topic (Stehr 1978:185; Zuckerman 1988:519–520). Part of this concerns the difficulty of obtaining comparative data on the knowledge production of different scientific apparatuses. Zuckerman, quoting Merton, writes, "'Although the most diverse social structures have provided some measure of support to science,' comparative data are far from simple to interpret since it is not just the survival of the sciences that is in point, but the 'ratio of scientific achievement to scientific potentialities'" (1988:519). At a less macro level, much of the academic debate about the ethos has concerned the effects of scientists' adherence to the knowledge they produce. A landmark was Ian Mitroff's (1974) contention that a set of "counter-norms," such as particularism, secrecy, and zealous interestedness, were necessary for a community to generate productive intellectual debate.

The dimensions of this relationship involving scientific autonomy have not been explored within the Mertonian tradition. While counter-norms can positively affect knowledge production (at least under certain circumstances), this tradition (almost) always conceives "external influences" as corrupting to both the ethos and knowledge production. Ironically, a major exception to this analytic trend is Merton's own *Science, Technology and*

Society in Seventeenth-Century England (1970) in which he documents the positive roles that political, economic, and military demands played in the growth of the scientific field and the role of Puritanism in its legitimation, attractiveness to powerful elites, and the codification of its normative structure. Though Merton's *historical* claims have been debated vigorously, researchers have not carried their implications into the analysis of other scientific communities.

Two Empirical Vignettes

I would now like to present two brief empirical vignettes that show different relationships between the scientific ethos and autonomy described in the canonical account of Merton and his colleagues. These examples, drawn from my ongoing projects in the sociology of contemporary genetics, show how scientific autonomy and aspects of the ethos can move in different directions rather than being mutually reinforcing. That is, they show the autonomy-ethos relationship organized in an opposite fashion to the way Merton and others claimed or assumed.

CRITICISM IN BEHAVIOR GENETICS

Behavior genetics, the field generating claims about the genetic causation of intelligence, personality, mental illness, criminality, homosexuality, and political attitudes, among many other traits, has a long history of controversy. This history is as old as the eternal "nature versus nurture" controversy and is rooted in social anxieties about the continuing impact of the legacy of eugenics and concerns that genetic science is a potential force for discrimination, inequality, and social control. Behavior genetics's most notorious controversies—spawned by Arthur Jensen in the early 1970s and Herrnstein and Murray's book *The Bell Curve* in the mid-1990s—have involved claims that differences in intelligence and social status between blacks and whites are attributable to genetic causes. These scandalous claims are elements of a large set of practices and statements both scientific and social that have led many scientists to perceive behavior genetics as a deviant scientific field. Critics from across the sciences have challenged the field over what they consider its shortcomings, scientific and otherwise, from the time of Jensen until the present.[3]

It is no surprise, then, that behavior geneticists have long resented their critics and have come to see them as a nearly intolerable impediment to the field's scientific progress. Here is a quote from an eminent behavior geneticist that I interviewed:

[Critics have] got an unfair advantage. They don't do research. It's one of our main gripes against the antigenetics [people]. They don't do any research. Do research to show how important the environment is, great; do research showing that genetics is no good. But, just to attack and attack. And they can attack faster than you can ever respond. So, you say, "But okay; you're saying this is important. We've studied that. We're going to study it. It isn't." But they're so far beyond it, they don't care. I mean, they don't say, "Oh right; okay." They say, "But here are twenty other things." And you know you could never catch up because they're not doing any research. They're just attacking anything that gets done. It's a very negative thing, and I find that if you respond to that it's never-ending. You'll never win anyway. So, I'd rather just do the research—take a longer view of it. So, it's for that same reason I don't answer—I wouldn't answer on either side of it. But, it does—you know sometimes seem kind of cowardly.

In this quote the message is "enough already," and we can sympathize with the sentiment expressed. Mitigating the impact of criticism—that is, securing the field's autonomy from its scientific naysayers—has been one of the field's most important collective projects.

But these efforts, which are too complicated to detail here, have had dramatic consequences for the integrity of organized-skepticism practices within behavior genetics. In the words of one behavior geneticist I spoke with, the field has become "clubbish" and closed to ward off its critics: "There was kind of this mindset, don't criticize each other . . . you stand by each other, and you don't hang your dirty laundry outside for people to see." Certainly, not every behavior geneticist would agree with this characterization of the field, but neither is it an idiosyncratic view of one member. Bits and pieces can be gleaned from many of my interviews. Here is a particularly clear example from one interviewee's description of his effort to get a critical meta-analysis of animal research on aggression published:

We sent it to [four of the journals] that had been the main ones that had published the original research. . . . [T]he reactions we got . . . were by and large completely illiterate. They had nothing to do with what we wrote but they were personal attacks basically saying, "How dare you do this? It's done by careful researchers, how dare you try to smear them?" and this sort of stuff. . . . And then what would happen is inevitably the editor would say, "Look, you know, our reviewers found this substandard" and "No, we're not going to give you a chance to rebut them. We just suggest you take it somewhere else." . . . We then sent it to a journal from biological researchers, the *Journal of Neurogenetics*, where it had no problem getting published.

The picture that emerges from these and other examples is that behavior genetics has developed a collective cultural allergy to certain forms of criticism because of the extreme pressure it has faced during its long history of controversy. For behavior geneticists, the ongoing problem of securing intellectual autonomy from their critics has appeared to be a condition of survival. But the particular ways they have gone about this have set the threshold quite low for what is considered acceptable criticism among members. The result, to put it bluntly, has undermined the field's own commitments to organized skepticism and constrained practices oriented toward those ends. The pursuit of scientific autonomy in behavior genetics has turned the norm of organized skepticism against itself.

PATIENT ADVOCACY IN MEDICAL GENETICS

One of the most dynamic areas of genetic medicine today is the search for genetic mutations that cause rare, often devastating, inherited diseases. To conduct this research, scientists need tissue samples from afflicted individuals and often their family members. The devastating consequences of these diseases and the isolation faced by families of disease sufferers have led many to form advocacy groups.[4] The rarity of these diseases makes it difficult for scientists to gather sufficiently large samples of afflicted individuals, so they often partner with advocates. Patient advocacy groups, or parents of afflicted children acting alone, are often instrumental in helping the scientists identify tissue donors and often donate funding and other resources to help push research along.

A key issue at stake in this setting is what Merton would call the norm of communalism, or the idea that the "substantive findings of science are a product of social collaboration and are assigned to the community. They constitute a common heritage . . . [and] property rights in science are whittled down to a bare minimum" (1973:273).[5] As many have observed, the ethic of communalism in the life sciences especially is becoming dramatically reorganized as commercial interests have come to be important forces (Thackary 1998; Krimsky 2003; Shorett, Rabinow, and Billings 2003). Private ownership affects not only the final application of knowledge, but also the direction and evaluation of research as well as scientists' abilities to collaborate, share data, and so forth. In the field of rare genetic disease research, many questions of ownership, control, and commercialization are on parade. Because of the rarity of these diseases, the market for research products might be extremely small, making commercial investment too risky a proposition; but genetic tests for given conditions can have huge market potential if they are used in pre- or post-natal screens for the population at large.

There is significant variation in how the ownership and control of research resources and products are organized among different genetic diseases. And the actions of patient advocates can have a large impact on these arrangements. Here is the first of two contrasting cases: Starting in the early 1980s, families with children suffering from Canavan disease (a degenerative brain disease) and a number of genetic disease advocacy groups worked with the medical geneticist Reuben Matalon to research the causes of the disease.[6] Disease advocates donated tissues and money, and in 1993 Matalon's laboratory cloned a gene variant responsible for Canavan disease, which led to the rapid development of a screening test. Families were hopeful that these developments would promote research on treatments while screening would lower the number of children born with the disease. But unknown to the patient advocates, Miami Children's Hospital (MCH) Research Institute, where Matalon's research had been conducted, filed a patent on the discovery, which was granted in 1997. MCH began commercializing the test and put highly restrictive licensing conditions on the patent which, among other impacts, had the effect of limiting scientists' access to a critical tool, thus hindering further research into the disease. Patient advocates felt betrayed and outraged. They brought suit against MCH in 2000. The court upheld the patent, and it is unclear exactly what concessions MCH made to advocates in the final 2003 settlement.

A second case had a very different outcome. Sharon and Patrick Terry were eager for scientific research when they learned their children had the rare genetic disease PXE.[7] Hoping to avoid subjecting their children to multiple blood draws when two groups of researchers asked them for tissue donations, the Terrys asked whether researchers might share their samples. When told that such sharing was not common practice in medical genetics, the Terrys anticipated the kinds of problems that the Canavan advocates experienced and organized an advocacy group, PXE International, to protect the disease sufferers' interests. In contrast to the Canavan groups, PXE International took a very active role in the research process. They took control of the patient recruitment and tissue collection process. These resources were offered to potential researchers on the condition that they would agree to share data and findings with other scientists and that they would allow PXE International a controlling stake in any patents that the research generated. PXE International entered into a close collaboration with one research group (members even learned genetic techniques and did shifts in the lab), and one of the founders was ultimately listed as a coauthor on the paper identifying the PXE mutation. PXE International has licensed its gene patent openly with the aim of promoting research and ensuring any treatments developed will remain accessible to the disease sufferers.

In the Canavan case, patient advocates adopted a fairly traditional relationship with scientists, acting as their patrons and clients at the margins without "interfering" in the research process. In the PXE case, patient advocates eschewed the margins, becoming intimately involved with researchers, not only asserting "property" ownership and putting conditions on its use, but also deeply engaging the research and researchers.[8] In both cases scientists faced a climate of commercialization that weakened their commitments to the norm of communalism, but in the PXE case the "extra" influence of patient advocates helped steer researchers back toward communalistic practices. In the Canavan site, scientists enjoyed incomplete, though relatively greater, autonomy, but exhibited a weaker form of the scientific ethos.

Debates about the Ethos and Autonomy of Science

Until the late 1970s or early 1980s, the ethos of science was a topic of vigorous sociological research and debate, but since then it has faded from attention. This is due in part to the way arguments about the ethos became embedded in a larger set of debates about the proper direction of the sociology of science between Merton-influenced institutional sociologists of science and "constructivist" sociologists of scientific knowledge. Harriet Zuckerman has observed that debates about the ethos of science became a microcosm of the broader disputes between these two parties:

> It seems to have provided an occasion for sociologists of science adopt-ing a relativist or phenomenological stance [i.e., the "constructivists"] to claim shortcomings not just of the normative theory but of the Mertonian research program, in general. It has also become an occasion for laying out alternative accounts of scientific practice; what norms are and their role in the production of knowledge; and last, how scientists behave in relation to them. (1988:516)

Debates about the norms had concerned the question of their specificity to science, the extent of scientists' adherence to them, whether Merton had characterized them accurately, and so on (see Stehr 1978; Zuckerman 1988).

In the late 1970s many dimensions of Mertonian institutionalism came under attack by the emerging constructivist sociology of scientific knowl-edge (SSK). Among these were the Mertonians' treatment of science as a special area of social life (where actors are distinctly truthful, rational, or disinterested) and the analytic separation of the contents of scientific knowledge from the institutional organization of science. For SSK ana-lysts, such self-imposed sociological limits would cede too much: accept-ing science's self-image as an accurate description (something sociologists would do with no other social group) and accepting as a priori precisely what needs to be explained—i.e., how scientists distinguish truth from fal-sity, how the social and cultural organization of science generate particular ideas about nature, and how science gained the cultural authority to be perceived as a special area of social life.[9]

The disagreement between the Mertonians and the SSK was partly un-derwritten by paradigmatic incommensurability in Kuhn's (1970) sense. Their cognitive interests and assumptions overlapped little. Much of this had to do with SSK's shift in explanation from "why" questions about scientists' professional actions and culture to "how" questions about sci-entists' knowledge-making practices (Zuckerman 1988:548; Knorr Cetina and Mulkay 1983). From the SSK's perspective, which views scientists as motivated by power and prestige just like everyone else, Merton's question, "why do scientists fight so fiercely over multiple discoveries?" (1973:286–324, 343–370), appears somewhat trivial. But for a Mertonian, any answer to the classic SSK question, "how do scientists construct facts?" necessitates unreasonably high expectations of the "social conditioning of knowledge" (Ben-David 1981). All this is to say that the two parties' mutual disregard concerned their different intellectual aims, assumptions, and traditions more than direct intellectual confrontations of different answers to the same question.

Two exceptions to this trend were Michael Mulkay and Thomas Gieryn who each sought to bridge this gap, though from different directions. Mulkay (1976, 1980), following the forcefully skeptical style of SSK, launched a probing critique of the Mertonian account of the ethos and autonomy of science. For example, reflecting SSK's Kuhnian-influenced turn to the content and cognitive aspects of science, Mulkay (1976) argued that social norms do not regulate scientists' actions beyond their impact on cognitive or technical norms of scientific practice. This was another way to say that explanations of scientists' actions cannot be separated from their disputes over the contents of knowledge. Later Mulkay (1980) invoked Wittgenstein's (1953) critique of the idea that "rules" can explain actions to argue against interpreting the "ethos" as a set of rules that are clearly related to or sufficient for explaining scientists' actions. This argument paralleled the SSK's Wittgenstein-inspired critique of "rationality" as providing sufficient justification to account for scientists' belief in the truth of given scientific facts (Bloor 1983). And Mulkay's argument that the ethos of science is best conceived as an "ideology" propagated by scientists and a "vocabulary of justification" they use to legitimate themselves to their patrons and other publics, reflects a general skepticism in the SSK about claims for science's special or privileged status as a realm of human endeavor (1976:653–4).

While Mulkay approached these issues having fully invested in the SSK critique, Thomas Gieryn, a student of Merton, sought to reimagine aspects of the Mertonian sociology of science in the light of SSK's constructivist insights rather than to side with one camp or the other. Gieryn developed and deployed his well-known concept of "boundary-work" (1983, 1999) in ways that take institutional functions of the scientific ethos and autonomy seriously, while understanding their symbolically constructed "ideological" character as well. His starting point is the demarcation of science from nonscience. Rather than seeing the difference as something inherent to science, as in Merton's view of the ethos providing a unique scientific culture (1973:267–278) or the rationalist view of it embodying particular cognitive procedures (e.g., Popper 1962), Gieryn views demarcation as "part of ideological efforts *by scientists* to distinguish their work and its products from nonscientific intellectual activities" (1983:781–2, emphasis in original). But in pointing out the constructed character of the lines between science and nonscience, he does not mean they are "ideological" in the sense of imaginary, false, dishonest, or superficial. While few SSK constructivists would put the matter so bluntly, the tendency to take science's nonautonomy as a starting point tends to presume something of this view. Gieryn, in contrast, shows how these "ideological efforts" correspond to the professional "strains and interests" scientists face (1983:782–3). As a result he can interpret scientific autonomy as simultaneously symbolically constructed, necessary for scientists' cognitive authority and thus their institutional and personal success, and variably manifested depending on the pressures of particular situations. In this analytic strategy the scientific ethos represents a symbolic repertoire for boundary-work, and it exerts normative force insofar as scientists invoke its elements in their efforts to distinguish themselves and discipline each other.

What's the upshot for the empirical vignettes presented above? I think there is a historical and an analytic point. The historical point is that as the sociology of science moved away from Merton, there was less interest in his characteristic concerns with the scientific ethos and autonomy. The overwhelming interest in knowledge production and scientists' practices changed assumptions: analysts assumed that *cognitively* or *practically* science was not autonomous (from society, culture, etc.) and the question of science's *institutional* autonomy tended to fade into the background. In addition, if science is composed of multiple "epistemic cultures" (Knorr Cetina 1999), then a unifying ethos hardly makes sense—this too faded from view. The analytic point is that each of the perspectives—Merton's institutionalism, Mulkay's constructivism, and Gieryn's synthesis—has blind spots and none can adequately dissect the kinds of dynamics between scientific autonomy and the ethos in my examples.

Let's consider Merton's functional institutionalism first. This analytic perspective tends to see the institutional structures of science as relatively fixed environments for scientists' actions and the contents of knowledge and cognitive practices as the targets of scientists' actions. Both are essentially "external" to the actions themselves, which are the proper target of sociological analysis. One implication has been noted by Nico Stehr, "the relative compatibility of cognitive and social elements within science is emphasized. Threats to such compatibility primarily come from sources external to science such as the state. Cognitive divisions therefore are deemphasized, because the theory of the institutional basis of science and its cognitive development reinforce each other" (1978: 177). It becomes difficult to see cognitive and social conflicts as intimately related, and the tendency is to translate cognitive conflicts into social ones. Merton's famous interest in multiple discoveries and priority disputes is a case in point. His approach seeks to use these occasions as a strategic research site to reveal the institutional imperatives and dynamics of conflict within science (1973:286–324, 343–382). But these analyses mostly take for granted the cognitive dimensions of multiple discoveries and the institutional structure of science seeing them as fundamentally external to the social conflicts among scientists.[10] Framing disputes this way makes it difficult to analyze the behavior genetics example from above. In that example, there is an intimate relationship between the cognitive and the social disputes. If we don't attend to the cognitive disagreement then it is impossible to see the social outcome as anything but "deviant"—that is, behavior geneticists seem to be "bad scientists" with an incomplete commitment to organized skepticism. But if we attend to the disagreement about scientific contents and practices, then we see their actions as practical imperatives of their community rooted in rationally justified scientific understandings. Here acknowledging the intertwined character of cognitive and social norms leads to a very different analysis than when we leave cognitive issues as background.

The examples I presented above suggest a different relationship between scientific autonomy, the scientific ethos, and knowledge production than Merton and associates might predict. In both examples greater scientific autonomy—i.e., a community of scientists having less interference from "external" parties—was associated with the institutionalization of some variant of the scientific ethos that is problematic from the perspective of Merton's ideal-type description. With the resources Merton provides, it is difficult to understand how greater autonomy could lead to a problematic ethos or how greater interference from nonscientific powers could lead closer to an ideal-typical ethos, as in the case of the PXE International collaboration with scientists. In the functionalist institutional analysis of science, even when autonomy is conceived as a variable, the tendency is to see decreasing autonomy as "interference" and thus inherently dysfunctional.

These analytic tendencies are closely related, I think, to a particularly constrained way of thinking about scientists' actions and conflicts. Merton is of course highly attuned to the competitive, conflict-filled character of scientific life. But his tendency has been to see the competition as concerning the rewards of a static and external institutional structure rather than the constitution of that structure itself—that is, the structure is an exogenous influence on the actions and not directly accountable to those actions. It becomes much easier to see how the influence of nonscientists like PXE International could have a "positive" influence on the ethos of a scientific community when we conceive of science as did Pierre Bourdieu as a twofold struggle among scientists both for rewards and recognition, and for the rules governing the definition and allocation of rewards and recognition (1975). Then it is possible to see scientific autonomy and norms of practice as ongoing products of actions and relationships with any number of concerned parties (either "inside" or "outside" science—though this distinction is part of what's negotiated), rather than as starting points from which external "interference" can promote deviance.

Now, Mulkay's critique of the ethos leaves us in a different position, but it is no better at providing resources to account for the dynamics in my empirical examples. Viewing the ethos as a "vocabulary of justification" can help explain some of the boundary-work that takes place in those settings, but it cannot account for why the actors I discuss would fight so hard to establish different norms as standards of practice. Strong skepticism about the autonomy of science might be a useful antidote to the assumption that science is a distinct and special social arena, but it leaves us equally disarmed in taking seriously the different ways that scientific autonomy might be constituted in the settings I discussed. The SSK focus on local cultures of scientific practice (e.g., Knorr Cetina 1999) also makes it difficult to consider common features of scientific practice and organization across settings. Mulkay's claim that "there is no single, coherent code dominant in science, but rather a diverse variety of formulations which can easily be used by scientists to challenge any particular rule-based assertion" (1980:123) may be a useful corrective to an inclination to see science as essentially unified under one logic (with variations being deviations). But the tendency to see science as a huge jumble of diverse communities each with their own local standards begins to undermine the notion that different scientific settings could share a common overarching logic and have lessons for each other.[11]

Gieryn's notion of symbolic boundary-work clearly helps explain parts of the behavior genetics case, but it helps less with other aspects of it and the rare diseases example. Clearly, behavior geneticists' negative views of their critics should be seen as boundary-work attempting to shore up the field's authority from outside assault. That such boundary work would affect organized skepticism in the field is less easy to explain in Gieryn's terms which, in emphasizing scientists' varying and inconsistent definitions of science, tend to portray boundary-work as voluntaristic and flexible. The behavior genetics example suggests a theoretical revision: boundary-work can leave a cultural residue in a field that affects collective norms but also individual dispositions (e.g., perceptions and judgments of acceptable scientific practice). In the two medical genetics examples, however, boundary-work was hardly an issue though the scientific ethos and autonomy were. One of the limits of the boundary-work perspective is that the focus on symbolic constructions of autonomy directs attention away from its other aspects, many of which are organizational and institutional.[12] Understanding the scientific ethos primarily as a set of resources for boundary-work makes it difficult to engage its elements as things in themselves—for example, varying communalistic arrangements in PXE versus Canavan research.

Revisiting the Ethos and Autonomy of Science

What I have been trying to show is that the Mertonian institutionalism and the two versions of the SSK critique are "right," but their analytic habits and characteristic disagreements have left sociologists of science few resources for simultaneously taking seriously the ethos and autonomy of science and the production of knowledge. In this section I'll seek to bring together aspects of the Mertonian and SSK perspectives to illuminate some aspects of the empirical vignettes. This synthesis transforms the analytic perspectives as well as the concepts of ethos and autonomy. What follows will necessarily be schematic and suggestive. Like Gieryn, my synthesis is driven by a focus on actors' struggles for social power as constituting the social organization of science, but I place no special emphasis on boundary-work or other symbolic dimensions of such struggles. None of this is to claim that a focus on social struggle is *the way* to bring together Merton and SSK or to focus attention on the autonomy/ethos relationship. Rather it quickly and clearly enables me to illustrate a version of this synthesis (which differs from Gieryn's) and the theoretical transformations it might produce.[13]

Using this focus generates at least four observations:

1. The scientific ethos and scientific autonomy (in these cases at least) are not abstract institutional imperatives, but are connected to actors seeking to serve what they perceive to be their interests through interaction with others. The ethos and autonomy can be seen as "outcomes," either settlements or crystallizations of particular relationships; or we can understand them as "resources" (either tacit or self-conscious) that are constructed in the course of their deployment in interaction. Thus "communalism" among PXE researchers is the product, in part, of an alliance between an advocacy group that has gained control over a vital resource and a research group that has helped them gain access and legitimacy in the scientific world. Together they have imposed communalistic rules concerning certain objects and practices on a certain community.

2. The meaning and manifestation of aspects of the scientific ethos and scientific autonomy vary between circumstances. The fate of "communalism" in the Canavan and PXE cases was very different. These are just two of many possible examples in the genetic disorder research field, which we might now interpret as a field of varying and competing communalistic arrangements whose contours are determined, in part, by the relationships and relative powers of researcher and advocate groups. Ethos and autonomy vary not only by their circumstances but also as principles unto themselves. The example of behavior genetics showed that organized skepticism comprised two separate things. Where we would "ordinarily" be inclined to view practices of peer review and "criticism" as connected and continuous, in behavior genetics they have manifested in contradictory ways comprising stakes of conflict within the field. Likewise "autonomy" varies across scientific locations and is itself comprised of many elements. Thus we always need to be clear about what we're talking about in deploying these concepts, framing them as: "Organized skepticism *about what?*" and "Autonomy *from this here* as opposed to *that over there.*"[14]

3. We cannot assign particular roles or tendencies to actors simply in terms of their locations "inside" or "outside" science. Behavior geneticists have developed a hostility toward certain types of organized skepticism that is typical, according to Merton, of extrascientific publics whose "comfortable power assumptions" might be challenged by scientific investigation (1973:264–6). But behavior geneticists' attitudes in this regard are based on their scientific convictions, not because they have, say, particular religious or economic interests at stake (as might a creationist or a pharmaceutical company with a faulty drug). In the other example, it is only through the "interference" of a group of nonscientists who are motivated primarily to help their children (not primarily by the pursuit of "truth") that the scientific norm of communalism could be secured among scientists within science. In this case, scientific autonomy (already compromised by commercialization) is at cross-purposes with communalism, and further social "interference" by patient advocates is serving the institutional imperative of science.

4. Anything might be at stake in a struggle over science: from rewards or recognition (as Merton conceived them), to social structures, to knowledge itself, and usually all three at once. At stake in the behavior genetics example are issues such as: Which individuals and which contributions are recognized as legitimate? Which tacit rules for engaging each other's work will be observed? And ultimately, what knowledge is collectively accepted as true (what version of reality is put forward)? This suggests that not only is it an empirical error to circumscribe one's analysis to certain aspects of science a priori (i.e., looking at the competitions between scientists but eliminating scientific content from consideration or focusing on the distribution but not the genesis of rewards) because it decides before asking what the "real contest" is. It is also to unwittingly endorse the victors of the "prior" contest, which was to establish the terms of struggle (e.g., what counts as prize worthy research).

I have tried to use these examples to show how to think about scientific autonomy and the ethos of science differently than did Merton or SSK critics. My aim has been to show how scientific autonomy and the scientific ethos are wrapped up in dynamics of social conflict as stakes and outcomes, how they are comprised of disparate elements, vary by circumstances, and are manipulated by different parties to such a degree that we should question whether there is a normal or most functional manifestation (at least insofar as we're talking about the real world). In short, I've tried to show how we might recast this aspect of Mertonian sociology of science by focusing it on dynamics of power and social conflict, thus utilizing many of the constructivist critiques's strengths, but moving beyond some of their limitations.

Conclusion

Why, in the end, should we care about the scientific ethos and its relationship to scientific autonomy? I mentioned one simple answer earlier: at stake is the "advancement of knowledge" as Merton would put it, or different possibilities for the construction or production of knowledge, to put it in more SSK-appropriate terms. Even those who would adopt radically constructivist perspectives on science and see science's claims to distinctiveness as ideological at heart would still likely prefer to see a relatively autonomous science committed to the ethos rather than one completely dominated by and serving the interests of corporate capitalism or the military.

Observers have noted that today science conforms less and less to the ideal-type images of the ethos and autonomous science (Krimsky 2003; Shorett, Rabinow, and Billings 2003; Ziman 2000). But the questions to ask are: How much? Where? Under what conditions? And, what are the effects on knowledge? Ultimately, the concern with these issues isn't about abstractions like the soul and values of science and academia but about the conditions under which scientists and other academics will work and the ends of their efforts. In their "Changing Norms of the Life Sciences," Shorett, Rabinow, and Billings write:

> Although many observers have noted the ethical implications of the changing modes of scientific production, few have examined their impact on science as a vocation and a way of life. Greater self examination by scientists and biotechnologists could yield important insights into the future practices of science. Proper scientific governance will require that members of the life sciences community take a more active position in public debates surrounding these changes. (2003:123)

As they note, the ability of the scientific profession to govern itself is at stake. Scientific governance has recently become a topic of growing sociological interest (Irwin 2008), and it's a good thing too, since sociologists turned away from the ethos and the questions it raises at just the historical moment when the set of transformations began that would take the life sciences so far from the old Mertonian image.

Mine is certainly not a lone voice in the wilderness. Scott Frickel and Kelly Moore (2006) have called for a "new political sociology of science," key to which is the combination of Mertonian institutionalism and constructivist concern with knowledge production. In addition, much recent work on social movements and science concerns the stakes and implications of "lay people's" challenges to scientific autonomy and impacts on the ethos, though such themes are most often left as an undercurrent. To take just one example, Brown et al. (2006) have shown how a coalition of breast cancer activists and scientists have pushed for paradigmatic change in breast cancer research—a shift from a reductionistic focus on physiology to a more holistic concern with environmental factors in disease etiology. The scientific ethos and autonomy could be fruitfully brought to the center of focus here: Perhaps cognitive reductionism is a developmental tendency of relatively autonomous fields. Perhaps autonomy doesn't free disinterestedness and organized skepticism, but constrains them in certain ways, so that particular kinds of "external" challenges can interrupt these constraints and the paradigmatic tendencies they promote. Perhaps not. But the point is that moving the scientific autonomy and ethos can raise very interesting possibilities for these lines of research, including new opportunities for comparison and generalization.[15]

Paying attention to the kinds of dynamics I discussed in my examples may open up different ways of thinking about the problem of commercialization and other "intrusions" on the autonomy of science. Ordinarily, critical observers see the commercialization of science as corrupting (e.g., Krimsky 2003). This perspective, of course, is dependent on explicit or implicit notions of a pristine state of science and its previous separation from such influences. The usual solution is to propose a shift back toward that pristine state and means by which science might achieve greater separation from corrupting influences. But what if scientific communities are routinely embedded in a complex web of relationships—oppositions and dependencies—like in my examples above? Well, then greater autonomy (at least of the most immediate varieties) wouldn't move these communities to the "pristine" state. For behavior genetics a pursuit of autonomy led to weakened organized skepticism. The medical genetics example is even more interesting here because it suggests that rather than rolling back commercial interests, it might be more effective for additional "external players" to enter the field. Of course the key question is, more effective at what? In this case it is building a science that is closely linked to patients' needs. This, of course, opens up many other urgent questions, but we have shifted the critical task away from defending an image of science that may be gone and may never have existed without losing our purchase on these issues through cynical rejections. It is through the pursuit of analytic strategies like these that Merton's concern with the scientific ethos and autonomy could again become centrally important to the critical sociology of science.

Notes

This chapter was drafted for the "Robert K. Merton: Sociology of Science and Sociological Explanation" conference and revised on October 2008. I would like to thank the National Science Foundation (SES 0328563) and the Robert Wood Johnson Foundation for supporting the research from which this paper draws. Any opinions, findings, and conclusions or recommendations expressed in this material are those of the author and do not necessarily reflect the views of the National Science Foundation or the Robert Wood Johnson Foundation.

1. Merton also acknowledged that this injunction was likely to make scientists insensitive to the broader social consequences of adhering to it, which include stirring up the public's hostility and resentment toward science.

2. See the literature reviewed by Stehr (1978:183–4) and Zuckerman (1988:518–9). See also Ziman 2000, esp. 56–82.

3. Current critiques include Balaban 2001, Joseph 2003, Kaplan 2000 and 2006, and Moore 2001.

4. The Genetic Alliance (www.geneticalliance.org) and the National Organization for Rare Disorders (www.rarediseases.org), umbrella organizations, together list about two-thousand patient advocacy groups as members.

5. Merton originally called this "communism." Barber (1952), perhaps responding to McCarthyite conservatism of the postwar period, relabeled it "communalism." This move is, of course, highly ironic for a theory about the autonomy of science.

6. On the Canavan case, see Greif and Merz 2007, McCabe and McCabe 2008, and Marshall 2000.

7. PXE (pseudoxanthoma elasticum) is a rare genetic disease causing mineral deposits that affect the skin, eyes, and cardiovascular and gastrointestinal systems. On the PXE case, see Terry and Boyd 2001, Terry et al. 2007, and Novas 2005.

8. This close collaboration was not always conflict free (Terry and Boyd 2001). And the advocates report that that on at least one occasion actually directing scientists away from tackling certain problems to keep them focused on the advocates' goals (Terry et al. 2007).

9. See Barnes 1977, Bloor 1991, and Shapin 1995 for overviews.

10. The approach doesn't focus on, for example, how scientific communities come to recognize two discoveries as essentially about the same thing. Harry Collins (1985) takes up this issue from a different direction in his analysis of scientific replication. He shows that scientists can never replicate each other's work beyond a reasonable doubt, so it becomes an important task to show how communities come to discriminate between reasonable and unreasonable doubts.

11. Fuchs (1992) complains that SSK reifies "Science" as a singular entity and thus gives up on the project of comparative explanation. But, the seemingly opposite tendency to analyze science as fragmented epistemic cultures (Knorr Cetina 1999) is little better because it tends to reify the "disunity of science" rather than posing common and varying features of scientific fields as an analytic problem.

12. This is not just an issue for Gieryn. Much of SSK (excluding the large part that is uninterested in autonomy, for example Latour's [1987] Actor Network Theory, which seeks only to trace associations among elements regardless of their "location" viz. boundaries of science) treats autonomy as symbolically or interactionally constructed as a background condition of successful science. For example, Shapin's (1994) account of virtual witnessing and Collins's (1985) notion of the core set concern the establishment of versions of autonomy for experimentation constructed through symbolic and practical action. Their accounts emphasize tacit action and the sedimentation of tradition and thus are not particularly voluntaristic, but neither are they institutional or organizational in the Mertonian sense.

13. My approach follows the analytic tradition of critical theory, which Craig Calhoun has defined as the "critique of received categories, critique of theoretical practice, and critical substantive analysis of social life in terms of the possible, not just the actual" (1993:63). For the critically minded SSK, Merton's account of science assumed and reinforced the important "received categories"—for example, science *versus* society, the separation of science as an institution from the content of scientific knowledge, the scientific ethos as an ideal type and the tracking of "deviance" from it. This is all true, but too often SSK work embodied the spirit of critical theory but failed to follow its full implications. For example, Mulkay's (1976, 1980) brilliant unmasking of the ethos's ideological functions and sociologists' assumptions about norms certainly challenged received categories and theoretical practice. But the subsequent SSK ten-

dency to see the ethos and autonomy as little more than ideological meant that analysts typically view them as barriers to "possible" emancipatory social projects, rather than as potentially crucial elements.

14. The same thing goes for the reward system: Are priority disputes the same everywhere? Are they motivated by recognition and the norm of originality, or intellectual property rights, and what's the difference? When do scientists seek recognition of their peers and when are they indifferent? Which peers are important? These last two are key questions in interdisciplinary fields like behavior genetics and aren't reflected in Merton's descriptions of the "reward system," which tend to portray it as unitary, unified, and centralized (at least by field but with little attention to variations between fields) as opposed to a set of multiple competing, overlapping, centripetally organized reward systems.

15. Such concerns might also make this field, which tends to be fairly celebratory of lay interventions in science, a bit more concerned (as was Merton) with the potential problems of democratizing science.

References

Balaban, Evan. 2001. "Behavior Genetics: Galen's Prophecy or Malpighi's Legacy?" In *Thinking about Evolution: Historical, Philosophical, and Political Perspectives*, ed. Rama S. Singh, Costas B. Kribas, Diane B. Paul, and John Beatty, 429–466. Cambridge: Cambridge University Press.

Barber, Benjamin. 1952. *Science and the Social Order*. Glencoe, IL: Free Press.

Barnes, Barry. 1977. *Interests and the Growth of Knowledge*. London: Routledge and Kegan Paul.

Bloor, David. 1983. *Wittgenstein: A Social Theory of Knowledge*. New York: Columbia University Press.

——. 1991. *Knowledge and Social Imagery*. Chicago: University of Chicago Press.

Bourdieu, Pierre. 1975. "The Specificity of the Scientific Field and the Social Conditions of the Progress of Reason." *Social Science Information* 14:19–47.

Brown, Phil, Sabrina McCormick, Brian Mayer, Stephen Zavestoski, Rachel Morello-Frosch, Rebecca Gasior Altman, and Laura Senier. 2006. "'A Lab of Our Own': Environmental Causation of Breast Cancer and Challenges to the Dominant Epidemiological Paradigm." *Science, Technology & Human Values* 31: 499–536.

Calhoun, Craig. 1993. "Habitus, Field, and Capital: The Question of Historical Specificity." In *Bourdieu: Critical Perspectives*, ed. Craig J. Calhoun, Edward LiPuma, and Moishe Postone, 61–88. Chicago: University of Chicago Press.

Collins, Harry. 1985. *Changing Order*. London: Sage Publications.

Frickel, Scott, and Kelly Moore. 2006. "Prospects and Challenges for a New Political Sociology of Science." In *The New Political Sociology of Science*, ed. Scott Frickel and Kelly Moore, 3–31. Madison: University of Wisconsin Press.

Fuchs, Stephan. 1992. *The Professional Quest for Truth*. Albany: State University of New York Press.

Gieryn, Thomas F. 1983. "Boundary-Work and the Demarcation of Science from Non-Science." *American Sociological Review* 48:781–795.

Greif, Karen F., and Jon F. Merz. 2007. *Current Controversies in the Biological Sciences*. Cambridge: MIT Press.

Irwin, Alan. 2008. "STS Perspectives on Scientific Governance." In *The Handbook of Science and Technology Studies*, 3rd ed., ed. Edward J. Hackett, Olga Amsterdamska, Michael Lynch, and Judy Wajcman, 583–607. Cambridge: MIT Press.

Joseph, Jay. 2004. *The Gene Illusion*. New York: Algora Publishing.

Kaplan, Jonathan. 2000. *The Limits and Lies of Human Genetic Research*. New York: Routledge.

——. 2006. "Misinformation, Misrepresentation, and Misuse of Human Behavioral Genetics Research." *Law and Contemporary Problems* 69:47–80.

Knorr Cetina, Karin. 1999. *Epistemic Cultures*. Cambridge: Harvard University Press.

Knorr Cetina, Karin, and Michael Mulkay. 1983. "Emerging Principles in Social Studies of Science." In *Science Observed*, ed. Karin Knorr Cetina and Michael Mulkay, 1–17. London: Sage.

Krimsky, Sheldon. 2003. *Science in the Private Interest*. Lantham, MD: Rowman-Littlefield.

Kuhn, T. S. 1970. *The Structure of Scientific Revolutions*. Chicago, University of Chicago Press.

Latour, Bruno. 1987. *Science in Action*. Cambridge: Harvard University Press.

Marshall, E. 2000. "Families Sue Hospital, Scientist for Control of Canavan Gene." *Science* 290: 1062.

McCabe, Linda, and Edward McCabe. 2008. *DNA: Promise and Peril*. Berkeley: University of California Press.

Merton, Robert K. [1938] 1970. *Science, Technology and Society in Seventeenth-Century England*. New York: Harper and Row.

——. 1973. *The Sociology of Science: Theoretical and Empirical Investigations*. Chicago: University of Chicago Press.

Merton, Robert K., and Thomas F. Gieryn. 1982. "Institutionalized Altruism: The Case of the Professions." In *Social Research and the Practicing Professions*, ed. Robert K. Merton, 109–134. Cambridge, MA: Abt Books.

Mitroff, Ian. 1974. "Norms and Counter-Norms in a Select Group of the Apollo Moon Scientists: A Case Study of the Ambivalence of Scientists." *American Sociological Review* 39:579–595.

Moore, David S. 2001. *The Dependent Gene*. New York: W. H. Freeman.

Mulkay, Michael. 1976. "Norms and Ideology in Science." *Social Science Information.* 15:637–656.

———. 1980. "Interpretation and the Use of Rules: The Case of the Norms of Science." In *Science and Social Structure: A Festschrift for Robert K. Merton*, ed. Thomas F. Gieryn, 111–125. New York: New York Academy of Sciences.

Novas, Carlos. 2005. "Genetic Advocacy Groups, Science and Biovalue: Creating Political Economies of Hope." In *New Genetics, New Identities*, ed. Paul Atkinson, Peter Glasner, and Helen Greenslade. London: Routledge.

Popper, Karl. 1962. *Conjectures and Refutations*. New York: Basic.

Shapin, Steven. 1994. *A Social History of Truth*. Chicago: University of Chicago Press.

———. 1995. "Here and Everywhere: Sociology of Scientific Knowledge." *Annual Review of Sociology* 21:289–321.

Shorett, Peter, Paul Rabinow, and Paul R. Billings. 2003. "The Changing Norms of the Life Sciences." *Nature Biotech* 21:123–125.

Stehr, Nico. 1978. "The Ethos of Science Revisited: Social and Cognitive Norms." *Sociological Inquiry.* 48:172–196.

Storer, Norman W. 1973. "Introduction." In *The Sociology of Science: Theoretical and Empirical Investigations*, ed. Robert K. Merton, xi–xxxi. Chicago: University of Chicago Press.

Terry, Sharon F. and Charles D. Boyd. 2001. "Researching the biology of PXE: Partnering in the Process." *American Journal of Medical Genetics.* 106:177–184.

Terry, Sharon F., Patrick F. Terry, Katherine A. Rauen, Jouni Uitto, and Lionel G. Bercovitch. 2007. "Advocacy Groups as Research Organizations: the PXE International Example." *Nature Reviews Genetics* 8:157–164.

Thackray, A., ed. 1998. *Private Science: Biotechnology and the Rise of the Molecular Sciences*. Philadelphia: University of Philadelphia Press.

Wittgenstein, Ludwig. 1953. *Philosophical Investigations*. Oxford: Blackwell.

Ziman, John. 2000. *Real Science*. Cambridge: Cambridge University Press.

Zuckerman, Harriet. 1977. "Deviant Behavior and Social Control in Science." In *Deviance and Social Change*, ed. Edward Sagarin, 87–138. Beverly Hills, CA: Sage.

———. 1988. "The Sociology of Science." In *Handbook of Sociology*, ed. Neil Smelser, 511–574. Newbury Park, CA: Sage.

8

Merton, Mannheim, and the Sociology of Knowledge

ALAN SICA

During the 1920s in Germany, Paul Honigsheim, Ernst Grünwald, Max Scheler, and Karl Mannheim introduced the term *Wissenssoziologie* into scholarly circles. This development was quickly and enthusiastically greeted in the United States by Albion Small, doyen of the Chicago School of sociology, who published a laudatory review in the September 1925 issue of the *American Journal of Sociology* which evaluated this new avenue in sociological thinking. Robert Merton learned about the sociology of knowledge while a graduate student at Harvard during the mid-1930s, partly through the influence of his sponsor, Pitirim Sorokin, and also from reading the work of recent German immigrants, such as Hans Speier. Some of Merton's first published pieces, which were later revised for inclusion in his most important book, dealt explicitly and in detail with the sociology of knowledge of the German type.

My chapter investigates Merton's analysis of this new way of looking at social knowledge, and tries to answer the question: Why did Merton, after initially writing positively, in particular, about Mannheim's *Wissenssoziologie*, turn against this strong current in European thinking, and in so doing, spoil the potential reception of Mannheim's ideas in the United States?

Put another way, how is it that a hermeneutic practitioner of such legendary care and wisdom seemed to lose his bearings when asked to deal with
the early documents in the sociology of knowledge? This is not an easy
question to answer, partly because of the complex arguments Mannheim
and his colleagues put forth, and partly because Merton is hard to second-
guess after an interval of seventy years. My chapter provides several plausible reasons for Merton's negative final judgments, and makes a case for
his having been mistaken in this position, at least in part.

I begin with a puzzle. That Robert Merton was a great scholar is a weary platitude. Surely, no U.S. sociologist in the twentieth century could
reasonably be called greater, especially if his teacher, Pitirim Sorokin, is
defined as Russian (Calhoun 2003). Ten years ago when he wore his son's
Nobel Prize in a celebratory group photo, everyone knew that Merton
should have had his own Nobel. It is also widely recognized that from his
earliest professional publications in his midtwenties, he exhibited the same
kind of verbal skill and precise analysis that typified his work for the next
sixty-five years; his writing and thinking were always virtuosic. In short,
Merton was already Merton at a tender age in the same way that Heifetz
was already Heifetz at sixteen when he took Carnegie Hall by storm. I
like to think of them together, both of Russian stock, since Merton, so he
told me, often heard Heifetz with the Philadelphia Orchestra, where as a
boy he would stand in the cheap section, soaking up the cultural capital
that was then available to the ambitious poor. Considering all this, my
self-assigned puzzle presents itself: how is it that Merton in 1940 could so
pitilessly attack Karl Mannheim and in so doing cast the Americanized
version of the sociology of knowledge into a denatured mode from which
it never recovered its original zest and promise? I cannot solve the puzzle
entirely, for to do that would require Merton's presence, so that he could
explain himself in those inimitable paragraphs of well-modulated reason-
ableness that characterized his oral and written testimony. But perhaps I
can lay out the primal scene of the puzzle's development.

Lewis Coser wrote a chapter for the Merton festschrift he edited in 1975
called "Merton's Uses of the European Sociological Tradition," which is unusual in the literature. Merton is often considered the quintessential American sociologist, far more so than Parsons, whose *Structure of Social Action*, of
course, is an absorbed reckoning with European genius—"there were profound differences in their respective approaches" (Coser 1975:88). The very
notion that Merton truly wrestled with continental thinkers, in the way that,

say, Habermas tried to decipher George Herbert Mead, seems less plausible than it might have been had Merton's subsequent work taken a different path. Even his avowed discipleship under Durkheim when he was young disappears from view once he hit his stride after World War II and became heavily involved in the fine points of empirical research: as Coser shrewdly observed, "He honors it [European sociological theory] chiefly by putting it to his own distinctive uses" (90). Raised in Philly, educated in Cambridge, a mandarin in New York, Merton for many midcentury sociologists represented the best the discipline had to offer that was homegrown, autochthonous, and justifiably proud of its nonderivative, non-European character.

That Coser's chapter very gently treats the issue at hand is hardly surprising, given his close relationship to Merton as teacher and friend. He writes, for instance, "I shall attempt to highlight his capacity to draw from many sources and, in a grand synthesizing effort, to rise above all of them" (85). By "all of them," he meant Marx, Weber, Durkheim, Scheler, Mannheim, Sorokin, and Coser's own favorite, Simmel. Coser also borrowed from Isaiah Berlin, referring to Parsons as the hedgehog and Merton the fox: "Parsons is of the company of Plato, of Dante, or of Nietzsche; Merton of that of Aristotle, of Montaigne, or of Erasmus" (88). I suspect both Parsons and Merton were very pleased to read these observations when they appeared, and not a little embarrassed by them.

Granting Coser's narrative all the persuasiveness it deserves, I want to tell a somewhat different story. I do not think that Merton's goal, particularly during his early scholarly adventures, was to "rise above all of them" in sheer theoretical terms. He was too alert to the contours and limits of genuine creativity, his own as well as others', to harbor such ambitions. Instead, I want to invoke again Harold Bloom's smallest and most useful book, *The Anxiety of Influence*. You will recall Bloom's argument from 1973, that a creative writer's biggest fear is to be viewed as the mere caboose of an earlier author's train—as nothing but a talented epigone. The "stronger" the writer, so says Bloom, the more creative the distortion of his predecessors' works. To use the most familiar example, Hemingway invented his quasi-journalistic prose style in order to distance himself from prior titans like Henry James, William Dean Howells, Theodore Dreiser, Sherwood Anderson (whom he shamelessly parodied in *The Torrents of Spring*), or any of his other rivals on the American scene. They overwrote, so he thought, thus he would underwrite, perhaps in friendly imitation of his friend Ezra Pound.

Similarly, I believe it meant a great deal to Merton not to be considered merely as someone's acolyte—neither Sarton's, nor Sorokin's, nor Durkheim's, nor Weber's, and especially not Parsons's. In the same way that Weber heartily complimented Marx and Engels for the strong creative impulse behind *The Communist Manifesto*, while in the next breath vigorously disputing their main points (Weber 1994:287), so, too, Merton accepted the wisdom and achievements within classic European social thought (as defined in part by Parsons's first book), but then trotted away from it in order to develop sociology along lines that were less aristocratic, less cynical, more tied to applied research, and less haughtily rendered. And also less politically charged, less historically anchored, less philosophically probing, and much less world-weary. The cultural and political experience of Europe between 1870 and 1925, capped by the wild popularity of Spengler's *Decline of the West*, did not sit well with the young Merton, even if he understood entirely the dynamics and meaning of that experience.

The Pareto cult at Harvard headed for eight years during the '30s by the physiological chemist Lawrence J. Henderson, to which Merton was entirely privy if not a core member, left no lasting or identifiable impression on his work. Bernard Barber, in his unique anthology of Henderson's sociological writings, clearly indicates that George Homans, Crane Brinton, Joseph Schumpeter, William F. Whyte, and Parsons fell for a time under the spell of Paretian theorizing (or Henderson's version of same), while Merton stepped adroitly to one side (Barber 1970:39–53). In sum, one could even say that Merton sincerely appreciated his European "colleagues-at-a-distance," to use a favorite phrase of his, but was not displeased that they stayed abroad. Like other ambitious young scholars of the time, Merton had to deal with several unpleasant facts of life during the late 1930s, well above and beyond those that typically affect young adults. The first, of course, was the diabolically miserable job market, which had been in place ever since he was a college student at Temple ten years before. The second was the even more diabolical stranglehold that fascism held on several major European countries. And lastly was the influx of mature, brilliant, and underappreciated Jewish and "dissident" refugee intellectuals who were suddenly competing with Americans for the few academic jobs that did open up. Clearly, Americans at this point, even the most sympathetic and cosmopolitan, likely held ambivalent views about European culture, political and otherwise. This becomes especially obvious when one considers the almost fawning

review by Albion Small in the September 1925 issue of *AJS* regarding a
collaborative work in German on the sociology of knowledge edited by
Max Scheler, and featuring five chapters by Weber's protean student, Paul
Honigsheim. Small bends over backward to alert his snoozing brethren
to the huge importance of this new line of thinking, with phrases that
must have seemed within a few years (and after Small's death six months
later) to have been overstated. He opens with avuncular bombast: "This
book deserves to rank and to function among the principal orienta-
tion-monuments for all sociologists. It affords an outlook for the widest
survey of the area of the adventure to which sociological pioneering is
committed" (262). Small then reminds his readers of the "omnipresent
group factor" in social life, the "detection of group phases" and other
"interindividual influences" that surround social knowledge: "While it is
true that sociology must deal with 'pauperism, prostitution, and plumb-
ing,' it is all the more true that sociology must take part in explaining
the highest, widest, and deepest reaches of the human mind. No previous methodological treatise has done as much to impress this fact as the
volume before us" (ibid.). After a concise summary of the book's contents, Small carries on his own long tradition of urging his colleagues to
broaden their perspectives:

> American sociologists will have to gird themselves for a kind of effort which
> has been conspicuous for its absence from our programs in recent years. . . .
> The argument leaves no uncertainty about the fact that at least in the field
> of "*Wissenssoziologie*," Germans and Americans have not occupied the same
> universe of discourse. . . . In spite of the handicap of unfamiliarity with its
> background, however, if they will exercise sufficient patience, Americans
> may ferret out the substance of the reasoning, and none of them who deal
> with methodology at all can afford to omit the attempt. . . . Obviously
> the methodology thus contemplated is in direct antithesis with prevailing
> sociological tendencies in the United States . . . this book opens up vistas
> of social relations compared with which our sociological searchings thus far
> have been parochial" (Small 1925:263–64).

Even if Small's opinion seems overheatedly positive, eleven years later, in
Vol 1, issue 4 of the *American Sociological Review*—the new journal of re-
bellion against Chicago's hegemonic control of the field—a series of five
reviews were grouped together by Howard Paul Becker as Book Review

Editor, which repay careful reading even today. It is in this context that Merton's Mannheim studies must be appraised.

The first review, eleven full and dense pages in length, and translated by Becker from a longer German version, is Alexander von Schelting's famous attack on Mannheim's 1929 book, *Ideologie und Utopie*. There are still Mannheim specialists who refer to von Schelting, born of Dutch ancestry one year after Mannheim, as his "nemesis" (Kettler and Meja 1995:207–12). His review was followed by Parsons's lengthy appraisal of von Schelting's own much admired study in German of Weber's methodology. After this, Hans Speier, a recent emigrant and Mannheim's first doctoral student at Heidelberg (Speier 1989:6), reviewed Ernst Grünwald's precocious, untranslated study in the sociology of knowledge. This was followed by Merton's analysis of a French work which, by means of *Wissenssoziologie*, offered an appraisal of ancient Greek thought. The final review of the set was Floyd House's astute examination of Karl Mannheim's *Mensch und Gesellschaft im Zeitalter des Umbaus*, translated into English four years later under the title *Man and Society in an Age of Reconstruction*. All five reviews, consuming twenty-two pages (664–86) of the journal, concern the sociology of knowledge. And all are written by excellent scholars whose opinions were already or would soon be highly regarded. In short, Becker, fascinated by German theorizing, felt it was useful to ask talented colleagues to evaluate with care this European strain of sociological reasoning in an early issue of *ASR*, and they complied.

There is no time now to recount the complex arguments that fill these sophisticated reviews—especially those drawn in detail by von Schelting in his dismantling of Mannheim, and Parsons in his creative misreading of von Schelting's Weber study. But it is clear from later work by Parsons and Merton that they accepted almost at face value von Schelting's dismissal of Mannheim's larger epistemological goals, freely quoting him as a solid reference point in everything they wrote that pertained to *Wissenssoziologie*. Merton, in fact, took the trouble within a year to outline in print von Schelting's thorny essay, which he called "a thoroughgoing critique," reducing it to seven key points (Merton 1937:499–501). This reduction became a standard substitute in the secondary literature for von Schelting's essay itself since, as always, Merton's prose and reasoning were pellucid. Von Schelting's prose, even for a German neo-Kantian professor, showed its philosophic roots. His writing style aside, von Schelting seemed to play the role of the "good, non-Jewish German" at Columbia between 1936 and

1939, offering courses on Weber in which graduate students, like Daniel Bell, would spend an entire semester translating the first few pages of *Wirtschaft und Gesellschaft* (Swedberg 1990:217–18); Page, 1982:27).

Von Schelting's central complaint against Mannheim was simple, even though the casuistic subtleties go on for pages: Mannheim's pursuit of what we would call a "privileged epistemological standpoint" could not, so he argued, deliver "objective knowledge," which for von Schelting and everyone else at the time was indeed the Holy Grail of social scientific work. It was important to show the Rockefeller Foundation and other interested parties that social science could deliver what now might be known as "actionable intelligence." Contrary to this hope, Mannheim's analysis of different social classes proved how one-sided they were, how unreflective, how self-serving, how blinded by their own practical interests, and how therefore unreliable as a guide to general social knowledge that could be set beside the achievements of the natural sciences as generalizable truth. For von Schelting, this was enough to sink Mannheim's entire enterprise—not to mention Mannheim's prospects for an academic career in the United States—at least from a strictly epistemological point of view.

However, just as Merton would do several years later, von Schelting ends his review by sharply distinguishing between Mannheim's failure as a theorist of knowledge versus his skill as an analyst of concrete cases of ideological distortion. This parallels Weber's reputation at the time, since "a number of his concepts . . . certainly prove workable and will greatly stimulate concrete research as well as abstract discussion" (von Schelting 1936:673). Setting aside Mannheim's "epistemological inconsistency," von Schelting admits that he "possesses incomparably sharp eyes for what can be called the ideological element in social thought" (ibid.:674). Since this comes after ten solid pages of unforgiving criticism, one wonders why von Schelting bothers with a quasi-retraction. Still, somehow Mannheim made his way in England, and von Schelting's critique, though fondly used by Parsons, Merton, and others, did not derail his project of a distinctive *Wissenssoziologie*.

In 1947, weeks before his death, Mannheim was offered an important UNESCO position (which, ironically, was given to von Schelting) that might well have brought him to the United States at the very time when Merton was establishing himself as the leader of the postwar generation of sociologists. I suspect this is one European thinker, seventeen years his senior, whom Merton would have liked not to have too close by. I do not say this cavalierly. Consider the broad similarities and differences between them. Both explosively smart Jewish intellectuals choosing to enter a new and highly suspect field of study that was already a victim of anti-Semitism in Europe and elsewhere, singled out for venomous attack by the radical right; both the children of foreigners, making their way in host countries not always sympathetic to their presence or their ambitions; both phenomenally well attuned to the intellectual currents swirling around them, yet both eager to establish an Archimedean point outside the maelstrom from which to evaluate dispassionately all that was going on; both fascinated with the social-psychological reality that inhabits personality, but more inclined to publish works that highlighted macroanalysis, preferring the Olympian view; both eager to link the humanities and social sciences in pursuit of objectively defensible knowledge.

Yet Mannheim's cultural heritage was almost unimaginably privileged in ways that Merton's clearly was not. Mannheim, born in Budapest to an Hungarian father and German mother, came naturally to a clutch of foreign languages and worldviews, while Merton had to teach himself Italian rapidly to suit Sorokin, and learned Latin, French, and German the standard, harder way in classrooms. Mannheim's blood relation was György Lukács, with whom he often interacted as a young man. Ernest Manheim, whom I interviewed on tape in 1980, remembered being at boarding school when Lukács and Karl Mannheim, Ernest's first cousin, would drop by on Sundays to talk about ideas. (Ernest Manheim's name and Karl's differ because the latter, like Merton, elected to change his at some point by adding an "n.")

Donald Levine reports (by way of Guy Oakes) that during the late '20s in Heidelberg, Karl Mannheim convened a seminar whose members included Marianne Weber, Hannah Arendt, Hans Gerth, and Hans Speier (Levine 1997; Speier 1989:5–9, 37–40). Among Mannheim's teachers were Emil Lask, Heinrich Rickert, and Edmund Husserl (Manheim 1947:471–72). He was also a research associate at the original Frankfurt School while waiting for his own professorship to be created in 1929, which means he had personal contact with Adorno, Horkheimer, Benjamin, and that crowd. In short, while Robert Merton was creating himself, Mark Twain-style, at the unaccredited Temple College under the kindly George E. Simpson, Mannheim was given intimate access to the crème de la crème of Central Europe's intelligentsia—those "free-floating intellectuals" about whom he later wrote so hopefully. It is therefore unsurprising (as Edward

Shils explained to me) that dealing interpersonally with Mannheim during the late '30s and early '40s in England was a trial because of his pomposity and self-importance—which, it must be noted, contradicts Speier's characterization of Mannheim as an effective and reasonable teacher at Frankfurt (ibid.). (Perhaps Shils himself learned how to play the role of Mighty Mandarin directly from Mannheim—whose *Ideology and Utopia* he translated in the summer of 1934 as a graduate student at Chicago. Louis Wirth paid him $90 to do the work, which comes to about $1400 in today's money, and no royalties ever came Shils's way although the book has been in print ever since.)

One easily recalls that pages 493 through 582 of *Social Theory and Social Structure* (in the enlarged edition of 1968) contain Robert K. Merton's lasting foray into what he called "The Sociology of Knowledge and Mass Communications." The three reprinted chapters that make up this part of the book include "The Sociology of Knowledge" (510–542) taken from the influential Gurvitch and Moore reader, *Twentieth Century Sociology* (Philosophical Library 1945); "Karl Mannheim and the Sociology of Knowledge" (543–562); and "Studies in Radio and Film Propaganda" (563–582), coauthored with Lazarsfeld, and first published in the *Transactions of the New York Academy of Sciences* for 1943. My task will be to discuss very lightly the first and second chapters, leaving aside the Lazarsfeld piece since it is so entirely different in ambition, substance, and technique—so different, in fact, that it seems anomalous when juxtaposed with the other chapters.

The introduction to this discrete and unusual section of the book he pointedly titled "*Wissenssoziologie* and Mass Communications Research" (493–509), insisting upon a very sharp distinction between the former and the latter, so much so that it could fairly have been called "*Wissenssoziologie versus* Mass Communications Research." An inside-dopester might have added a Shandean subtitle of the sort that Merton himself enjoyed attaching to his later writings, which might go like this: "Or Why Theodor Adorno and Paul Lazarsfeld Detested Each Other's Work on the Columbia Radio Research Project of the Late 1930s." A second, equally apt subtitle from an imagined eighteenth century could have read: "Why European Gloominess Has No Place at the Table of Optimistic American Social Science." Merton capsulized his general complaint in a formula often repeated in later years, especially by those science-besotted Americans who felt intrinsically superior to the "arm chair" theorists they imagined inhabited European universities, who had never experienced "empirical reality": "And gradually, the loose impression emerges which can be baldly and too simply summarized thus: the American knows what he is talking about, and that is not much; the European knows not what he is talking about, and that is a great deal" (Merton 1968:496). This is classic Mertonian syncretism: giving each side of an argument some credence for its rightful value, but refusing to allow either to reign supreme. Presumably, a Mertonian *Aufhebung* would emerge, dialectically transforming the weaknesses of each side into an improved synthesis. That this caricature of both constituencies is just that—funny to be sure but fundamentally unilluminating—never seemed to trouble those many Mertonians who became fond of quoting it, or alluding to it slyly without direct reference. It was just this sort of keen rhetoric that helped make Merton the favored "theorist" of those American social scientists after World War II who were at base antipathetic to "theory" per se, but knew they would need "some of that" in their work. Yet in some ways, and not without irony, such observations exemplified just the sort of intellectual gamesmanship that Mannheim had long before become expert at "deconstructing," especially in essays such as "Conservative Thought," and which Merton avoided considering as he probed the Mannheimian edifice.

Nearby in the same piece, Merton elaborates on the "European and American variants" of research, pointing out that they "have notably different conceptions of what constitutes raw empirical data." It's very clear that the European style irritates him, especially in the person of Mannheim:

If the intellectual status of an author is high enough and the scope of his attainments broad enough, his impressions, sometimes his casual impressions of prevailing beliefs, will be typically taken as reports of sociological fact . . . To seek a few illustrations is to find an embarrassment of riches. A Mannheim, for example, will summarize the state of mind of the "lower classes in the post-medieval period," saying that "only bit by bit did they arrive at an awareness of their social and political significance." Or, he may regard it as not only significant but true that "all progressive groups regard the idea as coming before the deed," this ostensibly being a matter of thorough observation rather than of definition. Or, he may submit an hypothesis as instructive as the following, an hypothesis compounded of several assumptions of fact: " . . . the more actively an ascendant party collaborates in a parliamentary coalition, and the more it gives up its original utopian impulses and with it its broad perspective, the more its power to transform society is likely to be absorbed by its interest in concrete and isolated details. Quite parallel to the change that may be observed in the political realm runs a change in the scientific outlook which conforms to political demands, i.e., what was once merely a formal scheme and an abstract, total view tends to dissolve into the investigation of specific and discrete problems." Suggestive and nearly apodictic, and if true, shedding so much light on so much that the intellectual has experienced and perhaps casually noted in the course of living in political society, such a statement tempts one to regard it as fact rather than as hypothesis. What is more, as is often the case with sociological formulations of the European variety, the statement seems to catch up so many details of experience that the reader seldom goes on to consider the vast labor of empirical research required before this can be regarded as more than an interesting hypothesis. It quickly gains an unearned status as generalized fact. (Merton 1968:496–97).

If one remembers that, according to his own statement, Merton collected and studied six thousand short biographies of early modern scientists while writing his dissertation, it is clear that his love of fact and reproducible data was immense, and he wanted to show that Mannheim had "not done his homework" before making such allegedly sweeping statements. And yet if Merton had referred to Mannheim's other work, where he clearly does indeed engage specific "data" of the very kind that Merton used in his own early work, he could not have accused him of committing brilliant hypothesizing masquerading as "established fact." It is also undeniable that Mannheim's generation was schooled on European history in ways quite unimaginable to an American scholar of the same period, and that "the data" which undergirded Mannheim's arguments very likely existed in forms common to that circuit of intellectual life, but remote from the American scene—partly no doubt because it was published in many languages. Merton's love of scientific method and of the history of science for its own sake collided with Mannheim's apparent disregard for workmanlike "testing" of hypotheses using readily available data. But based on a careful reading of Mannheim's oeuvre, one can quickly see that he was as interested in "the facts of the case" as was Merton. This is truly a case of misapprehension and misaccusation.

In 1939 Robert K. Merton, then twenty-nine years old, moved from Harvard, where he'd been a lecturer in the sociology department for three years following the acquisition of his doctorate, to Tulane University, where he became associate professor and chair of the department. He stayed for two years before removing to Columbia. He wrote that the exotic character of New Orleans attracted him (Merton 1996:354), and that Harvard's president had declared a moratorium on hiring, so there was no point in remaining any longer in Cambridge. Yet he was not alone in using Tulane as a suitable first job, despite its cultural and geographic remoteness from the eastern seaboard. He'd been preceded there by Luther Bernard, Louis Wirth, Ellsworth Faris, and Edward Reuter, all of whom, like himself, eventually becoming ASA presidents.

In the midst of this hejira, in 1940, he submitted an article to *The Journal of Liberal Religion* on Karl Mannheim and what was then still known as *Wissenssoziologie*. Only forty-seven libraries today own this journal, most of them being small theological seminaries; even the Library of Congress has but one issue; interestingly, Columbia's libraries own two full sets. The journal had begun the year before, and was edited by James Luther Adams while working at Meadville Theological School in Chicago, to which Adams had moved in 1937. The journal lasted one decade, from summer 1939 until summer 1949. It is entirely likely that very few readers of Merton's essay book, *Social Theory and Social Structure*, have noted or cared to note that his youthful evisceration of Mannheim and his ideas had originally appeared in such a minor venue, and that had it not been included in Merton's bestseller, it would surely by now be forgotten. These pages are uncharacteristically pungent and unforgiving when compared with Merton's usual modus operandi. Why this is the case is one puzzle I want to address.

Based on my longstanding interest in Mannheim's work, and my no less intense esteem for Merton's, I do not believe Merton gave Mannheim even half a chance to prove the utility of *Wissenssoziologie* along lines the latter chose to explore. And because Merton became who he became during the '50s and '60s, and because Mannheim died in 1947 at fifty-three from a congenital heart defect, thus unavailable to defend himself, *Wissenssoziologie* was abruptly converted into an Americanized "sociology of knowledge." As such it was entirely redesigned along the lines Merton had laid down as a very young scholar, barely out of graduate school. One must wonder how differently this subfield might have developed had Mannheim lived and been able to argue directly with Merton's prescription for a reconceptualized understanding of the interaction between knowledge and social forces. The political edge that Mannheim gave his version did not sit well with Merton, for it threatened to undercut the claims to scientific objectivity that the latter believed a valuable sociology of knowledge ought to exhibit.

It is true that Mannheim has had some stalwart defenders, including his own student, Kurt Wolff, who beginning in 1943 published several extended clarifications of what a Mannheimian *Wissenssoziologie* meant from the point of view of an insider (Wolff 1974:554–590). Wolff, like so many European refugees, was forced to bridge the enormous existential and scholarly gap between the worldviews of U.S. and continental academics. He put it simply when saying parenthetically, "there is probably an affinity between the sociology of knowledge and a European outlook" (Wolff 1974:58 n, 8). He also pointed out that the sociology of knowledge had endured a "precarious, transplanted existence, mainly in the United States" ever since 1933 when the Nazi takeover had dispersed its main proponents. But none of Mannheim's defenders was so broadly inventive as he himself, and his legacy suffered accordingly, while Merton's new direction prospered.

One must wonder why a writer as notoriously careful, scrupulous, even, one might argue, horrified at the prospect of factual or interpretative error could commit to print an article that is demonstrably misrepresentative of its principal target, Mannheim's masterpiece, *Ideology and Utopia*. Were he only here to explain himself, to provide the contextualizing subtleties that quickly become historical simulation when the key players are gone. Is it possible that Merton practiced bad-faith hermeneutics upon Mannheim's text, perhaps a unique instance in his entire oeuvre? Dare one hold such a thought? He was young and in a hurry; he was working under Sorokin and other egomaniacs at Harvard; he read and wrote at a blazing clip; and the word was out, so claimed von Schelting, that Mannheim's theory of knowledge was defective due to its relativistic tendency. With the stunning exception of *OTSOG*, Merton was never particularly fond of practicing *explication de texte*, perhaps wanting to distance himself from Parsons, much preferring developing sociology as a "real science." Hence his repeated invocation of the 1917 Whitehead apothegm regarding the benefits of forgetting one's past (from *The Organization of Thought*). But in this case, as with a few early pieces on Durkheim, he sets out to analyze and argue with an important theoretical text in close hermeneutic fashion. It is therefore only in these terms that his essays on the sociology of knowledge can be evaluated.

Let's begin with the gross facts of the case. Perhaps inspired by his contemporary Philadelphian, Edward Shils, Merton chose to focus on Mannheim's

principal collection of essays to that date, assembled in 1936 by Wirth and
Shils under the title *Ideology and Utopia*, most of which came from the lesser German edition published in 1929. This move allowed Merton, either
knowingly or not, to avoid considering Mannheim's most important work
of applied sociology of knowledge, his already famous essay, "Conservative
Thought." This ninety-page labor of sustained brilliance appeared in 1927
when Mannheim was thirty-four, as Merton notes in a Mannheim bibliography he includes in the chapter in question (Merton 1968:546n). He also
chose to slight several other, similarly ingenious studies that served as the
foundation of Mannheim's project: "On the Interpretation of *Weltanschauung*" (1921–22), "The Problem of a Sociology of Knowledge" (1925), "The
Problem of Generations" (1928), and "Competition as a Cultural Phenomenon" (1929). Mannheim experts agree that these lengthy articles form the
crux of his efforts to formalize his own version of *Wissenssoziologie* in the
face of competing and different programs being simultaneously advanced by
Max Scheler, Marcel Granet, Ernst Grünwald, Sorokin, many Durkheim-
ians, and others. One of the virtuosic features of Merton's early work is his
willingness to read deeply in German, French, and Italian texts when required. His own translations of Mannheim's and Weber's works are solid, so
it would not have been difficult for him to examine carefully these neglected
works by Mannheim had he chosen to do so. There is some evidence that he
did read them, since he mentions them fleetingly in the two chapters before
us. But it is only *Ideology and Utopia* that received his complete attention.

In the first item, the chapter in Gurvitch and Moore called "The Sociology of Knowledge," Merton tries to do what Mannheim had done, using
a similar title but at much greater length, exactly twenty years before, and
at almost the same age. This chapter is in fact a clever reworking of a fine
piece of juvenilia that Merton had published in Sarton's journal, *Isis*, in
1937, when he was twenty-seven. The major difference between the *Isis* article and the Gurvitch and Moore chapter is tone: the first is crisp, repor-
torial, and balanced; the latter is critical, polemical, and hermeneutically
aggressive. Perhaps Sarton's editing of *Isis* persuaded Merton to temper
his negative sense of Mannheim's mission. That this transformation of attitude occurred in relatively few years adds to the puzzle, although moving
from graduate student at Harvard to professor at Tulane and then rising
star at Columbia might well have affected Merton's scholarly vision.

It seems that assessing *Wissenssoziologie* was at that time one way for as-
piring intellectuals to demonstrate their high seriousness while still young.

Given its deeply epistemological nature, the new subfield must have seemed forbidding to the less philosophically inclined. Yet because of von Schelting's shellacking of Mannheim in *ASR*, Parsons, Merton, and other onlookers repudiated the sort of enthusiastic endorsement given to the sociology of knowledge by Albion Small in 1925. Yet neither von Schelting, Parsons, nor Merton assessed Mannheim's substantive, "concrete" case studies of the 1920s. The younger men, busy with other work, relied instead upon the purely methodological or epistemological attack given to them by von Schelting—whose motives are themselves worth examination—thus making it impossible for Mannheim's work to receive the kind of thorough study it would finally begin to enjoy among other readers in the late 1950s. It was then that his essays were translated and published in a half-dozen Routledge books as part of the "International Library of Sociology and Social Reconstruction," a robust and influential series which Mannheim himself had overseen during the '40s. But by then the potential audience for his labors had substantially shrunk, not a little influenced in this direction by the two chapters in Merton's essay book.

In the survey of *Wissenssoziologie* that Merton first wrote for *Isis*, retooled eight years later for Gurvitch and Moore, and finally included in *Social Theory and Social Structure*, he goes through a lot of Marx and Engels before getting to Mannheim. It's clear that he believes the sociology of knowledge is a leftwing invention, despite earlier, complementary noises made by Bacon, Nietzsche, Whitehead, Shakespeare, and others. Merton translates from an 1885 Hamburg edition of *The Eighteenth Brumaire* that is now quite scarce; his translation compares well with today's standard English edition. He also finds relevant materials from the *Manifesto, Contribution to the Critique of Political Economy, Das Kapital,* and *The German Ideology*. In all, he quotes from Marx and Engels about fifteen times. He summarizes part of the story this way:

> And throughout runs the basic theme of the unwitting determination of ideas by the substrata; the emphasis on the distinction between the real and the illusory, between reality and appearance in the sphere of human thought, belief, and conduct. And whatever the intention of the analysts, their analyses tend to have an acrid quality: they tend to indict, secularize, ironicize, satirize, alienate, devalue the intrinsic content of the avowed belief or point of view. Consider only the overtones of terms chosen in these contexts to refer to beliefs, ideas, and thought: vital lies, myths, illusions,

derivations, folklore, rationalizations, ideologies, verbal facade, pseudo-reasons, etc. (Merton 1968:512).

Aside from what one might call an aesthetic aversion to this sort of "acridness," Merton was troubled by this general attitude because it not only "debunked" (*Enthüllen*) ordinary illusions harbored by hoi polloi, but also put at risk the most elevated thoughts entertained by scientists and philosophers—the very company to which Merton aspired.

Merton put forth in the essay a "paradigm for the sociology of knowledge" that is Sorokinesque in its completeness, but is purely Mertonian in its refusal to be sucked into the debunking industry invented by Marx and Engels, then carried into the twentieth century by Pareto, Lukács, Scheler, and Mannheim. He also surveys dozens of other writers with something pertinent to say, from Sorokin to Bertrand Russell to Erich Fromm to Freud, C. Wright Mills, and Keynes. It remains a useful and evenhanded survey for the most part, and an important historical document in measuring how *Wissenssoziologie* was apprehended and reshaped to fit the American scene.

It is in the earlier essay, "Karl Mannheim and the Sociology of Knowledge," transplanted from the *Journal of Liberal Religion*, where Merton polemicizes in a fashion that is atypical, where his hermeneutic labors are sabotaged by hardly contained bile. He cites or quotes from *Ideology and Utopia* forty-five times in the course of the essay, along the way providing a useful short bibliography of Mannheim's work to date, mostly in German. Yet the stylistic easiness and helpfulness which characterized the *Isis* review of 1937 is not much in evidence. In its place one finds a fierce determination to beat Mannheim at his own game, and, like von Schelting, to spend 90 percent of the paper discussing his alleged "failures," saving a few words of praise for the final paragraphs. Within the thirty-five quotations from Mannheim's writings, Merton often inserted ellipses or used fragments, a pattern more often seen in polemics than in balanced exposition. There are to be sure laudable Mertonian features to the essay, but beside and among them are others that were more often found in the acerbic critiques which later made Sorokin infamous among his peers. It is a peculiar piece of work that does not fit well with Merton's other writings, and its strangest component is its willful failure to give Mannheim credit for what he accomplished. If *Ideology and Utopia* did not turn out to be, as Small called it, an "orientation-monument for all sociologists," it is surely one of the half-dozen most inventive and creative works of cultural sociology written during the twentieth century. It seems now that young man Merton somehow had to dispose of the work before perfecting his own version of *Wissenssoziologie* and the sociology of mass communications. It is likely that his bosom pal Lazarsfeld, with his strong orientation toward Big Science, and his suspicion of the "merely" theoretical, may have influenced Merton's displeasure with Mannheim at this stage.

One is forced to wonder how Mannheim and Merton would have interacted had the former moved to Morningside Heights along with Adorno and Horkheimer in the late '30s when Merton was making his place there. Could these two overpowering, gifted young scholars—one filled with dark forebodings, the other searching for the bright light of science—have helped each other understand the shortcomings of each others' *Weltanschauungen*?

References

Bloom, Harold. 1973. *The Anxiety of Influence: A Theory of Poetry.* New York: Oxford University Press.

Calhoun, Craig. 2003. "Robert K. Merton Remembered." *ASA Footnotes,* March.

Coser, Lewis A, ed. 1975. *The Idea of Social Structure: Papers in Honor of Robert K. Merton.* New York: Harcourt Brace Jovanovich.

Henderson, L. J. 1970. *On the Social System.* Ed. Bernard Barber. Chicago: University of Chicago Press.

House, Floyd. 1936. Review of Karl Mannheim, *Mensch und Gesellschaft im Zeitalter des Umbaus. American Sociological Review* 1:684–86.

Kettler, David and Volker Meja. 1995. *Karl Mannheim and the Crisis of Liberalism.* New Brunswick, NJ: Transaction Publishers.

Levine, Donald. 1997. Email to Alan Sica, June 10.

Manheim, Ernest. 1947. Obituary for Karl Mannheim. *American Journal of Sociology* 52:471–74.

Mannheim, Karl. 1936. *Ideology and Utopia: An Introduction to the Sociology of Knowledge.* With a preface by Louis Wirth. Trans. Edward Shils and Louis Wirth. New York: Harcourt, Brace, and World.

——. 1971. *From Karl Mannheim.* Ed. Kurt H. Wolff. New York: Oxford University Press.

Merton, Robert K. 1936. Review of Pierre-Maxime Schuhl, *Essai sur la formation de la pensée grecque: introduction historique a une étude de la philosophie platonicienne. American Sociological Review* 1:683–84.

———. 1937. The Sociology of Knowledge. *Isis* 27:493–503.

———. 1968. *Social Theory and Social Structure.* Enlarged ed. New York: Free Press.

———. 1996: *On Social Structure and Science.* Ed. Piotr Sztompka. Chicago: University of Chicago Press.

Page, Charles Hunt. 1982. *Fifty Years in the Sociological Enterprise: A Lucky Journey.* Amherst: University of Massachusetts Press.

Parsons, Talcott. 1936. Review of Alexander von Schelting, *Max Webers Wissenschaftslehre. American Sociological Review* 1:675–681.

Schelting, Alexander von. 1936. Review essay on Karl Mannheim, *Ideologie und Utopie. American Sociological Review* 1:664–674.

Small, Albion W. 1925. Untitled Review (Versuche zu einer Sociologie des Wissens, Max Scheler). *The American Journal of Sociology,* Vol. 31, No. 2:262–264.

Speier, Hans. 1936. Review of Ernst Grünwald, *Das Problem einer Soziologie des Wissens. American Sociological Review* 1:681–82.

———. 1989. *The Truth in Hell and Other Essays on Politics and Culture, 1935–1987.* New York: Oxford University Press.

Stark, Werner. 1958. *The Sociology of Knowledge: An Essay in Aid of a Deeper Understanding of the History of Ideas.* London: Routledge and Kegan Paul.

Swedberg, Richard. 1990. *Economics and Sociology, Redefining Their Boundaries: Conversations with Economists and Sociologists.* Princeton: Princeton University Press.

Weber, Max. 1994. *Weber: Political Writings.* Ed. Peter Lassman and Ronald Speirs. Cambridge: Cambridge University Press.

Wolff, Kurt H. 1974. *Trying Sociology.* New York: John Wiley and Sons.

9

The Ethos of Science and the Ethos of Democracy

RAGNVALD KALLEBERG

There is a tendency among many contemporary sociologists to regard Robert Merton's scientific contributions as primarily of historical interest, belonging to a finished, structural-functional phase in the history of the discipline. In the view of the present author, however, Mertonian insights and analytical approaches are as essential to an understanding of current problems as they were half a century ago. Merton warrants renewed attention as a contemporary classic. In this article I use a reconstructive approach and discuss contributions from Merton in order to improve our understanding of the relationship between science and democracy. The main focus is on the formation and collective certification of opinions in both areas and on the vital role of science for an enlightened public understanding of common problems and challenges in liberal democracies.

Focus, Approach, and Disposition

In his legendary essay from 1942, "Science and Democratic Social Structure" ([1942] 1968:604–615), Merton insisted on the positive relationships between the scientific and democratic social orders, and the intrinsic tensions between science and totalitarian governance. He was cautious in not presenting too strong a claim about the positive relationship, reminding the reader that science had developed in several different political orders, and that too little research of a historical-comparative nature was available. But he launched the "provisional assumption that 'science is afforded opportunity for development in a democratic order which is integrated with the ethos of science' (606). He was more definitive in his analysis of the negative relationship between science and "modern totalitarian society" where "anti-rationalism and the centralization of institutional control both serve to limit the scope provided for scientific activity" (615).

Merton's essay on science and democracy should be read together with "Science and the Social Order," published four years earlier ([1938] 1968:591–603). The topic analyzed there was the interdependence of science and other social institutions, with a particular focus on "the role of science in the Nazi state" (594). Merton compares the situation of science in a "liberal society" such as America with the situation in a "dictatorial state" (602). He argues that science is in an essentially better position in a liberal society, guaranteeing a high degree of autonomy to its different institutions. The young Merton—like the old—believes in value neutrality in science. Despite this, however, there can be no doubt about his approval of the following moral sentiment often found in scientific institutions: "Science must not suffer itself to become the handmaiden of theology or economy or state" (597). These two early articles fit well into the picture of Merton in this period. Politically, he was located left of the center, being antifascist and prodemocracy. He identified with persons, groups, and movements that fought against fascism and totalitarianism (Hollinger 1996; Merton 1996b; Enebakk 2007). These groups claimed that the scientific attitude favored democracy and that the ethos of science could contribute to an improvement of the general democratic culture in society. A leading individual here was Mark A. May, director of Yale's *Institute of Human Relations*. At the time he was obviously a more visible and influential social scientist than Merton. He advocated that the basic norms and values of science, such as honesty and freedom of inquiry, should also be cultivated and become central in the general culture of modern societies. The scientific spirit was in essence antifascist and prodemocratic (Hollinger 1996:87, 158–164). Merton shared these views.

Such a perspective on science in democracy was not maintained as a topic for research in the Mertonian tradition of science studies. In a revisit to Merton's concept of an ethos of science and its reception within the sociology of science, Stehr (1978) did not mention this theme as something that had been—or should be—pursued. In the beginning of the 1970s, Storer edited and introduced Merton's contributions to the sociology of science. He rightly insisted that the 1942 essay is "one of the most significant in the history of the sociology of science," but then added that it had acquired a "rather misleading title" due to the main theme of the first issue of the antifascist *Journal of Legal and Political Sociology* (Storer in Merton 1973:226). The original title from 1942 was "A Note on Science and Technology in a Democratic Order." In the three editions of *Social Theory and Social Structure* (1949, 1957, 1968), the title was modified to "Science and Democratic Social Structure." In *The Sociology of Science* (1973) Merton gave the essay a very different title, "The Normative Structure of Science" and later still, in *On Social Structure and Science* (1996), the title became "The Ethos of Science."[1]

Storer's argument is misleading. The content of the article made it appropriate to give it a title reflecting the interdependence of the scientific and democratic order. Merton was passionately interested in the fate of science and science-based technology in an age of increasing totalitarianism, be it Fascism, Nazism, or Communism. He noted the widespread mistake among scientists to think of science as being "in society but not of it": "A frontal assault on the autonomy of science was required to convert this sanguine isolationism into realistic participation in the revolutionary conflict of cultures" ([1942] 1968:605). The title was purposefully chosen as an articulation of an essential connection between science and the democratic order. Merton saw science as one of the basic institutions in modern, liberal society, influencing and being influenced by other institutions (Merton 1968:538–542, 1970:vii–xxxii; Zuckerman 1989).

In my view research topics related to interdependencies between science and democracy should be regarded among the most important in sociology. The development and maintenance of enlightened understanding in well-functioning publics, as public discourse in mass media, is essential for opinion and will formation in democracies. The scientific and scholarly disciplines are primary sources for reliable knowledge and valid insight. Thus, several key issues are in question: the relationships between the ethos of science and the ethos of democracy; the rationality of opinion formation in the two orders; and the contribution of academics as public intellectuals influencing public definitions of situations. Widespread misinformation, scientific illiteracy, and distorted public agendas are among the problems for contemporary democracies. A more adequate balance and dialogue between science and society than we often have today is essential (Kalleberg 2000:237–250, 2008:17–23, 38–42).

In order to contribute to a better understanding of the relationships between the ethos of science and the ethos of democracy, I discuss Merton as a contemporary contributor, taking as my point of departure the two articles on science and democracy published seventy years ago (in 1938 and 1942), and applying a reconstructive approach (Kalleberg 2007:147–152). Such a reconstructive approach is oriented to the maintenance of valid insight in the contributions analyzed, and to the identification of mistakes that should be rejected and weak points that should be improved and clarified. There are weak and untenable points in Merton's works. He can, for instance, be criticized for holding on to a scientistic conception of the tasks of social science, for assuming that normative opinions cannot be defended or criticized with cognitively convincing reasons; there are also problems with his functionalist explanations (Bernstein 1976:7–18; Kalleberg 2007:145,152–153, 2009a; Elster 1983:55–68). However, such valid criticism should not mislead us to commit a hyperfunctionalist fallacy, assuming that if some elements in the larger Mertonian theoretical structure have to be rejected, then the whole structure breaks down and should be located in the museum of sociology. The (unintended) consequence of such an approach would be to undermine the cumulative nature of sociology as a scientific discipline.

Sociologists using a reconstructive approach often focus on basic practices in society or concepts and perspectives in science. Merton often used a kind of reconstructive approach, for example when clarifying and explicating paradigms for functional analysis, structural analysis, and the sociology of knowledge (Merton 1968:73–138, 1976:109–144, 1968:510–542). But he did not have an explicit conception of this approach, for instance as part of a typology of three types of empirical approaches: studies based on primary data, integrations of insights from existing studies, and reconstructive studies (Kalleberg 2007:147–149). Merton had, at most, a "protoconcept" of such reconstructive activity, "an early rudimentary . . . and largely unexplicated idea /rather than/ a concept" (Merton 1990:338). One example is what Merton labels "establishing the phenomenon," the task of providing a reliable answer to the question: "Is it really so?" (1987:4). His recommendation is this: "Take care to establish a phenomenon (or historical event) before proceeding to interpret or explain it" (5). As I interpret this advice, it has two components: (1) be sure that the phenomenon actually exists (or has existed) and (2) be sure to identify the phenomenon in an adequate way.[2]

Commenting on the long history of discussion about his original "formulation" of the ethos of science, he underlines the controversies as an example of "organized skepticism" at work, "replete with incentives and rewards, for finding flaws, errors and other shortcomings as well as previously unnoticed potentialities in those knowledge claims" (1990:339). Merton's underlining here of the identification of "previously unnoticed potentialities" is an apt description of reconstructive work focused on existing studies. Three standard components can be identified in such work: (1) conserving and reformulating earlier insights, not suppressing them because of committing the "fallacy of the latest word" (Merton 1984); (2) criticizing by finding shortcomings and errors; and (3) developing potentialities and new insights, preferably shown to be compatible with the theory under scrutiny.[3]

The first section of the article focuses on the formation and change of opinions in social contexts, be it within scientific communities, in everyday communication, or in political debate. We need a conception of *homo sociologicus* as a reasoner in order to improve our documentation and analysis of how reasons (opinions, ideas) are formulated and publicly "certified" (Merton [1942] 1968:606). Reasons are social phenomena and their quality depends on cultural norms and institutional arrangements. Such a conception is compatible with Merton's work, and can improve our understanding of how opinions (reasons, ideas) are formed and transformed in different social contexts. In the next section I take a closer look at Merton's rudimentary, but eminently fruitful, conception of the ethos of democracy and how it is related to science. All institutions are in this view characterized by an ethos, built on a set of values, norms, positions (statuses), and role sets. Merton's bold claim is that the institutional imperative of universalism is the dominant, guiding principle in the ethos of democracy. Because the norm of universalism basically requires unrestricted rational and open discussions, Merton's claim opens up for the importance of open and rational discussions in democratic orders and also—I shall argue—for the role of university academics participating in democratic discourse. In the last section it is inquired whether a regular task for academics should be to influence public discourse using scientific knowledge. The answer offered is that to be a public intellectual is part of the academic role set, where the academic contributes to public discourse with scientific knowledge, in communication with individuals in citizen roles. Merton did not work out an explicated conception of such a role and institutional task. This generated tensions in his own sociology of science and in relation to his own academic practice as a public intellectual.

Homo Sociologicus as Reasoner

Similar to many other social scientists, Merton had an underdeveloped conceptual apparatus for documenting and analyzing the formation and change of opinions in social interaction. This is a serious problem because reasons are essential for our analysis and explanation of social action and interaction. With Merton's structural, functional, and norm-sociological resources, it is not possible to give a convincing analysis of the formation and change of descriptive and normative opinions (Kalleberg 2007, 2009a). Nor is that possible with traditional rational-choice theory, based on its narrow conception of rationality, restricting it to instrumental rationality, cost-benefit analysis, and a one-sided focus on the consequences of acts (Boudon 1996, 1998, 2006b).

In order to improve our analytical resources for capturing what is actually taking place in social interaction, we also have to understand *homo sociologicus* as a reasoner, a rational being compelled by its own nature to base its actions on a definition of situations (with reasons), and with responsibility for its own action or inaction (Kalleberg 2007:144). This does not imply that human beings are not also products of social circumstances, and in general only partly responsible for what takes place. But we are not merely "obedient puppets" (Merton [1957] 1973:294); we have a degree of individual autonomy to define situations and act on the basis of those definitions.

A widespread scientistic prejudice among many social scientists is that normative issues should be kept outside scholarly discourse, because in principle they cannot be settled rationally with convincing reasons. After the normative turn in social theory from the 1970s, however— with contributions from theorists such as Rawls, Habermas, Sen, Dahl, and

Boudon—the concept of rationality has been broadened so as to include not only descriptive but also normative reasons (see Kalleberg 2009a). Descriptive reasons have to do with the identification and description of states of affairs, including explanations of change and stability and guesses about possible and probable futures. Normative claims have to do with the evaluation of actions and situations, and with the recommendation of what to do or to avoid. With the help of reasons, descriptive and normative opinions are presented, discussed, accepted, modified, or rejected.

Examples of normative-empirical research, such as criticism of scientific misconduct (see Jones 1993), assessments of democratic citizenship (see Lafferty 2002), and normative argumentation for why democracy is more legitimate than dictatorship (see Dahl 1989), are instances relatively common in scholarly discourse. It is thus a legitimate scientific task for a sociologist of science to document and criticize violations of the norm of universalism in scientific communities, be it among French nationalistic scientists during World War I, physicists in Germany in the interwar period, or African-American sociologists during the 1960s (Merton [1942] 1968:608, [1938] 1968:592–596, [1972] 1973b[1972] 1973a:102–112).

How do actors persuade each other about the facts of situations and about the appropriate evaluation of a state of affairs in open discussions? In this view, they are convinced by arguments, a kind of legitimate "power" in the interplay of reasoners arguing and listening to each other (Kalleberg 2007:146). This is not the only mechanism for social coordination in social life. Obviously, there are several others at work, for instance brute force and outright manipulation intended to deceive others. But open discussions are nevertheless a basic form of social coordination. We all know, including from personal experience, that reasons acted upon are not always descriptively true and normatively appropriate. They may be both false and unfair. Human beings are not only reasonable beings, but also fallible ones. But (socio)logically the possibility of truth and normative rightness is the condition making it possible to be wrong, not the other way around. Because we can be right we can also be wrong.[4]

The reasoning individual defines situations and acts on that basis. The actors can, for instance, be entangled in processes of self-fulfilling prophecies, in the certification of scientific knowledge, or the evaluation of alleged scientific misconduct, such as the Baltimore case (see Kevles 1998). Some points about reasoners may be illustrated with an examination of Merton's analysis of the ethos of science and of self-fulfilling prophecies.

Reasons and the testing of reasons are essential in scientific communities. Merton underlines "the disinterested pursuit of truth" ([1957] 1973:321) in science and speaks occasionally about opinions and reasons as "truth claims" ([1942] 1968:607), the "validity of claims" ([1938] 1968:608), and "knowledge claims" (1990:339). Such validity claims have to be presented, defended, and discussed by peers in the relevant scientific community, and eventually accepted or rejected. It may also be the case that an agreement emerges that it is too early to have an opinion because new evidence and arguments are needed. Here we have a social process of argumentation where the validity of opinions is at stake. Merton underlines the decisive importance of developing propositions "consonant with observation and with previously confirmed knowledge" ([1942] 1968:607), that is, checking for truth and coherence. In his 1942 article, Merton tries to place cognitive truth claims outside of the sociology of science, but does not succeed. And how could he? Such cognitive interaction is embedded in social space and historical time. It "must refer to social processes among scientists, processes that can and should be described and analyzed by sociologists and historians as other interaction processes" (Kalleberg 2007:141).

The phenomenon focused on in the 1942 article is the normative regulation of scientific behavior and the institutional and cultural interdependence of science with other institutions. Well-functioning scientific communities are moral communities where prescriptions about universalism and organized skepticism and proscriptions against particularistic and ethnocentric criteria are essential. The institutional imperatives of science are not local conventions; they are moral obligations and can backed with compelling normative reasons. They constitute and maintain scientific communities characterized by cultural integrity and institutional autonomy. Cultural integrity in science means that only the influence of better arguments shall govern the formation and "certification" of opinions among participants (Merton [1942] 1968:606).

Definitions of situations in everyday life are regularly both descriptive and normative. When we define something as a "problem," we not only assume a given state of affairs, but also that the situation is not as it ought to be. Implicitly, we usually also presuppose that something could and should be done. The solution must be both feasible (that it could happen) and desirable (that it should happen). Only individuals are "reasoners" in the sense used here, engaged in an explicit or implicit conversation. In everyday reasoning we sometimes base the reasoning on anonymous rumors that may also be incorrect. Let me illustrate this and some general points with Merton's most famous essay, "The Self-Fulfilling Prophecy."[5]

The basic analytical insight is formulated as follows: "public definition of a situation. . . . becomes an integral part of the situation and thus affects subsequent developments" (Merton [1948] 1968:477). Merton starts with the sociological parable about banks going bankrupt because of self-fulfilling prophecies. Mr. Smith has heard from his friend Mr. Jones that *The Last National Bank* is insolvent. He has no reason to think that his friend is untruthful. He takes his definition of the situation seriously and accepts it as descriptively true. Mr. Smith also thinks that the implicit normative advice is appropriate: "You should quickly withdraw your money in order to safeguard your family!" Both persons are rational in the sense that they listen to and evaluate descriptive and normative reasons and act on that basis. It is strangely overlooked, by Merton himself as well as the sociological community, that he here also criticizes actors and institutions and even recommends what could and should be done. Such critical and constructive scholarly practice is inconsistent with his own theory of value-neutral science, and with his assumption that normative opinions in fields studied are not based on (cognitive) reasons and not open to cognitive criticism (Kalleberg 2007:152–154, 2009a:256–259). A basic claim is worth quoting once more, with his own italics: "The self-fulfilling prophecy is, in the beginning, a *false* definition of the situation evolving a new behavior which makes the originally false conception come *true* . . . and perpetuates a reign of error . . . misleading rumor created the very conditions of its own fulfillment. . . . Such are the perversities of social logic" ([1948] 1968:477). One of his examples concerns the bank going bankrupt. In another, "the gentleman from Mississippi" (481), believing first that educational resources should not be wasted on inferior Blacks, subsequently implements a school policy in accordance with such a prejudice, and points to the low number of educated black people, confirming with real evidence the inferiority of this group. Such "anti-Negro charges which are not patently false are only speciously true. The allegations are true in the Pickwickian sense" (477) that self-fulfilling prophecies are in general true.

When analyzing discriminating opinions and actions concerning Jews and Blacks, in the section on in-group virtues and out-group virtues, Merton criticizes the everyday inferences used in the social field as "moral alchemy" (482). By engaging in such irrational everyday alchemical processes, leading in-groups are able to "transmute" in-group virtues into out-group vices. "Is the in-group hero frugal, thrifty and sparing? Then the out-group villain is stingy, miserly and penny-pinching" (482). The reasons and reasoning in the social field analyzed are irrational, and therefore "we must examine the moral alchemy through which the in-group readily transmutes virtue into vice, and vice into virtue" (482). There can be no doubt that Merton here is a social critic. He unmistakably criticizes the social reality he has first described, emphasized with normative expressions like "tasteless ethnocentrism," "scrambled logic," "self-hypnosis" and "specious evidence" (481–482).

The English word "rational" comes from the Latin word "ratio," meaning "reason" or "ability to give and listen to reasons" in order to defend and explain one's opinions and actions. The word "rational" is here used in accordance with this etymological meaning, and includes both descriptive and normative reasons. To understand interaction processes, it is necessary to understand the reasons and reasoning of actors. As articulated by Boudon: "[A] good theory is one that explains a social phenomenon by making it the consequence of understandable behavior on the part of the individuals concerned" (2006a:107). A necessary condition for an adequate description of actors in a given context is an understanding of their reasons. That is also required for explaining unintended consequences and aggregated effects. Explanations in the social sciences are based on (sociocultural) reasons, not on (natural) causes (see Kalleberg 2007:145–146, 2009a:263, and references there).

For Merton, science is "a sort of micro-model for social reality as such" (Sztompka 1986:3). We can therefore use the understanding of opinion formation in science to understand and explain formation of opinions more generally. An example of such an analytical strategy can be found in Boudon's work, as when he points to "the type of reasons which lead scientists to believe in the truth of their scientific theories" (1996:147), in order to illustrate how opinions are generally formed. Discussions in science "are not different in nature . . . from the ones we find at work in ordinary life" (ibid.). The major generalized insight to be gained from such a cognitivist perspective on reasoners is that individuals (also) form and change opinions, and act on them, because they think they have good (enough) reasons to do so.

The formation and testing of reasons in scientific communities is an intensively collective process. To underline this, Merton talks about the norms of science as "institutional imperatives" ([1942] 1968:606) governing the participants. Participants in processes of organized skepticism are required both to open up for new knowledge and insight from peers, and to critically evaluate the new claims. There can be neither private nor secret formation of scientific knowledge. The open process is the best we have to achieve valid claims. But to be rational is also to have an insight into one's own fallibility. We may be wrong and do wrong, and we may be brought to understand that by criticism from others or by self-criticism. In the next section we shall see that similar requirements and institutional imperatives also govern—to varying degrees—participants in democratic processes of opinion and will formation.

Universalistic Deliberation in the Legitimate Circulation of Power in Democracies

In the two articles from 1938 and 1942, Merton is at his most explicit in arguing for a positive relationship between science and democracy. He organizes the discussion along two dimensions: cultural integrity (i.e., an adequate ethos of science) and institutional autonomy. In both dimension he looks at the interplay of different cultural ethoses and social institutions. He focuses on the perverting institutional and cultural effects of the Nazi State on German science. The integrity and autonomy of science was under attack.

The discussion of institutional autonomy is short but the main argument is clear enough. In a liberal, democratic society, the different institutions have a high degree of autonomy, they are not controlled from one center of power as in a "totalitarian society" ([1938] 1968:602). He uses contemporary German sources and Edward Hartshorne's (1937) detailed study of the reorganization of German universities after the Nazis came to power in 1933 to back his arguments about the perverting effects of a "dictatorial state" ([1938] 1968:602). The Nazi State reformed the institutions of higher education to serve its own purposes and introduced a hierarchical leadership principle incompatible with a collegial culture.[6]

The main focus in the two early articles is the cultural integrity of science, analyzed with the help of the values and norms of an ethos of science. The essential relationship between science and democracy is not only made explicit in the discussion of institutional autonomy, but also in the discussion of the norm of universalism. Merton's main thesis is this: "However inadequately it may be put into practice, the ethos of democracy includes universalism as a dominant guiding principle" ([1942] 1968:609).

It is not straightforward to explicate what this means and where it leads us; Merton does not elaborate the thesis much in the two articles, nor does he do so later. But it seems reasonable to hold on to the two dimensions of his concept of universalism, partly related to arguments, partly to actors ([1942] 1968:607–609). The norm requires that argumentation collectives shall be established and maintained. When knowledge claims are evaluated in well-functioning scientific communities the only thing that matters is the quality of documentation and argumentation. Only reasons based on "impersonal criteria: consonant with observation and with . . . confirmed knowledge" shall influence opinion formation in this context ([1942] 1968:607). In Merton's perspective truth-claims cannot be validated in an ethnocentric way, which is a violation of the norm. To prevail, the claims have to withstand a universalization test, including all kinds of probing arguments and criticism. In general, "particularistic criteria of validity" ([1942] 1968:607), for example reference to the sex or ethnicity of the reasoner, are forbidden according to the institutional imperative of universalism.

If we accept the widening of the concept of rationality as presented in the previous section, and also recognize normative claims as legitimate in scientific discourse, social scientists do not have to behave as critics in disguise. There are, for instance, cognitively robust reasons for affirming the norm of universalism as indispensable in scientific communities, obliging scientists only to be influenced by the better arguments when participating in scientific discourse. This normative statement, the explicit acceptance of the norm of universalism, is not a subjective preference only based on emotions and maintained by external sanctions, as Merton tends to assume because of his narrow concept of rationality; it is a valid statement based on convincing reasons (Kalleberg 2009a).

The insight that normative claims can be cognitively valid, that is, defended, criticized, and decided with reasons, has wide-ranging consequences for the social scientific understanding of public discourse. Democratic deliberation not only consists of opinion formation of a descriptive kind, for instance documenting and explaining widening or shrinking income gaps in a population, or the percentage of a population that has health insurance; it also consists in the formation of evaluations of states of affairs, including normative opinions of what to do or not to do. Habermas identifies this second kind of opinion formation as "will-formation" (e.g., 1996:338–341). Lindblom labels the same type of deliberative process "volition": It might be called a "judgment," but "volition" has the advantage of stressing commitment or will (1990:21). Definitions of situations consist both of a descriptive understanding of states of affairs, a normative evaluation of the established phenomena, and an opinion of what (not) to do.

The second meaning of universalism in Merton's contributions concerns actors, the individuals who are discussing reasons ([1942] 1968:608). The scientific community shall be open to all competent persons, not excluding participants because of race, nationality, sex, or religion. Merton undoubtedly put so much stress on this aspect of the norm because of the perversions in the German system after the Nazis came to power. They wanted, for instance, to get rid of Jews in German universities, as documented by Hartshorne (1937). Several new laws were introduced in the years 1933 to 1935 that excluded "Non-Aryans" from getting university exams in professions such as business and various medical fields. Jews were the largest group of university teachers dismissed, and only because they were Jews (1937:84, 99–100). Merton articulated the norm violated here as follows: "Universalism finds further expression in the demand that careers be open to talents. . . . To restrict scientific careers on ground other than lack of competence is to prejudice the furtherance of knowledge" ([1942] 1968:608–609). Merton is acutely aware that the ethos of science is constantly under pressure, more or less seriously, in any society and from different sources, such as the state, the market, and religion. Science is a community of peers stimulating unrestricted discussions. It has to be protected constantly from internal and external opinions and norms that weaken or distort its ethos.[7]

This second aspect of universalism in science permits the construction of a bridge from science to a basic norm of the ethos of democracy, the political equality of its members, be it in a nation or an institution. Who are the competent peers in democratic orders? In a democratic structure all normal adults are members of the demos, presupposed to be free and equal. Robert Dahl convincingly argues "that ordinary people are, in general, *qualified* to govern themselves" (1989:97) and concentrates an essential normative insight in the "Presumption of Personal Autonomy": "*In the absence of a compelling showing to the contrary, everyone should be assumed to be the best judge of his or her own good or interests*" (100, italics in the original).

Merton does not discuss the other norms of the ethos of democracy and their relationship to the institutional imperatives of democracy. The bundle of norms can be referred to with the acronym CUDOSH: communism (or communalism), universalism, disinterestedness, originality, skepticism, and humility (Kalleberg 2007:142). It is reasonable to argue that Merton also assumed an internal connection between the other norms and the ethos of democracy. One such reason is that the values and norms of the ethos of science are internally connected and difficult to distinguish from each other. The other norms basically point to the importance of open forums designed in such a way that the participants are obliged—by legitimate institutional imperatives—to rely only on arguments and strive to find the better ones. The imperatives of *organized skepticism* and *communism* point unequivocally to the importance of unrestricted discussions. The norm of *originality* is also important in democratic processes; citizens are often forced to develop new responses to unexpected problems and challenges such as the economic crisis between the two World Wars or the contemporary ecological challenges. The norms about *disinterestedness* and *humility* require that participants listen to arguments and modify or reject their own views on that basis and accept their own understanding as limited when compared to the community of inquirers. The last two norms are essential when translated into the requirements of democratic forums. The norm of disinterestedness requires impartiality. This is important in a democratic structure where the members try to find solutions that support the common good, and where they have to grant other members the same degree of freedom and equality that they presuppose for themselves (Dahl 1990:6–21).[8] The norm of humility requires that participants in democratic discourse are willing to listen to others and take the role of others based on the insight that each person's understanding is limited when evaluating the feasibility and desirability of alternatives. The diversity of values, norms, and interests is enormous in a large-scale political democracy.

DELIBERATION AND DEMOCRACY

Merton never presented a detailed analysis of the ethos of democracy, the institutional imperatives characteristic of a democratic order and its institutional arrangements. In this he was typical in contemporary sociology; an underdeveloped conception of democracy is generally a serious deficit in the discipline. But Merton insisted that universalism—rational discussion among free and equal persons in open forums—is a dominant, guiding principle in a well-functioning democratic order. In an explicated and further developed Mertonian perspective, open and rational discussions are essential both in scientific and democratic communities. In a general sense well-functioning scientific and democratic communities are regulated by the force of better arguments. Leading theorists of democracy underline free and open discussions as central to developing an enlightened understanding among members, be it in the governance of states or individual organizations. In his procedural understanding of a democratic process, Dahl underlines that members of the democratic demos should have the chance to gain "enlightened understanding" (1989:110–111, 180–182, 306–308). He insists on the importance of "inquiry, discussion, and deliberation" (1998:39). Dahl reminds his readers—and fellow social scientists, many of whom are impaired by historical provincialism—that this is an old idea, referring to the famous speech made by Pericles in 431 BC: "instead of looking on discussion as a stumbling block in the way of action, we think it an indispensable preliminary to any wise action at all" (ibid.). The focus on discussions among free, equal, and reasonable members of the demos has become more common in democratic theory during recent decades, often under the heading of "deliberative democracy" (e.g., Chambers 1996; Guttman and Thompson 1996; Elster 1998).

The basic insight to be learned from science and translated into an understanding of a democratic ethos is that freedom of expression is based on an insight into human fallibility. To secure that more well-founded opinions emerge in public discourse, it is crucial that opinions can be corrected and modified in confrontation with the opinions of others, just as in science. The norms regulating argumentation in scientific communities are also at work in the deliberations of democratic forums. Well-functioning scientific communities can each be described as a kind of ideal deliberative democracy, only regulated by the force of better arguments among free, rational, and equal people.

Despite similarities it is nevertheless obvious that deliberation in science and democracy takes place under very different conditions. Parliaments and political-administrative institutions are not only discussion forums, they are representative bodies responsible for acting on behalf of the demos. Decisions based on the majority principle are necessary and legitimate in democratic systems, as an adjustment to the requirement of political equality and to the need for ending discussions and implementing laws and political decisions (Dahl 1989:135–152; Habermas 1996:179–180). To use the principle of majority in a scientific forum in the same way as it is used in a parliament would be irrational and illegitimate.

Merton is a sociologist passionately interested in structurally based tensions and in sociological ambivalences (1976). There are tensions in role sets and there are tensions between the larger orders in society, such as the incompatibility between the ethos of the market stimulating secrecy and the ethos of science stimulating total openness ([1942] 1968:612). This does not mean market or independent scientific institutions should be abolished; both are functionally necessary in a pluralistic, functionally differentiated society. The challenge is to find ways of isolating and combining conflicting ethoses, of defending them against each other, and of balancing them. Market values can endanger the ethos of science (cf. Bok 2003). The ethos of science has to be defended against the "invasion of norms" ([1938] 1968:597) from other institutional ethoses so that science does not become "the handmaiden of theology or economy or state" (597). This interest in finding balances between conflicting expectations in role sets and between incompatible ethoses of different institutions is a core perspective in Merton's work. Sztompka (1986:5, 241–245) appropriately describes it as a "pervasive *leitmotif*" in Merton's work, and labels it the classicist theme, an Aristotelian approach to find a "golden mean" among the conflicting norms, values, interests, and institutional orders of a modern society.

One of the most fruitful elements in Merton's sociological approach is his insistence on the importance of institutions and historical traditions (e.g., 1975:73–89, 109–144; 1985). Actors create organizations and institutionalized practices, but then they anonymously influence the creators in all kinds of ways. From everyday life in science and society, we may know that it can be difficult to maintain such a demanding perspective. Mainstream critics of Merton in science studies, for instance, have not been able to maintain an understanding of the ethos of science as an institutional phenomenon with long historical traditions, but misidentified it as only individual ideals (see Kalleberg 2007:137–138, 150, 152). From everyday life we all know how easy it is to forget a structural perspective and instead find individual scapegoats. Merton is a master in keeping the "sociological imagination" (Mills 1959) alive, focusing on individuals, institutions, and traditions. A basic challenge in modern democratic theory is to design a democratic ethos that forces us, as citizens, in a way similar to how scientists are forced by institutional imperatives. Scientists act the way they do primarily because there is something special in the institutional context, not with themselves as individuals. A similar argument for freedom of expression in a democratic society is the need for open forums to develop and maintain enlightened public understanding (Berendt 2005:7–13; NOU [1999] 2005:27–28).

Habermas has developed a conceptual framework for the description, analysis, and evaluation of opinion and will formation in constitutional democracies with market economies (1996:341–387, 1998:273 – 288). There are three basic media of social coordination: money (the market), power (the state and hierarchical organizations), and solidarity (civil society). The robustness of his model has to do with the realistic understanding of the importance of well-functioning markets, including firms that also are hierarchies. The importance of authoritative state regulations in pluralist democracies, in the last instance backed with a monopoly on the legitimate use of physical force, is also explicitly accepted in the model. But social coordination in civil society cannot be achieved in terms of commercial transactions or in command structures; it requires communication where actors listen to each other and come to an understanding of situations and what to do.

Constitutional democracies are in need of a vibrant civil society, for instance that which comes from participating in voluntary associations and open discussions in mass media, uncoupled from commercial and state regulation. In order to ensure sustainable cultural and political reproduction in deliberating democracies, an infrastructure of public forums has to exist to ensure enlightened public understanding and to counterbalance the institutional pressures from business enterprises, state regulations, lobby groups, PR, and the entertainment industry. In the ideal-typical model of *the legitimate democratic circulation of power*, the starting point is outside of the formal political institutions (Habermas 1996:315–328, 341–387; 1998:282–285). Formal and informal publics have their basis in civil society, informal networks, social movements, non-profit and non-governance associations, schools, universities, mass media, and churches. The "public sphere can get its impulses and inputs from *citizens* who resonate their private experience of social problems" (Habermas 1998:283). This kind of modern society is built around social orders regulated by different and partly conflicting values and norms. We need well-functioning markets and authoritative state regulations, but we also need forums free from market imperatives and state regulations. "The *public sphere* can best be described as a network for communicating relevant issues and contributions, while opinions are weighted by the affirmative and negative responses they receive" (Habermas 1998:284). *Public opinion* formed in undistorted forums in civil society can be transformed into *communicative power* by legislating bodies enacting laws or cabinets forming political programs. This kind of power can later be transformed into legitimate *administrative power* by ministries actually implementing laws and political programs. The constitutive normative idea of democratic theory points to a "self-legislating community where all members enjoy equal private and public autonomy so that the addressees of valid laws can at the same time regard themselves as the authors of these laws" (Habermas 1998:281).

Habermas is, of course, aware of the fact that the normative model is not identical with actual practices in existing democracies. Such a model is not only a basis for a critical analysis of existing conditions; it also points to desirable possibilities for the further development of democracies. Habermas has concentrated this insight into the thesis of modernity as an unfinished, historical project (see Kalleberg 2008:18–22). In a parallel way of thinking, seeing the idea of democracy as embedded in a project to be more fully realized in the future, Dahl has suggested distinguishing between "polyarchy" (existing, partly realized democracies) and "democracy" fully realized (Dahl 1989:322–341). No one has given a more succinct and moving expression of the idea of democracy as an unfinished historical project than Abraham Lincoln in his Gettysburg Address.[9]

The Academic Role Set: Academics as Public Intellectuals

Should academics—as academics—influence opinion and will formation in society? Is there, or should there be, a specific role for such activity as part of the role set of academics? Do, or should, academic institutions as such have a responsibility to contribute scientific knowledge and insight to public discourse? In earlier contributions I have argued that we should answer these questions in the affirmative (Kalleberg 2000, 2005a:300–324, 2008). There is a a legitimate role as public intellectual in the role set of Western academics. Scientific disciplines located in research universities are—ideal-typically—bundles (or constellations) of five tasks, resulting in five types of outcomes: 1) *research* resulting in publications conveying new knowledge; 2) *teaching and study* resulting in educated students; 3) dissemination, i.e., *popularization and public discourse* resulting in both improved scientific literacy in a broader public and contributions to enlightened democratic discourse; 4) *expert* activity resulting in improvements for clients, such as medical treatment of patients; and 5) *institutional governance* resulting in functioning institutions. This general typology of the tasks of an academic discipline is the institutional basis for a fivefold role set. An academic position such as a professorship entails five corresponding roles (with their subroles): researcher, teacher, public intellectual (or disseminator, popularizing and taking part in public discourse), expert, and academic citizen. This analysis can be applied to all kinds of scientific and scholarly disciplines, whether chemistry, sociology, history, or law.

As far as I know, only in Norway does there exist a reasonably representative documentation of popularization and participation in public discourse among university academics. Several survey studies, based on questionnaires sent to all academic personnel in Norwegian universities, document that the activity of dissemination is quite widespread among Norwegian academics and has been stable over time. For instance, during a three-year period (1998–2000), 60 percent of all social scientists published at least one popular article (on average 2.2 articles) and half participated at least once in public discourse. It is worth noting that it is the more productive scientists that also are the more productive popularizers and debaters (Kyvik 2005). There are many case studies and general reflections, often historically oriented, that document and discuss this academic role in different societies (e.g., Coser 1970; Brunkhorst 1987; Jacoby 1987; Habermas 1989; Bender 1993; Hollinger 1996; Bender 1998; Furet 2004; Slagstad 2004; Myhre 2008).

In academic fields such as sociology, history, theology, and archaeology, it is often only possible to make an analytical distinction between the first (science) and third (dissemination) disciplinary activity in the fivefold bundle of activities. Excellent scientific contributions are also at the same time regular contributions to a general audience of citizens. A few examples in book form are Arlie Hochschild's *The Managed Heart: the Commercialization of Human Feeling* (2003), John Dominic Crossan and Jonathan L. Reed's *In Search of Paul: How Jesus' Apostle Opposed Rome's Empire with God's Kingdom* (2005), and Ian Kershaw's *Fateful Choices* (2007). Merton's essay on self-fulfilling prophecies is a classic in the article format.

Popularization and participation in public discourse is based on a tradition in Western Europe and North America going back to the Enlightenment requiring that academics should make sure that knowledge of general interest was translated from the esoteric language of specialized disciplines and made accessible for broader publics (Kalleberg 2008:21). In this way academics can contribute to public discourse and enlightened public understanding. There is no generally accepted terminology used to identify this activity. The Norwegian case is typical, where expressions (in English translation) such as "disseminator," "popularizer," "public enlightenment," "participant in public discourse," and "public intellectual" are used more or less interchangeably.

WHO ARE ACADEMICS AS DISSEMINATORS COMMUNICATING WITH?

When engaged in dissemination and public discourse, academics communicate with nonspecialists and laypersons outside of their own field. The general audience of outsiders is not only located outside of academia, but also inside other specialized academic disciplines. Natural scientists may, for example, read much history, and social scientists may enjoy reading popularizations written by natural scientists. How should we identify the complementary role of the academic as disseminator and public intellectual? Or to reformulate the question and relate it to myself and my fellow sociologists: What is our role as sociologists when reading Steven Jay Gould's books or listening to a public debate among natural scientists about climate changes? Or to give the question a historical twist: What was the role of the general American readership—obviously including academics of all kinds—when they read Gunnar Myrdal's masterpiece *An American Dilemma* (1944)? This book, by a Swedish sociologist and economist, deeply influenced how racial issues were (re)defined in the United States and had an impact on the landmark decision of the Supreme Court in 1954, desegregating public schools. Before its second edition in 1965, it had been sold in more than one hundred thousand copies (Southern 1987).[10]

Roles are related to other, complementary roles. We can speak about role pairs such as researcher and peer, teacher and student, professional expert and client, and academic leader (such as chair person) and member (such as professor and student). The interaction in role pairs is regulated by the reciprocal expectations of duties and rights. I suggest that we identify the roles complementary to academic disseminators as citizen roles. Analytically it can be fruitful to distinguish between "cultural" and "political" citizens. Esoteric research specialists popularize their knowledge for us as cultural citizens. Normally that requires both a translation to a language we understand and a condensed, short presentation so that it is not too time consuming to understand it. As cultural citizens we are interested in scholarly and scientific knowledge and insight as cultural values in their own right. Merton's essay on self-fulfilling prophecies and his book *On the Shoulders of Giants* (1965) are cultural values in their own right, comparable to Montaigne's essays or Laurence Sterne's fabulous novel *Tristram Shandy*. Such citizen roles require something of the occupants different from being a colleague, a client, or a kind of customer to be entertained. But here it is difficult to introduce something other than analytical distinctions. It is (also) entertaining to read Gould and it may, of course, be useful to listen to popular lectures about geography or physiology.

As responsible political citizens, we are obliged to educate ourselves rationally in a complex world, whether about climate change, the quality of schools, or international conflicts. In such processes of education and enlightenment we also need the input from specialists in different fields. One of the basic arguments for freedom of expression is that our limitations may be reduced when exposed to counterarguments and required to defend our own positions. The intended result of academic work in this role is communication of scholarly knowledge and insight improving the processes of opinion and will formation taking place in the different forums in civil society. In face-to-face settings and in meetings or discussions in mass media, communication has to be real, participants have to be willing to learn from each other and to answer a well-founded critique. "In a process of enlightenment, there are only participants" (Habermas 1994:101). There can be no talk about scientistic philosopher kings; impairments among professionals are a too well-known phenomenon, as are lay impairments (Lindblom 1990:175–209). Organized skepticism, the "rigorous policing" in publics, is essential both in scientific and democratic discourse.

A PUBLIC INTELLECTUAL WHO LACKED THIS TASK IN HIS OWN CONCEPTION OF ACADEMIC ROLE SET

It is illuminating to use Mertonian concepts to analyze the academic role of the intellectual, for instance, framing it within his sophisticated conception of role set (1968:41–45, 422–438) and "institutionalized motivation" ([1957] 1973:294). But we may also shift orientation and ask about Merton's conception of the academic role set, and if this set includes the role of disseminator and debater. In an article on aging and age structure in science, he argues that the status (position) of scientist is the institutional basis for a fourfold role set, indicated by the terms "research," "teaching," "administration," and "gate keeping" (Merton [1972] 1973b:519–522). In my view it is fruitful to reword and relocate his gate-keeping role. It naturally belongs as a subtask within three of the roles in the fivefold role set presented above: in research (as recruiting members of research groups); in teaching and study (as admitting people to PhD programs); and in institutional governance (as employing academics in universities). Reformulated in my terminology, Merton's conception of the academic role set comprises three basic roles: research, teaching, and institutional governance. Merton discusses professions such as engineer, doctor, and lawyer in several publications (e.g., Merton et al. 1983). It is therefore unproblematic to add academics as experts (or professionals) as a fourth role in his typology, in accordance with the typology presented above.

But the role of popularization and participation in public discourse is missing from Merton's conception of the academic role set. This is surprising. The lack of a concept for this kind of activity creates tensions in Merton's work, not only in relation to the societal movements and academic traditions he belonged to as a young man, but also to his own academic practice and theoretical ambitions throughout his career. As we have seen, the young Merton defined himself as a public intellectual, insisting on the dissemination of a scientific culture into the general culture of society. In the history of Columbia University, the mature Merton is identified as an important public intellectual (McCaughey 2003:375ff), and in other studies as an example—a role model—of a public intellectual (Bender 1993:77; Hollinger 1996:80–96, 133–134). There is an inconsistency between his own academic practice and his theory about it.

Merton's essay "The Self-Fulfilling Prophecy" is one of the best ever published by an academic in the role of public intellectual; it is an exemplar in the Kuhnian sense. This essay was first presented to a general audience in the *Antioch Review* during the summer of 1948. Here Merton both introduced a basic theoretical perspective on social interaction and an eminently relevant perspective on how to criticize and change social realities. In an article from 1989 he informs us: "I had deliberately decided to publish that paper in a journal for the general reader rather than in an academic journal. For I thought then, precisely forty years ago, as I still do now, that the concept of the self-fulfilling prophecy held direct and significant implications for the conduct of social life; I wanted to have it become more quickly and widely known than is ordinarily the case with the diffusion of technical sociological ideas into the public consciousness" (1989:311).

This apt comment makes it even stranger that he did not identify this role as part of the legitimate role set of academics. He wanted the concept of self-fulfilling prophecy to be widely known so that it could become integrated into everyday life and influence ordinary definitions of situations. To achieve this, he had to communicate with a wide, general audience, to exert an influence on the prevailing definitions of situations. In the 1938 article Merton presents an interesting analysis of different forms of social coordination in liberal and dictatorial societies: "In a liberal society, integration derives primarily from the body of cultural norms toward which human activity is oriented. In a dictatorial structure, integration is effected primarily by formal organization and centralization of social control" ([1938] 1968:602). This distinction is only mentioned and not further developed. It could be connected to the model about the legitimate circulation of power in a liberal democracy presented in the foregoing section. In such self-governing societies that regard its adult inhabitants as equal, free, and rational members of demos, the rationality of the processes of cultural reproduction and political discourse is essential. Building an infrastructure that channels scientific knowledge and insight into these processes is the basic legitimation of the role of academic as public intellectual, and as such is vitally important.

Why did Merton not recognize this role? We cannot simply point to a difference between European and American traditions as an explanation, a fact we are reminded of if we compare Merton and Parsons. In the classic study of the modern research university, *The American University* (1973), Parsons and Platt distinguish between four fundamental functions for universities: 1) research and graduate training (in graduate schools); 2) general education (in colleges); 3) the training of professional practitioners (in professional schools); and 4) contributions to "societal definitions of the situation" by "intellectuals" (268). Their conception of the intellectual task is similar to what in this article has been called "dissemination" (popularization and public discourse). As intellectuals, academics communicate with a "diffuse public, both inside and outside of the university, but *always* with a segment outside" (275). Compared to "the practitioners of applied professions," the "analogy to the *client* population . . . lies in the intellectually interested public" and public forums in liberal democracies (282, 293).[11] They observe that the intellectual function "has not become so formally institutionalized in organizational divisions of the university system," as is the case with the others (6, 292). It is interesting to note that Parsons and Platt see nothing natural in the lack of an institutional infrastructure in the American research university. Instead, they speak about a "structural vacuum" and recommend the development of a more adequate infrastructure (292).

Today, there seems to be a widespread, renewed interest in American sociology about academics as public intellectuals. Michael Burawoy's presidential address to the American Sociological Association in 2004 was on the importance of "public sociology" (Burawoy 2005; also Clawson et al. 2007; Nichols 2007). This movement among American sociologists has stimulated similar debates in other parts of the world (see, e.g., *The British Journal of Sociology* no 3, 2005; Jacobsen 2008). But whereas the problem with Merton in this context is the lack of a concept of the academic as public intellectual, Burawoy's conception of public sociology encompasses too much. It undoubtedly includes dissemination and participation in public discourse, but it also includes other disciplinary activities such as teaching, expert activity for client groups (for instance, in local community development), and PR for sociology as a discipline. The analytical distinctions between "public sociology" and political activity outside disciplinary activity are also too unclear (Kalleberg 2005).

One could also compare Merton with mainstream traditions in American academic and public life, giving the same surprising result. Some of the leading contributors within American pragmatism—such as John Dewey and George H. Mead—belonged to the same generation as Durkheim and Weber. They were radical democrats and commonsense thinkers, not only insisting that science was enlightened common sense, but also that science should enlighten common sense and general political discourse. In his classic book *The Public and its Problems* (1927), Dewey warns against the twin perversions of "academic specialism" with little or no connection to social relevance, and a "public" filled with advertisements and "propaganda," which creates a culture of "sensations" (168). He recommends the development and design of genuine publics characterized by "debate, discussion, and persuasion," where scientific "dissemination" has an important place, fused with the use of art (182–84, 208–9). It is not difficult to draw the long intellectual lines of the American academic in public life, from Benjamin Franklin and Thomas Jefferson, through Dewey and Mead, to C. W. Mills (1959) and Lindblom (1990).

Merton knew well the European traditions of public enlightenment, which strongly influence American research universities. The academic culture that, for simplicity, we call the Humboldt tradition has been essential for the development of universities and general academic cultures in the West for the last two centuries, including in the United States (Clark 1995:1–4, 19–37,

219–222). There was a strong German influence on the design and development of the leading institutions in the United States during the last century (Clark 1995:116–124). The four tasks documented and analyzed by Parsons and Platt—research, teaching, the training of professionals, and the role of the "intellectual"—are easy to reconcile with the ambitions of the Humboldt model (Habermas 1989; Kalleberg 2000). The subrole of public intellectual is related to what the Berlin reformers who designed the Humboldt university defined as the task of enlightenment (*Aufklärung*) (Kalleberg 2008:20–22).

It is surprising that Merton did not introduce an "intellectual task" as a general task in the academic role set with a corresponding role as public intellectual. His noncognitivism with regard to normative analysis may be an important element in the explanation of that. Public intellectuals have to make normative judgments about social relevance and present normative arguments for recommendations and warnings. In my view the task of dissemination and participation in public discourse with scientific knowledge is not only compatible with Merton's practice and reasoning, it is also an improvement on the Mertonian structural analysis of the interdependencies between science and society.

In this area as a field of interaction for deliberating citizens, institutional redesign is essential to achieve better balances between market, state, and civil society. We need to develop more appropriate institutions, role sets, and practices to stimulate the interplay between science and other knowledge institutions—the role of the school system is pivotal—in public discourse (Kalleberg 2000, 2008). A recent change in the Norwegian constitution concerning the freedom of expression is an interesting example on the macro level of a nation. The commission suggesting the revision argued for the importance of rational deliberation in democracy (see NOU [1999] 2005). There are several interesting ideas in the new article on the freedom of expression, including this clause on the maintenance and development of an adequate institutional infrastructure: "The State authorities shall create conditions that facilitate open and enlightened public discourse." This underlines the responsibility of the democratic state—representing the common interests of citizens as free and equal members of the demos—for ensuring that individuals and groups in practice are given opportunities to express their opinions and meet relevant and rational opposition. State support for mass media, public funding of schools and universities, and public support of the arts and non-governmental organizations are mentioned as examples.

Notes

1. This story about titles is even a little more complicated. The title of the essay given on its opening page in 1942 is actually "A Note on Science and Democracy" (115). On the page giving the contents of the journal's first issue, however, the essay is titled "A Note on Science and Technology in a Democratic Order," and this was the one that Merton referred to as the original title when republishing it.

2. Another example of implicit reconstructive analysis can be found in his conceptualization of paradigms as the "identification and organization of what has been implicit in work of the past rather than the invention of new strategies for research" (1968:69). Although he was ambivalent about it in his research practice, Merton tended to assume that such activity was "theoretical" and not "empirical." I have problematized and criticized this interpretation (2007:147–152).

3. The first task is important in this kind of reconstructive research, because some classic contributors—for instance Plato, Hobbes, Tocqueville, and Weber—also remain contemporaries (Habermas 1984:140). The use of classics as contemporaries is a peculiar research strategy in social science and the humanities, a phenomenon of no or little importance in the natural sciences. Good examples of the three components in reconstructive studies can be found in Habermas's work on Mead (1998b) and Boudon's (2006a) on Tocqueville. In a review of a *Festschrift* for Merton, Boudon (1977:1356) mentions Stinchcombe's chapter as a contribution of the same kind, establishing that it is possible to identify "a general theory of social action in Merton's work" and making an "effort to make explicit this implicit general theory."

4. In a clarification of Austin's distinction between illocutions and perlocutions in the analysis of speech acts, Habermas argues that the strategic use of language is parasitic on "the use of language with an orientation to reaching understanding" (Habermas 1984:286–195, quote from 288).

5. When Merton in 1994 received the National Medal of Science from the American President, his analysis of self-fulfilling prophecies was explicitly mentioned as part of the motivation.

6. Hartshorne (1937:38–39) noted the similarity of the perversion of the humanistic Humboldt ideals in "the National Socialist, the Italian Fascist, the Russian Communist, or the Japanese Imperialist university of our days." Interestingly, he also noted the affinities between this kind of university and Plato's ideas about nondemocratic rule by a meritocracy. On the Harvard sociologist Edward Hartshorne (1912–1946) and his impressive work on and in Germany, see Gerhardt 2009.

7. Nazi Germany and what led to it interested Merton as "an extreme and therefore illuminating case of a more general relationship" (1968:587–588) between science and the political order. He criticized those who would forget this experience "as an exceptional and pathological case, with no implications for the more general situation"

(ibid.), assuming that they and their society have nothing to learn from it. Recently, the historian Fritz Stern has presented a similar argument, insisting that "no country is immune to the temptations of pseudo-religious movements of repression such as those to which Germany succumbed. . . . the lessons I had learned about German history had a frightening relevance to the United States today" (2006:4). Merton was well aware of pressures in the United States on academic freedom. One example was during World War I when everything German came under pressure after the United States entered the war in 1916, including pressures on academics in Merton's own university, Columbia University (see Weiler 2008). Another example was the McCarthy period. The study *The Academic Mind: Social Scientists in a Time of Crisis* represents a high point in the achievements of the Columbia University's *Bureau of Applied Social Research* (Lazarsfeld et al. 1958).

8. It is ironic that so many contemporary social scientists tend to regard such points of view as idealistic, pointing to the realism in the tradition from Adam Smith, supposedly only treating human beings as self-centered and greedy. But Adam Smith is the author of a classic text in moral sociology and sociology of emotions, *The Theory of Moral Sentiments* (1759), where he insists on our natural, unavoidable solidarity with others and the influence of a well-informed, impartial spectator in the emergence and improvement of social and moral norms. The similarities between Adam Smith and George Herbert Mead are striking. On Smith as a classic in sociology, see Kalleberg 2009.

9. To quote 49 of the 272 words of the Gettysburg Address: "our fathers brought forth on this continent a new nation, conceived in Liberty, and dedicated to the proposition that all men are created equal . . . .It is for us the living rather to be dedicated to the unfinished work which they who fought here have thus far so nobly advanced." Wills (1992) gives a masterly interpretation of the text and its context. Merton also opens up for such a historical perspective on democracy as an unfinished historical project, as when speaking about "obstacles to the path of full democratization" (1968a:610). At the end of the essay on self-fulfilling prophecies, he discusses "appropriate institutional and administrative conditions" that put an end to vicious social circles, and approvingly quotes Tocqueville's claim that "the field of possibilities is much more extensive than men living in their various societies are ready to imagine."

10. Merton assisted the psychologist Kenneth Clark "to put together the much-debated Social Science Brief on desegregation in the public schools for Brown v. Board of Education" (Merton 1996:349). His studies on an integrated community, mentioned in the essay on self-fulfilling prophecies, were important in this context.

11. Merton mentions the same analytical distinction in his codification of a paradigm for sociology of knowledge and in his discussion of the "intellectual" in public bureaucracy (1968:263, 266, 536–537), but does not elaborate it.

References

Barendt, Eric. 2005. *Freedom of Speech.* 2nd ed. Oxford: Oxford University Press.

Bender, Thomas. 1993. *Intellect and Public Life: Essays on the Social History of Academic Intellectuals in the United States.* Baltimore: Johns Hopkins University Press.

——. 1998. "Politics, Intellect, and the American University, 1945–1995." In *American Academic Culture in Transformation*, ed. T. Bender, C. E. Schorske. Princeton: Princeton University Press, 17–54.

Bernstein, Richard. 1976. *The Restructuring of Social and Political Theory.* New York: Harcourt Brace Jovanovich.

Bok, Derek. 2003. *Universities in the Marketplace: The Commercialization of Higher Education.* Princeton, NJ: Princeton University Press.

Boudon, Raymond. 1977. Book review of *Festschrift* to Merton, ed. L. A. Coser. *American Journal of Sociology* 82 (6):1356–1361.

——. 1996. "Generalizing the 'Rational Choice Model' into a Cognitivist Model." *Rationality and Society* 8 (2):123–150.

——. 1998. "Limitations of Rational Choice Theory." *American Journal of Sociology* 104:817–828.

——. 2004. *The Poverty of Relativism.* Oxford: The Bardwell Press.

——. 2006a. *Tocqueville for Today.* Oxford: The Bardwell Press.

——. 2006b. "Are we doomed to see the *homo sociologicus* as a rational or as an irrational idiot?" In *Understanding Choice, Explaining Behavior*, ed. J. Elster, O. Gjelsvik, A. Hylland, and K. Moene, 25–42. Oslo: Unipub.

Brunkhorst, Hauke. 1987. *Der Intellektuelle im Land der Mandarine.* Frankfurt: Suhrkamp.

Burawoy, Michael. 2005. "2004 American Sociological Association Presidential address: For Public Sociology." *The British Journal of Sociology* 56:259–294.

Camic, Charles, and Neil Gross. 2001. "The New Sociology of Ideas." In *The Blackwell Companion to Sociology*, ed. J. Blau, 236–249. Cambridge: Blackwell.

Chambers, Simone. 1996. *Reasonable Democracy: Jürgen Habermas and the Politics of Discourse.* Ithaca: Cornell University Press.

Clark, Burton. 1995. *Places of Inquiry: Research and Advanced Education in Modern Universities.* Berkeley: University of California Press.

Clawson, Dan, Robert Zussman, Joya Misra, Naomi Gerstel, Randall Stokes, Douglas L. Anderton, Michael Burawoy. 2007. *Public Sociology: Fifteen Eminent Sociologists Debate Politics and the Profession in the Twenty-first Century.* Berkeley: University of California Press.

Coser, Louis. 1970. *Men of Ideas: A Sociologist's View.* New York: Simon and Schuster.

Crossan, John D., and Jonathan L. Reed. 2005. *In Search of Paul. How Jesus' Apostle Opposed Rome's Empire with God's Kingdom.* London: SPCK.

Dahl, Robert A. 1989. *Democracy and its Critics*. New Haven: Yale University Press.

——. 1990. *After the Revolution? Authority in a Good Society*. Rev. ed. New Haven: Yale University Press.

——. 1998. *On Democracy*. New Haven: Yale University Press.

Dewey, John. [1927] 1954. *The Public and its Problems*. Athens: Swallow Press/Ohio University Press.

Elster, Jon. 1983. *Explaining Technical Change*. Cambridge: Cambridge University Press.

——, ed. 1998. *Deliberative Democracy*. Cambridge: Cambridge University Press.

Enebakk, Vidar. 2007. "The Three Merton Theses." *Journal of Classical Sociology* 7 (2):221–238.

Furet, Frank. 2004. *Where Have All the Intellectuals Gone?: Confronting 21st Century Philistinism*. London: Continuum.

Gerhardt, Uta. 2009. "Nachwort. Nazi Madness: Der Soziologe Edward Y. Hartshorne und das Harvard-Projekt." In *Nie mehr zurück in dieses Land. Augenzeugen berichthen über die Novemberpogrome 1938*, ed. U. Gerhardt & T. Karlau, 319–358. Berlin: Propyläen.

Guttman, Amy, Dennis Thompson. 1996. *Democracy and Disagreement*. Cambridge: Cambridge University Press.

Habermas, Jürgen 1989a. "The Idea of the University: Learning Processes." In *The New Conservatism*, ed. J. Habermas, 100–127. Cambridge: MIT Press.

——. 1989b. "Heinrich Heine and the Role of the Intellectual in Germany." In *The New Conservatism*, ed. J. Habermas, 71–99. Cambridge: MIT Press.

——. 1992. "Individuation through Socialization: On George Herbert Mead's Theory of Subjectivity." In *Postmetaphysical Thinking*, ed. J. Habermas, 149–204. Cambridge: MIT Press.

——. 1994. "What Theories Can Accomplish—and What They Can't." In *The Past as Future*, ed. J. Habermas. (Interviewed by M. Haller), 99–120. Cambridge, UK: Polity Press.

——. 1996. *Between Facts and Norms. Contributions to a Discourse Theory of Law and Democracy*. Cambridge: MIT Press

——. 1998. "Civil Society and the Constitutional State." In *Habermas and the Korean Debate*, ed. Sang-Jin Han, 273–288. Seoul: Seoul National University Press.

Hartshorne, Edward Y. 1937. *The German Universities and National Socialism*. London: George Allen and Unwin Ltd.

Hochschild, Arlie R. 2003. *The Managed Heart: the Commercialization of Human Feeling*. 2nd Ed. Berkeley: University of California Press.

Hollinger, David A. 1996. *Science, Jews, and Secular Culture: Studies in Mid-Twentieth-Century American Intellectual History*. Princeton: Princeton University Press.

Jacobsen, Michael H., ed. 2008 *Public Sociology: Proceedings of the Anniversary Conference Celebrating Ten Years of Sociology in Aalborg*. Aalborg, Denmark: Aalborg University Press.

Jacoby, Russell. 1987. *The Last Intellectuals: American Culture in the Age of Academe*. New York: The Noonday Press.

Jones, James H. 1993. *Bad Blood: The Tuskegee Syphilis Experiment*. Rev. ed. New York: Free Press.

Kalleberg, Ragnvald. 2000. "Universities: Complex Bundle Institutions and the Projects of Enlightenment." In *Comparative Social Research*. vol. 19, 219–255.

——. 2005a. "What Is 'Public Sociology'? Why and How Should It Be Made Stronger?" *The British Journal of Sociology* 56 (3):387–393.

——. 2005b. "Samfunnsvitenskapenes oppgaver, arbeidsmåter og grunnlagsproblemer"/The Tasks, Methods and Basic Problems of the Social Sciences." In *Introduksjon til sammfunnsfag*, ed. F. Engelstad C. E. Grenness, R. Kalleberg, R. Malnes, 92–193. Oslo: Gyldendal Akademisk.

——. 2007. "A Reconstruction of the Ethos of Science." *Journal of Classical Sociology* 7 (2):137–160.

——. 2008. "Sociologists as Public Intellectuals in the Norwegian Project of Enlightenment." In *Academics as Public Intellectuals*, ed. Sven Eliaeson and Ragnvald Kalleberg, 17– 48. Newcastle: Cambridge Scholars Publishing.

——. 2009a. "Can Normative Disputes Be Settled Rationally? On Sociology as a Normative Discipline." In *Raymond Boudon: A Life in Sociology*, vol. 2, ed. Muhamed Cherkaoui and Peter Hamilton, 251–269. Oxford, UK: The Bardwell Press.

——. 2009b. "Adam Smith as a Classic in Sociology". Unpublished paper, presented to an international conference, University of Oslo, August 27–29.

Kershaw, Ian. 2007. *Fateful Choices: Ten Decisions that Changed the World 1940–1941*. New York: The Penguin Press.

Kevles, Daniel J. 1998. *The Baltimore Case: A Trial of Politics, Science, and Character*. New York, NY: W.W. Norton and Co.

Kyvik, Svein. 2005. "Popular Science Publishing and Contributions to Public Discourse among University Faculty," *Science Communication* 26 (3):288–311.

Lafferty, William M. "Varieties of Democratic Experience: Normative Criteria for Cross-National Assessments of Citizenship," *Bürger und Demokratie in Ost und West: Festschrift für Hans-Dieter Klingemann*, ed. D. Fuchs, E. Roller, and B. Wessels, 50–72. Wiesbaden: Westdeutscher Verlag.

Lazarsfeld, Paul F., W. Thielens, Jr. 1958. *The Academic Mind: Social Scientists in a Time of Crisis*. Glencoe, IL: The Free Press.

Lindblom, Charles. 1990. *Inquiry and Change: The Troubled Attempt to Understand and Shape Society*. New Haven: Yale University Press.

McCaughey, Robert A. 2003. *Stand, Columbia: A History of Columbia University in the City of New York, 1754–2004*. New York: Columbia University Press.

Merton, Robert K. [1938] 1968. "Science and the Social Order." In *Social Theory and Social Structure*, 591–603.

———. [1938] 1970. *Science, Technology and Society in Seventeenth Century England*. New York: Howard Fertig.

———. [1942] 1968. "Science and Democratic Social Structure." In *Social Theory and Social Structure*, 604–615.

———. [1948] 1968. "The Self-Fulfilling Prophecy." In *Social Theory and Social Structure*, 475–490.

———. [1957] 1973. "Priorities in Scientific Discovery." In *The Sociology of Science: Theoretical and Empirical Investigations*, 286–324.

———. 1968. *Social Theory and Social Structure*. Enlarged ed. New York: The Free Press.

———. [1972] 1973a. "The Perspectives of Insiders and Outsiders." In *The Sociology of Science: Theoretical and Empirical Investigations*, 99–136.

———. [1972] 1973b. "Age, Aging, and Age Structure in Science." In *The Sociology of Science: Theoretical and Empirical Investigations*, 497–559. With H. Zuckerman.

———. 1973. *The Sociology of Science: Theoretical and Empirical Investigations*. Ed. and with an introduction by Norman W. Storer. Chicago: The University of Chicago Press.

———. 1976. *Sociological Ambivalence and Other Essays*. New York: The Free Press.

———. 1984. "The Fallacy of the Latest Word: The Case of 'Pietism and Science'." *American Journal of Sociology* 89 (5):1091–1121.

———. 1985. *On the Shoulders of Giants*. New York: Harcourt, Brace, Jovanovich, Publishers.

———. 1987. "Three Fragments from a Sociologist's Notebooks: Establishing the Phenomenon, Specified Ignorance, and Strategic Research Materials." *American Review of Sociology* 13:1–28.

———. 1989. "Unanticipated Consequences and Kindred Sociological Ideas: A Personal Gloss." In *L'Opera di R. K. Merton e la Sociologica Congemporanea*, ed. Mongardini and Tabboni, 307–329. Genova: Edizioni Culturali Internazionali Genova.

———. 1990. "STS: Foreshadowing of an Evolving Research Program in the Sociology of Science". In *Puritanism and the Rise of Modern Science. The Merton Thesis*, ed. Cohen, 334–371. London: Rutgers University Press.

———. 1996a. *On Social Structure and Science*. Ed. and introduced by Piotr Sztompka. Chicago: University of Chicago Press.

———. 1996b. "A Life of Learning". In *On Social Structure and Science*, 339–359.

Merton, Vanessa, Robert K. Merton, Elinor Barber. 1983. "Client Ambivalence in Professional Relationships: The Problem of Seeking Help from Strangers." In *New

Directions in Helping. Vol. 2, Help-Seeking, ed. B. M. DePaulo, A. Nadler, J. D. Fisher, 13–44. New York: Academic Press.

Mills, Charles. W. 1959. *The Sociological Imagination*. Oxford: Oxford University Press.

Myhre, Jan E. 2008. "Academics as intellectuals: Studying Norwegian Academics and Intellectuals in the Public Sphere." In *Intellectuals in the Public Sphere in Britain and Norway after World War II*, ed. J. E. Myhre, 183–208. Oslo: Unipub.

Myrdal, Gunnar, with the assistance of Richard M. E. Sterner and Arnold M. Rose. 1944. *An American Dilemma: The Negro Problem and Modern Democracy*. New York: Harper and Brothers.

Nichols, Lawrence T., ed. 2007. *Public Sociology: The Contemporary Debate*. New Brunswick: Transaction Publishers.

NOU. [1999] 2005. *"There Shall Be Freedom of Expression." Proposed New Article 100 of the Norwegian Constitution: Report of Commission Appointed by Royal Decree on 26 August 1996*. Oslo: Ministry of Justice and the Police, The Norwegian National Commission for UNESCO.

Parsons, Talcott, and Gerald M. Platt. 1973. *The American University*. Cambridge: Harvard University Press.

Restivo, Sal. 1995. "The Theory Landscape in Science Studies: Sociological Traditions." In *Handbook of Science and Technology Studies*, ed. Jasanoff et al., 95–110. London: Sage.

Slagstad, Rune. 2004. "Shifting Knowledge Regimes: The Metamorphoses of Norwegian Reforms." *Thesis Eleven* 77:65–83.

Smith, Adam. [1759] 2002. *The Theory of Moral Sentiments*. Cambridge: Cambridge University Press.

Southern, David W. 1987. *Gunnar Myrdal and Black-White Relations. The Use and Abuse of An American Dilemma, 1944–1969*. Baton Rouge: Louisiana State University Press.

Stehr, Nico. 1978. "The Ethos of Science Revisited." In *The Sociology of Science*, ed. J. Gaston. Chicago: University of Chicago Press.

Stern, Fritz. 2006. *Five Germanys I Have Known*. New York: Farrar, Straus, and Giroux.

Sztompka, Piotr. 1986. *Robert K. Merton: An Intellectual Profile*. New York: St. Martin's Press.

Weiler, Bernd. 2008. "Thus Spoke the Scientist: Franz Boas' Critique of the Role of the United States in World War I". In *Academics as Public Intellectuals*, ed. S. Eliaeson and R. Kalleberg, 65–86. Newcastle: Cambridge Scholars Publishing.

Wills, Gary. 1992. *Lincoln at Gettysburg: The Words that Remade America*. New York: Simon and Schuster.

Zuckerman, Harriet. 1989. "The Other Merton Thesis." *Science in Context* 3:239–267.

10

Merton's Sociology of Rhetoric

PETER SIMONSON

I am persuaded that he didn't really appreciate
the value of what he said there.
—Robert K. Merton, *On the Shoulders of Giants*

A quarter of the way into his critical 1941 review of Karl Mannheim's sociology of knowledge, Robert K. Merton mobilized an epithet that summarized the shortcomings he saw in the Marxist theory of ideology, and set it off from an intellectually rigorous and epistemologically sound sociology of knowledge. Polemical, anti-intellectualistic, and argumentatively suspect, the theory of ideology was "akin to rhetoric rather than science" (Merton [1941b] 1968:548). Since Merton was committed to sociology as a scientific endeavor, there was little doubt about the valence of the "rhetoric" epithet, which functioned to distance the kind of work he championed from its competitors, and to distance science from rhetoric.

As a matter of fact, the story was more complicated. Merton's own trajectory to that point revealed a subtle and interwoven relation between science and rhetoric, one not suggested by the traditional and formulaic dichotomy he fell back upon. That formulaic boundary-work, which was itself as rhetorical as it was scientific, was perhaps of a piece with the mood of Merton's anti-Mannheim essay, described by Alan Sica as "uncharacteristically pungent and unforgiving when compared with Merton's usual modus operandi" (Sica, Chapter 8 of this volume). I might say that the pungent and unforgiving were in fact semiregular Mertonian moods, as C. Wright Mills among others could later attest, but I agree with Sica that the 1941 article presents a puzzle. I will also suggest that the epigraph Merton selected for that article offers an unintended clue about how to read it, which Sica's chapter and my own in different ways follow out: "But indeed language has succeeded until recently in hiding from us almost all the things we talk about."

The quote could have been Freud's, but was actually penned by I. A. Richards. It appeared in Richards's important *Principles of Literary Criticism* (1925), though Merton somehow couldn't bring himself to mention that source, either in the epigraph or in his article's twelfth footnote, where Richards again warrants quotation, but his book's manifestly unscientific title does not. Merton recognized, however, that Richards, the Cambridge-trained philosopher and literary critic, knew something about language, and the ways it could obscure the subjects we talk about. For two decades, Richards had charted meaning and misunderstanding in a series of significant books, most recently *The Philosophy of Rhetoric* (1936), which had set out "to revive an old subject," rhetoric, whose reputation had sunk so low "that we would do better just to dismiss it to Limbo than to trouble ourselves with it—unless we can find reason for believing that it can become a study that will minister successfully to important needs" (3). Surveying Merton's work before and after 1941, I would argue that rhetoric ministered successfully to a range of his own needs, both scholarly and personal. The epithet in the Mannheim review, prying rhetoric from science, functions to hide from view the part played by rhetoric in Merton's thinking to that point, and to deflect attention from rhetoric's role in his subsequent writings, including his sociology of science.

As Merton himself confessed to me, in a conversation two years before his death, rhetoric was a "very important" resource for him. How should we take that confession? One route would lead to Merton the wordsmith and prose stylist. His lectures captivated classroom, professional, and occasional public audiences, from his days as an instructor at Harvard in the 1930s through the autobiographical "Life of Learning" speech he delivered to the American Council of Learned Societies in 1994 (when with casual elegance he mentioned that he was born Jewish, a fact he had generally kept from public view before then).[1] His writing was famously described in a 1961 *New Yorker* profile as being crafted "too well for a sociologist," a story that also remarked on his facility with "metaphor and other literary devices—so rarely used in sociology as to be called Mertonisms by some of his associates"

(Hunt 1961:62, 44). His editing of other people's manuscripts is legendary, totaling some two-hundred-and-fifty books and two thousand articles in the "back-of-the-envelope estimate" he offered in the "Life of Learning" speech ([1994] 1996:357). And his love for words, which he habitually deployed with analytical precision and investigated with historical and sociological aplomb, served as the dispositional midwife for a long string of concepts and publications, running from "the serendipity pattern" to "the Kelvin dictum" and beyond (e.g., Merton 1945; Merton, Sills, Stigler 1984; Merton and Barber 2004; see Zuckerman and Camic, Chapters 11 and 12 of this volume). Though Merton felt some ambivalence when people praised his style and his talent for coining terms—fearing such encomia diminished his substantive scholarly contributions—it would not be unreasonable to conclude that his confession that rhetoric had been "very important" to him was an index of his lifelong devotion to words and cultivation of the arts of using them through speech and writing.

I think Merton was saying more, however, some of which lay latent in the manifest comments he made to me about rhetoric late in his life. The immediate prompt for his response was my observation that four of the six chapters of his first freestanding published book, *Mass Persuasion* (1946), opened with long quotations from classic texts in the rhetorical tradition—Plato's *Gorgias* and *Phaedrus*, Aristotle's *Rhetoric*, and Thomas Hobbes's *Art of Rhetorick*. He told me he wanted to remind propaganda researchers that the subject they studied was an old one. As I have since discovered, reading through his published and unpublished papers before 1946, Merton was knowledgeable about the terms and texts of the European rhetorical tradition, and had longer standing interest in rhetoric's twentieth-century variant, mass-mediated propaganda, which dated back at least to his graduate school years at Harvard. This familiarity and interest led him to describe twentieth-century propaganda as the historical offspring of ancient and early modern rhetoric. More consequentially, Merton's encounters with propaganda and rhetoric in the late 1930s helped stoke some of the foundational insights in his early sociology of science and catalyzed formative moments in the development of his scientifically guided sociology. It turns out that rhetoric and science were intertwined in Merton's work, to a degree he almost certainly didn't realize when he confessed that rhetoric had been very important to him.

Drawing upon a mixture of historical evidence and neopragmatist re-description, I want to argue that amongst all else he did in his remarkable nine-decade life, Robert K. Merton laid the groundwork for a sociology of rhetoric. The label is mine, but I like to think that Merton too might accept it, as the sort of reconceptualization of earlier work for later purposes that he profitably engaged in himself, from his earliest publications onward.[2] Richard Rorty (1991) made the case for recontextualization as form of inquiry, and he provides the philosophical grounding for my methodology here. I believe that redescription and recontextualization of Merton's work in terms of the rhetorical tradition is warranted by both the historical evidence and the potential interpretive payoff. On the evidentiary side, Merton makes use of terms, concepts, distinctions, and texts that arise in the intellectual tradition of rhetorical study that dates back to classical antiquity. That tradition classically defined rhetoric as both the art (*tekhnê*) of addressing the many through speech (for purposes of persuasion, instruction, or entertainment), and the kind of discourse produced by that art—oratory, sermons, and other modes of public address. Remarkably pliable, the intellectual tradition came to inform a variety of discursive practices over the centuries, extending beyond the spoken word to new media and to modes of inquiry and address practiced by elites in communication with one another. As I will show, Merton both drew upon rhetorical vocabulary and cast his attention to varieties of rhetorical discourse, from modern back to medieval times, which in turn provided the empirical base for what I am calling his sociology of rhetoric.

The interpretive payoff of recasting Merton rhetorically is potentially manifold. Within the contexts of this volume, it provides the historical run-up to Charles Camic's and Harriet Zuckerman's accounts of Merton's program of sociological semantics, which took off with the "serendipity" study of the 1950s, and accelerated in the last twenty years of his life. Merton paid careful attention to words and language throughout his life. Before embarking on that body of research Camic and Zuckerman deftly describe, Merton nourished his sociological interest in language through the entwined inventional springs of rhetoric and mass communications research. While "sociological semantics" is a label that nicely channeled Merton's scientific aspirations, "the sociology of rhetoric" indexes his persistent humanistic self, and casts his work as part of a longer historical conversation. For all his focus upon developing a professionalized, scientifically oriented sociology, Merton maintained bifocal attention to grander historical tales, too. By taking the opening provided by the historical evidence, I hope both to bring out Merton's humanist side, and contribute to the dialogue between rhetoric and sociology that dates back in the United States to the 1930s and '40s, through figures such as Merton, Richards, Kenneth Burke, Louis Wirth, and Hugh Dalziel Duncan (on whom, see Kenny 2008; Simonson 2010a).

While Merton's corpus as a whole invites itself to be read as a contribution to the rhetorical tradition, I focus here on a smaller body of his work, centered upon his propaganda and mass communications research of the 1940s, and extending backward to his seminal pre-1945 sociology of science, and forward to his stem-winding *On the Shoulders of Giants* (1965), letting them stand in as representatives of Merton's early, middle, and later sociologies of rhetoric. In each of the three periods, rhetoric and science function as counterparts and complements. He investigates rhetorical dimensions of science by reading printed texts, and he brings scientific scrutiny to the study of rhetoric through focused interviews, content analysis, and surveys analyzing radio and motion picture propaganda. In the early period, the 1930s, popular rhetoric was a vehicle through which Merton figured the ethos of science. In the middle period, the 1940s, science was a vehicle through which Merton figured mass communicated propaganda. In the later period, after 1950, his substantive interest returned to science and, in *On the Shoulders of Giants*, the rhetorical figures of elite discourse. In the early and later periods, Merton attended centrally to science and sometimes considered its rhetorical dimensions. In the middle period, he attended centrally to rhetoric and analyzed it from a scientific perspective. The first two had Merton engaged with *popular* rhetoric and propaganda—of scientific, civic, and, to a lesser extent, religious sorts. The post-1950 Merton, however, was far more ensconced in the sociological and discursive worlds of *elites*, a focus that matched his own personal trajectory into the highest echelons of professionalized sociology, and the beginning of his research program in sociological semantics. As a preface to tracing these developments and a means of throwing them into broader historical relief, I'll begin with a few comments about the classical rhetorical tradition Merton drew upon, and the twentieth-century revival of the subject, of which he was part.

Rhetoric: The Long and Wide View

The Greek word *rhetôrikê*, from which Merton's 1941 epithet was derived, was a neologism likely coined by Plato early in the fourth century B.C. to designate the activity of public speakers (Schiappa 2003). In the Greek-speaking world of his day, a *rhêtôr* was someone who regularly spoke in the political assembly. The *-ikê* suffix meant "art of," though Plato doubted that rhetoric was a true art (or *tekhnê*), that is, an activity guided by rational principles which might be established through dialectical inquiry and its characteristic methods of definition and division of a subject matter into its constituent parts. As Edward Schiappa has argued, it was one of many *-ikê* terms Plato coined, among them others that designated verbal arts, including dialectic (*dialektikê*) and eristic (*eristikê*)—the art of philosophical dialogue aimed at the discovery of truth (of which Plato's teacher Socrates was master), and the art of no-holds-barred contentious debate aimed at individual victory (often associated with the educational methods of Socrates's contemporary, the sophist Protagoras). Plato's early dialogue, the *Gorgias*, canonically established the term and concept of "rhetoric" in the Western intellectual tradition, and helped give it the negative valence that Merton drew upon. In the view that emerged from the *Gorgias*, rhetoric was both morally and epistemologically suspect—a form of flattering the masses that was more experiential knack than true art.

Though the term and concept of rhetoric was canonically established in written form through the *Gorgias*, it was almost certainly "orally published" (to borrow a Mertonism [1980]) in conversations with students at Plato's Academy. The most important of those students was, of course, Aristotle, whose subsequent treatise, *On Rhetoric*, offered a full-blown theoretical conceptualization of the art, its key parts, and its species. While Plato questioned rhetoric's status as a legitimate, theoretically grounded intellectual discipline, Aristotle took up a more empirically minded view, pointing out that "it is possible to observe" (*theôrein*, to see or "theorize") why some efforts at persuasion succeed, and that "such observation is the activity of an art" (*Rhetoric* 1.1.2).[3] While Plato was sharply critical of rhetoric's epistemological and moral status and privileged dialectic as a mode of inquiry, Aristotle took a more favorable view, calling rhetoric the counterpart (*antistrophos*) of dialectic: both were naturally occurring human activities that could be applied to any subject matter—dialectic "to test and uphold an argument," reach necessary conclusions, and issue in knowledge; rhetoric "to defend . . . and attack" particular positions and issue in probable or contingent judgments (1.1.1). Though both were natural, there was also the sense that dialectic was an activity reserved for the few, who carried it out in dialogues with each other, while rhetoric was the art of addressing *hoi polloi*, and issued in something less than certified knowledge. Merton would draw upon these understandings in his own work.

Subsequent generations of teacher-theorists built upon and extended Plato, Aristotle, and other Greek writers on the arts of speech. They codified and organized rhetoric in terms of five overarching categories that constituted the classical canon—invention, arrangement, style, memory, and delivery, a schema that both sequentially mapped the process of rhetorical production and provided a theoretical vocabulary for analyzing the efforts of others. In *De Oratore*, Cicero, the single most influential figure in the tradition, drew rhetoric and dialectic together under the heading of "eloquence," true knowledge spoken artfully. In *On Christian Doctrine*, Augustine, a former teacher of rhetoric, brought the pagan art into the Christian fold, joined rhetoric to hermeneutics, and laid the groundwork for establishing preaching as a theoretically informed rhetorical endeavor. In the Middle Ages, rhetoric was institutionalized as part of the classical trivium—along with grammar and dialectic, the arts of language, which prepared students for and complemented the arts of measurement represented in the four disciplines of the quadrivium (mathematics, geometry, astronomy, and music). Though classically an art of speech and embodied address, rhetoric found application in other media forms as well, from ancient letter writing to print discourse in the Renaissance. At various times, it also provided an architectonic method for organizing and engaging in other arts and sciences. The discipline has always had its critics—proponents of dialectic, logic, antirhetorical theology, and, later, empirical scientific inquiry chief among them—but as an art of communication and inquiry, it has proved both useful and resilient.[4]

Rhetoric is thus an intellectual tradition and a kind of discourse, and, to fast-forward in time, the twentieth century brought a revival of the tradition and a proliferation and mediated transformation of the discourse. Indeed, among all else that it was, the twentieth was The Rhetorical Century. This was partly owing to its ushering in a dramatic volumetric expansion of discourse traditionally classified as rhetorical—addressed to the many, and strategically aimed at persuasion, entertainment, education, or (perhaps less frequently) spiritual uplift. Powerful new technologies and techniques emerged that communicated, disseminated, and fundamentally reshaped rhetoric in its varied guises—motion pictures, radio, television, advertising, and public relations, to name a few. Along with words and sounds, images proliferated widely, reproduced and disseminated through mechanical and electronic means, each in their own ways moving or, as Merton would term it, "narcotizing" audiences (Lazarsfeld and Merton 1948). Industrial methods and bureaucratic organizations displaced individuals as the loci of rhetorical production, accelerating and rationalizing processes pioneered by church and state. The interwar years seemed awash with competing propagandas—political, commercial, religious, educational (Sproule 1997). New fields of study emerged that analyzed these and related phenomena, including the academic study of journalism (in the first decade of the century), film theory (1910s), propaganda analysis (1920s), public opinion research (1930s), radio research (1930s), mass communications research (1940s), cultural studies (1960s), and media studies (1980s). All were interdisciplinary affairs, grafted onto existing social sciences and humanities, and all picked up and extended traditional topics of rhetorical inquiry. Rarely was this genealogical connection made manifest, nor did scholars in these fields typically draw explicitly upon rhetorical texts and understandings, but there were a few exceptions. Merton was one of them.

After suffering more than a century of decline, rhetoric was revived as an explicit topic by philosophers and literary critics between and immediately after the world wars. Responding both to the changing communicative world around them and to exigencies internal to their disciplines, an array of important thinkers considered rhetoric anew and brought it to bear upon the problematics of the era. Among the key critics were Richards (1893–1979), Burke (1897–1993), Richard Weaver (1910–1963), and Marshall McLuhan (1911–1980). On the philosophical side, Martin Heidegger (1889–1976), Richard McKeon (1900–1985), and Chaim Perelman (1912–1984) all lectured or wrote on the subject.[5] Merton read and drew upon Richards and Burke in the 1930s and '40s, collaborated with McKeon in the 1950s, and intellectually sparred with McLuhan in professional and public contexts in the 1950s and '60s.[6] While Merton has not been grouped with these thinkers as part of the twentieth-century revival of rhetoric, I would argue that he belongs there as someone who developed a sociology of rhetoric that functioned as a counterweight and complement to the literary and philosophical approaches taken by his contemporaries. He worked it out in close work with the ideas and practices of science.

Rhetoric, Propaganda, and the Ethos of Science

Merton's early sociology of rhetoric had him wading through propaganda in figuring the normative ethos of science. As I have detailed further elsewhere, Merton had longstanding interest in propaganda (Simonson 2005). He was exposed to academic opinion on the subject as an undergraduate at Temple, where in the spring of 1931, he carefully penned class notes for Frederick Lund's Social Psychology course. Propaganda, language, and public opinion were interrelated topics in it, as they would be for Merton over the course of his career.[7] Papers from his Harvard years reveal his knowledge of common and semiarcane classical rhetorical terminology: for instance *enthymeme*, Aristotle's term for the shorthand rhetorical version of the syllogism, which Merton uses to characterize Durkheim's reasoning and John Creedy's propaganda analysis; and *periphrasis*, the Latin term for roundabout expression, which Merton used to chastise his own prose in self-editing marginalia in a paper he wrote for Talcott Parsons.[8]

He sought for himself a leaner, modernist prose style, absent embellishments but not artfulness or wit. He found models for that style when he turned to dissertation research in 1933, and plunged himself into seventeenth-century England. Rhetoric commanded major attention in early modern Europe (Rebhorn 2000), where proponents of Ciceronian eloquence did battle with those who rejected it as a barrier to philosophical clarity, scientific discovery, or religious piety. Puritan religious leaders and their fellow-traveling scientific brethren were among those who rejected the Ciceronian tradition, favoring perspicuity and a less adorned style to which Merton would also be drawn. He almost certainly encountered Thomas Hobbes's *Art of Rhetorick* (1681) while doing his dissertation research, and read Hobbes's Aristotelian gloss on rhetoric as "that Faculty, by which we understand what will serve our turn, concerning any Subject to win belief in the hearer." One of the keys to Merton's subsequent influence as a sociologist was precisely his own command of this Hobbesian faculty.

The dissertation led Merton through two characteristic rhetorical forms of seventeenth-century England—Puritan sermons, and the "words," "apologia," and "eloquence" of the scientists of the era (Merton [1938] 2001:82, 84, 88). This rhetorical discourse turned out to be pivotal to his broader argument, and the idea of "the ethos of science" that would eventually grow out from it. As indices of Puritan values and attitudes, Merton turned to "sermons and similar exhortations directed primarily toward the actual behavior of individuals," which, he argued, "not only reflected but also reinforced the dominant sentiments of the day" (60)—an understanding of communicative power that would find its way into his media research a decade later (Lazarsfeld and Merton 1948:100–108). Such rhetoric was the discursive manifestation of what Merton (following Sumner and Weber) termed "the Puritan ethos."[9] He had not yet coined the phrase "ethos of science," but for evidence of what he called scientists' "chief motive forces," he turned, among other sources, to Robert Boyle's "highly commended apologia of science" (*Some Considerations Touching the Usefulness of Experimental Natural Philosophy*), and "the resonant eloquence of that 'veritable apostle of the learned societies,' Francis Bacon," whom Merton called "one of the principal propagandists in favor of positive social evaluation of science" ([1938] 2001:83, 84, 88). The vocabulary of "motives," meanwhile, Merton drew from Burke's *Permanence and Change*, which he quoted from directly in an article published out of the dissertation, where he defended the methodological soundness of working from scientists' publicly expressed motives for their activities.[10] Burke and seventeenth-century rhetorical discourse were moving Merton closer to formulating the ethos of science.

In the last half of the 1930s, Merton's attention shifted from seventeenth-century science and propaganda to its twentieth-century variants. In 1936, after attending lectures delivered for Harvard's three-hundred-year anniversary, he typed notes to himself observing that "the attitudes of laymen toward the scientist and scientific propositions are largely the outcome of deliberate propaganda (dispensed by the scientist in the schools, by the preachers in church, by 'science news' services in newspapers, by 'popularizers' of science, etc)" (Merton n.d. [1936?], Sociology of Knowledge notebook, RKM, personal files). A year later, he explored rhetoric more systemically in dialectical inquiry with the "Parsons's Sociological Group," which considered among other topics "the problem of transition from power to rational authority, through the intermediary forms of persuasion and propaganda." The group, which kept track of its quasi-Socratic dialogues through rotating scribes, considered "a possible analogy between rational and coercive persuasion, and the Platonic dialectic and rhetoric." They aimed to define and distinguish propaganda and persuasion, and notes reveal Merton taking a leadership role in the process.[11]

His mind primed by considerations of science and propaganda, in the summer of 1937 Merton traveled to Europe, for the first time, ostensibly to improve his German by studying in Austria. In July, he slipped across the border into Germany, visited Heidelberg (where Parsons had done his graduate work in sociology), and collected pamphlets and other propaganda on Nazi and Jewish science. He exercised his German through careful reading and annotation of them.[12] Returning to the United States in September, he sent a note to George Lundberg, a section organizer for the American Sociology Society meetings in December. In July, Merton had agreed to give a report there of his study, "Patterns of Friendship." Now, other issues pressed harder. Merton inquired about presenting a different paper, "'Social Sources of the Repudiation of Science' (or Social Sources of the Revolt against Science)." Lundberg replied with interest, querying, "Am I right in assuming that you are referring to the German situation?" Merton responded,

> You are certainly correct in inferring that I deal with the Nazi situation, but this is treated as only one case in point. Other less obvious political instances as well as this extreme example of political sources of the repudiation of (some aspects of) science are considered. . . . In most general terms, I trace the sources of antagonism between scientists and representatives of other institutionalized spheres of human behavior, so that the theological, political, economic, etc. instance of such antagonism can be seen as special cases of a more general uniformity. The "scientific code" which, whether tacitly assumed or overtly expressed, can be shown to govern scientific research is involved as an important factor in such repudiations. In other words, I present a sociological theory of "the revolt(s) against science" which, I believe, accounts for the incidence and occurrence. I flatter myself that I shall be able to preserve an impartial attitude while dealing with a subject which, even (?) to a group of sociologists, is charged with emotional dynamite. This theory has grown out of a more or less continuous survey of relevant facts over a period of three years.[13]

Though he may have been surveying the relevant facts for three years, it was Merton's firsthand encounter with the "emotional dynamite" of Nazi propaganda that crystallized his thinking, as is evident when one surveys the footnotes for the published article "Science and the Social Order," which offered his first formulation of the concept he now called "the ethos of science" (Merton 1938). Through some version of what Burke (1935) called "perspective by incongruity," Merton came to recognize the ethos of science by way of the Nazi rhetoric that challenged it.[14]

In 1939, Merton moved on from Harvard to a two-year stint at Tulane, the site of intellectual production for the Mannheim review that opened my essay here. In apparent preparation for that review, he read Arthur Schopenhauer's *The Art of Controversy* (1830 [trans. 1896]), and typed up notes in dialogue with the book's claims. "Thus, Aristotle was correct in putting RHETORIC AND DIALECTIC together as both AIMING AT PERSUASION—the difference lies in the MODES OF PERSUASION; the first using devices which are directed at emotional bases of assent; the second compelling assent in terms of certain IMPERSONAL RULES OR CRITERIA." Merton went on to make the link between dialectic and "the INSTITUTION OF SCIENCE [which] is so designed as to provide RULES OF THE GAME with impersonal rules of evidence and pre-established criteria of validity" (Merton, notes to Schopenhauer's *The Art of Controversy*, n.d. [1940?], RKM, personal files, caps as typed). Merton would align himself, epistemologically and methodologically, on the side of science, dialectic, and impersonal criteria. But he was about to set off on a more thoroughgoing sociological inquiry into the rhetorical side of persuasion instead.[15]

Tulane provided him several roles through which to deepen his thinking on the subject. In September of 1939, after the Nazis invaded Poland, he played the academic expert and gave a public lecture on the role of propaganda among combatant nations. In April of 1940, as the Germans struck north into Denmark and Norway, he played the role of citizen and radio aficionado (he had built several receivers growing up), and sat transfixed, "wasting . . . too much time listening to short-wave European broadcasts," as he confessed to his undergraduate mentor, George E. Simpson. "I rationalize it by saying that it's valuable propaganda material which I can use in discussion of that subject. And, incidentally, I'm gradually becoming convinced that the field of propaganda, with all its implications, is practically the field of social psychology" (RKM to George E. Simpson, April 21, 1940, RKM, personal files). As a classroom instructor, Merton played out his conviction later that year, when he planned a course on Social Psychology that would feature propaganda as a main subject.[16] His interests were drifting further toward language, and he drew material for the course from a paper he was drafting, entitled "Ethnic Epithets: A Study in Language as a Means of Social Control."[17] In a recent publication, he had rejected the view that "overt behavior is 'more real' than verbal behavior" and that "verbal responses are simply epiphenomenal" (Merton 1940b:21).

The language of propaganda drew Merton's attention, but he was critical of studies to date. "Current analyses of the effectiveness of propaganda presuppose some knowledge of the demonstrable results of propaganda," he wrote. "In point of fact, systematic materials on such effects are notably wanting" (Merton and Johnson 1940–41).

A year later, Merton was teaching at Columbia, and was soon joining forces with Paul Lazarsfeld in an effort to remedy that epistemological want.

Building a Science of Propaganda and Mass Communications

If, in the Harvard and Tulane years, Merton used rhetoric as an invention-al source for insights into science, in his first decade at Columbia he mobilized science and dialectic as methods for generating knowledge about rhetoric. He worked under the intellectual signs of "propaganda" and "mass communications research," gathered in *Social Theory and Social Structure* as "the sociology of opinion and mass communications," counterpart (*antistrophos*) to the sociology of knowledge, as two "species of that genus of research which is concerned with the interplay between social structure and communications" ([1949] 1968:493). During the 1940s, he laid the groundwork for an empirically grounded cultural sociology of rhetoric, understood in its classic sense of discourse addressed to the masses, and operating in the realm of popular opinion (*doxa*) and belief (*pistis*).[18] This was a project he conducted during and after the war, in dialogue with Paul Lazarsfeld, and with significant assistance from the typically unsung women of the Office of Radio Research (ORR, rechristened the Bureau of Applied Social Research [BASR] in 1944) (on the women of the BASR, see McCormack, 2009; "Women in Media Research").

I've given detailed historical accounts of Merton's 1940s communications research elsewhere. The punch line is this: when Merton joined forces with Lazarsfeld at the ORR, a prepared mind met an opportunity structure that bore serendipitous fruit—a body of empirical and theoretical writings and a longstanding partnership that helped establish the contours of postwar American (and, to a certain degree, world) sociology. Propaganda and mass communications research was the anvil upon which the team of "Lazarsfeld and Merton" was forged, providing the base upon which they worked out the blend of codified methodologies, middle-range theory, and empirical research that defined the mainline of Columbia sociology. That semicoerced research also gave Merton the occasion to formulate (or rhetorically invent) some of his earliest middle-range theoretical concepts, including "the boomerang response," "pseudo-*Gemeinschaft*," "local and cosmopolitan influentials," "public image," "the status conferral function," "the narcotizing dysfunction," and, less directly, "the self-fulfilling prophecy." It also gave him experience overseeing organized research teams, which he would continue afterward in his famous unpublished public housing study (Merton et al. 1951), as well as his important research on medical education (Merton et al. 1957). It came in what was arguably Merton's most political decade as a trained sociologist, when left democratic sensibilities competed with the professionally identified liberalism that fully won the day with him by the early 1950s.[19]

Seizing openings Merton himself provided, I am here redescribing his propaganda and mass communication research as a scientifically oriented sociology of rhetoric. There were historical precedents for such scientific study. To take the long view, in the *Phaedrus* Plato ventriloquized Socrates to say that a true art of oratory would be able to classify different audiences and different rhetorical appeals, determine how some "are affected by this or that kind of speech in this or that way," and give an dialectically scrupulous account as to why (§271). Aristotle extended the project with a general classification of different kinds of audiences, and suggestions about what rhetorical topics (*topoi*) might move each (*Rhetoric* 2.12–17). More generally, by linking the art of rhetoric to observations of why some efforts at persuasion succeed (1.1.2), he opened the door to empirical study. The quasiscientific impulse to categorize audiences and specify the means through which discourse moved them resonated, among other places, in the Scottish Enlightenment, where philosophers such as George Campbell linked rhetoric to the faculty psychology of the era. An early nineteenth-century German treatise, *Über Declamation als Wissenschaft* (1801), imagined a science of public speech, and others in Europe and America would follow suit over the next century and later (Conley 1990:244–49). Most of these efforts to establish a science of rhetoric drew upon psychology or the philosophy of mind. Merton and Lazarsfeld would in the 1940s push in more sociological directions, though Lazarsfeld, too, got there by way of psychology (which he had studied in Vienna), and Merton via social psychology—a term he would use to categorize some of his propaganda research in the 1940s (e.g., *Mass*

Persuasion: The Social Psychology of a War Bond Drive), before grouping it with the sociology of opinion and mass communication.

Surveying the work as a whole, I would say that Merton's sociology of rhetoric during the 1940s was characterized by eight interrelated qualities that blended traditional dialectical methods with modern social science. In collaboration with Lazarsfeld and the woman researchers of the Bureau, Merton (1) drew upon and questioned received wisdom, often with an eye toward the long-range view; (2) forged definitions; (3) codified empirical research methodologies; (4) organized small- and larger-scale investigations of radio, film, and print; (5) uncovered and amplified complexities and ironies of propagandistic effort; (6) formulated middle-range theoretical concepts; (7) advised practitioners; and (8) provided broader cultural interpretations of rhetorical processes writ large, which sometimes included distinctly critical elements. Some of these qualities are more prevalent than others, but all were clearly present during the 1940s, a pivotal decade in his intellectual life.

The first seven qualities are evident in the early-season fruits of Merton's labors in the field with Lazarsfeld, a paper initially delivered to writers of wartime propaganda, later republished as the sole representation in *Social Theory and Social Structure* of Merton's sociology of mass communication. Though originally published as "Lazarsfeld and Merton" (1943), the prose style is Merton's, and I suspect he included it in his own collection of essays because he was functionally its lead author. Proclaiming "it is long since time to halt discussions of propaganda in the large; discussions which have all the fascination of speculation uncontrolled by empirical inquiry," the piece proceeds with dialectical soundness by offering a definition, and promising to make it "hold throughout our discussion" (Lazarsfeld and Merton 1943; in Merton 1968:563). The definition was a twentieth-century gloss on Aristotle: "We understand by propaganda any and all sets of symbols which influence opinion, belief or action on issues regarded by the community as controversial" (ibid).[20] Like Aristotle, too, who understood rhetoric in terms of the persuasive in a particular case (*Rhetoric* 1.2.1), the paper declared that "[t]o bring certain problems of propaganda into clear focus, we must turn to propaganda in the particular, and develop definite procedures for testing our interpretations" (563–64).

The continuities between rhetoric and propaganda research were made explicit in *Mass Persuasion*, based on a 1943–44 study of the popular entertainer Kate Smith, and her marathon war bond drives held on the CBS radio network. Here Merton began to offer broader cultural interpretations of rhetoric and make critical observations about how it was manifest and studied within the social contexts of the era. "In every age, the artifices of rhetoric have moved men to act—or to refrain from action," Chapter 1 begins, using a name for the audience that helps obfuscate the fact that women constituted 88 percent of those moved to act by Smith and interviewed for the study.

Techniques of persuasion are known to have a long history and they have, probably, a longer prehistory. But never before the present day has the quick persuasion of masses of people occurred on such a vast scale. The trivial and the large decisions alike are made the object of deliberate control. Large populations are brought to prefer a given brand of soap or hair tonic or laxative. Or, predisposed by their conditions of life, large masses are persuaded to follow a political leader who means many things to many men. Loyalties are captured and control of mass behavior temporarily ensured. Masses of men move in paths laid down for them by those who persuade (Merton, Fiske, and Curtis [1946] 2004:1).

The situation was grim, and potentially overwhelming, but scientific method might, if not save the day, at least shed some light on it, and contribute to the epistemological progress of rhetoric in the process. "As long as we continue to speculate about the arts of persuasion and propaganda we shall have little to add to what Aristotle, Bacon, Hobbes and Bentham had to say each in his own day," he went on. "Only by closely studying actual instances of mass persuasion will we come to understand it workings more fully" (ibid, 1–2). As further illustration of the continuity of his project, Merton, as I mentioned earlier, opened four of the book's seven chapters with extended epigraphs from classical rhetorical texts (Plato, Aristotle, Hobbes)—joined by others from Tocqueville, Robert Lynd, Julian Huxley, Lewis Mumford, Kate Smith, and one of her die-hard fans, a pastiche of epigraphic voices that mapped onto the politics and cultural particularities of the rhetorical case study Merton in the mid-1940s was conducting. In an age where entertainers had become popular idols, the means of moving mass audiences had taken new figure and cultural shape. What Weber had once termed "the charisma of rhetoric" ([1922] 1978:244) was particularly evident in a situation where a flag-drenched celebrity sold war bonds to the worried mothers of American soldiers.

Merton's sociology of rhetoric, then, was built upon the labors of organized research, much of it carried out in the contexts of the war, but put into the broader service of understanding the dynamics of the new communications media of the twentieth century. That effort, in turn, led Columbia research teams to do something not much done by students of rhetoric before then, namely asking audiences systematic questions about their experiences with appeals directed at them. Herta Herzog, Lazarsfeld's second wife and a key member of the Office of Radio Research from 1937 to 1943, had helped pioneer what Lazarsfeld and Merton referred to as "interviews of a special type, which we shall call the 'focused interview'" (Lazarsfeld and Merton 1943; in Merton 1968:570). However, Merton and Lazarsfeld's third wife, Patricia Kendall, were assigned the task of writing the article that codified the methodology publicly, and Merton would garner recognition for it. Observing that the interview grew out of the Bureau's "studies of the social and psychological effects of mass communications," Merton and Kendall (1946) laid out procedures and analytical schemas for the method, which they distinguished from other types of research interviews. The new method—one of the few major social scientific methods to be developed within the contexts of communications research—was a means to investigate "the *subjective experiences* of persons" who "have been involved in *a particular concrete situation*: they have seen a film; heard a radio program; [or] read a pamphlet, article, or book" (541). To be conducted properly, the film, radio program, or written matter needed to be scrutinized in advance through content analysis, a method developed by another sometime propaganda researcher, the political scientist Harold Lasswell. Blending Aristotelian attention to the particular case with the Platonic dream of matching specific kinds of discursive appeals with specific kinds of audiences, the focused interview provided a methodological tool for developing a sociological science of rhetoric.[21]

Methodologically disciplined empirical research put Merton and company in a position to uncover rhetorical complexities and amplify their ironies. Focused interviews drew attention to unintended meanings that audience members drew from propaganda efforts. "The boomerang response"—a locution Merton had used (and perhaps coined) when talking about propaganda in his Tulane social psychology class—was a name for one kind of ironic consequence, where the actual effect was opposite that intended. Long before Stuart Hall and Birmingham Cultural Studies drew attention to gaps between the encoding and decoding of messages, Columbia audience research found and analyzed the phenomenon. Whether it be public health campaigns that issued in skepticism about medical experts, wartime propaganda aimed at cultivating goodwill toward allies that promoted ethnocentric nationalism, or tolerance propaganda that intensified racial prejudice, Merton was attuned to the ironies of mass-mediated rhetoric, and to its limits in achieving the desired ends of those who produced it. This was of course a piece with his longer-standing awareness of unanticipated consequences, first formulated in his classic piece at Harvard (Merton 1936b).[22] Pretesting propaganda through content analysis and focused interviews represented one way to head off unwanted boomerangs. In his role as Lazarsfeldian "administrative researcher" at the Bureau, serving clients like the Office of War Information and CBS, Merton communicated with producers about possible boomerangs and ineffective appeals. Advising practitioners, too, was a component of Merton's sociology of rhetoric.

Merton's ironic eye was at its best in "The Self-Fulfilling Prophecy" ([1948] 1968), a classic essay that was partly an outgrowth of his longer attention to racial and ethnic epithets.[23] One of his most public articles (it first appeared in the *Antioch Review*), "The Self-Fulfilling Prophecy" can be read as a kind of ironic extension of a view of rhetoric as world-creating force that runs from the Sophist Gorgias through the Transcendentalist Ralph Waldo Emerson. Drawing on examples such as runs on banks during the Depression, Merton showed how "public definitions of a situation (prophecies or predictions) become an integral part of the situation and thus affect subsequent developments" (Merton [1948] 1968:477). In the case of the bank run, an initial prophecy—that the bank was on the verge of insolvency—drove people to withdraw their money, which in turn made the bank insolvent. "The self-fulfilling prophecy is, in the beginning, a *false* definition of the situation evoking a new behavior which makes the originally false conception come *true*" (ibid). In contrast to humanists like Emerson, who believed that prophetic orators could move audiences through willful intention, Merton gave us an ironic sociological alternative: prophecies operating on their own, through collective processes, and sometimes contrary to the wishes of those who uttered them.

"The self-fulfilling prophecy" was one of a number of middle-range concepts that Merton forged during the 1940s, others of which pertained more directly to his propaganda and communications research. Like the *Antioch Review* essay, which included an extended sociological critique of

U.S. racial and ethnic prejudice, the middle-range concepts in Merton's mass communications research were sometimes embedded within broader observations and moderate, scientifically muted, left-liberal critiques of American social life. One can see this critical impulse, for instance, in the Kate Smith study, which introduced the notion of "pseudo-Gemeinschaft"—"the mere pretense of common values in order to further private interest," a condition Merton suggested was commonplace in the U.S. culture of advertising and salesmanship (Merton, Fiske, and Curtis [1946] 2004:144).[24] In *Mass Persuasion*, too, the more neutral sounding "public image" indexed the carefully cultivated but contradictory public personae of Smith, enhanced by publicists and press releases for pseudo-events like "the National Father's Day Committee," which, Merton wryly noted, had awarded the unmarried singer "the 'coveted' Eisenhower medal . . . because she had labored successfully to 'cement fine relationships' between fathers and their children" (151). Even more critically pointed was his idea of "the narcotizing dysfunction"—the first specification of any dysfunction in his emerging functionalist theory—which named the way in which "the vast supply of communications may elicit only a superficial concern with the problems of society, and this superficiality often cloaks mass apathy" (Lazarsfeld and Merton 1948:105).[25]

The Tulane and early Columbia years were Merton's most political period, though professional identifications nearly always trumped citizenly alternatives, even in this era (see Simonson, 2010b) He entertained hopes of reaching a larger reading public with *Swayed by Smith*, the working title for the manuscript that became *Mass Persuasion*, and intended to show them how a popular entertainer could serve as "Ideological Balm for the Underprivileged," as he titled one chapter in the book's penultimate draft. This was about the same time that Merton gave a rather striking class lecture, "Institutional Ideologies and Propaganda," where he set his sights on the broad cultural structure and sketched the roles played by competing ideologies in a social environment marked by uncertainty and skepticism. "Ideologies structure our evaluations by supplying us with a ready-made vocabulary of encomium and opprobrium, with a preexisting set of value laden terms to apply to various situations, words that are nominally descriptions but in fact evaluations of situations, events, persons, and behavior," Merton wrote, staking out a position close to Burke's in *Permanence and Change*. "They include epithets like un-American radical, red, nigger, agitator, wholesome, free enterprise, free speech, liberty, decency, etc."

Ideologies helped structure the symbolic realm, while propaganda was the vehicle through which epithets and other key terms were in particular cases mobilized. "Ideologies have a social basis," he went on, drawing out the social structures of which they were part. "[W]hat is decisive in the success or failure of the counter-ideologies is the underlying conditions of power and organization." Merton took up a middle position on their sociological status. "It is not contended that the struggle of ideologies are simply epiphenomenal, but it is not sufficient to consider these as the determining factors in social change" (Merton 1943). Aware of the links between propaganda and competing ideologies, and interested in ways of combining his social scientific expertise and left-liberal political sympathies, Merton wrote Harold Laski in December of 1945 and offered his services to the British Labor Party.[26] Though skeptical of all pieties, Merton in the 1940s articulated a sociology of rhetoric with broader political resonance.

A History of Scientific Figuration: On the Shoulder of Giants

After he was burned in a minor McCarthy Era episode during the presidential election campaign of 1952, Merton seems pretty well to have abandoned whatever occasional daydreams he entertained about politics as a vocation.[27] Instead of moving any further in cultivating what Weber had called "the ethos of politics as a 'cause'" ([1919] 1978:214), Merton committed himself fully to the ethos of science, in its professionalized sociological variety. Not unrelated, he ended his marriage of convenience with the sociology of mass communication, and returned to his first and abiding love, the sociology of science. His studies of language persisted in the 1950s and '60s, but more at the margins of his main sociological work. There was the unpublished "serendipity" book, set aside semifinished in 1958, but more famously *On the Shoulders of Giants*, his stem-winding "Shandean postscript" of a book begun as a letter in the fall of 1959 and published in book form six years later. In contrast with his 1930s and '40s sociologies of rhetoric, in the '50s and '60s he turned almost exclusively to looking at the ways that elites communicated amongst themselves, charting the flow and usage of their words.

This is the work that would grow into the "sociological semantics" of the last three decades of his life, an elevated scientific-sounding name for a program of study that might also be captured by the slightly seedier sounding "sociology of rhetoric." Merton wasn't about slumming though, linguistic or otherwise, and attending to elite language use was somehow fitting for a man ensconced in the highest echelons of the sociological profession, who devoted the bulk of his research energies to science and sociological theory, and spent the majority of his time discoursing silently or out loud with the fellow scholars (living and dead) who populated his primary reference group. By the second edition of *Social Theory and Social Structure* (1957), Merton was a long ways away from the rhetorical performances of lowbrow popular entertainers like Kate Smith, and the critical edge with which he discussed her. He purged by more than half the book's indexed references to "ideology."[28] The term was a conceptual holdover from another era.

On the Shoulders of Giants was a far different project. Begun and carried out as a letter to Lazarsfeld's son-in-law, the Harvard historian Bernard Bailyn, the published product was a two-hundred-and-ninety-page epistolary-style frolic in the fields for Merton. At its base *OTSOG*, as Merton came to call it, was a study of the history and circulation of a rhetorical figure, that of dwarves standing on the shoulders of giants, which had been most famously deployed by Sir Isaac Newton in his aphorism, "If I have seen further, it is by standing on the shoulders of giants." Merton was a bit unclear about what to call his main object of study. He had once called Newton's saying an "epigram" (Merton 1957:646), but in *OTSOG* it variously became an "aphorism" (or "Aphorism"), a "figure" (or "figure of speech" or "figurative expression"), a "simile" (or "similitude"), a "sententious saying," and a "gnome."[29] All are traditional rhetorical terms that name devices of argument (which fall under the canon of invention) or expression (which fall under the canon of style).

Merton's awareness of the aphorism dated back to the mid-1930s, when his mentor, the historian of science George Sarton, published a query about the saying's origins, in his journal *Isis*. A response by R. E. Ockenden followed in the next issue. Between them, the scholars established that the saying, though often attributed to Newton, was actually quite older, and they cited twelve different usages of it dating back to the twelfth-century philosopher, Bernard of Chartres.[30] In 1942, Merton quoted what he called "Newton's remark" as support for the idea of a scientific communalism, one of the four scientific norms ([1942] 1968:611–12), which he followed with a footnote declaring that "Newton's aphorism is a standardized phrase which had found repeated expression from at least the twelfth century," and citing the two *Isis* entries.[31] As he later recounted in his epistle-book to Bailyn,

"Between 1942, when I first wrote the note, and 1949, when I reprinted the allusion without further comment, I had been industriously collecting . . . every little nut of an allusion to the epigram and providently storing it away" ([1965] 1993:2). This collecting took place at the same time that he was considering ethnic epithets and the language of popular, mass-mediated propaganda. Merton was in a different inventional space, however, when he brought out the epigram in his 1957 Presidential Address to the American Sociological Society, in the contexts of his analysis of priority claims among scientists (Merton 1957:646). Merton mailed a copy of the address to Bailyn, who answered with a note of his own, wondering about the history of the saying, which in turn prompted Merton's book-length response.

The project allowed Merton to tickle his Anglophile sensibility, spend time in his superbly equipped home office in a grand Tudor house with views of the Hudson River, and send supremely talented graduate students like Stephen Cole and Harriet Zuckerman to track down sources for him in the library (before, finally, "reluctantly but dutifully," having to go off to do some library research of his own [182]). Built upon the activity of Merton reading, *OTSOG* was in basic ways a hermeneutical project. In form, it was a self-conscious imitation of Laurence Sterne's *Tristam Shandy*, taking on the non-linear narrative style that features digression ("that most essential tool of the writer's craft" [124n]) as its main structuring principle. In the best manner of imitation (*imitatio*), a staple of traditional rhetorical education, Merton creatively appropriated the exemplar and bent it to his own purposes. The result was a kind of sociologically oriented *explication de texte*, aimed at tracing the history of the giants-and-dwarves figure, and using it as an opportunity to discourse with erudition and wit upon themes in the sociology of science that he had pursued in well different style elsewhere—priority claims, reward structures, "obliteration by incorporation," adumbrationism, conceptual schemes, functions and dysfunctions, and the relation of the history of ideas to the creation of knowledge in the present. Merton scoured the texts of his intellectual forebears and offered interpretive commentary more playful than anything in the Augustinian or Talmudic hermeneutic traditions that preceded it. Saturated with irony and word play, *OTSOG* brought sociology to the humanistic borderlands between rhetoric and poetic, calling attention to its own artifice in the process.[32] It was a well-wrought modernist text.

As a contribution to the sociology of rhetoric, *OTSOG* straddled what Merton in a different context called history and systematics. The straddling was implied in Merton's cleverest naming of his circuitous investigation, a third of the way into the book. "By this time, we might describe the Aphorism, in a fit of alliterative paronomasia, as a mnemonic gnome about gnomes on the shoulders of giants," he wrote. "And that, I suppose, makes me a gnomologist—twice over" (74). *Gnōmē* is the Greek word for a saying or maxim (the word literally means "thought"), which, Aristotle argued, could play a part in rhetorical reasoning (*Rhetoric* 2.21).[33] Before offering up his clever pun, Merton had observed that the saying "in one form or another, was being repeated on all sides by men who were rushing into print to help win the battle of the books during the seventeenth century" (74). That is, he had found that the *gnōmē* was deployed by both defenders of antiquity, who used it to argue that the ancients were giants, and by defenders of modernity, who emphasized that we moderns can see further. The *gnōmē* was mnemonic in the double sense that it both cued those who used it to remember the predecessor "giants" who had built the cultural base upon which their own epistemological advances depended; and it cued Merton and fellow historians of the saying to the long lineage of writers who had made use of it before Newton. Merton's clever phrasing captured the way in which his own project both traced the history of a rhetorical figure among men of science and learning *and* lay preliminary groundwork for a broader theoretical account of rhetorical figuration within the frameworks of the sociology of science—thus history and systematics.

Historically, Merton reconstructed the "chain of transmission of the simile" (217), from Newton and seventeenth-century England back and forward in time. He showed how the saying was used in various contexts for sometimes competing purposes, and he probed ways in which it was fragmented, recombined, and otherwise modified along the way. In roundabout reflexive fashion, he followed the figure from Barlett's *Familiar Quotations* and the second edition of Robert Burton's *Anatomy of Melancholy* (1624), through Newton's correspondence with Robert Hooke (1675/6), George Herbert's *Jacula Prudentum* (1640), John of Salisbury's twelfth-century *Metalogicon* (with an assist from George Sarton's 1933 *Introduction to the History of Science*), and then back to "the more nearly subterranean region's of [seventeenth-century] small talk, tracts, and quarrelsome books" (42), including the Anglican bishop Godfrey Goodman's *The Fall of Man* (1616) and the Calvinist clergyman George Hakewill's *Apologie* (1627).

Merton's tour-de-figuration meandered across the English Channel, and through the French, Spanish, and Italian Renaissance, where he reached beyond the pale of Protestant and Catholic aphorists to include the great crypto-Jewish Spanish humanist Juan Vives and the Jewish-Italian historian Azariah de Rossi. The latter took up a view of ancients and moderns that sounded a lot like the one held by *OTSOG*'s author.[34] It prompted Merton "to retrace the Italo-Hebraic tradition of the Aphorism back to the late thirteenth-century author . . . Zedekiah ben Abraham 'Anav" and his teacher, Isaiah of Trani, a Talmudist who in turn had picked up the aphorism from the gentiles (241). Like Merton himself, the simile moved among cultures, cutting a cosmopolitan figure for itself.[35]

Beyond being a history of rhetoric-in-use, *OTSOG* provided preliminary starting points for a sociologically oriented rhetorical theory of elite discourse. I will mention two of them, which, per Merton's style, dwell within the middle range. First, he linked the social uptake and effectivity of the *gnōmē* to the self images of the rhetors who used it (or perhaps were used by it). "[T]hose previously disposed to self-derogation resonate to the Aphorism once they encounter it," Merton suggested. "This is not a simple matter of cause-and-effect in which the ideological content of the Aphorism produces a contraction of self-image among those exposed to it but a far more complex matter of endlessly interacting forces in which prior disposition makes for both exposure and response to the Aphorism which in turn reinforce subsequent exposure and response" (239). This relation between exposure to rhetoric and audience disposition was one that the Office of Radio Research had worked out by the early 1940s, while engaged with the problems of building interest in public affairs or cultural programming—those with a preexisting taste for classical music, for example, were most likely to seek out and benefit from classical programming on the radio. Here Merton transferred the basic idea to a different realm, indexed less to the cultural tastes of mass audiences than to the dispositions of individual scientists and scholars.

The second theoretical starting point I will mention reveals a great deal about Merton's own rhetorical distaste for certain kinds of public wrangling. He called it "the Hooke-Newton-Merton sociological theory of the perverse effects of public debate upon intellectual clarity (not to say integrity)" (142). Like a confession on the analyst's couch, the theory surfaced initially in one of the book's countless digressions. The author circled back to it several times, though, associating it also with Plato (and "the basic distinction between noisy contention in public and peaceful discussion in private" [143n]) and with Juan Vives (and his low opinion of public disputation and "'pandering to the audience, as it were to the public in the theatre'" [61–2]). Merton's own formulation of the theory, which served as pretext to these digressions from the main *OTSOG*-ial quest, had arisen in a 1959 paper still fresh in his mind when he started the letter to Bailyn. He had delivered the paper, "Social Conflict over Styles of Sociological Work," at a plenary session of the Fourth World Congress of Sociology in Stresa, Italy, four months before he began his letter-book to Bailyn. He quoted from the Stresa paper early in *OTSOG*, suggesting it remained prominent in his mind. Among "men of sociological science," he observed "'polemics have more to do with the allocation of intellectual resources among different kinds of sociological work than with a closely formulated opposition of sociological ideas. . . . Since the conflict is public, it becomes a battle for status more nearly than a search for truth'" (24–25).

The immediate foreground for these observations was the publication of C. Wright Mills's *The Sociological Imagination*, whose eloquent vituperation of Parsonian grand theory and Lazarsfeldian abstracted empiricism lay down the gauntlet for a more public, politically engaged form of sociology. Instead of taking on Mills directly, Merton chose to diminish his book through indirect means, in a professional paper and a Shandean Postscript.[36] He abstracted himself from the particulars of the case at hand and made general quasiscientific observations about the nature of scholarly polemic as such. At Stresa and in *OTSOG*, Merton drew a line between the real epistemological business of science and the "perverse," merely rhetorical effects of public debate. Mills and his *Sociological Imagination* fell on the wrong side of this line, a point Merton made through studious avoidance of "noisy contention in public" about whether or not Mills was right. Deeper into the 1960s, however, a new generation of sociologists embraced public contentiousness, took Mills as a hero, and struck out in decidedly post-Mertonian directions. The intellectual economy of the field came to be powered by engines different than in 1959. For some, Merton's star had faded.

Taking Stock

Looking back, we can say that, as a foray into the sociology of rhetoric, *On the Shoulders of Giants* was light years away from the Kate Smith study.

Instead of propaganda directed at popular audiences, deeply enmeshed with patriotic sentiment, commercial entertainment, and national media industries, *OTSOG* plumbed a single rhetorical figure as it wound its way through elite discourse across the centuries. It was a kind of sociological antiquarianism, high-Renaissance wit meets mid-century Mertonian sociology, carried out through leisurely textual pursuit of a saying over time. An erudite and literary study, *OTSOG* has attracted a very impressive list of admirers, including Stephen J. Gould, Denis Donaghue, and a lot of other people who are both a hell of a lot smarter than I am, and possess far more cultivated literary tastes. I agree the book is impressive, but also admit that reading it can feel like listening to the scholarly equivalent of a long diddling guitar solo, played by a virtuoso musician maybe a bit too impressed with his riffs.

To throw the project into perspective, one might compare *On the Shoulders of Giants* to three other books of the era that weighed in on rhetoric broadly conceived—Raymond Williams's *Culture and Society* (1958), Marshall McLuhan's *Gutenberg Galaxy* (1962), and Jürgen Habermas's *Structural Transformation of the Public Sphere* (1962). While Merton the sociologist was moving in textual and literary directions, the literary scholars Williams and McLuhan were making observations about society, and Habermas was melding philosophy, history, and sociology together in a grand and fertile blend. All three took up mass media, which Merton had left behind in the 1940s, and offered long historical views of larger-scale social and political transformations. While Williams was tracing the evolution of "culture," and embracing his working-class Welsh background, Merton meandered through his books to trace the figure of dwarves standing on the shoulders of giants and repressed his own working-class Jewish roots. McLuhan meanwhile was living out a convert's Catholicism and finding sea changes as he peered back toward the same Renaissance Merton moved through more delicately, while Habermas embraced the ways of Critical Theory and excavated the structural transformation of publicness from classical antiquity to the present. Each of the four men would influence traditions of thinking and research on media, but by the time of *OTSOG*, Merton's own work on the subject was nearly two decades behind him. No American academic of Merton's stature weighed in broadly on the mass media in the 1960s. Mills was dead. Lazarsfeld was onto other things, and never had much interest in public work anyway. One can make the case that, given his position of leadership and knowledge, Merton should have been writing about narcotizing dysfunctions and contradictory media images instead of veering back into his rarified studies in the sociology of science. Part of me wants to hold him responsible for choosing the wrong kind of rhetoric to study, and reneging on his civic obligations.

But another part of me wants to give Merton a more charitable read, and emphasize his until-now unrecognized contributions to the understanding of rhetoric. As I have tried to show, from the 1930s on, Merton stirred science into rhetoric and rhetoric into science. He folded sociological method and middle-range theory into the traditional study of rhetoric, and brought them to bear on forms of rhetoric that were anything but traditional. Without always acknowledging that he was doing so, Merton explored rhetorical dimensions of science and used them as platforms for peering more deeply into what he considered the essence of the institution. In the process, he updated ancient insights about the nature of rhetoric, and he offered a sociological counterpart to literary and philosophical approaches to the newly revived subject. These were significant accomplishments, historically and theoretically.

Gazing back across the three periods I have sketched, I would say that rhetoric served Merton variously as portal, object of study, and mode of expression. As a portal, rhetoric served as an entry point into other substantive areas, including the ethos of science and mechanisms of ethnic and racial prejudice. As an object of study, rhetoric was something for Merton to scrutinize and occasionally have fun with, from mass propaganda in the 1940s to scientific figuration two decades later. As a mode of expression, rhetoric was a vehicle for Merton's *logos*, from the lectures and conversations that captivated live audiences, to the essays he composed with typographic grace, and left behind for us. Through the embodied memories of those who heard him, and the printed pages that lay waiting for new readers, this *logos* is what remains of the man. Merton's was a species of scholarly eloquence, less broadly resonant than Mills's or David Riesman's, but striking nonetheless. It remains a model of intellectual craftsmanship—elegant, learned, analytically precise, witty.

As Merton confessed without fully apprehending, rhetoric was very important to him.

Notes

1. "As a *New Yorker* profile by Morton Hunt put it some 35 years ago, I was born 'almost at the bottom of the social structure' in the slums of South Philadelphia

to working-class Jewish immigrants from Eastern Europe," Merton said ([1994] 1996:342). Hunt had mentioned many things about Merton, but the fact that his parents were Jewish was not one of them.

2. Consider, for instance, the resonant opening of an early classic: "In some one of its numerous forms, the problem of unanticipated consequences of purposive action has been treated by virtually every substantial contributor to the long history of social thought. The diversity of context and variety of terms by which this problem has been known, however, have tended to obscure the definite continuity in its consideration"—a point he underscored with a footnote that observed, "Some of the terms by which the whole or certain aspects of this process have been known are: Providence (immanent or transcendental), Moira, *Paradoxie der Folgen*, *Schicksal*, social forces, heterogony of ends, immanent causation, dialectical movement, principle of emergence and creative synthesis" (Merton 1936b:894).

3. This and subsequent quotations come from George A. Kennedy's translation of the *Rhetoric* (Aristotle 2007).

4. For good single-volume histories of rhetoric since classical antiquity, see Conley 1990, Kennedy 1999, and Barilli 1989. For an attempt to consider rhetoric outside European bounds, see Kennedy 1998. For philosophical and historical accounts of rhetoric as an architectonic art, see the unjustly neglected and brilliant essays by Richard McKeon collected in McKeon 1987 and 1990, and in Garver and Buchanan 2000. For a fine historical account of the trivium, see Marshall McLuhan's published 1943 dissertation (2006). For a recent volume considering the idea of a rhetorical tradition, see Graff, Walzer, and Atwill 2005.

5. For brief accounts of Richards, Burke, Weaver, McKeon, and Perelman on rhetoric, see Conley 1990:260–310. For a discussion of Heidegger's early reading and 1924 lectures on Aristotle's *Rhetoric,* see Gross and Kemman 2005. Other important literary theorists and philosophers turned to rhetoric in the second half of the century, including Wayne Booth, Paul de Man, Stanley Fish, and Henry Louis Gates (on the literary side); Ernesto Grassi and Hans Blumenberg (on the philosophical side); and Walter Ong (theologian, historian, media theorist).

6. Richards and C. K. Ogden's *Meaning of Meaning* (1923) was recommended reading for Clyde Kuckholn's class, Contemporary Theories and Methods of Cultural Anthropology, which Merton audited at Harvard in the fall of 1938; Merton's reading notes on the 1927 edition of the book are among his personal papers, and he quotes from Richards in early 1940s work (Merton 1941b, 1944). Kenneth Burke's *Permanence and Change* (1935) was an important book for Merton, giving him conceptual ammunition to address the dysfunctions of bureaucracy by means of Burke's discussion of Veblen's "trained incapacity" and Dewey's "occupational psychosis," as well as what Merton called Burke's own "almost echolalic phrase, 'people may be unfitted by being fit in an unfit fitness'" (Merton [1940a] 1968:252). *Permanence and Change* also

led Merton to the dictum he later called "the Burke Theorem"—a way of seeing is also a way of not seeing; a focus on object A involves the neglect of object B (Merton 1984)—and may have contributed to Merton's thinking about cultural and sociological "orientations" (Merton 1944, 1945). Merton's collaboration with McKeon culminated in McKeon, Merton, and Gellhorn (1957). Merton sparred with McLuhan in a seminar at Columbia in 1955 (Marchand 1989:132), and again on educational television in 1966, WNDT-TV's 90-minute symposium, "McLuhan on McLuhanism" (Simonson, 2010b:159–60).

7. Propaganda was "1. any deliberate attempt to manufacture public opinion, irrespective of moral content 2. chief characteristic is emotional appeal"; language understood as "medium of communication and control in social situations"; and public opinion was "1. not unanimous" but marked by "2. [the] concept of publics" (RKM, class notes to Social Psychology, Temple College, Spring 1931; RKM, personal files).

8. Durkheim as enthymemist and Merton as periphrasist both appear in "Some Considerations of Durkheim's Methodology" (Merton 1932). Merton characterized John Creedy's method of propaganda analysis as "nothing more or less than the formulation of a syllogism from an enthymeme" in a document he prepared for a Social Psychology course he cotaught at Tulane with Hiram Johnson in the spring of 1941 ("On Creedy's Document Analysis," RKM, personal files).

9. Turner (2007) writes that "Merton's core notion of *ethos* appears in Weber repeatedly, and particularly in *The Protestant Ethic*, where it is used to deal with the early capitalists' distinctive orientation toward work. But in Merton's "A Note on Science and Democracy," he goes on, "the reference [for *ethos*] is to Sumner" (169). Though he stops short of saying that Merton took the term from Weber without acknowledging so, such is the implication of Turner's analysis. I think it just as likely that William Graham Sumner's *Folkways* was in fact the source. I find three passing uses of the term "ethos" in *The Protestant Ethic*, none defined (Weber [1904–5] 1958:51, 52, 67), though he would come closer to a definition in "Protestant Sects and the Spirit of Capitalism" (1906); and uses the term prominently in his 1919 lecture, "Politics as a Vocation." Sumner, on the other hand, gives it a prominent place near the opening of his book, under the heading "Purposes of the Present Work," and follows with a definition: "The Greeks applied the term 'ethos' to the sum of the characteristic usages, ideas, standards, and codes by which a group was differentiated and individualized in character from other groups" (Sumner [1906] 1940:36). Aristotle used *ethos* in something like this sense in the *Rhetoric* (2.12–17), though the groups whose *ethē* he discusses are differentiated more by social status (age, wealth, "good birth," and political power) than by cultural orientation and mores (cf. Calhoun 2007:8–9).

10. Explaining his intent "to determine the extent to which the values of the Puritan ethic stimulated interest in science by surveying the attitudes of the contemporary [i.e., seventeenth-century] scientists," Merton allowed that while scientists' publicly

avowed motives may represent rationalizations, "these conceivable rationalizations themselves are evidence (Weber's *Erkenntnismitteln*) of the motives which were regarded as socially acceptable, since, as Kenneth Burke puts it, 'a terminology of motives is moulded to fit our general orientation as to purposes, instrumentalities, the good life, etc'" (Merton [1936a] 1968:629). Merton was not the only young sociologist of knowledge to incorporate Burke's terminology of motives: C. Wright Mills took the issue conceptually further in an article four years later (Mills 1940; see also Kenny 2008).

11. On May 4, for instance, the scribe reported, "The attempt to find a water-tight definition seemed at this stage unattainable, and here Merton made the helpful suggestion that we temporarily abandon the attempt to define propaganda, and that we take the general field denoted by that concept and treat separately three of its major aspects . . . The specific types of motivation of A (the propagandist), the influence exercised on B (the propagandee), and the content of propaganda, the techniques used—from the point of view of the objective observer." These were questions Merton would raise six years later in analyzing Kate Smith's all-day radio war bond drive (Merton, Fiske, and Curtis [1946] 2004). Merton also drew attention to cases where propaganda "used the authority of science in a biased way," and pulled the group back when it drifted into "a discussion of Pareto's list of residues as an example of convincing without logical basis," warning "that this line of thought would carry us to an examination of all of rhetoric" (Parsons's Sociological Group, Reports of Meetings, January 12 and May 4, 1937; RKM, personal files). For brief discussions of the Parsons' Group, see Gerhardt 2003:65–67 and Simonson 2005:280–82.

12. See for instance his heavily annotated copy of Bernhard Rust and Ernst Krieck, *Das nationalsozialistische Deutschland und die Wissenschaft* (1936), in RKM, personal files. Rust and other Nazi writers on science are referenced in most of the first twenty-one footnotes of "Science and the Social Order" (Merton [1938] 1968:591–96).

13. RKM to George A. Lundberg (GAL), October 4, 1937; GAL to RKM, October 7, 1937; RKM to GAL, October 8, 1937; all in RKM, personal files.

14. Merton amplified the ethos of science in his more famous "norms of science" essay four years later. Though more repressed, rhetorical elements remained part of the general evidentiary base for the more systematic formulation: "Although the ethos of science has not been codified, it can be inferred from the moral consensus of scientists as expressed in use and wont, in countless writings on 'the scientific spirit' and in moral indignation directed toward contraventions of the ethos," Merton wrote ([1942] 1968:605–606). For another take on rhetorical elements of Merton's ethos of science, see Prelli 1989. For excellent accounts of the historical contexts of Merton's formulation with regard to scientific thought and politics, see Hollinger [1983] 1996, Turner 2007, and Huff 2007.

15. A decade later, Merton updated the traditional distinction between rhetoric and dialectic in the introductory essay to the section of *Social Theory and Social Structure* entitled "The Sociology of Knowledge and Mass Communications" (cf. Sica,

Chapter 8 of this volume). Playing the part of rhetoric was "the sociology of opinion and mass communications," which "deals with the masses" and is concerned "with public opinion, with mass beliefs, and with what has come to be called 'popular culture.'" Playing opposite was "the sociology of knowledge," which "comes to deal with the intellectual élite" and analyzes "more esoteric doctrines, or those complex systems of knowledge which become reshaped and often distorted in their subsequent passage into popular culture" (Merton [1949] 1968:495).

16. Among the paper topics suggested for students were propaganda in education, the press, revolutions, reform (e.g., for social work), and cartoons, as well as the relation of propaganda and counterpropaganda, and the place of linguistic symbols in propaganda analysis (Merton and Johnson 1940–41).

17. The ethnic epithet study never came to publication, and I have not found any existing drafts among his papers. I suspect that he folded it into "The Self-Fulfilling Prophecy," which considered, among other phenomena, "how the very same behavior undergoes a complete change of evaluation in its transition from the in-group Abe Lincoln to the out-group Abe Cohen or Abe Kurokawa," and touched on epithets directed at Jews: "Was Abe Lincoln eager to learn the accumulated wisdom of the ages by unending study? The trouble with the Jew is that he's a greasy grind, with his head always in a book, while decent people are going to a show or a ball game" (Merton [1948] 1968:483). Merton himself may have experienced such epithets, and so knew firsthand about their function as agencies of social control.

18. Rhetorical realms identified in a quote from Hobbes's *Art of Rhetorick* that Merton quoted in *Mass Persuasion* (Merton, Fiske, and Curtis [1946] 2004:20).

19. For more detailed accounts of the history and contemporary significance of Merton's communications research, see Simonson and Weimann 2003 and Simonson 2004, 2005, 2006. For a fuller story of his political development, see Simonson 2010b.

20. "If, however, the topic is regarded as beyond debate," Lazarsfeld and Merton go on, "it is not subject to propaganda" (Merton 1968:563). Compare Aristotle: "Its [i.e., rhetoric's] function [*ergon*] is concerned with the sort of things we debate and for which we do not have [other] arts and among such listeners as are not able to see many things together or to reason from a distant starting point. And we debate about things that seem capable of admitting two possibilities; for no one debates things incapable of being different" (*Rhetoric* 1.2.12).

21. As Merton and Kendall made clear at the end of their article, focused interviews were best used in combination with quantitative research. "When the interview precedes the experimental or statistical study, it is used as a *source of hypotheses*, later submitted to systematic test." In other cases, the order is reversed, and the focused interview serves "*to interpret previously ascertained experimental findings*" (Merton and Kendall 1946:557; cf. Merton's account of the focused interview in Lemann 2000). Put

in rhetorical language, these might be termed the inventional and hermeneutic functions of the focused interview.

22. As an ironist, Merton had elective affinities with Burke (who in turn resonated with the irony of Veblen). As he confessed much later in a letter, "I too am persuaded that irony pervades culture and society, not least as seen from a Burkean perspective" (RKM to Alan G. Gross, April 9, 1987, RKM, personal files).

23. See in particular his discussion of the "moral alchemy" of converting characteristics considered positive in dominant groups into negative traits when they appear in minorities (Merton [1948] 1968:480–84, which I quote from in footnote 17 above). Borrowing from Burke without citing him directly, Merton noted, "Through the adroit use of these rich vocabularies of encomium and opprobrium, the in-group readily transmutes its own virtues into others' vices" (483).

24. On every side, Americans "feel themselves the object of manipulation, . . . the target for ingenious methods of control, through advertising which cajoles, promises, terrorizes; . . . through cumulatively subtle methods of salesmanship which may simulate values common to both salesman and client for private and self-interested motives." Listeners felt a "magnified 'will to believe'" in Kate Smith's sincerity as a consequence of living in a society "which has foregone a sense of community ('Gemeinschaft') and has substituted . . . the mere pretense of common values in order to further private interest ('pseudo-Gemeinschaft')" (Merton, Fiske, and Curtis [1946] 2004:142, 144).

25. "It is termed *dys*functional rather than functional on the assumption that it is not in the interest of modern complex society to have large masses of the population politically apathetic and inert," the paper suggested, in an assumption that wouldn't be shared by all observers (Lazarsfeld and Merton 1948:105; see also Simonson and Weimann 2003). Merton had briefly mentioned the general idea "dysfunctions" in a short critique of Parsonian grand theory delivered at the 1947 meetings of the American Sociological Society (Merton 1948:168).

26. Merton asked Laski for a job "studying the 'effectiveness' of the Labor Party program of education and propaganda," saying that it was "a sad commentary on 'social science' that its skills have been put in the service of testing the effectiveness of advertisements, but not of progressive political and economic propaganda" (RKM to Harold Laski, December 15, 1945, RKM, personal files).

27. On the 1952 event, when Merton's signing of a published statement of criticism about Republican vice presidential candidate Richard Nixon prompted a dirty-tricks-like media smear campaign, see "Nixon Fund Vicious, Say 23 at Columbia," *New York Times*, October 6, 1952:n.p.; Jack Doherty, "9 Anti-Nixon Profs Tinted by Red Probe," *New York Daily News*, October 9, 1952:3; "Link Nine Professors to Communist Fronts," *Columbia Spectator*, October 9, 1952:1, 2, 4; "9 Nixon Fund Critics Listed in Red Probe," *Chicago Tribune* October 9, 1952 "Political Battle at Columbia Rages," *New York Times*, November 2, 1952:n.p.; all found in RKM, personal files.

28. In the Index to the 1949 edition, under "Ideology" the reader was directed to the pages of five different articles: "Social Structure and Anomie," "The Self-Fulfilling Prophecy," "The Sociology of Knowledge," "Karl Mannheim and the Sociology of Knowledge," and "Science and Democratic Social Structure" (the later-renamed "norms of science" classic). In the enlarged 1957 edition, only the two review-type sociology of knowledge chapters are thus indexed. In 1949, "ideology" was a term Merton still used for his own work. In 1957, it referred to positions held by others.

29. For *aphorism* see Merton [1965] 1993:1, 55, 266, passim; for *figure* and related names, 56, 73, 139, 158, 160; *simile* and *similitude*, 73, 74, 153–54; *sententious saying*, 40; *commonplace*, 76, 259 (and, in the 1993 Postface, 312n); *gnome*, 74, 178.

30. Observing that Newton's maxim "is very remarkable because it implies belief in the progress of science, a belief which was apparently so rare in ancient and mediaeval times that it is often thought of as being specifically modern," Sarton went on to note that the idea of progress, though interesting in its own right, "derives an additional interest from the fact that it had to compete against an antagonistic idea, namely the conception of a primordial golden age," which, he had found, "still obtained in the seventeenth century" (Sarton 1935:109). The countervailing beliefs in progress and a primordial golden age was one of the themes Merton pursued in *OTSOG*, which discussed the twelve authors Sarton and Ockenden (1936) found who had deployed the saying: Bernard of Chartres, John of Salisbury, Henry of Mondeville, Didacus Stella, Robert Burton, Alexander Neckam, Peter of Blois, Guy de Chauliac, Alexandre Dionsye, François Martel, George Herbert, and Samuel Taylor Coleridge. (Merton indexed all save Dionsye and Martel, who make cameo appearances on page 229 of *OTSOG*.)

31. Ironically, given that scholarly precision and imprecision would be a steady topic in *OTSOG*, Merton got the date wrong for the Ockenden reply (which he had as 1938), an error that would persist through subsequent reprintings of the article in the first two editions of *Social Theory and Social Structure* and in *OTSOG* itself before finally being corrected in the third edition of *Social Theory and Social Structure* (1968).

32. Merton frequently described the artifice in explicitly rhetorical terms, as for instance when he summarized his investigative labors thus far in a form he identified as a "hendecachordal anaphora," an eleven-fold repetition of the same word (241–44); or when he identified his project as "the subdued enunciation of basic truths in the middle ground that lies between shouting and total silence, which I think is called meiosis"—an understated rhetorical style often marked by irony (274).

33. "A *gnōmē* . . . is an assertion of a generality, and people enjoy things said in general terms that they happen to assume ahead of time in a partial way; for example, if someone had met up with bad neighbors or children, he would accept a speaker's saying that nothing is worse than having neighbors or that nothing is more foolish than begetting children" (*Rhetoric* 2.21.15).

34. "Azariah plainly belongs to the progressivist wing of the Aphorism's users," having taken up a "composite of traditionalism and modernism" that allowed him to sustain both "his loyalty to tradition and his belief in a progressively enlarged truth." In matters of reflection and empirical science, Merton quoted Azariah as saying, "there is an ongoing process that adds link to link and strand to strand, finally reaching the point where, with indispensable help of earlier generations who themselves despaired of success, the well-digger who follows after these earlier unsuccessful efforts, can now labor successfully and exclaim: 'I have dug and I do drink!'" And then Merton's observation: "With this concluding anecdote of the egotistic well-digger, Azariah points the moral and puts all of us Johnny-come-latelies in our diminutive places" (236); cf. "The Functions of Classical Theory" (Merton 1968:35–38). For a more explicit and developed reading of postwar Columbia sociology in the contexts of Jewish intellectual history, see Peters 2006; for Merton in the Jewish tradition, see Simonson 2010b.

35. Merton would follow the figure forward in time from seventeenth-century England as well, though in far less loving detail than he displayed in excavating its Newtonian prehistory, devoting just ten pages to it (260–270).

36. In the Stresa paper, Merton referred to Mills and *The Sociological Imagination* once, as part of a "few general observations [that] may provide a guide through the jungle of sociological controversy" that preceded the excerpt quoted in *OTSOG*: "It would be instructive to compare the extent of dispersion around the dominant trend of sociological work in the United States, which are periodically subjected to violent attacks from within, as in the formidable book by Sorokin, *Fads and Foibles in Modern Sociology*, and in the recent little book by C. Wright Mills which, without the same comprehensive and detailed citation of seeming cases in point, follows much the same lines of arguments as those advanced by Sorokin" (Merton [1961] 1973:55). Mills's name wouldn't soil the pages of *OTSOG*. For a marvelous account of the fissure between Mills and Lazarsfeld and Merton, see Summers 2006.

References

Aristotle. 2007. *On Rhetoric: A Theory of Civic Discourse*, 2nd ed. Trans. George A. Kennedy. New York: Oxford University Press.

Barilli, Renato. [1983] 1989. *Rhetoric*. Trans. Giuliana Menozzi. Minneapolis: University of Minnesota Press.

Burke, Kenneth. 1935. *Permanence and Change: An Anatomy of Purpose*. New York: New Republic.

Calhoun, Craig. 2007. "Sociology in America: An Introduction." In *Sociology in America: A History*, ed. Craig Calhoun, 1–38. Chicago: University of Chicago Press.

Conley, Thomas M. 1990. *Rhetoric in the European Tradition*. Chicago: University of Chicago Press.

Garver, Eugene, and Richard Buchanan. 2000. *Pluralism in Theory and Practice: Richard McKeon and American Philosophy*. Nashville: Vanderbilt University Press.

Gerhardt, Uta. 2003. *Talcott Parsons: An Intellectual Biography*. Cambridge: Cambridge University Press.

Gross, Daniel. M., and Ansgar Kemman, eds. 2005. *Heidegger and Rhetoric*. Albany, NY: SUNY Press.

Habermas, Jürgen. [1962] 1989. *The Structural Transformation of the Public Sphere*. Trans. Thomas Burger. Cambridge: MIT Press.

Hollinger, David A. [1983] 1996. "The Defense of Democracy and Robert K. Merton's Formulation of the Scientific Ethos." In *Science, Jews, and Secular Culture: Studies in Mid-Twentieth-Century American Intellectual History*, ed. David A Hollinger, 80–96. Princeton: Princeton University Press.

Huff, Toby E. 2007. "Some Historical Roots of the Ethos of Science." *Journal of Classical Sociology* 7:193–210.

Hunt, Morton. 1961. "How Does it Come To Be So?" *New Yorker* 36 (November 28):39–63.

Kennedy, George A. 1998. *Comparative Rhetoric: An Historical and Cross-Cultural Introduction*. New York: Oxford University Press.

——. 1999. *Classical Rhetoric and Its Christian and Secular Tradition*. 2nd ed. Chapel Hill: University of North Carolina Press.

Kenny, Robert Wade. 2008. "The Glamour of Motives: Kenneth Burke within the Sociological Field." *KB Journal* 4 (2). http://kbjournal.org/kenny.

Lazarsfeld, Paul F., and Robert K. Merton. 1943. "Studies in Radio and Film Propaganda." *Transactions of the New York Academy of Sciences* 6 (December):58–79. Reprinted in *Social Theory and Social Structure*, 563–582

——. 1948. "Mass Communication, Popular Taste, and Organized Social Action." In *The Communication of Ideas*, ed. Lyman Bryson, 95–118. New York: Harper.

Lemann, Nicholas. 2000. "The Word Lab." *The New Yorker*. (October 26):100–101.

Marchand, Philip. 1989. *Marshall McLuhan: The Medium and the Messenger*. New York: Ticknor and Fields.

McCormack, Naomi. 2009. *Out of the Question: Women, Media, and the Art of Inquiry*. DVD. Philadelphia, PA: Annenberg School for Communication, University of Pennsylvania.

McKeon, Richard. 1987. *Rhetoric: Essays in Invention and Discovery*, ed. Mark Backman. Woodbridge, CT: Ox Bow Press.

——. 1990. *Freedom and History and Other Essays: An Introduction to the Thought of Richard McKeon*, ed. Zahava K. McKeon. Chicago: University of Chicago Press.

McKeon, Richard, Merton, Robert. K., and Gellhorn, William. 1957. *The Freedom to Read: Perspective and Program.* New York: R. R. Bowker.

McLuhan, Marshall. 1962. *The Gutenberg Galaxy: The Making of Typographic Man.* Toronto: University of Toronto Press.

——. [1943] 2006. *The Classical Trivium: The Place of Thomas Nashe in the Learning of His Time,* ed. W. Terrence Gordon. Berkeley: Gingko Press.

Merton, Robert K. 1932. "Some Considerations on Durkheim's Methodology." RKM, personal files.

——. 1936a. "Puritanism, Pietism, and Science." *Sociological Review* 28:1–30. Reprinted in *Social Theory and Social Structure,* 628–660.

——. 1936b. "The Unanticipated Consequences of Purposive Social Action." *American Sociological Review* 1:894–904.

——. 1938. "Science and the Social Order." *Philosophy of Science* 5:321–337.

——. [1938] 2001. *Science, Technology and Society in Seventeenth-Century England.* New York: Howard Fertig Publishers.

——. 1940a. "Bureaucratic Structure and Personality." *Social Forces* 18:560–68. Reprinted in *Social Theory and Social Structure,* 249–260

——. 1940b. "Fact and Factitiousness in Ethnic Opinionnaires." *American Sociological Review* 5:13–28.

——. 1941a. "Intermarriage and the Social Structure: Fact and Theory." *Psychiatry* 4:361–374.

——. 1941b. "Karl Mannheim and the Sociology of Knowledge." *Journal of Liberal Religion* 2: 125–47. Reprinted in *Social Theory and Social Structure,* 543–62.

——. 1943. "Institutional Ideologies and Propaganda." Class lecture, Columbia University. RKM, personal files.

——. 1944. "Memorandum on the Family in the Depression." RKM, personal files.

——. 1945. "Sociological Theory." *American Journal of Sociology* 50:462–47. Reprinted as "The Bearing of Sociological Theory on Empirical Research," in *Social Theory and Social Structure,* 139–155.

——. 1948. "Discussion of Talcott Parsons, 'The Position of Sociological Theory.'" *American Sociological Review* 13:164–68.

——. [1948] 1968. "The Self-Fulfilling Prophecy." Reprinted in *Social Theory and Social Structure,* 475–490.

——. 1949. "Patterns of Influence: A Study of Interpersonal Influence and Communications Behavior in a Local Community." In *Communications Research, 1948–49,* ed. Paul F. Lazarsfeld and Frank Stanton, 180–19. New York: Harper and Brothers.

——. [1949] 1968. "Introduction to Part III, The Sociology of Knowledge and Mass Communications." Reprinted in *Social Theory and Social Structure,* 493–509.

——. 1957. "Priorities in Scientific Discovery." *American Sociological Review* 22:635–59.

——. [1961] 1973. "Social Conflict over Styles of Sociological Work." Reprinted in *The Sociology of Science*, 47–69.

——. [1965] 1993. *On the Shoulders of Giants: A Shandean Postscript*. Chicago: University of Chicago Press.

——. 1968. *Social Theory and Social Structure*. Enlarged edition. Glencoe, IL: Free Press.

——. 1973. *The Sociology of Science: Theoretical and Empirical Investigations*. Ed. and with an Introduction by Norman W. Storer. Chicago: University of Chicago Press.

——. 1980. "On the Oral Transmission of Knowledge." In *Sociological Traditions from Generation to Generation: Glimpses of the American Experience*, ed. Robert K. Merton and Matilda White Riley, 1–35. Norwood, NJ: Ablex.

——. [1994] 1996. "A Life of Learning." Reprinted minus introductory commentary in *On Social Structure and Science*, ed. Piotr Sztompka, 339–359. Chicago: University of Chicago Press.

Merton, Robert K., and Elinor Barber. 2004. *The Travels and Adventures of Serendipity: A Study in Sociological Semantics and the Sociology of Science*. Princeton: Princeton University Press.

Merton, Robert K., Marjorie Fiske, and Alberta Curtis. [1946] 2004. *Mass Persuasion: The Social Psychology of a War Bond Drive*. New York: Howard Fertig Publishers.

Merton, Robert K., and Hiram Johnson. 1940–41. Lectures on Social Psychology. Tulane University. RKM, personal files.

Merton, Robert K., and Patricia L. Kendall. 1946. "The Focused Interview." *American Journal of Sociology* 51:541–557.

Merton, Robert K., George G. Reader, and Patricia L. Kendall. 1957. *The Student-Physician: Introductory Studies on the Sociology of Medical Education*. Columbia University Bureau of Applied Social Research.

Merton, Robert K., David L. Sills, and Stephen M. Stigler. 1984. "The Kelvin Dictum and Social Science: An Excursion into the History of an Idea." *Journal of the History of the Behavioral Sciences* 20:319–331.

Merton, Robert K., Patricia Salter West, and Marie Jahoda. 1951. *Patterns of Social Life: Explorations in the Sociology and Social Psychology of Housing*. Columbia University Bureau of Applied Social Research.

Mills, C. Wright. 1940. "Situated Actions and Vocabularies of Motives." *American Sociological Review* 5:904–913.

Ockenden, R. E. 1936. "Answer to Query no. 53." *Isis* 25:51–52.

Peters, John Durham. 2006. "The Part Played by Gentiles in the Flow of Mass Communication: On the Ethnic Utopia of *Personal Influence*." *Annals of the American Academy of Social and Political Science* 608:97–114.

Prelli, Lawrence. 1989. "The Rhetorical Construction of Scientific Ethos." In *Rhetoric in the Human Sciences*, ed. Herbert W. Simons, 48–68. London: Sage.

Rebhorn, Wayne A. 2000. *Renaissance Debates on Rhetoric*. Ithaca, NY: Cornell University Press.

Richards, I. A. 1936. *The Philosophy of Rhetoric*. London: Oxford University Press.

Rorty, Richard. 1991. "Inquiry as Recontextualization: An Anti-Dualist Account of Interpretation." In *Objectivity, Relativism, and Truth: Philosophical Papers, vol. 1.,* 93–110. Cambridge: Cambridge University Press.

Rust, Bernhard, and Ernst Krieck. 1936. *Das nationalsozialistische Deutschland und die Wissenschaft*. Hamburg: Hanseatische Berlagsanstalt

Sarton, George. 1935. "Query no. 53." *Isis* 24:107–9.

Schiappa, Edward. 2003. *Protagoras and Logos: A Study in Greek Philosophy and Rhetoric*, 2nd ed. Columbia, SC: University of South Carolina Press.

Schopenhauer, Arthur. 1896. *The Art of Controversy and Other Posthumous Papers*, trans. T. Bailey Saunders. New York: MacMillan.

Simonson, Peter. 2004. "Introduction." In *Mass Persuasion*, ed. Robert K. Merton, xi–xlv. New York: Howard Fertig Publishers.

——. 2005. "The Serendipity of Merton's Communications Research." *International Journal of Public Opinion Research*, 17:277–297.

——. 2006. "Celebrity, Public Image, and American Political Life: Rereading Robert K. Merton's *Mass Persuasion*." *Political Communication* 23:271–284.

——. 2010a. "A Cultural Sociology of Rhetoric: Hugh Duncan's Forgotten Corpus." In *Reengaging the Prospect(s) of Rhetoric*, ed. Mark Porrovecchio. New York: Routledge.

——. 2010b. "Merton's Skeptical Faith." In *Refiguring Mass Communication: A History*. Urbana, IL: University of Illinois Press.

Simonson, Peter, and Weimann, Gabriel. 2003. "Critical Research at Columbia: Lazarsfeld and Merton's "Mass Communication, Popular Taste, and Organized Social Action." In *Canonic Texts in Media Research: Are There Any? Should There Be? How About These?*, ed. Elihu Katz, John D. Peters, Tamar Liebes, and Avril Orloff, 12–38. Cambridge: Polity Press.

Simpson, George E. 1936. *The Negro in the Philadelphia Press*. Philadelphia: University of Pennsylvania Press.

Sproule, J. Michael. 1997. *Propaganda and Democracy: The American Experience of Media and Mass Persuasion*. New York: Cambridge.

Summers, John. 2006. "Perpetual Revelations: Mills and Lazarsfeld." *Annals of the American Academy of Social and Political Science* 608:25–40.

Sumner, William Graham [1906] 1940. *Folkways*. New York: Blaisdell Publishing Company.

Turner, Stephen. 2007. "Merton's 'Norms' in Political and Intellectual Context." *Journal of Classical Sociology* 7:161–78.

Weber, Max. [1919] 1978. "Politics as a Vocation." In *Selections in Translation*, 212–225.

———. [1922] 1978. The Nature of Charismatic Domination. In *Selections in Translation*, 226–250.

———. [1904–05] 1958. *The Protestant Ethic and the Spirit of Capitalism*. Trans. Talcott Parsons. New York: Charles Scribner's Sons.

———. 1978. *Selections in Translation*. Ed. Walter G. Runciman, trans. Eric Matthews. Cambridge: Cambridge University Press.

Williams, Raymond. 1958. *Culture and Society, 1780–1950*. New York: Harper and Row.

"Women in Media Research." 2009. *Out of the Question: Women, Media, and the Art of Inquiry*. http://www.outofthequestion.org/Women-in-Media-Research.aspx (accessed 9 January 2010).

11

On Sociological Semantics as an Evolving Research Program

HARRIET ZUCKERMAN

"Sociological semantics" is a distinctly Mertonian research program that takes words, phrases, aphorisms, slogans, and other linguistic forms as subjects of inquiry. This essay examines the origins of sociological semantics and its evolution, and comments on some directions future research might take. I write as Robert Merton's one-time student, as his frequent collaborator, and as his wife and partner for forty-two years.[1]

The Travels and Adventures of Serendipity: A Study in Sociological Semantics and the Sociology of Science—by Merton and his coauthor Elinor Barber (2004)—is my point of departure. Its history is unconventional, to say the least, having been completed (more precisely, almost completed) in 1958 and then remaining "carefully unpublished" for almost forty-five years (Merton 2004a:x).

The protracted pause between *Serendipity's* near completion and its ultimate publication has had the paradoxical effect of making Merton's first contribution to the research program and his last the very same, despite his having written copiously in the interim on subjects he would come to label "sociological semantics." For those familiar with Merton's work, it will come as no surprise that there was a foreshadowing of things to come before he settled down to work on *Serendipity*.

In 1949, in "Bureaucratic Structure and Personality," he beguilingly calls attention to the sociological potentials of the study of words: "The diagnostic significance of such linguistic indices as epithets has scarcely been explored by the sociologist. . . . A sociological study of 'vocabularies of encomium and opprobrium should lead to valuable findings'" (1949 in 1968b:258n24). The significance of words as "strategic research materials" (1987) in sociology was evidently in his mind at least a decade before the beginning of the Serendipity project.

Through the years, as his various contributions to sociological semantics accumulated, he became convinced that the study of "culturally strategic language" held sociological promise in general, not only in the particular cases he explored (1997:225). And this conviction led him to consider the problematics sociological semantics would address, that is, what questions such inquires would have to consider and the research procedures that would be fruitfully employed to study them. His multiple publications suggest that such procedures would include archival forays, the content analysis of texts and quantitative and qualitative analyses of the appearances of particular words or phrases in all manner of writings in one language and in multiple languages where appropriate. Dictionaries would, of course, be key sources for the systematic study of the appearance of words, their meanings, and the transformations in them through time and space (2004:245–250).[2] Using these procedures, separately and together, makes it possible to track who coined particular words, under what circumstances, for what purposes, and how their use changed or if they disappeared altogether.

Appropriately enough, Merton gave serious attention to what this research program should be called and he ruminated at length on a number of possibilities. These included Historical Semantics, Sociological Rhetoric, and Social Linguistics, all of which he rejected as misleading or inappropriate for the purpose. Eventually, sociological semantics emerged as the best of the lot (2004a:x). It is no coincidence that the term appears in the subtitle of *Serendipity* as "*A Study in Sociological Semantics and the Sociology of Science.*" His intent, clearly, was to call attention to sociological semantics and to pique readers' curiosity as to what exactly it (they) might be.

Merton had a lifelong love affair with language for its own sake and believed it was far more than a vehicle for communication. (His large collection of dictionaries of all sorts is material testimony to his affection for words. His library held a hundred or more, including a full set of *The Oxford English Dictionary* with all its supplements, multiple copies of Webster's, unabridged and abridged, foreign language dictionaries, dictionaries of scientific and technical terms, such staples as Brewer's *Dictionary of Phrases and Fables*, and such specialized volumes as the *Dictionary of Saints* and the *Dictionary of Angels*.[3]) Almost from the outset of his career,[4] he sought apt terms or phrases for concepts and phenomena not because new terms could be clever substitutes for common words but instead because he thought that precise terminology actively contributed to the development of science and scholarship. Evocative terms can illuminate phenomena heretofore unobserved, they can sharpen the meaning of concepts that otherwise could be obscure, they could underscore the similarities between phenomena that, on the face of it, appear to be entirely different, and a compact term can help ensure that a concept not "slip from view" (1968a:15). Consider only a few of the concepts he probed and the terms he introduced that have since found their way into the general language: self-fulfilling prophecy, unanticipated consequences, Matthew Effect, and influential.

Merton's intense engagement with words and his studies in sociological semantics might seem to have been connected with the "linguistic turn" in philosophy. As far as I know, they were not, despite his having read and reread Wittengenstein and the works of philosophers and scientists who were members of the Vienna Circle. This remains an open question. However, there is no evidence that his interest in sociological semantics was encouraged by J. L. Austin's investigation of "speech acts" (1962) and its immense influence in philosophy, linguistics, and literary studies. And it would be quite misleading to claim that his sociological semantics anticipated the development of "speech act theory" or stimulated the now widespread interest in "performativity" in studies of gender and politics or science studies. (See Butler 1990; Pickering 1995; Callon 1998; MacKenzie 2006, 2007). The absence of citations referring to the linguistic turn, speech act theory, or performativity in his papers on sociological semantics, despite his habit of keeping his intellectual debts straight via detailed footnotes, suggests that to the extent he considered these matters, he concluded that these developments were different from those he pursued.[5] And for good reason, since speech act theory focuses on "doing things with words," to paraphrase Austin, while various strains of performativity analysis treat, as Butler has put it, "the reiterative power of discourse to produce the phenomena that it regulates and constrains." In science studies, such explorations have focused on the specific case of finance theory and its effects on market behavior. They are all about words and more or less contemporaneous with sociological semantics but their objectives and modes of inquiry are otherwise unconnected.[6]

Thus claims that Merton anticipated Austin or Butler or Callon or MacKenzie are also unwarranted. Merton was decidedly impatient with unwarranted claims of anticipation, including those which cast him as having ideas in advance of others when he was up to something different. He was particularly sensitive to the differences between discoveries and prediscoveries, genuine anticipations and pseudoanticipations and adumbrations in the history of science and indeed went to great pains to distinguish between them (1968a:13–14).[7]

Merton did not define "sociological semantics" in one fell swoop but he said enough about its objectives and provided more than sufficient examples of such investigations to make its reconstruction unproblematic. For example, in the preface to *Serendipity*, he wrote that sociological semantics "examines the ways in which [words] acquire new meanings as [they] diffuse through different social collectivities" (2004a:x).[8] Elsewhere, he and his coauthors observe that "simple phrases, aphorisms, dicta—their ability to summarize, epitomize, exemplify, or even create complex programs of research or action—has long been known" (Merton, Sills, and Stigler 1984:319). He also took note of classes of words and phrases meriting sociological attention, including slogans, niche words, loan words (words taken from one language and adopted without translation into another), vogue words, nonce words, idioms, eponyms (to which he paid considerable attention in his analyses of the allocation and misallocation of credit in science), neologisms,[9] epithets and compliments, words that are profane and those that are sacred, and words whose history, use, and meanings, both lost and acquired, would tell much about social life but are rarely examined systematically.[10] Two assumptions underlying inquiries in sociological semantics are that words can be cues to or indicators of the existence of significant social phenomena and that words are not inert labels but have their own effects on social action.

Thus, sociological semantics explores:

- The origins of particular words and phrases and the social standing of their originators;

- The social patterning of their use;
- The changing meanings attached to them, that is, their evolution;
- Their modes of diffusion;
- The consequences, intended and otherwise, of their use;
- And the conditions of their survival or disappearance.

In gross quantitative terms, Merton published seventeen papers of varying length, three books, and the massive compendium *Social Science Quotations*, all, in one sense or another, bearing on sociological semantics, exemplifying its practice, or addressing the role language plays in science and scholarship.[11] Most of these treat the historical development and social implications of particular words and constructs as well as the social contexts in which they arose, were transmitted, and changed or maintained their meanings. The size of this corpus makes it clear that sociological semantics was no passing interest for Merton.

This is not the place to review the each of these contributions, though as a group, they show the evolution of Merton's thinking about words and about what their study could convey about social phenomena. I turn instead to Merton's study of the origins of the word *scientist* as a single case in point (1997).[12]

This exemplary piece opens with three observations, the first from Balzac, "What a splendid book could be written about the life and adventures of a word"; the second, an injunction from C. S. Pierce to William James, "I wish you would reflect seriously on the moral aspect of terminology"; and the third from Lucien Febvre "to probe the history of a word will not be labor lost"(1997:225). Merton takes these as encouragement for his "continue[ing] excursions into the sociological history of *culturally strategic* words by examining the genesis and de-gendered evolution of the English word *scientist*"(1997:225). And culturally strategic the word turns out to be. Introduced in 1834, two centuries after the emergence of modern science in England, the word had many critics and few if any advocates despite its being proposed by the academically impeccable William Whewell. Whewell was Professor of Mineralogy and later of Moral Philosophy at Trinity College, Cambridge, a Fellow of the Royal Society of London, and cofounder and president of the British Association for the Advancement of Science.[13] Indeed, Whewell proposed the word not once but twice, and both times it was rejected roundly for being a hybrid of a Latin root and a Greek suffix. Even "Darwin's bulldog," the generally forward thinking anatomist T. H. Huxley, "considered 'scientist' as degraded as the word 'electrocution' and [the word] was [also] condemned by the Duke of Argyll, Lord Rayleigh and Sir John Lubbock" (Merton 1997:232). For Merton, "the bastard word *scientist*" flouted "then and there rules of word formation . . . [that] prohibited such miscegenation between the Latin stem and the Greek suffix" (1997:235).

The record suggests that its obviously epicene character had nothing to do with the disdain the new coinage evoked.

From a sociological perspective, the word *scientist* evokes a whole set of associations—not only those concerning views prevailing at the time about how new words should be formed but also about the unity of the sciences and the demarcation of science from other kinds of cognitive activities, about the process of specialization of scientific knowledge and scientific inquiry, the cultural imagery of science, the legitimation of words and concepts, and not least, about the place of women in scientific inquiry and their distinctive sensibilities in perceiving natural phenomena.[14]

Drawing on all manner of documentary materials in a search for appearances of the word "scientist," Merton's first treats its "prime" origins, and then turns to the resistance the word encountered, its subsequent dormancy, and its ultimate acceptance owing to the growing significance and power of science. The next section, titled the "The Epicene Word Scientist," takes on that property of the word, and examines its absence of gender specificity and much more, including the contention that "there is a sex in minds."[15] The last takes up the weighty question of who can legitimately be called a scientist and where the boundaries lie between science and nonscience.

But these important subjects do not exhaust the possibilities for further inquiry into sociological semantics suggested by study of the word *scientist*. At least three additional themes deserve attention since each is relevant to the probability that new coinages will survive. The first is whether and in what respects a given word emerges in response to a socially recognized *need*. The second pertains to the *contexts* in which words are invented, what Merton called the "enabling contexts of creation" The history of the word *scientist* suggests that the same contexts can at one and the same time encourage the inventions of new words and discourage their further use. The third is that inventions of new words, like inventions of all sorts, are apt to produce *unintended consequences*. Once a word or phrase has been proposed, it often has consequences, over the short and the long run, that were altogether unintended by its originator.

Invention as a Response to Need

The documentary material on which Merton draws demonstrates "recurrent" demands for a word to describe those who "cultivate science" in general[16] rather than in each of the sciences specifically. At the time, terms for scientific specialists such as chemist and geologist were well established but no term existed for the collective other than "Men of Science" or "Scientific Men." In 1830, "cultivators of natural science" was suggested by the Scottish educator and agricultural chemist, James F. W. Johnston. Not surprisingly, that unwieldy label did not take hold.[17] However, Johnston's proposal of the term indicates that Whewell was not alone in thinking that some way had to be found to designate all those who did science.

Whewell's first attempt was made in an altogether indirect fashion. In an anonymous review (later acknowledged to be his) of a book by Mary Somerville, Whewell wrote, there is a:

> want of any name by which we can designate the students of the knowledge of the material world collectively. We are informed that this difficulty was felt very oppressively by the members of the British Association for the Advancement of Science at their meetings at York, Oxford and Cambridge. . . .[Whewell then goes on to say,] some anonymous gentleman proposed that by analogy with the word *artist*, they might form *scientist*, and added that there could be no scruple with this termination when we have such words as *sciolist, economist* and *atheist*—but this was not generally palatable. (Quoted in Merton 1997:227)

It was in this doubly anonymous proposal that the word *scientist* appeared in print for the first time. But if there was a need for such a word, evidently *scientist* failed to satisfy it at the time. It did not take hold. It would not be until 1847 that Whewell once more proposed the word, this time under his own name in the second edition of his *Philosophy of the Inductive Sciences*: "We need very much a name to describe a cultivator of science in general. I should incline to call him a Scientist." Again, his proposal not only failed to find support, once again it was vigorously rejected. Whewell would use the word in print one more time, in 1851, in a lecture in which the phrase "men of science" appears three times. Still, at the end, he resorts to using "scientist" followed by the phrase "if I may use the word." Merton observes that "One could scarcely ask for a more eloquent expression of an ambivalent affirmation-and-denial of a terminological brainchild" (1997:234).

Other evidence also suggests that there was recognition that a word for "cultivators of natural science" was needed and not just by Englishmen. Ever thorough, Merton searched American dictionaries and found a listing for *scientist* in the 1864 *Webster's* with an attribution to someone named "Gould." No other identifier was provided. The 1890 edition of *Webster's* also contained the word *scientist* but now, it was attributed to Benjamin A. Gould, a well-known American astronomer and President of the American Association for the Advancement of Science (AAAS). A hunch led Merton to guess that if Gould had used the word, it ought to have been in a speech he made to the AAAS, the kin-organization to the British Association that Whewell had founded and over which he had presided. This then led to a long search through the undigitized nineteenth-century proceedings of the AAAS and then to Merton finding what he privately referred to as his "smoking gun." Gould had indeed used the word in 1869 in an address to the AAAS in which he also said that he had proposed the word twenty years earlier as a general label for those who sought natural knowledge. Merton concluded that the Whewell-Gould invention must have been a multiple independent coinage rather than a transatlantic migrant. Thus, however much need there was on both continents for the word *scientist*, it plainly did not win the day in either place for some time.

There is surely more to be learned about the role need plays in the invention of words and in their survival. Indeed, it suggests the hypothesis that words coming into language in response to perceived need should have a better chance of acceptance and continued use than those invented for other reasons. In the instance of the word *scientist*, however, perceived need failed initially to guarantee the word's success. It was after that need was reinforced by historical change that *scientist* came into widespread use. Merton did not explicitly pursue the relationship between need and the invention of words any further than taking note of it but he might well have done so, since he had been occupied with that relationship as early as his doctoral dissertation, which dealt, in part, with the sources of innovation in science and technology and with the well-known proposal that "need is the mother of invention." He coolly noted there that the relationship can go both ways, need may call forth invention but invention also has a way of evoking needs (1938:234–261).

Contexts of Invention and Contexts of Reception

As we have seen, the need for a word that would refer to cultivators of natural knowledge was recognized initially among members of the tight network of Victorian academics and scientists and among those in the more extended network of interested laymen, many of whom were members of the British Association for the Advancement of Science. These groups served as "sociocognitive micro- and macro-environments" for invention, that is, they were "conducive to the development of new ideas" (1979, 2004b:264–268).[18] It seems clear from the history of the word *scientist*, however, that the very same sociocognitive environments which supported the invention of the new word were the same ones that mounted resistance to it. Prevailing norms about proper language formation in this instance trumped the power of need.

The word also failed the mellifluence test, evoking complaints about what seemed to Victorian ears to be an excess of "s" sounds, especially in the plural. Merton observes that "sociology," also a Latin and Greek hybrid, and which came into being around the same time,[19] did not fare much better, nor did Whewell's coinage *physicist* inspire enthusiasm. Its plural form also provoked "auditory discomfort" as it "contains "four sibilant consonants [that] fiz like a squib." Resistance to certain new words mobilized in specified sociocognitive environments seems to be a worthy problem in sociological semantics, as is the capacity of such environments to have encouraged their invention.

The Fate of Words and Their Uses:
Unanticipated Consequences

Coining words, like other purposive actions, can have unanticipated consequences even if their specifics cannot be predicted in detail. The meaning attached to new words and their uses is apt to depart from the intentions of their coiners.

If Whewell meant to invent a word for those who pursued scientific inquiry in general, he was apparently unaware that his word was gender free, much less having the intent that it be so. Indeed, Whewell's review of Mary Somerville's *On the Connexion of the Physical Sciences* provides evidence that Whewell did not think of women as suitable practitioners of science. At the time, of course, there were precious few who were. Somerville, whose obituary referred to her as "the queen of science," was admired for her understanding of esoteric scientific knowledge and her ability to write about it in a way that was comprehensible to laymen and laywomen. She was, however, not a scientific investigator. Instead, she was a gifted interpreter of the scientific contributions of others (Merton 1997:238).[20] Whewell, despite his admiration for Somerville, did not believe that men and women thought about natural phenomena in the same way and that while women might have special perceptual abilities, these were distinctly limited. In that same review, Whewell, as Merton puts it, "launched . . . on a veritable ocean of sex-laden and gender-laden reflections [that] proved at times to be perceptibly if unwittingly patronizing":

> Notwithstanding all the dreams of theorists, *there is a sex in minds* [sic] . . . One of the characteristics of the female intellect . . . is a clearness of perception, as far as it goes; with them, action is the result of feelings; thought, of seeing; their practical emotions do not wait for instruction from speculation; their reasoning is undisturbed by the prospect of its practical consequences. . . . Their course of action is not perturbed by the powers of philosophic thought, even when the latter are strongest. The heart goes on with its own concerns, asking no counsel of the head; and, in return, the working of the head (if it does work) is not impeded by its having to solve questions of casuistry for the heart. . . . what [women] understand they understand clearly; what they see at all, they see in sunshine. (Quoted in 1997:240)

With convictions such as these, one would be hard put to argue that Whewell intended his new word to include both men and women who pursued science, much less to champion the equality of the sexes.

That the word *scientist* ultimately came into common and unproblematic use was, as noted earlier, a response to the emerging significance of the sciences in England and the United States. The acceptance of the word took time and its being gender free would seem to have become relevant only when the number of women pursuing scientific work began to multiply.

However, the use of the term *men of science* stubbornly persisted despite its growing inaptness. As late as the 1960s, the standard source in the United States for biographical information on scientists was the multivolume *American Men of Science*, so titled despite its having included women among its listings from its first edition in 1906 onward. It was not until 1971 that the title of the twelfth edition was changed to *American Men and Women of Science, Formerly American Men of Science*.[21] Five years later, the 1976 edition lost its extension and became simply *American Men and Women of Science*.

Merton musters further evidence on the long transition from "man of science" to the gender-free word *scientist* in successive editions of the *Oxford English Dictionary*, "the grandest of English dictionaries," known familiarly as the "OED." From 1914 onward, the word *scientist* was defined as "a man of science." This formulation remained through the publication of the supplement (between 1982 and 1986). It was not until 1989 with the second edition of the OED that the gendered definition was abandoned and in its place the neutral, "A person with expert knowledge of a science; a person using scientific methods" was substituted (1997:242–243).

So much for sociological analysis of the word *scientist* and its emergence, rejection, and ultimate survival. One might well be reluctant to accept a single case as convincing evidence for the value of studying the sociological semantics. Abundant support for this conjecture, however, can be found among the papers and books constituting the Mertonian corpus on the subject.

Merton was well aware of the value of earmarking new subject matters for sociological inquiry.[22] His doctoral dissertation treated the rise of modern science in seventeenth-century England (1938), a far from conventional subject for sociologists to study at the time. He was convinced however that science and its institutional arrangements were manifestly worthy subjects of study. Evidently, he concluded some decades later that words, phrases, slogans, and other semantic objects would also provide new and important opportunities for investigation.[23] Merton knew a good idea when he had one or when a good idea chose him as its discoverer. As the economist, Robert M. Solow put it:

There is no mystery in the fact that he [Bob Merton] was unappeasably attracted to all kinds of ideas, especially ideas about social institutions, but really about anything. What is more mysterious is that somehow ideas were attracted to him, as if he were some kind of intellectual flypaper. If we took any six of us here and put us in a room with Bob Merton and released an idea somewhere near the chandelier, the odds are two to one that it would flutter down and come to rest on Merton. You realize what that means: the random idea had a two-thirds probability of finding its way to Merton and a probability of just one-eighteenth of coming to rest on one of us. And we are intelligent, idea-friendly people or we wouldn't be here. He must have emitted some pheromone-like come-on [for ideas] (2004:17–18).

Merton was doubly convinced that language is an untapped fund of sociological knowledge and an unexamined force in social life, one to which sociologists might well pay further attention. These convictions lie at the heart of the proposed research program on sociological semantics. Should that program take hold, it would not be the first time that Robert Merton broke new ground and fathered a line of inquiry. It would, however, be the last.

Appendix

ROBERT MERTON'S CONTRIBUTIONS TO SOCIOLOGICAL SEMANTICS

1960. "'Recognition' and 'Excellence': Instructive Ambiguities." In *Recognition and Excellence*, ed. Adam Yarmolinsky, 297–328. New York: Free Press.

1961. "Now the Case for Sociology: The Canons of the Anti-Sociologist." *New York Times Magazine*, July 16.

1965/1985/1993. *On the Shoulders of Giants: A Shandean Postscript.* NY: The Free Press. Subsequent editions in English published by Harcourt Brace Jovanovich and by University of Chicago Press.

1969/1972. "Sociology, Jargon and Slangish," In *Sociology: Theories in Conflict*, ed. R. Serge Denisoff, 52–58. Belmont, CA. Wadsworth Publishing Co. (Originally published in The *Subterranean Sociologist*, 1969)

1975. "On the Origin of the Term: Pseudo-Gemeinschaft." *Western Sociological Review* 6:83.

1979. *The Sociology of Science: An Episodic Memoir.* Carbondale, Illinois, University of Southern Illinois Press.

1980. "On the Oral Transmission of Knowledge." In *Sociological Traditions from Generation to Generation: Glimpses of the American Experience*, ed. Robert K. Merton and Matilda White Riley, 1–35. Norwood, NJ: Ablex Publishing Co.

1981. Our Sociological Vernacular," *Columbia Magazine*. November:42–44.

1984. "Socially Expected Durations: A Case Study of Concept Formation in Sociology." In *Conflict and Consensus: In Honor of Lewis A. Coser*, ed. W. W. Powell and Richard Robbins, 262–283. New York: Free Press.

1987. "Three Fragments from a Sociologist's Notebook: Establishing the Phenomenon, Specified Ignorance, and Strategic Research Materials." *Annual Reviews*, 13:1–28.

1988/1997. "De-Gendering 'Man of Science': The Genesis and Epicene Character of the Word Scientist." In *Sociological Visions*, ed. Kai Erikson, 225–253. New Haven: Yale University Press. (1988 edition published in Italian "Le Multiplici origine e il carrettere epicene del termine inglese Scientist," *Scientia: L'Imagine e il Mondo*. Commune di Milano, 273–293.)

1989/1998. "Unanticipated Consequences and Kindred Sociological Ideas: A Personal Gloss." In *L'Opera di Robert K. Merton e la sociologica contemporanea*, ed. C. Mongardini and S. Tabboni, 307–329. Genova: ECIG. Published in the United States in 1998. "Unanticipated Consequences and Kindred Sociological Ideas: A Personal Gloss." In *Robert K. Merton and Contemporary Sociology*, ed. Carlo Mongardini and Simonetta Tabboni, 295–318. New Brunswick: Transaction Publishers.

1992. "Patterns in the Scholarly Use of Quotations," Social Science Research Council *ITEMS* 46, 4:75–76.

1993. "Genesis of the Field of 'Science, Technology and Society (STS)." *Journal of Science Policy and Research Management* (Japanese).

1995. "Opportunity Structure: The Emergence, Diffusion, and Differentiation of a Sociological Concept, 1930–1950." In *Advances in Criminological Theory: The Legacy of Anomie Theory*. Vol. 6, ed. Freda Adler and William S. Laufer, 3–78. New Brunswick, NJ: Transaction Publishers.

1995. "The Thomas Theorem and The Matthew Effect." *Social Forces* 74, 2:379–424.

Merton, Robert K., and Elinor Barber. 2004. *The Travels and Adventures of Serendipity. A Study in Sociological Semantics and the Sociology of Science*. Princeton: Princeton University Press, 2004. Italian Edition: 2002 as *Viaggi e avventure della Serendipity: Saggio di semantica sociologica e sociologica della scienza*. Bologna: Il Mulino.

Merton, Robert K., David L. Sills and Stephen M. Stigler. 1984. "The Kelvin Dictum and Social Science: An Excursion into the History of an Idea." *Journal of the History of the Behavioral Sciences* 20 (October): 319–331.

Merton, Robert K., and Alan Wolfe. 1995. "The Cultural and Social Incorporation of Sociological Knowledge." *The American Sociologist* 26, 3 (Fall):15–38.

Sills, David L., and Robert K. Merton, eds. 1991. *Social Science Quotations: Who Said What, When, and Where. International Encyclopedia of the Social Sciences*, Vol. 19. New York: Macmillan.

ANTICIPATION

1949/1968. "Bureaucratic Structure and Personality." In *Social Theory and Social Structure*. Enlarged Edition. New York: Free Press. P. 258, note 24: "The diagnostic significance of such linguistic indices as epithets has scarcely been explored by the sociologist. . . . A sociological study of "vocabularies of encomium and opprobrium should lead to valuable findings."

UNPUBLISHED MANUSCRIPTS

1977. "Unanticipated Consequences and Kindred Sociological Ideas: A Retrospective Essay." In *Unanticipated Consequences of Social Action: Variations on a Theme*, ed. Robert K. Merton. Working paper 37 (Two versions, one dated 1977 and the second dated 1978.) Columbia University Special Collections Library, Robert K. Merton Archive.

1978. "E. M. Forster, The Little Old Lady, Thought and Attention." Letter to Gerald Edelman, Thanksgiving Day. 24 plus 9 pp addendum. Columbia University Special Collections Library, Robert K. Merton Archive.

Notes

This is a revised version of remarks presented at the conference on "Robert Merton's Work on the Sociology of Science and Sociological Explanation," held at Columbia University on August 9–10, 2007. At that meeting I learned that Charles Camic's paper on Merton as a historian of ideas and my own paper on sociological semantics were unexpectedly and fruitfully complementary. (See Camic's essay in this volume.) Subsequently, we jointly assembled comprehensive bibliographies of Robert Merton's work bearing on each subject. (See the appendix to this essay.)

1. I have found no graceful way of referring to the originator of sociological semantics. Identifying him as Robert Merton or more tersely as Merton puts us at an uncomfortable distance but I have concluded that using the informal Bob in this context is unacceptable. Hereafter, he shall be Robert Merton or Merton, just as he is in texts by other authors.

2. For one example, see Merton's tracing the evolving the definition of the word "serendipity" in dictionaries over the course of the twentieth century and its metamorphosis from an attribute of phenomena or events to an "individual disposition." (2004b:245–50).

3. I do not count sets of the *Dictionary of National Biography*, the *Dictionary of American Biography*, the *Dictionary of Scientific Biography*, and an array of concordances of various sorts.

4. While at Harvard, Merton was research assistant to Pitirim A. Sorokin, who was then working on the monumental *Social and Cultural Dynamics*. Merton reports making the "audacious suggestion" that Sorokin drop his central term "sensuous" and substitute "the far less connotational word 'sensate'" for cultures emphasizing "the satisfaction of material needs and desires," one of the triad of cultural types on which Sorokin's analysis rested. The other types were, of course, "ideational" and "idealistic." "The suggestion was grounded in the belief that John Milton's word 'sensuous' . . . hardly corresponded to the intended meaning." Evidently, Sorokin was convinced by his young assistant since the term "sensate" was used thereafter. Merton goes on to comment wryly some fifty years later that *The Oxford English Dictionary Supplement* (4:55) ascribes the sociological use of the word "sensate" to P. A. Sorokin (Merton 1988:25n5).

5. Merton was greatly interested in Donald McKenzie's papers, which he read in draft form. It is not unreasonable to think that his interest in part was due to MacKenzie's analysis of the role Merton's economist son, Robert C. Merton, played in the formulation of options pricing theory.

6. Nor does sociological semantics, as Merton conceived it, have more than a distant relationship to "conversational analysis" along the lines Emanuel Schegloff has pursued, despite Schegloff having been a colleague at Columbia (Schegloff 1968). He read Shegloff's papers and they talked, but their objectives were quite different. Merton was more in tune with the development of Charles Bazerman's thinking about and studies of the emergence of the scientific paper and with Bazerman's further work on scientific rhetoric (2000). Bazerman attended the seminar on the sociology of science that Merton and I taught at Columbia and the three of us talked severally about it.

7. Merton observes in the context of writing about prediscoveries, rediscoveries, anticipations, and adumbrations that "A suitable vocabulary is needed to designate varying degrees of resemblance between earlier and later formulations of scientific ideas and findings" (1968a:13). Such distinctions are critical to getting the history of science right and they are central to identifying authentic, independent, multiple discoveries in science, phenomena in the development of science Merton returned to over and over again.

8. As he put it, *Serendipity* is not a work in "'*historical* semantics' but was, rather an early exercise in what can be better described as a barely emerging '*sociological* semantics' that examines the ways in which the word *serendipity* acquired new meanings as it diffused through different social collectivities" (2004a:x).

9. All apart from his skill in devising new words, Merton took seriously the study of neologisms in the history of sociology and the history science more generally. In "Three Fragments," he lists no fewer than fourteen sociological neologisms meriting historical research and analysis (1987:25–26).

10. A conspicuous counterexample of the general inattention to the sociological implications of words is Stanley Lieberson's study of the changing popularity of children's first names over time and in a variety of communities. He uses the patterning of names to exceptional effect in analyzing changing tastes and preferences and their use in the emergence of a more general theory of social change. (See, for example, 2000).

11. See the appendix to this article for a comprehensive bibliography of Robert Merton's work bearing on sociological semantics. Merton's files recently yielded up two additional unpublished items. The first is a collection of papers assembled in 1977 on "unanticipated consequences" and kindred ideas and includes papers by Albert Cohen, Richard Henshel, Gary Marx, Sam Sieber, and Merton himself. It was under contract at the time Merton decided to set it aside. There is no indication in the file why he did so. Another is a long "epistolary essay," written in 1978 to the neurobiologist Gerald Edelman, which probes the implications of the phrase uttered by the elderly Mrs. Moore in E. M. Forster's *A Passage to India*, "How do I know what I think until I hear what I say?" Merton took this as the occasion to probe the connections between thinking and speaking. Both manuscripts are available in the Columbia University Library Special Collections, Robert K. Merton Archive.

12. An earlier version of the paper was published in 1988 in Italian. Successive editions of this paper were delivered at the meetings of the American Philosophical Society, Harvard University's Department of the History of Science, The Rockefeller University, The New York Academy of Sciences, and the University of Oslo prior to publication (1997:253n54). These multiple drafts and multiple deliveries testify that Merton was a believer in revisions via "oral publication" much like publishing successive revised editions of books is a standard mode in the scholarly world.

13. See Morrell and Thackray 1982 for the significance of the Asssociation in British society.

14. This account of the sociological value found in exploring the emergence of the word *scientist* is a condensed version of what appears in Merton 1997:226.

15. That Whewell was convinced that "there *is* a sex in minds" [my italics] makes it ironic for him to have coined a term that was gender free. As Merton notes, Londa Schiebinger's *The Mind Has No Sex?* serves as a counterpoint to this declaration, following the claim by the seventeenth-century French social philosopher François Poullain de la Barre, "L'ésprit n'a point de sexe."

16. As Merton observes, the call for a general term for "students of the material world" presupposes a common identity among them and thus, to some degree, unity among the sciences.

17. Merton (1997:229) reports that this plea-cum-proposal was published by Johnston in "Meeting of the Cultivators of Natural Science and Medicine at Hamburgh, in September 1830," *The Edinburgh Journal of Science* N.S. IV April 1831:189–244 at 218.

18. The affinity between sociocognitive environments and Ludwik Fleck's "thought collectives" unsurprisingly did not escape Merton attention. Fleck's rarely read, difficult German text, *Genesis and Development of a Scientific Fact* (1935), was in a sense rediscovered when Thomas Kuhn referred to it in *The Structure of Scientific Revolutions* (1962). It was subsequently translated and edited by Merton and Thaddeus J. Trenn. Not unconnected are the "evocative environments" and their role in stimulating Nobel prizewinning research. (Zuckerman 1977:131, 172–173)

19. August Comte had the same misgivings about the word *sociology* and rightly so, as the field it described was said in one English journal to be "barbarously termed" (Merton 1997:231).

20. Despite her large following, Somerville was not a full-fledged but only "an *honorary* . . . member of several Royal Societies" (Merton 1997:238).

21. With that change in 1971 came another. Social scientists had initially been included but were separated out from physical and biological scientists and came to occupy their own set of volumes. So much for the unity of the sciences.

22. Undertaking the study of new subject matter is related to, but not the same as, selecting "strategic research sites" or "strategic research materials." In the latter instance, the investigator knows what problems are to be investigated and a search is made to identify the "material that exhibits the phenomena to be explained or interpreted to such advantage and in such accessible form that it enables the fruitful investigation of previously stubborn problems" (Merton 1987:10–11). Studying an entirely new domain usually means that the problems are not yet known nor are the phenomena to be explained altogether clear.

23. However, he was less than convinced that sociological semantics could become a separate sociological subspecialty. Rather, he predicted without much elaboration that in the end it would become a "distinct subspecialty of [the well-established field of] sociolinguistics" (2004:251n22).

References

Austin, John L. 1962. *How to Do Things with Words*. Cambridge: Harvard University Press.

Bazerman, Charles. 2000. *Shaping Written Knowledge*. Madison, WI: University of Wisconsin Press.

Butler, Judith. 1990. *Gender Trouble: Feminism and the Subversion of Identity*. London: Routledge.

Callon, Michel. 1998. "Introduction: The Embeddedness of Economic Markets in Economics." In *The Laws of the Markets*, ed. Michel Callon, 1–57. London: Blackwell Publishers.

Fleck, Ludwik. [1935] 1977. *Genesis and Development of a Scientific Fact*. Ed. Thaddeus J. Trenn and Robert K. Merton and trans. Fred Bradley and Thaddeus J. Trenn. Chicago: University of Chicago Press.

Kuhn, Thomas. 1962. *The Structure of Scientific Revolutions*. International Encyclopedia of Unified Science, Volume 2:2. Chicago: University of Chicago Press.

Lieberson, Stanley. 2000. *A Matter of Taste: How Names, Fashions, and Cultures Change*. New Haven: Yale University Press.

Mackenzie, Donald. 2006. *An Engine, Not a Camera: How Financial Models Shape Markets*. Cambridge, MA: MIT Press.

——. 2007. "Is Economics Performative? Option Theory and the Construction of Derivative Markets." In *Do Economists Make Markets? On the Performativity of Economics*, ed. Donald MacKenzie, Fabian Muniesa and Lucia Siu, 54–86. Princeton: Princeton University Press.

Merton, Robert K. 1936. "The Unanticipated Consequences of Purposive Social Action." *American Sociological Review* 1:894–904.

——. 1938. *Science, Technology and Society in Seventeenth-Century England*. In *Osiris*, ed. George Sarton. Bruges: St. Catherine's Press, 1938 and New York: Howard Fertig Press, 2001.

——. [1948] 1968. "The Self-Fulfilling Prophecy." In *Social Theory and Social Structure*, 475–490. Enlarged Edition. New York: Free Press.

——. [1949] 1968. "Bureaucratic Structure and Personality." In *Social Theory and Social Structure*, 249–260. Enlarged Edition. New York: Free Press.

——. 1960. "'Recognition' and 'Excellence' Instructive Ambiguities." In *Recognition and Excellence*, ed. Adam Yarmolinsky, 297–328. New York: Free Press.

——. 1961. "Now the Case for Sociology: The Canons of the Anti-Sociologist." *New York Times Magazine* July 16.

——. [1965/1985] 1993. *On the Shoulders of Giants: A Shandean Postscript*. NY: The Free Press. Subsequent editions published by Harcourt Brace Jovanovich and by University of Chicago Press.

——. 1968. "On the History and Systematics of Sociological Theory." In *Social Theory and Social Structure*, 1–38. Enlarged Edition. New York: Free Press.

——. [1969] 1972. "Sociology, Jargon and Slangish." In *Sociology: Theories in Conflict*, ed. R. Serge Denisoff, 52–58. Belmont, CA: Wadsworth Publishing Co. (Originally published in *Subterranean Sociologist*)

——. 1975. "On the Origin of the Term: Pseudo-Gemeinschaft." *Western Sociological Review* 6: 83.

——. 1977. "Unanticipated Consequences and Kindred Sociological Ideas: A Retrospective Essay." In *Unanticipated Consequences of Social Action: Variations on a Theme*, 1–37. Unpublished manuscript. Columbia University Special Collections Library, Robert K. Merton Archive. A second edition of this paper is dated 1978.

——. 1978. "E. M. Forster, 'The Little Old Lady,' Thought and Attention." Letter to Gerald Edelman. Thanksgiving Day. 24 plus 9 pp in addendum. Columbia University Special Collections Library, Robert K. Merton Archive.

——. 1979. *The Sociology of Science: An Episodic Memoir.* Carbondale, IL: University of Southern Illinois Press.

——. 1980. "On the Oral Transmission of Knowledge." In *Sociological Traditions from Generation to Generation: Glimpses of the American Experience,* ed. Robert K. Merton and Matilda White Riley, 1–35. Norwood, NJ: Ablex Publishing Co.

——. 1981. "Our Sociological Vernacular." *Columbia Magazine,* November: 42–44.

——. 1984. "Socially Expected Durations: A Case Study of Concept Formation in Sociology." In *Conflict and Consensus: In Honor of Lewis A. Coser,* ed. W. W. Powell and Richard Robbins, 262–283. New York: Free Press.

——. 1987. "Three Fragments from a Sociologist's Notebook: Establishing the Phenomenon, Specified Ignorance, and Strategic Research Materials." *Annual Reviews* 13:1–28.

——. 1988. "The Sorokin-Merton Correspondence on 'Puritanism, Pietism and Science,' 1933–34." *Science in Context* 3:1, 293–300.

——. [1988] 1997. "Le Multiplici origine e il carrettere epicene del termine inglese Scientist." In *Scientia: L'Imagine e il Mondo,* 273–293. Commune di Milano.

——. [1989] 1998. "Unanticipated Consequences and Kindred Sociological Ideas: A Personal Gloss." In *L'Opera di Robert K. Merton e la sociologica contemporanea,* ed. C. Mongardini and S. Tabboni, 307–329. Genova: ECIG.

——. 1992. "Patterns in the Scholarly Use of Quotations." *ITEMS* 46 (4):75–76.

——. 1993. "Genesis of the Field of 'Science, Technology and Society (STS).'" *Journal of Science Policy and Research Management* (Japanese).

——. 1995a. "Opportunity Structure: The Emergence, Diffusion, and Differentiation of a Sociological Concept, 1930–1950." In *Advances in Criminological Theory: The Legacy of Anomie Theory,* Vol. 6, ed. Freda Adler and William S. Laufer, 3–78. New Brunswick, NJ: Transaction Publishers.

——. 1995b. "The Thomas Theorem and The Matthew Effect." *Social Forces* 74:379–424.

——. 1997. "De-Gendering 'Man of Science': The Genesis and Epicene Character of the Word Scientist." In *Sociological Visions,* ed. Kai Erikson, 225–253. New Haven: Yale University Press. (English edition of earlier publication in Italian.)

——. 1998. "Unanticipated Consequences and Kindred Sociological Ideas: A Personal Gloss." In *Robert K. Merton and Contemporary Sociology,* ed. Carlo Mongardini and Simonetta Tabboni, 295–318. New Brunswick: Transaction Publishers.

——. 2004a. Preface to *The Travels and Adventures of Serendipity. A Study in Sociological Semantics and the Sociology of Science,* ed. R. K. Merton and E. Barber, ix–x. Princeton: Princeton University Press, 2004.

———. 2004b. "Afterword: Autobiographical Reflections on The Travels and Adventures of Serendipity." In *The Travels and Adventures of Serendipity. A Study in Sociological Semantics and the Sociology of* Science, R. K. Merton and E. Barber, 230–298. Princeton: Princeton University Press.

Merton, Robert K., and Elinor Barber. 2002. *Viaggi e avventure della Serendipity: Saggio di semantica sociologica e sociologica della scienza.* Bologna: Il Mulino:

———. 2004. *The Travels and Adventures of Serendipity: A Study in Sociological Semantics and the Sociology of Science.* Princeton: Princeton University Press.

Merton, Robert K., and David L. Sills, eds. 1990. *Social Science Quotations: International Encyclopedia of the Social Sciences,* Vol. 19. New York: Macmillan Publishing Company.

Merton, Robert K., David L. Sills, and Stephen M. Stigler. 1984. "The Kelvin Dictum and Social Science: An Excursion into the History of an Idea." *Journal of the History of the Behavioral Sciences,* 20 (October):319–331.

Merton, Robert K., and Alan Wolfe. 1995. "The Cultural and Social Incorporation of Sociological Knowledge." *The American Sociologist* 26:15–38.

Morrell, Jack, and Arnold Thackray. 1982. *Gentlemen of Science: Early Years of the British Association for the Advancement of Science.* Oxford: Oxford University Press.

Pickering, Andrew. 1995. *The Mangle of Practice: Time, Agency and Science.* Chicago: University of Chicago Press.

Schegloff, Emanuel A. 1968. "Sequencing in Conversational Openings." *American Anthropologist,* New Series 70:1075–1095

Schiebinger, Londa. 1989. *The Mind Has No Sex?* Cambridge: Harvard University Press.

Whewell, William. 1840. *The Philosophy of the Inductive Sciences, Founded Upon Their History,* 2 vols. London. 2nd ed. 1847.

Zuckerman, Harriet. 1977. *Scientific Elite: Nobel Laureates in the United States.* New York: The Free Press.

12

How Merton Sociologizes the History of Ideas

CHARLES CAMIC

The work of Robert Merton presents a paradox. At all stages of his career, Merton's writings display breathtaking intellectual-historical erudition, an understanding of ideas and thinkers from the past that seems to know no limit and which stands unrivalled among sociologists of the twentieth century. In a footnote of an article published when he was barely twenty-six, Merton mentions casually that "Machiavelli, Vico, Adam Smith (and some later classical economists), Marx, Engels, Wundt, Pareto, Max Weber, Graham Wallas, Cooley, Sorokin, Gini, Chapin, [and] von Schelting" are among "*some* of the *modern* theorists" who concerned themselves with the "unanticipated consequences of purposive action" (1936:894 [emphasis added]). In a midlife essay on "problem-finding in sociology," he comments that "in science as in everyday life, explanations are sometimes provided for things that never were" and then lightly tosses off the following elaboration:

We need hardly review the long list of notorious episodes of this kind in the history of thought. Consider only Seneca explaining why some waters are so dense that no object, however heavy, will sink in them or why lightning freezes wine; Descartes explaining why the pineal gland could exist only in man just a short time before Niels Stensen discovered it in other animals; Hegel solemnly explaining why there could be only seven planets and none between Mars and Jupiter just as Piazzi was discovering Ceres in that very region; the talented physiologist Johannes Muller explaining why the rate of transmission of the nerve impulse could never be measured just a few years before Helmholtz proceeded to measure it; J. S. Mill explaining the impossibility of sound statistical studies of human behavior long after Quetelet and others had conducted such studies. (1959:xiii)

Twenty years later, looking for a simple and convenient illustration of the "logic [of experimental control] built into multivariate analysis," Merton thinks nothing of interjecting that: "One periodically needs to recall from one's student days the pertinence of the story told by Diogenes Laertius about Diogenes the Cynic who, when shown the votive tablets suspected by sailors who had escaped shipwreck 'because they had made their vows,' inquired 'Where are the portraits of those who perished in spite of the vow?'" (1977:34).

Hundreds of such examples appear throughout the Mertonian oeuvre, which at times seems barely able to contain the swell of Merton's immense knowledge of the history of ideas. For sociologists, however, all of this has long been overshadowed by the opening pages of his most widely read work, *Social Theory and Social Structure*, where Merton argues in favor of the "systematics of sociological theory" as against the "history of sociological theory." For decades, this argument has furnished seemingly incontrovertible evidence that, *as a sociologist*, Merton abjured the history of ideas except insofar as past ideas were directly relevant for contemporary sociological analysis. This view, at any rate, has long stood as the received wisdom about Robert Merton and the history of ideas. The first section of this chapter reviews this interpretation. The second section examines a very different aspect of Merton's thought by drawing on a neglected set of writings dating mainly from late in his career. The claim of this section is that, in these writings, Merton fuses the intellectual-historical and sociological dimensions of his thinking to produce an original and fertile historical sociology of the genesis and diffusion of ideas (and the linguistic forms that enfold them). The third section briefly speculates on the relationship between the two sides of Merton's work.

I

The received wisdom about Merton and the history of ideas rests on high textual authority. Barely a page into the 1949 and 1957 editions of *Social Theory and Social Structure*, Merton speaks forcefully of the need to differentiate of the "history of theory" from the "systematics of theory." Applying this distinction to the field of sociology, Merton equates "systematics" with "currently operating" or "utilizable sociological theory," which "represents the highly selective accumulation of those small parts of earlier theory which have thus far survived the tests of empirical research," whereas "the history of theory includes also the far greater mass of conceptions which fell to bits when confronted with empirical test, [among these] the false starts, the archaic doctrines and the fruitless errors of the past." Conceptions of the latter kind, in Merton's view, "may be a useful adjunct to the sociologist's training"—"exercises in the conduct of intellectual inquiry"—but "little of what [many of the intellectual] forerunners [of sociology] wrote remains of pertinence to sociology today." Hence, to confound "history" and "systematics" is to perpetrate a "fatal confusion," which Merton states that he will avoid (in the book that follows) by dealing "*not* with the history of sociological theory but with the systematics of certain theories with which sociologists now provisionally work" (1949:4–5, 1957:4–5 [emphases modified]; cf. 1948:165).

Expressed in such sharp prose, these are not noticeably ambiguous sentences. Even so, in the third edition of the book, Merton returns to the subject, clarifying that his insistence on the distinction between history and systematics aims not to condemn, but rather to encourage "the writing of authentic histories" of sociology by "the authentic historian of ideas"—in this case, the "historian of sociology" (1968:2, 17, 35). While strongly affirming this point, however, Merton continues to insist that for "the *sociologist qua sociologist,* rather than as historian of sociology," "the study of classical writings can be either deplorably useless or wonderfully useful": the first when "anemic practices of mere commentary" and "sterile exegesis" dominate; the second when "the present uses of past theory" guide the engagement with classical predecessors, and sociologists confine their intellectual-historical forays mainly to "following up and developing the [currently promising] theoretical leads of significant predecessors" (1968:35, 30 [emphasis modified]).

That this is Merton's position and that this is the viewpoint that informs many of his substantive writings are not issues at all in dispute among those who have engaged his work. To the contrary, restatements of this motif from *Social Theory and Social Structure* serve to anchor the major exegetical writings on Merton, as well as the edited volumes devoted to the analysis of his thought, all of which agree that "Merton is quite faithful to [his] professed policy" of orienting instrumentally to the intellectual past, drawing upon it only to the degree that doing so furthers contemporary theory and empirical research (Sztompka 2000:15–16; see also Sztompka 1986, 1996; Crothers 1987, 2003; Clark, Modgil, and Modgil 1990; Coser 1975a; Mongardini and Tabboni 1998).

So established, this interpretation has generated what appears to be an obvious corollary: the claim that, as a sociologist, Merton advocated an ahistorical approach to the history of ideas, an approach largely unconcerned with the historical context, with the specific places and periods, in which past ideas originated and subsequently developed. This is the contention, for example, of Lewis Coser—of all of Merton's distinguished students, the scholar who was probably the most knowledgeable about intellectual history. In Coser's view, the analytical procedure that Merton regularly follows when treating social thinkers from the past "is to surgically remove those layers and tissues of a thinker's thought that show the mark of his time, his place, his milieu, so as to be able better to expose that vital core of his message which transcends the various existential limitations that might have entered into his perspective. . . . By stripping [the] time-and-place-bound elements from the intellectual productions of the past, it becomes possible for Merton to incorporate past contributions into the body of current paradigms which can become springboards for future advance" (1975b:87).[1]

As his wording indicates, Coser seeks to characterize Merton's practice as ahistoricizing not to criticize but rather to celebrate Merton for his "creative appropriation" of the past, his ability to extract "theoretical gold [from] the most unlikely . . . quarries" (1975b:96; Coser and Nisbet 1975:7). In contrast, other scholars view this same "stripping" practice as fundamentally objectionable, a major obstacle to the sociological study of intellectual history. In this vein, for instance, Robert Alun Jones reproaches Merton for severely limiting sociologists (as distinct from historians) in regard to "the questions [they] might put to the past and . . . the answers [they] might expect in return" (1983a:132). Moreover, according to Jones, the issues which "the hypothetical adherent of Merton's methodological injunctions [(to distinguish history from systematics) will fail to] yield anything which we might recognize as an account of past social actions" that has historical validity (1983a:132–33; see also Jones 1977, 1983b).

At stake here in regard to Merton is one of the fundamental questions to consider in reckoning with the work of any major figure in the sociological tradition: to what extent does he or she offer an approach that accommodates history and the variety of time and place? Insofar as the history at issue is the history of ideas, both Coser, speaking in favor of Merton, and Jones, writing in opposition, urge the same verdict: namely, that Merton's approach is ahistorical, disregarding the time-and-place-bound elements of the intellectual productions of the past so as to appropriate what holds relevance for those questions, and only those questions, that form part of the present-day systematics of sociological theory. And, perhaps not surprisingly in the face of this agreement among the different scholarly parties, this judgment of Merton has held firm for several decades, provoking no dissent of any kind. For all this, however, overlooked evidence suggests a need to reopen the case.

II

The interpretation of Merton that Section 1 describes was well established by the mid-1970s. Yet, at just this time, Merton was actively engaged in another line of work which would provide one of his main focus points during the last twenty years of his life. Looking backward from the full corpus of writing that Merton eventually produced in this vein, one can, to be sure, find harbingers of these later developments at earlier stages in his career. In his graduate student days, Merton found dictionaries and volumes devoted to quotations and new words "irresistible" (Merton 2004b:239; see also Merton and Barber [1958] 2004:141). As a junior scholar, he observed the great "variety of terms" that different cultures use to capture the phenomenon of unintended consequences and expressed "hopes to devote a monograph. . . . to the history and analysis of this problem" (1936:894n3). At midcareer, he marked "ideas [and] categories of thought" as central topics for the sociology of knowledge ([1945] 1973:12) and turned attention, in a monograph on a World War II bond drive, not only to the rhetoric of persuasion—quoting Hobbes on the power of "*Words* [that] are most grateful to the Ear"—but also to the significance of popular "slogans" ([1946] 2004:20, 33–35; for discussion of Merton's concern with rhetoric, see Simonson 2004, 2010). Simultaneously, he launched the sociology of science and, in doing so, included among its topics the "words" and "concepts" that natural scientists use (Merton and Barber [1958] 2004:67).

From the mid-1950s onward, however, these various undercurrents began to push to the fore and intersect into what gradually emerged as a major research project in its own right. The signal turn in this direction was Merton's 1958 study (with Elinor Barber) of the word "serendipity," though more than four decades lapsed before this study appeared in print (supplemented by extensive additional research on the subject that Merton carried out in his final years) (Merton 2004b). In the interim, Merton published, sometimes in the deceptively quiet guise of autobiographical fragments, a wide range of related studies, among them: *On the Shoulders of Giants* ([1965/1985] 1993), "The Origin of the Term Pseudo-Gemeinschaft" (1975), *The Sociology of Science: An Episodic Memoir* (1977), "The Kelvin Dictum" (with Stigler and Sills, 1984), "De-Gendering 'Man of Science'" (1989 [German], 1997 [English]), "Opportunity Structure" (1995a), and "The Thomas Theorem" (1995b) (see also Merton 1980, [1982] 1984, [1985] 1993, 1998, and Merton and Wolfe 1995). With David Sills, he also produced the massive volume *Social Science Quotations* (1990) and examined the use of quotations as a sociointellectual phenomenon (Sills and Merton 1992a, 1992b).

While this body of work exceeds many times over the opening chapter of *Social Theory and Social Structure*, it remains virtually unknown among sociologists both in terms of its individual items and as a totality. Regarding the totality, Sztompka offers a brief paragraph on Merton's late concern with "the fate of scientific concepts and phrases" (2000:21) and Crothers (2003a) a slightly more extended report (see also Crothers 1987:30–31), but here the scholarly literature stops.[2] And the individual items have hardly fared better, with the equivocal exception of the study of serendipity, which appeared shortly after Merton's death and was widely reviewed in this context. What is more, when sociologists have remarked on some of the separate pieces, the tendency has been to view these as entertainment rather than as contributions to a serious intellectual project, as in Coser's characterization of *On the Shoulders of Giants* as a "delightful and whimsical book" (1975b:86), Crothers's description of the same book as an exercise "couched in a delightful Shandean mode" (1987:39), and

Sztompka's gloss of Merton's article on the Kelvin dictum as an "intellectual game" (1986:101). To date, only humanists (and scientist-humanists) have probed a few of these writings more deeply, albeit not with the purpose of elucidating their sociological contribution (see Donoghue 1985, 1997; Eco 1990; Gould 1990; Holton 1997; Schulman 2003).

That Merton himself viewed these writings in light of a larger intellectual project, rather than as occasional amusements, is something that he made increasingly explicit, however. The earliest direct indication of this larger project appears when, in the original subtitle to their monograph on serendipity, Merton and Barber glossed their work as "a study in historical semantics" (see Merton 2004a). Thirty years later, Merton retitled this project, greatly enlarged in the interim, when he laid out the writings that he then had in progress in the form of a "menu": a listing of forty-six topics from his working files that he offered to the editors of the *Annual Review of Sociology* as possible subjects for an invited autobiographical essay. Fourteen of these topics he grouped together for the occasion under the broader rubric of "Neologisms as Sociological Concepts: History and Analysis," presenting these topics as follows (1987:25–26):

1. On The Origin and Character of the Word *Scientist*
2. Self-Exemplifying Ideas: in the Sociology of Science and Elsewhere
3. Influentials: Evolution of a Concept
4. Institutionalized Evasions and Other Patterned Evasions
5. SED: Socially Expected Durations as a Temporal Dimensions of Social Structure
6. Homophily and Heterophily: Types of Friendship Patterns
7. "Whatever Is, Is Possible": A Brief Biography of the Theorem
8. Opportunity Structures: A Brief Biography of the Concept
9. "Haunting Presence of the Functionally Irrelevant Status": The Structural Analysis of Status-Sets
10. "Phatic Communion": Malinowski's Need of a Cognitive Conduit
11. Comte's "Cerebral Hygiene" and the Presumed Dangers of Erudition for Originality
12. *Veritas Filia Temporis*: Temporal Contexts of Scientific Knowledge
13. *Pseudo-Gemeinschaft* and Public Distrust
14. The Travels and Adventures of Serendipity: A Study in Historical Semantics and the Sociology of Science (with Elinor Barber)

Six related items appear elsewhere on the same menu: "The (William) James Distinction: Acquaintance With and Knowledge About"; "The (Kenneth) Burke Theorem: Seeing as a Way of Not Seeing"; "The (L. J.) Henderson Maxim: It's a Good Thing to Know What You Are Doing"; "OBI: Obliteration (of Source of Ideas, Methods, or Findings) *by* Incorporation (in Canonical Knowledge)"; "'Trained Incapacity': A Case of OBI"; and "The Adumbrationist Credo: What's New is Not True; What's True is not New" (1987:24–25). Five of these twenty titles—the items numbered 1, 5, 8, 13, and 14—correspond to studies that Merton eventually published, while the fifteen others remain (presumably) still among his unpublished papers. But, remarkably, twenty of Merton's forty-six working sociological files at this career stage appear to focus on the history of particular "words," "concepts," "neologisms," "theorems," "distinctions," "maxims," and other linguistic expressions.

In 1995, looking back to this menu, Merton characterized the enumerated studies, significantly, as "part of *a research program* centered on 'Sociological Words, Concepts and Paradigms'" (1995a:4n1 [emphasis added]), and two years later he referred to several of them collectively again—this time along with *On the Shoulders of Giants* and his articles on the Kelvin dictum and the Thomas theorem—as among his continuing "excursions into the sociological history of culturally strategic words" (1997:225, 245n4; cf. 1995b, 381–382). Finally, in the preface that he wrote to accompany the long-delayed publication of his study of serendipity, he states that he and Barber altered their 1958 subtitle to "a study in sociological semantics" because they now understood their work as "an early exercise in what can be better described as a barely emerging '*sociological* semantics'" (2004a:x [Merton's emphasis]).

Why Merton's nomenclature shifted over time is an intriguing biographical question that is outside the scope of this chapter. Of concern, instead, are the basic tenets of the research program to which he variously alluded and the implications of this program for understanding his work more generally. In this regard, the thesis of this section is that the studies that comprise Merton's sociological semantics constitute a rich and novel contribution to the sociological analysis of the history of ideas and, furthermore, that this contribution necessitates the revision of the accepted view that, as a sociologist, Merton accommodated the history of ideas only insofar as the intellectual products of the past were of relevance for advancing the present-day systematics of sociological theory.

That the received image of Merton as an ahistorical thinker requires some correction may already be suggested by the sheer number of separate lines of investigation that he included among his "excursions into the sociological history of culturally strategic words"—somewhere between a dozen and two dozen historical studies (depending on how one counts the unpublished items to which he refers). Notable as well, considering that Merton rarely undertook writing projects of monograph length, is that three of the five monographs that he did author during his career—*Serendipity*, *On the Shoulders of Giants*, and *The Sociology of Science: An Episodic Memoir*—fall among these intellectual-historical works (as, in different ways, do his other two monographs, his dissertation-book, *Science, Technology and Society in Seventeenth Century England* [1938] 1970, and *Mass Persuasion* [1946] 2004). What is more, in the course of these monographic studies and several of his shorter semantic inquiries, Merton immersed himself in original historical research, using extensive collections of documents (unpublished in some cases), during which whatever concerns he may have had with the systematics of contemporary sociological theory remained subterranean at best. Still further, as Merton presents them, these works had as their task the investigation of consequential subjects in modern intellectual history, including (re *On the Shoulders of Giants*) "the enduring tension between tradition and originality in the transmission of the growth of knowledge" ([1994] 1996:358); the "role of measurement in scholarship" (re "The Kelvin Dictum") (Merton, Sills, and Stigler 1984:319); and "the historically changing access of women to the world of scientific inquiry" (re "Man of Science") (1997:226). And the solid historiographic achievement of these works has indeed drawn praise from intellectual historians (see esp. Gould 1990).

But what has any of this to do with Merton as sociologist, as distinct from a moonlighting intellectual historian? Here a striking point to appreciate about all of these writings is how much they depart from the conventional genres of the intellectual historian. This is so because Merton's historical studies offer very little in the way of detailed textual exegesis, analysis of the life and times of particular thinkers, or examination of the evolution of specific intellectual movements or doctrines.[3] To be sure, historical particulars deeply interest Merton (see below). Here, as elsewhere in his sociological work, however, his tendency is to regard the particulars as instances of something broader. To this end, he is careful to present his historical projects—even when they deal with recent intellectual developments in which he himself played a central role—each as an "episode [that] provides a strategic research site" or a "case study" (1995b:380, 1977:77, [1982] 1984:263, 1995a:4): that is to say, a case study in sociological semantics, his "research program" on "culturally strategic words" and related terms.

As to the features of this program, however, Merton was laconic, reticent to put forth his novel agenda too baldly. This hesitancy recalls Stinchombe's comment (1975:26–27) about Merton's reluctance to formulate his signature approach to social structure as a fully general theory. So, just as Stinchombe was led to reconstruct Merton's general theory of social structure from its component parts, Merton's research program on sociological semantics must be drawn out and assembled from his various writings on the subject. When one undertakes this reconstruction, however, what emerges is a coherent sociological program tacitly based on four central tenets (see also Zuckerman, Chapter 11 of this volume).

The *first* of these tenets is Merton's claim that *ideas, as well as their linguistic carriers, constitute a wide and important area for sociological investigation.* Spanning across the writings under consideration here, one sees Merton devoting attention to the history of aphorisms, citations, coinages, concepts, credos, dicta, eponyms, ideas, linguistic innovations, maxims, neologisms, niche-words, paradigms, phrases, proto-concepts, pseudo-facts, quotations, slogans, terms, theorems, and (most simply) words—to alphabetize his expansive (and not especially tidy) vocabulary. On two occasions (1997, 2004b), he pointedly takes as his epigraph Lucien Febvre's maxim that "in writing the history of a word, one never wastes one's effort; whether the trip is short or long, monotonous or eventful, it is always instructive";[4] and in his semantic investigations, Merton explicitly identifies multiple reasons why words, in all their varied manifestations, furnish highly instructive objects of analysis for the sociologist. Specifically regarding "new words and phrases" in the natural sciences, the social sciences, and the humanities, for example, Merton observes:

> Intellectual life requires new expressions. In the natural sciences . . . new concepts, facts, and instruments require new words to designate them, and scientists are, in fact, continually coining such words. It is easy to justify the need for neologisms in the natural sciences—the newly designated element, fact, or uniformity is new in the sense of having been previously unknown . . . In the social sciences and in the humanities, new words and

phrases have other functions. The use of a new characterizing word or phrase, the drastic redefinition of an old word, the resurrection of a term fallen into disuse is *an integral part of the development of new perceptions and interpretations.* The social scientist must often use new terms to distinguish the systematic abstractions he makes . . . from the commonsense abstractions of the layman. [Hence,] *the sheer importance of words in the social sciences.* The humanist who is seeking to reinterpret human experience often uses new words or phrases to reexpress "old truths." (Merton and Barber [1958] 2004:67 [emphases added])

Turning from words that are new to more extended linguistic configurations of greater age, Merton (writing with Sills) stresses as well the significance of familiar quotations, advising researchers to take "the frequency and nature of quotations in society as objects of study in themselves" and pointing out the diverse social functions of quotations, including their capacity to "serve as instruments for the intergenerational transmission of knowledge," scientific and literary knowledge in particular (Sills and Merton 1992a:75). Likewise, looking in *Mass Persuasion* beyond the academic realm to the broader public sphere, Merton describes the decisive role of popular "slogan[s in] crystalliz[ing] and epitomiz[ing] the feelings and the tensions" of the men and women who were involved in the wartime bond drive with which his study deals ([1946] 2004:33). Generalizing this last point, Merton elsewhere (with Sills and Stigler) emphasizes "the power of simple phrases, aphorisms, slogans, dicta—their ability to summarize, epitomize, exemplify, *or even create complex programs of research or action*" (Merton, Sills, and Stigler 1984:319 [emphasis added]). Repeatedly, his individual semantic projects attest by means of empirical examples to this same conviction: namely, to Merton's belief in "power of phrases . . . and the ideas behind them" (Merton, Sills, and Stigler 1984:319). Arguably, this insight stands as one of his most distinctive contributions to the sociological tradition.[5]

But Merton then adds a *second* plank to his research program. Having brought ideas and their semantic expressions into focus, what he then proposes is that *the sociologist should examine the origins of these ideas and expressions and their paths of diffusion*—their "travels and adventures," as he likes to say (e.g., Merton and Barber [1958] 2004; Merton, Sills, and Stigler 1984:319). With this step, he foregrounds two of the most central sociological questions that such phenomena raise. On several occasions, Merton tellingly refers to his historical inquiries as biographies, biographies of a novel kind: "the biography of a sociological idea" ([1965/1985] 1993:25, 1995b:379n2), the "biography of an idea" ([1982] 1984:267), the "biography of a theorem" (1987:25), the "biography of a concept" (1995a:4)—shorthand in each case for an analysis of the focal object's beginnings as well as of its subsequent course of historical development. And, in each of these instances, these are exactly the issues that Merton's account then covers, as he implicitly forges a model for future studies in sociological semantics. Regarding beginnings, for example, he traces the aphorism "on the shoulders of giants" to its moment of "origin" ([1965/1985] 1993), proceeds likewise with the words "serendipity" ([1958] 2004) and "scientist" (1997) (see also Merton 1975), analyzes the "formation" of the concept "socially expected durations" ([1982] 1984:263) and of several key concepts in the sociology of science (1977:75ff.), and probes the "emergence" of the idea of "opportunity structure" (1995a:3ff.). As he studies the birth of such words and ideas, moreover, Merton also considers instances of stillbirths and entirely adverted moments of conception—he thus writes of intellectual opportunities that were a "total miss" (as well as some that were a "near miss")—viewing these as possibilities that were foreclosed, abandoned, or overlooked as a result of the conceptual and linguistic choices of historical actors (1977:51, [1985] 1993:xx). This line of inquiry embodies his commitment to Kenneth Burke's doctrine that "a way of seeing is also a way of not seeing—a focus upon object A involves a neglect of object B" (Merton 1977:95, quoting Burke 1940).

In addition to the question of origins, Merton examines the forms of diffusion that concepts and other expressions undergo historically. Here, the dominant theme of his analysis is that the "fate" of any expression is "contingent," entirely dependent on later developments, viz., on "what others make" subsequently of the newly created word, phrase, idea, etc. (1977:107, [1985] 1993:xx).[6] According to Merton, these subsequent "responses [can] vary . . . from out-and-out rejection of the word, to passive recognition of its existence, to active interest in . . . its continuing usage, . . . to the taking for granted of both its meaning and usage" (Merton and Barber [1958] 2004:61). Yet another alternative is the eventual abandonment of the expression due to its debasement or overusage (Merton and Barber [1958] 2004:65). Among these possibilities, "resistance," traceable to the "dispositions" and interests of the members of potentially recipient social-intellectual "communities," is an especially commonplace outcome (1977:107–08, 1997:230, 233), though even those expressions that survive may continually meet "startling changes in [their] meaning" as they become "slightly or drastically modified by the social context of [their] use" (Merton and Barber [1958] 2004:51, 4). Complicating this situation further, "initial diffusion"—which itself may occur quickly or following decades of delay—must be distinguished from "secondary (derivative or serial) diffusion" (1995b:385, 388). For, at later points in time too, the possibilities are multiple. In the instance of quotations, for example, Merton distinguishes how successive users may alternatively "echo," "parody," or "reverse" the wording or the sense of a previous statement, as well as "misattribute" or "obliterate" its original source (Sills and Merton 1992a, 1992b).

Diverse as they are, however, these outcomes are not random. To the contrary, as Merton suggests via his *third* programmatic move, *sociological analysis can identify the general social processes and mechanisms responsible for turning such episodes in the directions that they took historically*—whether that of "successful" or "failed" emergence, "successful" or "failed" diffusion, or any of the numerous variations in between. Examining, for example, how historian-philosopher Thomas Kuhn came to develop during the 1950s his distinctive views of science, Merton unpacks Kuhn's early academic career and uncovers therein processes of "institutional serendipity," the action of "local influentials," and the self-reinforcing dynamics of "the reward system" in higher education (1977:80–105). Likewise, probing the origin and diffusion of the concept of opportunity structure in American sociology in the mid-twentieth century, Merton (1995b) points to some of these same processes, as well as to the mechanisms of "oral publication," "student-mentor ambivalence," and "socially organized skepticism." And, in an analysis of the fractured diffusion among sociologists of the original source of the famous "Thomas theorem," Merton takes account of additional processes such as the simultaneous appearance of multiple independent discoveries and "the Matthew effect" (1995a:382).

By no means does Merton claim that these specific processes are always operative. The particular processes just named are processes identified and described elsewhere in Merton's oeuvre, chiefly in the writings that make up his sociology of science (see esp. Merton 1973, 1980); and they return in his analyses of Kuhn, the concept of opportunity structure, and the Thomas theorem because the modern academic milieu that Merton examines in these case studies happens to overlap substantially with the world of modern science, thus furnishing a locus for many of the same features—the academic reward system, the Matthew effect, organized skepticism, etc. Whether and to what degree sociologists would find the same processes or, instead, uncover different mechanisms in other contexts—say, in the kinds of contexts where political slogans originate and diffuse—is a question that Merton leaves open for researchers who investigate these other contexts. However, with regard to the academic context that Merton does consider in the studies under discussion, an important point bears notice. Critics of Merton's sociology of science have frequently faulted his approach for neglecting the *content* of scientific work, that is, for directing attention to the social-organizational processes characteristic of the scientific enterprise but overlooking the formation and development of scientific ideas, concepts, etc. Merton's semantic studies, however, significantly belie this charge, for when he invokes the academic reward system, the Matthew effect, organized skepticism, and related social processes in his semantic studies, Merton does so in order to address matters of content explicitly—the origins of Kuhn's ideas, the emergence and spread of the opportunity structure concept, the partial diffusion of the Thomas theorem. In these works, in other words, such processes and mechanisms become integral to Merton's account of the substance of the intellectual changes that he examines.

If this is Merton's analytical procedure, it would nonetheless seem to beg an overarching question. However well mechanisms of the sort he refers to in the studies just cited capture the social processes by which the ideas and concepts at issue originated and then spread, still absent is an explanation for why these processes, as opposed to other processes, obtained in the instances where Merton finds them: why, for example, the mechanisms relevant to the emergence and diffusion of Kuhn's ideas only partly coincide with those implicated in the emergence and diffusion of the concept of opportunity structure? Merton's program for sociological semantics is not yet done, however. Rather, with the addition of its *fourth* and final component, he holds that *the sociologist can construct an explanation for the processes and mechanisms that operate in a particular episode by analyzing the social-structural position of the historical actors involved in the genesis and diffusion of the ideas and expressions under investigation.*

At different moments in the development of his semantics program, Merton articulates this explanatory argument using a somewhat different vocabulary. For instance, in his study of serendipity, his explanatory thesis is that linguistic terms acquire new meanings as they are "refracted through the patterns of thought of different *social and intellectual circles*" (Merton and Barber [1958] 2004:65 [emphasis added]), whereas *On the Shoulders of Giants* observes how the aphorism in question mutated according to different "contexts" and their accompanying patterns of "*social relations*" ([1965/1985] 1993:5, 134 [emphasis added]). After his work on the edition and translation of Ludwik Fleck's *Genesis and Development of a Scientific Fact* (1979), Merton occasionally used Fleck's concept "*thought collectives*" (e.g., 1987:1 [emphasis added]). Almost simultaneously and continuing for the rest of his career, however, he gravitated toward a family of related concepts of his own coinage.

These are Merton's concepts of an "intellectual microenvironment" (1977, 1984), a "cognitive microenvironment" (1995a), or what he finally calls "*a sociocognitive microenvironment*" (2004b:260–69 [emphasis added]; cf. 1995b; the first use of the latter term seems to be 1995a:19). By these equivalent terms, he means in the first instance the local "social and cognitive network," or "sociometric structure," in which men and women of ideas engage in "direct interaction" with one another (1977:99, 73, 1995a:5). In Merton's view, such "interpersonal milieux" constitute the "structural contexts" that lie at the core of sociological explanations for the "formation of ideas" and the ways in which ideas, along with the expressions that carry them, subsequently diffuse (1977:73–75, 93, 1995a:5).

But why assign so much explanatory significance to sociocognitive microenvironments? Merton makes clear that he does this for the reason that a sociocognitive microenvironment constitutes an "opportunity structure" which furnishes differential access to ideas, concepts, information flows, and other resources to those actors who self-select, or are institutionally selected, into such a milieu and who then differentially make use of the sociointellectual possibilities that its reward system encourages or discourages (1977:75–77, 89–93, 1995a:8–9ff.).[7] In addition, different local microenvironments differ in the extent to which they are sites of the processes mentioned above (institutional serendipity, practices of oral publication, socially organized skepticism, etc.) and, hence, of the sociointellectual effects of these mechanisms (Merton 1977:102 speaks of "serendipity-prone microenvironments," a concept he later elaborates [2004b]). Also relevant, however, are the trajectories of women and men of ideas across "*successive microenvironments*"—since the order of succession can reinforce, complement, or nullify the impact of a prior microenvironment—as well as the location of these actors both in nonlocal "extended networks" operating "at-a-distance" (e.g., "invisible colleges") and in the larger "macro-environ-ment" (1977:86, 99, 5 [emphasis added], 1995a:34, 44, 1995b:410).

Merton mobilizes this general explanatory argument throughout his late semantic studies but, importantly, not in a one-size-fits-all manner. Rather, he goes to lengths in each instance to specify the argument. For Merton, how the various factors just identified happen to operate (and thus to shape the emergence and diffusion of ideas and other linguistic expressions) is something that is contingent on the historical circum-stances of the case, that is, on the particulars of the structural con-texts—the specific sociocognitive environments—under examination. Accordingly, Merton urges "fine-grained analysis, [such as is] possible in an individual case-study," the "tracing [of] the *fine-grained* social-and-cognitive interactions that have affected [the] work" in question (1977:101, 84 [emphasis in original]). To this end, each of his own case studies (esp. 1977, 1995a, 1995b, 2004b) draws on a range of historical materials—including, for the projects on Kuhn, the Thomas theorem, and the concept of opportunity structure, correspondence in which he himself was involved—to carry out a detailed reconstruction of the per-tinent microenvironments and the trajectories across them of the rel-evant historical actors.[8]

The result is a series of writings substantially at variance with the Coser-Jones claim that Merton's approach to the history of ideas is an ahistori-cal one which "strips [away the] time-and-place-bound elements from the intellectual productions of the past" and fails to yield accounts that have historical validity. Indeed, rather than "remove those layers and tissues . . . that show the mark of [thinkers'] time, place, and milieu," Merton's case studies incorporate precisely these elements as the necessary means to in-stantiate and ground his general argument about microenvironments and to establish its validity in regard to specific historical examples. In this way, he takes a research program which starts from an interest in the historical importance of particular ideas, concepts, words, and other expressions, which seeks to understand the historical origins and diffusion of those expressions, and which examines the social processes and mechanisms un-derpinning these historical developments, and he then caps this program with an explanatory account that only comes to life when historically specified. To be sure, Merton regards his semantic studies not as com-pleting this program but simply as pointing forward to future research; but this qualification by no means diminishes his accomplishment. Unfinished though it is in his hands, Merton's program constitutes a historical sociology of ideas which has no equivalent in the annals on scholarship and which remains vital, opening up fertile territory that sociologists have yet to explore and going further still to richly exemplify how to conduct this original path of inquiry so as to contribute at once to the historical understanding of the intellectual past and to the present advance of a nascent subfield of sociology.[9]

III

What then, if anything, is the relationship between the Merton of Section I and the Merton of Section II? The simple answer is that Merton did not say. More than this, he apparently felt no need to address the question, or even to raise the matter as an issue, satisfied with the harmonious coexistence between his "systematics of sociological theory" and his "sociological semantics." This, at any rate, is a reasonable inference from those autobiographical occasions when Merton placed *Social Theory and Social Structure* and *On the Shoulders of Giants* (his favorites among his works) side by side, contrasting them solely in terms of style of argument and mode of presentation (see Merton [1994] 1996).

Viewed in terms of Merton's career, this is not surprising, for the systematics and the semantics were the products of different periods and problematics, and for many years they remained essentially independent paths of intellectual interest. Merton's program to develop the systematics of sociological theory and (in pursuit of this program) his concern to distinguish systematics from the history of sociological theory and to dissuade sociologists from exegeses of older theories lacking in contemporary relevance was a line of work that crystallized in the mid-1940s amid a debate in American sociology, particularly with Talcott Parsons, over the nature of sociological theory and about the practices that could foster theory development within the field of sociology (see Sztompka 1986). The semantics program began to take shape a decade later when Merton's research in the sociology of science combined with his knowledge of the history of ideas to draw his attention to certain expressions—"serendipity," "on the shoulders of giants"—which illuminated salient aspects of modern science and whose origins and diffusion invited historical investigation (see Merton 2004b). In conducting historical studies of these particular expressions, however, Merton was in no sense writing the "history of *sociological theory*"; hence, his strictures on historical work of that kind were hardly pertinent.

The two programs veered toward each other only subsequently. This occurred when Merton not only extended his semantic research program to include all manner of other strategic words, terms, phrases, slogans, maxims, and the like, but went even further and actually carried out *historical case studies of ideas and concepts from sociological theories of the past*—e.g., the Thomas theorem. At this point, he was engaged in producing chapters in the history of sociological theory which had little evident bearing on the present-day systematics of sociological theory—and a hasty assessment of these writings might conclude that Merton's late practice was in this way in conflict with his earlier teachings.

This discrepancy is more apparent than real, however. It derives from entangling two separate issues that may arise with regard to past sociological works: (1) Do these works contain material that is relevant to the contemporary systematics of theory?; and (2) Do these works furnish instructive objects for sociological analysis: that is, ideas, concepts, words, and other linguistic expressions whose historical emergence and spread are ripe for sociological explanation? Only to the extent that these questions are interlinked, such that a negative answer on the first precludes asking the second, are Merton's systematics and semantics at odds. For Merton himself, however, these two issues are disconnected and orthogonal. Consequently, regardless of the contemporary usefulness of, say, the Thomas theorem for theories in organizational sociology or social psychology—and, from Merton's standpoint, this is indeed a question that sociologists in these areas should pose as a precondition for pursuing this aspect of W. I. Thomas's work—the genesis and diffusion of the theorem remains a compelling research topic for sociologists seeking to further the project of sociological semantics.

This fundamental and neglected distinction only comes to light, though, when one considers Merton's program for the systematics of sociological theory and his program for sociological semantics in tandem. Insofar as scholars keep to the received wisdom and examine the systematics of sociological theory in isolation, they will almost inevitably continue to overgeneralize Merton's argument on this score, interpreting it to require a more restricted and ahistorical approach to intellectual history on the part of the sociologist than is consistent with Merton's oeuvre as a whole. This standard interpretation of Robert Merton, however, not only misrepresents the implications of his systematics, it also obscures his major and still untapped achievement with regard to the historical sociology of ideas.

Notes

In 2004, the editor of the journal *Contexts* asked me to write a review of Robert Merton's book (with Elinor Barber) *Serendipity* and to frame the review by saying something about Merton's intellectual career more generally. When I finished drafting my review, I sent it to Harriet Zuckerman for suggestions; these she very generously offered, adding that I should read Merton's 1997 companion essay "De-Gendering 'Man of Science': The Genesis and Epicene Character of the Word *Scientist*." The present chapter is the product of the research that resulted from that fruitful recommendation, and I am deeply grateful to Harriet Zuckerman for leading me to this line of research, which (as I have since learned) converges in several ways with her own recent work on Merton's legacy, including her chapter in this volume. In the period since, I have also benefited from reading her chapter as well as from her very extensive comments on previous drafts of the current chapter.

1. One should not construe this passage to imply an aversion on Coser's own part to studying the history of sociological thought in a comprehensive manner. To the contrary: Coser saw many advantages to reading the work of earlier sociological thinkers, and he commended Merton's determination "to inventory the whole storehouse of European sociological and social thought and to select a much greater array of ideas from a much wider variety of sources" than had American sociologists who preceded him (1975b:88).

2. The singular and outstanding exception to this statement is Harriet Zuckerman's chapter in this volume.

3. Cf. Merton (1977:75), where Merton himself distinguished his approach from that of the intellectual historian.

4. On both occasions, Merton also cites Balzac: "What a beautiful book would one compose if one narrated the life and adventures of a word." (In both instances, Merton leaves the two quotations in French; I owe the present translations to Ivan Ermakoff.) The quotations bear comparison with Whitehead's statement, which Merton made famous by using it as the epigraph of *Social Theory and Social Structure*: "A science which hesitates to forget its founders is lost."

5. Merton quotes a 1978 letter of his to Albert Cohen in which he casually comments: "I truly believe that important ideas generally have a lot of consequences" (1995a:43).

6. One of the principal arguments of Bruno Latour has been that "the fate of a [scientific] statement is in later users' hands" (1987:59), and scholars in science studies

often associate this notion with Latour. Merton, however, entered this principle into the literature of the field well in advance of Latour.

7. Here, one sees Merton deftly tailoring what Stinchombe (1975) constructs as Merton's general theory of social structure specifically to fit the questions at stake in his sociological semantics.

8. That Merton pursued this detailed reconstructive work into his 80s and 90s is indicative of the significance that he attached to it.

9. For a more general discussion of this subfield—the sociology of ideas—see Camic and Gross 2001.

References

Camic, Charles, and Neil Gross. 2001. "The New Sociology of Ideas." In *Blackwell Companion to Sociology*, ed. Judith R. Blau, 236–49. Malden, MA. Blackwell.

Clark, Jon, Celia Modgil, and Sohan Modgil, eds. 1990. *Robert K. Merton: Consensus and Controversy*. London: Falmer.

Coser, Lewis A., ed. 1975a. *The Idea of Social Structure: Papers in Honor of Robert K. Merton*. New York: Harcourt Brace Jovanovich.

——. 1975b. "Merton's Uses of the European Sociological Tradition." In *The Idea of Social Structure: Papers in Honor of Robert K. Merton*, ed. Lewis A. Coser, 85–100. New York: Harcourt Brace Jovanovich.

Coser, Lewis A., and Robert Nisbet. 1975. "Merton and the Contemporary Mind: An Affectionate Dialogue." In *The Idea of Social Structure: Papers in Honor of Robert K. Merton*, ed. Lewis A. Coser, 3–10. New York: Harcourt Brace Jovanovich.

Crothers, Charles. 1987. *Robert K. Merton*. London: Tavistock.

——. 2003. "Robert K. Merton and the History of Sociology." *RCHS* [Research Committee on the History of Sociology] *Newsletter* June:7–13.

Donoghue, Denis. [1985] 1993. Afterword to *On the Shoulders of Giants: A Shandean Postscript*, by Robert K. Merton, 291–300. Chicago: University of Chicago Press.

——. 1997. "Strange Relation." In *Sociological Visions*, ed. Kai Erikson, 263–274. Lanham, Maryland: Rowman and Littlefield.

Eco, Umberto. [1990] 1993. Foreword to *On the Shoulders of Giants: A Shandean Postscript*, by Robert K. Merton, ix–xviii. Chicago: University of Chicago Press.

Fleck, Ludwik. 1979. *Genesis and Development of a Scientific Fact*. Trans. Thaddeus J. Trenn and ed. Robert K. Merton. Chicago: University of Chicago Press.

Gould, Stephen Jay. 1990. "Polished Pebbles, Pretty Shells: An Appreciation of *OTSOG*." In *Robert K. Merton: Consensus and Controversy*, ed. Jon Clark et al., 35–47. London: Falmer.

Holton, Gerald. 1997. "On Robert Merton, Mary Somerville, and the Moral Authority of Science." In *Sociological Visions*, ed. Kai Erikson, 255–62. Lanham, Maryland:
Rowman and Littlefield.

Jones, Robert Alun. 1977. "On Understanding a Sociological Classic." *American Journal of Sociology* 83:279–319.

——. 1983a. "On Merton's 'History' and 'Systematics' of Sociological Theory." In
Functions and Uses of Disciplinary Histories, ed. Loren Graham et al., 121–42. Dor-
drecht: Reidel.

——. 1983b. "The New History of Sociology." *Annual Review of Sociology* 9:447–69.

Latour. Bruno. 1987. *Science in Action*. Cambridge: Harvard University Press.

Merton, Robert K. 1936. "The Unanticipated Consequences of Purposive Social Action." *American Sociological Review* 1:894–904.

——. [1938] 1970. *Science, Technology and Society in Seventeenth-Century England*.
New Jersey: Humanities Press.

——. [1945] 1973. "Paradigm for the Sociology of Knowledge." In *The Sociology of Science:
Theoretical and Empirical Investigations*, 7–40. Chicago: University of Chicago Press.

——. [1946] 2004. Mass Persuasion: The Social Psychology of a War Bond Drive.
New York: Fertig.

——. 1948. "The Bearing of Empirical Research upon the Development of Social
Theory." *American Sociological Review* 13:505–515.

——. 1949. *Social Theory and Social Structure: Toward the Codification of Theory and
Research*. Glencoe, IL: Free Press.

——. 1957. *Social Theory and Social Structure*. Revised and enlarged edition. Glencoe,
IL: Free Press.

——. 1959. "Notes on Problem-Finding in Sociology." In *Sociology Today: Problems
and Prospects*, ed. Robert K. Merton et al., ix–xxxiv. New York: Basic Books.

——. [1965/1985] 1993. *On the Shoulders of Giants: A Shandean Postscript*. Chicago:
University of Chicago Press.

——. 1968. "On the History and Systematics of Sociological Theory." In *Social Theory
and Social Structure*, enlarged edition, 1–38. New York: Free Press.

——. 1973. *The Sociology of Science: Theoretical and Empirical Investigations*. Chicago:
University of Chicago Press.

——. 1975. "On the Origin of the term *Pseudo-Gemeinschaft*." *Western Sociological
Review* 6:83.

——. 1977. "The Sociology of Science: *An Episodic Memoir*." In *The Sociology of Science in Europe*, ed. Robert K. Merton and Jerry Gaston, 3–141. Carbondale, IL:
Southern Illinois University Press.

——. 1980. "On the Oral Transmission of Knowledge." In *Sociological Traditions from
Generation to Generation*, ed. Matilda W. Riley and Robert K. Merton, 1–35. Norwood, NJ: Ablex Publishing Corporation.

———. [1982] 1984. "Socially Expected Durations: A Case Study of Concept Formation in Sociology." In *Conflict and Consensus: In Honor of Lewis A. Coser*, ed. W. W. Powell and Richard Roberts, 262–83. New York: Free Press.

———. 1984. "Texts, Contexts and Subtexts: An Epistolary Foreword." In *The Grammar of Social Relations*, ed. Jay Weinstein, ix–xliv. New Brunswick, New Jersey: Transaction Books.

———. [1985] 1993. "Preface to The Vicennial Edition." In *On the Shoulders of Giants: A Shandean Postscript*, xix–xxv. Chicago: Chicago University of Chicago Press.

———. 1987. "Three Fragments from a Sociologist's Notebooks: Establishing the Phenomenon, Specified Ignorance, and Strategic Research Materials." *Annual Review of Sociology* 13:1–28.

———. [1994] 1996. "A Life of Learning." In *Robert K.Merton: On Social Structure and Science*, ed. Piotr Sztompka, 339–59. Chicago: University of Chicago Press.

———. 1995a. "Opportunity Structure: The Emergence, Diffusion, and Differentiation of a Sociological Concept, 1930s–1950s." In *The Legacy of Anomie Theory*, ed. Freda Adler and William S. Laufer, 3–78. New Brunswick, New Jersey: Transaction Publishers.

———. 1995b. "The Thomas Theorem and the Matthew Effect." *Social Forces* 74:379–422.

———. 1997. "De-Gendering 'Man of Science': The Genesis and Epicene Character of the Word *Scientist*." In *Sociological Visions*, ed. Kai Erikson, 225–53. Lanham, Maryland: Rowman and Littlefield. (An earlier German version of this essay dates from 1989.)

———. 1998. "Unanticipated Consequence and Kindred Sociological Ideas: A Personal Gloss." In *Robert K. Merton and Contemporary Sociology*, ed. Carlo Mongardini and Simonetta Tabboni, 295–318. New Brunswick, NJ: Transaction Publishers.

———. 2004a. "Preface." In *The Travels and Adventures of Serendipity*, by Robert K. Merton and Elinor Barber, ix–x. Princeton: Princeton University Press.

———. 2004b. "Afterword: Autobiographical Reflections on *The Travels and Adventures of Serendipity*." In *The Travels and Adventures of Serendipity*, by Robert K. Merton and Elinor Barber, 223–298. Princeton: Princeton University Press.

Merton, Robert K., and Elinor Barber. [1958] 2004. *The Travels and Adventures of Serendipity.* Princeton: Princeton University Press.

Merton, Robert K., David L. Sills, and Stephen M. Stigler. 1984. "The Kelvin Dictum and Social Science: An Excursion into the History of an Idea." *Journal of the History of the Behavioral Sciences* 20:319–31.

Merton, Robert K., and Alan Wolfe. 1995. "The Cultural and Social Incorporation of Sociological Knowledge." *The American Sociologist* 26 (no. 3):5–13.

Mongardini, Carlo, and Simonetta Tabboni, eds. 1998. *Robert K. Merton and Contemporary Sociology.* New Brunswick, New Jersey: Transaction Publishers.

Sills, David L., and Robert K. Merton, eds. 1990. *Social Science Quotations: Who Said What, When, and Where. International Encyclopedia of the Social Sciences*, vol. 19. New York: Macmillan.

——. 1992a. "Patterns in the Scholarly Use of Quotations." *Items* (Social Science Research Council) 46:75–76.

——. 1992b. "Social Science Quotations." *Current Comments* (Institute of Scientific Information) October 26:4–8.

Simonson, Peter. 2004. Introduction to *Mass Persuasion: The Social Psychology of a War Bond Drive*, by Robert K. Merton, xi–xlv. New York: Fertig.

——. 2010. "Merton's Sociology of Rhetoric." Chapter 8 of this volume.

Stinchombe, Arthur L. 1975. "Merton's Theory of Social Structure." In *The Idea of Social Structure: Papers in Honor of Robert K. Merton*, ed. Lewis A. Coser, 11–33. New York: Harcourt Brace Jovanovich.

Sztompka, Piotr. 1986. *Robert K. Merton: An Intellectual Profile*. New York: St. Martin's Press.

——. 1996. "Introduction." In *Robert K. Merton: On Social Structure and Science*, ed. Piotr Sztompka, 1–20. Chicago: University of Chicago Press.

——. 2000. "Robert K. Merton." In *The Blackwell Companion to Major Contemporary Social Theorists*, ed. George Ritzer, 12–33. Malden: Blackwell.

Zuckerman, Harriet. 2010. "On Sociological Semantics as an Evolving Research Program." Chapter 11 of this volume.

Contributors

CRAIG CALHOUN is president of the Social Science Research Council and University Professor of Social Sciences at NYU. He received his doctorate from Oxford University, following earlier study at Columbia University, and has also been a professor at the University of North Carolina and Columbia University. His most recent book is *Nations Matter: Culture, History, and the Cosmopolitan Dream* (Routledge, 2007). He has also edited *Sociology in America* (University of Chicago Press, 2007), and *The Public Mission of the Research University* (with Diana Rhoten, Columbia University Press, 2010).

CHARLES CAMIC is John Evans Professor of Sociology at Northwestern University. His research examines the development of the social sciences in the United States between 1880 and 1940 and focuses on the social processes by which new ideas take shape. He is currently completing a book on Thorstein Veblen and the origins on institutional economics. Recent publications include *Social Knowledge in the Making*, edited with Michele Lamont and Neil Gross (University of Chicago Press, 2010) and *Essential Writings of Thorstein Veblen*, edited with Geoffrey Hodgson (Routledge, 2010).

CYNTHIA FUCHS EPSTEIN is Distinguished Professor of Sociology at the Graduate Center of the City University of New York. Her work explores the impact of categorical distinctions in society and their enforcement, as reported in *Deceptive Distinctions* (Yale University Press, 1988). Her research has focused particularly on inequality between women and men in the legal profession. Among her books are *Women In Law* (Basic Books, 1982; 2nd edition, 1993) and *Fighting for Time: Shifting Boundaries of Work and Social Life, edited with Arne Kalleberg* (Russell Sage Foundation, 2004).

THOMAS F. GIERYN is Vice Provost for Faculty and Academic Affairs, Rudy Professor of Sociology, and adjunct professor in the Department of History and Philosophy of Science at Indiana University. His research focuses on the cultural authority of science and the significance of place for human behavior and social change. His recent publications include *Cultural Boundaries of Science: Credibility on the Line* (University of Chicago Press, 1999) and the forthcoming *Truth Spots: How Places Legitimate Beliefs and Claims.*

RAGNVALD KALLEBERG is professor of sociology in the Department of Sociology and Human Geography at the University of Oslo. His research interests include the history of sociology, universities as knowledge organizations, academic intellectuals, and research ethics. Some of his recent publications include "A Reconstruction of the Ethos of Science" (*Journal of Classical Sociology*, 2007) and "Can Normative Disputes be Settled Rationally?" in *Raymond Boudon: A Life in Sociology*, edited by M. Cherkaoui and P. Hamilton (The Bardwell Press, 2009).

AARON L. PANOFSKY is assistant professor of public policy with a joint appointment in the Center for Society and Genetics at the University of California, Los Angeles. His research interests center on the sociology of science and knowledge, with a specific focus on the field of genetics. His recent publications include "Behavior Genetics and the Prospect of 'Personalized Social Policy'" (*Policy and Society*, 2009) and "Generating Sociability to Drive Science: Patient Advocacy Organizations and Genetics Research" (*Social Studies of Science*, forthcoming).

ALEJANDRO PORTES is Howard Harrison and Gabrielle Snyder Beck Professor of Sociology at Princeton University. His research focuses on issues of immigration, economic sociology, comparative development, and

Developing World urbanization. Some of his recent publications include *Immigrant America: A Portrait*, 3rd edition, with R. G. Rumbaut (University of California Press, 2006) and *Economic Sociology: A Systematic Inquiry* (Princeton University Press, 2010).

ROBERT J. SAMPSON is Henry Ford II Professor of the Social Sciences at Harvard University. His work explores crime, the life course, neighborhood effects, and the social structure of the city. His recent publications include "Moving to Inequality: Neighborhood Effects and Experiments Meet Social Structure" (*American Journal of Sociology*, 2008) and the forthcoming *Neighborhood Effects and the Social Structure of the City* (University of Chicago Press).

ALAN SICA is professor of sociology at Pennsylvania State University. He is currently editor of the ASA journal, *Contemporary Sociology*. His research interests include classical and contemporary social theory, the history of sociology, and the sociology of culture. Some of his recent publications include the coedited volumes *Comparative Methods in the Social Sciences* (Sage, 2006) and *The Disobedient Generation: Social Theorists in the Sixties* (University of Chicago Press, 2005).

PETER SIMONSON is associate professor in the Department of Communication at the University of Colorado at Boulder. He teaches rhetoric and his research interests include the intellectual history of communication and rhetorical and mass communication theory. His recent publications include *Why?* (Princeton University Press, 2006) and *Contentious Performances* (Cambridge University Press, 2008).

CHARLES TILLY (1929–2008) was Joseph L. Buttenwieser Professor of Social Science at Columbia University. His research explored the relationship between large-scale social change and contentious politics, particularly in Europe after 1500. Some of his most recent publications include *The Politics of Collective Violence* (Cambridge University Press, 2003) and *Contention and Democracy in Europe, 1650–2000* (Cambridge University Press, 2004).

VIVIANA A. ZELIZER is Lloyd Cotsen '50 Professor of Sociology at Princeton University. Her current research explores the interplay of economic activities and personal ties, especially intimate ties, both in everyday practice and in the law. Some of her recent publications include *The Purchase of Intimacy* (Princeton University Press, 2007) and *Economic Lives: How Culture Shapes the Economy* (Princeton University Press, 2010).

HARRIET ZUCKERMAN is senior vice president of the Mellon Foundation and Professor Emerita at Columbia University, where she was professor of sociology until 1992. Her research examines the social organization of science and scholarship. Amongst other scholarly works, she is the author of the 1979 book *Scientific Elite: Nobel Laureates in the United States* and, most recently, the coauthor of *Educating Scholars: Doctoral Education in the Humanities* (Princeton University, 2010) and "Recent Trends in Funding for the Academic Humanities and Their Implications" (*Daedalus*, 2009).

Index

academic freedom, 208n7

academics: as disseminators and popularizers, 199, 200, 201, 203, 204, 205, 206; and institutional governance, 199, 202–3; as public intellectuals, 199, 200–201, 204–6; research in, 199, 202–3; reward system of, 286; role sets of, 187, 199–204, 206; teaching and study by, 199, 202–3

Adams, James Luther, 175

adaptation, 58–59

administrative power, 198–99

Adorno, Theodor, 171, 172

adumbration, 32, 36–38

advertising, 133, 220–21, 232, 245n24

African Americans: racial discrimination against, 8, 26, 114, 201, 231–32, 240; self-fulfilling prophecies about, 98–99, 190–91, 231, 245n23; and specified ignorance, 42

Alexander, Jeffrey, 79

ambivalence: normative, 123; in research, 121; and social roles, 84–85, 121, 132; sociological, 11, 65, 67, 85–86, 87, 140, 196; student-mentor, 285

American Association for the Advancement of Science (AAAS), 260

American Dream, 63, 84

American Journal of Sociology, 4

American Men and Women of Science, 263

American Sociological Association (ASA), 4, 8, 9

American Sociological Review, 9, 168–69

American University, The (Parsons and Platt), 204–5, 206

An American Dilemma (Myrdal), 201

Anatomy of Melancholy (Burton), 236

Anderson, Sherwood, 166

An Engine, Not a Camera: How Financial Models Shape Markets (MacKenzie), 104, 129

anomie theory, 2, 16, 64, 67, 84; and cultural values, 86; debate over, 63–64. *See also* deviance

anthropology, 39; social, 27n22, 118

anti-Semitism, 171: in Germany, 87, 194; Merton's experiences with, 25n1, 83 . *See also* Jews

Anxiety of Influence, The (Bloom), 166

A Passage to India (Forster), 268n11

Apologie (Hakewill), 236

Arendt, Hannah, 171

Aristotle, 166, 222; on rhetoric, 216, 219, 227, 228, 229, 236

Art of Controversy, The (Schopenhauer), 225

Art of Rhetorick (Hobbes), 216, 222, 244n18

Augustine, 220

Austin, J. L., 255

Azariah de Rossi, 237, 247n34

Bacon, Francis, 178, 223, 229

Bailyn, Bernard, 22, 234

Bakke, E. W., 98

Balzac, Honoré de, 257, 291n4

Barber, Bernard, 167

Barber, Elinor. *See Travels and Adventures of Serendipity, The*

Barnes, Barry, 104–5, 130

Bartlett's *Familiar Quotations,* 236

Barzun, Jacques, 13

Bazerman, Charles, 267n6

Becker, Howard Paul, 168–69

Beckert, Jens, 100

behavior genetics, 144–46, 152, 154, 155, 156, 159

Bell, Daniel, 170

Bell Curve, The (Herrnstein and Murray), 144

Benjamin, Walter, 171

Bentham, Jeremy, 229

Berlin, Isaiah, 166

Bernard, Luther, 175

Bernard of Chartres, 22, 234, 246n30

Billings, Paul R., 157

biotechnology, 133, 134, 157

Birmingham Cultural Studies, 230

Blau, Peter, 9, 19, 68–69

Bloom, Harold, 166

Blumenberg, Hans, 241n5

Boas, Franz, 39

boomerang response, 227, 230–31

Booth, Wayne, 241n5

Borges, Jorge Luis, 37

Boudon, Raymond, 187–88, 191, 207n3

boundary-work: concept of, 150; in science, 127–28, 151, 153, 154, 214

Bourdieu, Pierre, 84, 89, 153; honors Merton, 87; as rival of Merton, 124, 125, 126; on social capital, 34, 44

Boyle, Robert, 223

Brewer's *Dictionary of Phrases and Fables,* 255

Brinton, Crane, 4, 167

British Association for the Advancement of Science, 257, 259, 261

British Labor Party, 233, 245n26

Broome, Leonard, 83

Brown v. Board of Education, 20, 26n15, 201, 208n10

Bunche, Ralph, 4

Burawoy, Michael, 205

bureaucracy: as ideal type, 40; Merton research on, 2, 8, 16, 26n13

Bureau of Applied Social Research, 20, 21, 66, 231; projects and funding, 2, 9, 226, 230

Burke, Kenneth, 218, 221, 224; Merton and, 223, 232, 241–42n6, 243n10, 245nn22–23, 284

Burke Theorem, 241–42n6

Burt, Ronald, 60

Burton, Robert, 236, 246n30

Bush, Vannevar, 132

Butler, Judith, 255–56

Calhoun, Craig, 1–28, 69, 160n13

Callon, Michel, 103–4, 109n6, 129

Camic, Charles, 21, 22–23, 217, 273–92, 297

Campbell, George, 227

Canavan disease, 147–48

capitalism, 5, 103, 157. See also economy

Carnegie, Andrew, 3

Causes of Delinquency (Hirschi), 66

censorship, 8, 20

Center for Advanced Study in the Behavioral Sciences, 9, 27n18

Cerulo, Karen, 79

Chapin, F. Stuart, 273

Chauliac, Guy de, 246n30

Chicago School in sociology, 69, 70, 164; and applied research, 66; factional struggles with, 9, 168; influences on Merton, 10; social disorganization tradition of, 74n2

Chomsky, Noam, 119

Cicero, 220

Clark, Kenneth, 26n15, 208n10

class: and consciousness, 82, 170; distinctions, 98, 101–2, 108n2; and social status, 83

cloning, 134

Cohen, Stanley, 66

Colbert, Jean-Baptiste, 49

Cole, Jonathan, 19, 136n1

Cole, Stephen, 19, 235

Coleman, James, 9, 19, 72; and community research, 69, 70, 71; on intellectual atmosphere at Columbia, 66, 68; on micro-macro link, 70, 75n7; on theory and research, 68–69

Coleridge, Samuel Taylor, 246n30

collectivity, 70–73; analytical properties, 70, 71; global properties, 70, 71; and identity, 81; and individual, 54, 69–71, 75n7; in-groups and out-groups, 57, 98–99, 190–91; structural properties, 70, 71. See also social groups

Collins, Harry, 123, 160nn10–11

Columbia School in sociology, 9, 75n7, 227; style and approach of, 19–20, 67–70

Columbia University: intellectual atmosphere at, 66, 68; Merton career at, 6–7, 10, 203, 226, 232; student protests during 1960s, 13, 21; during World War I, 208n7

commercialization, 133, 147, 148, 156, 158–59

communalism, 87, 142–43, 155; and "communism," 159n5; and democratic ethos, 194, 195; as scientific and ethical norm, 125, 146–47, 148, 154, 156, 234

communicative power, 198, 223

Communist Manifesto, The (Marx and Engels), 167, 178

community: research, 70–71, 72–73; social theory of, 72–73

Comte, August, 269n19

conceptualization, 15, 22–23

conformity, 35, 140

constructivism: of Merton and
Lazarsfeld, 69–70; and scientific
ethos, 126, 128, 141, 149, 151, 157, 158
*Contribution to the Critique of Political
Economy* (Marx), 178
conversational analysis, 267n6
Cooley, Charles Horton, 10–11, 273
Coser, Lewis, 9, 19, 85, 278; on Merton
and European sociology, 165–66; on
Merton's "ahistorical" perspective,
276, 277, 288, 291n1
Coser, Rose Laub, 19, 85
cost-benefit paradigm, 45–46, 187
Creedy, John, 222, 242n8
crime, 6, 65; and deviance, 63–64, 66–67
criminology, 65, 67, 74n3
critical theory, 160n13, 239
Crossan, John Dominic, 200
Crothers, Charles, 278
culture: contradictions within, 85; and
deviance, 57, 86, 98; goals and values
in, 35, 97–98; and opportunity
structure, 84; and politics, 201–2; and
science, 5, 81, 123, 124, 126, 127, 189;
and serendipity, 99; and social class,
98, 108n2; sociology of, 79, 81, 86,
90n1, 226; and time, 88–89
Culture and Society (Williams), 239
Cuvillier, Armand, 38

Dahl, Robert, 187–88, 194, 196, 199
Dante Alighieri, 166
Darwin, Charles, 134
Decline of the West (Spengler), 167
defining the phenomenon, 34, 186
de Man, Paul, 241n5
democracy: and dictatorship, 188, 204;
and freedom of expression, 195–96,
197, 202, 206; and human fallibility,
196; and institutional and historical

traditions, 197; majority principle
in, 196; and market economies,
198; normative claims and models,
193, 194–95, 198–99; and political
equality, 194, 196; and polyarchy, 199;
and science, 183, 184–85, 192; and
universalism, 186, 192, 194, 195
democratic rights violations: under
McCarthyism, 8, 245n27; during
World War I, 188, 208n7
demography, 65, 74n3, 134
De Oratore (Cicero), 220
Descartes, Rene, 274
deviance, 2, 16, 35, 140; and crime,
63–64, 66–67; and cultural values,
57, 86, 98; and paradigms, 27n23
Dewey, John, 205, 241n6
dialectic, 219, 225, 226, 243–44n15
dialectical materialism, 38
Dictionary of Angels, 255
Dictionary of National Biography, 2
Dictionary of Saints, 255
Didacus Stella, 246n30
Diogenes Laertius, 274
Dionyse, Alexandre, 246n30
disentanglement, 129, 131
disinterestedness, 87, 125, 142–43, 158;
and democratic ethos, 194, 195
Division of Labor in Society (Durkheim),
25n5
Donaghue, Denis, 239
Dreiser, Theodore, 166
Duncan, Hugh Dalziel, 218
Durkheim, Émile, 1–2, 117, 205, 222;
on crime and deviance, 66; defends
philosophical realism, 129; *Division
of Labor in Society*, 25n5; *The
Elementary Forms of Religious Life*,
80; as enthymemist, 242n8; influence
on Merton, 79–80, 166, 167, 176; as

structural-functionalist, 119, 131; on studious ignorance, 43; *Suicide*, 65, 79

dysfunctions, 23, 95, 114–15, 116–17, 118, 245n25; narcotizing, 227, 232, 239

ecometrics, 72

economics, 103–4; behavioral, 44–45; grand theories in, 45–46; and intimate relations, 102; market theory, 129–31, 134; performativity in, 103–6, 109n6, 109n9, 130; rational action theory, 45–46, 47; and uncertainty, 100–103. *See also* Finance theory

economy: financial debacle of 2008, 107–8; informal, 43–45; market, 106–8, 134, 198

Eighteenth Brumaire of Louis Bonaparte, The (Marx), 178

Elementary Forms of Religious Life, The (Durkheim), 80

elites: downplaying of privileges by, 42; Merton study of, 218, 233, 234; use of language by, 217, 234

Emerson, Ralph Waldo, 231

empirical research: abstraction from, 20; interpretation of, 18; Merton as noted practitioner of, 2; Merton on, 14–15, 33; methods of, 12, 19; normative, 188; in science, 27n25; and theory, 14, 68. *See also* research

emulation, 58

Engels, Frederick, 38, 167, 178–79, 273

Epictetus, 80

epithets: ideological, 232–33; racial and ethnic, 231, 235, 244n17; and rhetoric, 214, 215, 231, 245n23; sociological study of, 244n17, 254, 256, 266

Epstein, Cynthia Fuchs, 19, 20, 79–91, 160n11, 297

Erasmus, Desiderius, 166

establishing the phenomenon, 33–35, 49, 186

ethnocentrism, 189, 191, 193, 231

evolutionary theory, 75n12, 134

exclusion, 57, 58; as Merton concern, 59–60

exploitation, 58, 59–60

Fall of Man, The (Goodman), 236

Faris, Ellsworth, 25n5, 175

fascism, 167, 183, 184. *See also* Nazi Germany

Fateful Choices (Kershaw), 200

Febvre, Lucien, 257, 282

finance theory, 105, 109n9, 256. *See also* economics

Fish, Stanley, 241n5

Fleck, Ludwik, 269n18, 287

focus group, 7, 230, 231, 244–45n21; coinage of term, 2, 36, 69

Forster, E. M., 268n11

Foucault, Michel, 84

Foundations of Social Theory (Coleman), 70

framing, 56, 129, 131

Frankfurt School, 171

Franklin, Benjamin, 102, 205

Frazier, E. Franklin, 4

freedom of expression, 195–96, 197, 202, 206

Freud, Sigmund, and Freudianism, 34, 179

Frickel, Scott, 158

Fromm, Erich, 179

functional analysis, 13, 114; paradigm for, 115, 118, 119. *See also* structural analysis

functional institutionalism, 149, 151–52, 154, 158

functionalism, 131, 132; and dysfunction, 232, 245n25; Merton and, 13, 89–90;

functionalism (*Continued*)
of Parsons, 14, 18, 38, 119; rejection
of, 13, 14; structural, 14, 27n22,
28–29, 125

gambling, 108n2, 130
Gans, Herbert, 20–21
Gates, Henry Louis, 241n5
generalization, 33, 55, 118, 158; scientific
role of, 15, 16
*Genesis and Development of a Scientific
Fact* (Fleck), 269n18, 287
genetically modified organisms, 134
German Ideology, The (Marx and Engels),
178
Gerth, Hans, 171
Gettysburg Address, 199, 208n9
Gieryn, Thomas F., 11–12, 23, 113–36,
150–51, 298
Gini, Corrado, 273
Gluckman, Max, 27n22
Goffman, Erving, 66
Goodman, Godfrey, 236
Gorgia (Plato), 216, 219
Gould, Benjamin A., 260
Gould, Steven Jay, 201, 202, 239
Gouldner, Alvin, 9, 13, 19, 21, 27
Granet, Marcel, 177
Grassi, Ernesto, 241n5
Greenspan, Alan, 107–8
Grünwald, Ernst, 164, 169, 177
Gutenberg Galaxy (McLuhan), 239

Habermas, Jürgen, 166; on democratic
opinion formation, 187–88, 193,
198, 199; on rhetoric and language,
207n4, 239
Hakewill, George, 236
Hall, Stuart, 230
Hartshorne, Edward, 192, 207n6

Harvard University: Merton at, 4, 25–
26n6, 174, 175; Pareto cult at, 167
health care, 47, 133; public campaigns,
231. *See also* medical genetics; patient
advocacy
Hegel, Georg Wilhelm Friedrich, 274
Heidegger, Martin, 221
Heifetz, Jascha, 165
Helmholtz, Hermann von, 274
Hemingway, Ernest, 166
Henderson, Lawrence J., 4, 167
Henry of Mondeville, 246n30
Herbert, George, 236, 246n30
Herzog, Herta, 230
Hirschi, Travis, 66
Hirschman, Albert O., 108n4
history: of ideas, 20, 21, 273–74, 289–90;
as shaper of social processes, 56; socio-
logical, 11, 275, 279–80, 289–90
Hobbes, Thomas, 207n3, 229, 277–78;
Art of Rhetorick, 216, 222, 244n18
Hochschild, Arlie, 200
Holmes, George C., 4
Homans, George, 167
Honigsheim, Paul, 164, 168
Hooke-Newton-Merton theory on
public debate, 237–38
Hooten, Earnest, 26n11
Hopkins, Charles H., 25n4
Horkheimer, Max, 171
Houdini, Harry, 3–4
House, Floyd, 169
housing, 8, 26nn14–15, 68, 69, 227
Howe, Irving, 83
Howells, William Dean, 166
humility, 194, 195
Hunt, Morton, 240n1
Husserl, Edmund, 171
Huxley, Julian, 229
Huxley, T. H., 258

Hyman, Herbert, 82

ideal types, 15, 40
Idea of Social Structure, The: Papers in Honor of Robert K. Merton, 96
ideas: history of, 20, 21, 273–74, 289–90; Merton attraction to, 20, 263–64, 273–74, 282, 291n5; social determination of, 117. *See also* knowledge
ideology, 234, 246n28; and propaganda, 232–33; scientific ethos as, 150, 151, 157
Ideology and Utopia (Mannheim), 169, 172, 176, 177, 179
ignorance. *See* specified ignorance
immigrants and immigration: and remittances, 102–3; and sociological ambivalence, 86; and specified ignorance, 42; and unanticipated consequences, 46–47
inequality, 63, 98, 144; mechanism-centered analysis of, 57–60
influentials, 227, 255
informal economy, 43–45
In Search of Paul: How Jesus' Apostle Opposed Rome's Empire with God's Kingdom (Crossan and Reed), 300
institutional governance, 199, 202–3
institutions: in civil society, 198–99; as concept, 34–35; ethos of, 186; importance of, 197; and institutional controls, 107, 183; and institutional imperatives, 87, 141, 152, 155, 156, 186, 189, 191–92, 195, 197; science as institution, 2, 23, 128, 131, 142, 160n13, 197
International Library of Sociology and Social Reconstruction, 178
intimate relations, 102–3
Introduction to the History of Science (Sarton), 236

in vitro fertilization, 134
Iraq war, 47, 86
irony, 95, 246n32; Merton use of, 231, 235, 245n22, 246n32
Isaiah of Trani, 237
Isis, 177

Jacula Prudentum (Herbert), 236
James, Henry, 166
James, William, 10–11, 37
Jasso, Guillermina, 85
Jefferson, Thomas, 205
Jensen, Arthur, 144
Jews: epithets against, 244n17; and inequality, 98–99; "Jewish science," 87, 224; Merton's Jewish background, 3, 6, 167, 215, 239, 240–41n1; persecution by Nazis of, 87, 194. *See also* anti-Semitism
John of Salisbury, 236, 246n30
Johnson, Hiram, 242n8
Johnston, James F. W., 259, 268n17
Jones, Robert Alun, 276–77
Journal of Classical Sociology, 28n27
Journal of Liberal Religion, The, 175
Journal of Political Economy, 25n6
justice theory, 85

Kahneman, Daniel, 46
Kalleberg, Arne, 88
Kalleberg, Ragnvald, 23, 182–208, 298
Kapital, Das (Marx), 178
Katz, Jack, 64, 68, 74n2
Kendall, Patricia, 7, 230
Kepler, Johannes, 27n25
Kershaw, Ian, 200
Keynes, John Maynard, 179
knowledge: production of, 9, 12, 133, 143, 151, 152, 158; and scientific autonomy and ethos, 141–44; social

knowledge (*Continued*)
  conditioning of, 150; and sociology of
  science, 122–24. *See also* ideas
Knowledge for What? (Lynd), 85
Kluckhohn, Clyde, 241n6
Kuhn, Thomas S., 119, 269n18; Merton
  on, 285, 286; and paradigms, 27n23,
  114, 143, 149

language: and dictionaries, 96, 98, 254–
  55, 260, 266n3, 277–78; of elites, 234;
  Merton's love of, 96, 216, 254–55, 277;
  and propaganda, 226; and under-
  standing, 207n4, 215; of war, 120,
  136n2. *See also* rhetoric; sociological
  semantics; word definition and
  origin; words and phrases
Language of Social Research, The
  (Lazarsfeld and Rosenberg), 70
Laplace, Pierre-Simon, 43
Lask, Emil, 171
Laski, Harold, 233, 245n26
Lasswell, Harold, 230
Latour, Bruno, 160n12, 291–92n6
Lazarsfeld, Paul, 19, 239; constructivism
  of, 69–70; criticized by Coleman,
  75n7; left-wing views of, 24–25n1; as
  Merton collaborator, 2, 6–7, 9, 172,
  226–27, 228; Merton disagreements
  with, 27n18, 27n21; methodological
  approach of, 70–71, 73; retirement and
  death, 21; works: *The Language of
  Social Research,* 70; *Mass Persuasion: the
  Social Psychology of a War Bond Drive,*
  8, 26n16, 69, 216, 228–29, 232, 281, 283;
  "Patterns of Influence: A Study of
  Interpersonal Influence and Communications Behavior in a Local Community," 26n16; *Personal Influence,* 68
Levine, Donald, 96, 171

Lévi-Strauss, Claude, 119
Lieberson, Stanley, 268n10
life insurance, 101–2
Lincoln, Abraham, 199, 208n9
Lindblom, Charles, 193, 205
Lipset, Seymour Martin, 19, 68–69
Louis XIV, 49
Lubbock, John, 258
luck, doctrine of, 98
Lukács, György, 171, 179
Lund, Frederick, 222
Lundberg, George, 224
Lynd, Robert, 6–7, 24–25n1, 85, 229

Machiavelli, Niccolò, 96, 273
MacIver, Robert, 7, 38
MacKenzie, Donald, 129, 256, 267n5;
  on economic performativity, 103–5,
  107, 108, 109n6, 109n9, 130, 131
*Managed Heart: the Commercialization
  of Human Feeling, The* (Hochschild),
  200
Manheim, Ernest, 171
Mannheim, Karl: biographical
  information, 171–72, 175; Merton's
  attacks on, 165, 172–74, 175–76,
  179; similarities and differences
  with Merton, 170–72; and
  sociology of knowledge, 117,
  164; von Schelting criticisms of,
  169–70; works: "Competition as
  a Cultural Phenomenon," 177;
  "Conservative Thought," 173, 177;
  Ideology and Utopia, 169, 172, 176,
  177, 179; *Mensch und Gesellschaft im
  Zeitalter des Umbaus,* 169; "On the
  Interpretation of *Weltanschauung,*"
  177; "The Problem of a Sociology of
  Knowledge," 177; "The Problem of
  Generations," 177

markets: market economies, 106–8, 134, 198; theory of, 129–31, 134, 256

Martel, François, 246n30

Marx, Karl, and Marxism, 13, 166; on false consciousness, 82; grand theory of, 38, 41; Merton criticisms of, 38, 178–79, 214; on sociology of knowledge, 117; as structuralist, 119; and unexpected in social life, 96, 273; Weber on, 41, 167

mass communication: Merton research on, 2, 8–9, 26n16, 226–27, 230, 239; and propaganda, 218, 220–21, 226–27. *See also* propaganda

Massey, Douglas, 60

Mass Persuasion: the Social Psychology of a War Bond Drive (Merton, Fiske, Curtis), 8, 26n16, 69, 281; discussion of rhetoric in, 216, 228–29,232, 283

Masterman, Margaret, 114

Matalon, Reuben, 147

materialism, 38, 64, 74n2

Matthew Effect, 255, 285, 286

May, Mark A., 183

Mayo, Elton, 4

McCarthyism, 159n5, 208n7; Merton and, 8, 25n1, 233, 245n27

McKenzie, Donald, 267n5

McKeon, Richard, 221, 242n6

McLuhan, Marshall, 221, 239, 242n6

Mead, George Herbert, 80, 166, 205, 208n8

Meaning of Meaning (Richards and Ogden), 241n6

means-end paradigm, 45, 46

mechanism-process accounts, 56–57, 60

mechanisms. *See* social mechanisms

medical genetics, 146–48, 154, 160n7

Menjívar, Cecilia, 103

Mensch und Gesellschaft im Zeitalter des Umbaus (Mannheim), 169

Merton, Robert C. (son), 104, 105–6, 130, 165, 267n5

Merton, Robert K.: "ahistorical" perspective of, 274, 275, 276–77, 281, 288; attraction to ideas, 20, 263–64, 273–74, 282, 291n5; childhood and youth, 3, 240–41n1; coins commonly used terms, 2, 12, 22, 32, 35, 36, 94, 140–41, 216, 255; at Columbia, 6–7, 9, 10, 13, 203, 226, 232; on crime and deviance, 63, 64; as cultural historian and sociologist, 86–87, 96; on democracy and dictatorship, 204; dictionary study by, 96, 98, 254–55, 260, 266n3, 277–78; distaste for polemics, 90, 237; eclipse of during 1960s, 13, 18, 21, 89; as editor, 5, 216; and European sociology, 5, 165–66, 167; as graduate student, 2, 5, 9; at Harvard, 4, 25–26n6, 174, 175, 241n6; on history of sociology, 279–80; on ideas, 273–74, 291n5; influenced by Durkheim, 5, 79–80, 166, 167, 176; influenced by Sarton, 4; influenced by Thomas, 10, 80; influenced by Weber, 5, 15, 32–33, 49, 80, 166; influence on sociology of, 1, 2, 6, 7, 12–17, 21, 24, 165, 166; as ironist, 231, 235, 245n22, 246n32; Jewish roots, 3, 6, 167, 215, 239, 240–41n1; knowledge of foreign languages, 22, 171, 223–24, 243n12; on Kuhn, 285, 286; legacy, 1–24, 35, 49, 64, 107; love of language and words, 96, 216, 254–55, 277; on Marx and Engels, 178–79; as mentor and model, 1, 19, 94; name change of, 3–4, 6, 83; neglect and underappreciation of,

Merton, Robert K. (*Continued*)
3, 12, 14, 24, 79, 89, 90, 90n1;
obliteration by incorporation of,
3, 10, 12–13, 90; political views of,
20, 24–25n1, 183, 203, 227, 232; on
propaganda, 224, 228, 229; prose
style, 1, 5–6, 215–16, 222; as public
intellectual, 187, 203; pungency of,
179, 214–15; reconstructive approach
of, 185–86; on reference group theory,
11; and research, 2, 33, 68, 281; and
rhetorical tradition, 217, 218, 222–23,
241n2; right-wing attacks on, 171;
and Robert C. Merton (son), 105,
165; scholarship qualities of, 1, 9,
24, 82, 165, 166, 255; on science
and knowledge, 141; on scientific
discoveries, 267n7; on scientific
ethos, 23, 202–3, 243n14; on self-
fulfilling prophecy, 190–91; on social
mechanisms, 57; on society and
human behavior, 14–15; on sociology
of knowledge, 172–74; on sociology
of science, 23; on specified ignorance,
43; stereotyped as "functionalist,"
89–90; on structural analysis, 118–19,
135; as teacher, 19, 94, 230–31, 232;
at Temple College, 4, 167, 171;
on theory and research, 14–15, 33,
68; trip to Austria and Germany,
223–24; at Tulane, 6, 174–75, 225,
230, 232, 242n8; on unanticipated
consequences, 95; unpublished
papers, 24, 54–55, 216, 227, 268n11,
279–80, 281; on words and rhetoric,
225, 254, 256, 267n8, 282–83
Merton, Robert K. — works:
"Bureaucratic Structure and
Personality," 10, 26n13, 254; Charles
Horner Haskins 1994 lecture, 25n3,
215; "Civilization and Culture," 5;
Contemporary Social Problems, 27n19,
66; "Continuities in the Theory of
Social Structure and Anomie," 57;
"The Course of Arabian Intellectual
Development, 700-1300 A.D.", 5;
"De-Gendering 'Man of Science'",
278; "Fluctuations in the Rate
of Industrial Invention," 5; "Karl
Mannheim and the Sociology of
Knowledge," 172, 179, 246n28; "The
Kelvin Dictum," 278–79; "Manifest
and Latent Functions," 27n23; *Mass
Persuasion: the Social Psychology of a
War Bond Drive,* 8, 26n16, 69, 216,
228–29, 232, 281, 283; "Multiple
Discoveries as Strategic Research
Site," 28n26; "The Normative
Structure of Science," 87; "On
Sociological Theories of the Middle
Range," 67–68, 73; *On the Shoulders
of Giants,* 21, 22, 124–25, 202, 218,
233, 234–39, 246n30, 246n31, 278,
281, 284, 287, 289; "Opportunity
Structure," 278; "The Origin of
the Term Pseudo-Gemeinschaft,"
278; "Patterns of Influence: A
Study of Interpersonal Influence
and Communications Behavior
in a Local Community," 26n16;
*Science, Technology and Society in
Seventeenth Century England,* 5, 131,
143–44, 222–23, 281; "Science and
Democratic Social Structure," 182–83,
184, 186, 189, 207n1; "Science and
Military Technique," 5; "Science
and the Social Order," 86–87, 183,
224; "The Self-Fulfilling Prophecy,"
57, 98, 107, 190, 203–4, 231; "Social
Conflict over Styles of Sociological

Work," 238; "Social Policy and Social Research on Housing," 26n14; *Social Science Quotations,* 257, 278; "Social Structure and Anomie," 10, 27n23, 32, 35, 57, 63, 67, 84, 114; *On Social Structure and Science,* 184; *Social Theory and Social Structure,* 9, 10, 25n4, 27n17, 36, 37–38, 87, 96, 172–74, 175, 178, 184, 228, 274, 275, 289; "Social Time: A Methodological and Functional Analysis," 88; *Sociological Ambivalence,* 86, 87, 121; *The Sociology of Science,* 28, 113, 184, 278; "Studies in Radio and Film Propaganda," 172; "The Sociology of Knowledge and Mass Communications," 172–74, 177, 243–44n15; "The Thomas Theorem and the Matthew Effect," 80, 89, 91n4, 278; "Three Fragments From a Sociologist's Notebook," 33; *The Travels and Adventures of Serendipity,* 21, 54, 79, 81, 95, 99, 253–54, 256, 267n8, 278, 281, 286–87; "The Unintended Consequences of Purposive Social Action," 5, 9, 46, 94–95, 97
Metalogicon (John of Salisbury), 236
Methodology of the Social Sciences (Weber), 43
Miami Children's Hospital (MCH), 147
microenvironments, 54, 135, 287–88
middle-range theories: as empiricist-positivist notion, 73; as fusion of theory and research, 68; mechanisms of, 54–55, 60; Merton notion of, 13, 15–16, 18, 20, 33, 39–41, 60, 227, 231–32
Mill, J. S., 274
Millo, Yuval, 104
Mills, C. Wright, 179, 205, 239, 240; attacks sociology's ties to power

structure, 18–19, 20, 21, 27n21, 238; Merton sponsors at Columbia, 13, 27n21; offends Merton, 18–19, 20, 27n21, 215; *The Sociological Imagination,* 27n21, 238, 247n36
Milton, John, 267n4
The Mind Has No Sex? (Schiebinger), 268n15
Mitroff, Ian, 143
modernity, 127, 199, 236
Montagu, Montague Francis Ashley, 6
Montaigne, Michel de, 166, 202
Moody, James, 123–24
Moore, Kelly, 158
Moore, Wilbert, 42
moral alchemy, 190, 191, 245n23
"moral hazard" syndrome, 47
Mulkay, Michael, 150, 153, 160n13
Muller, Johannes, 274
Mumford, Lewis, 229
Muniesa, Fabian, 109n6
Myrdal, Gunnar, 201
"Myth of Social Class and Criminality, The" (Tittle, Villimez, and Smith), 64

names: children's, 268n10; and culture theory, 82–83
narcotizing dysfunction, 227, 232, 239
Nazi Germany, 176, 225; Merton study of, 223–24; persecution of Jews in, 87, 194; science in, 6, 142, 183, 192, 207–8n7, 224, 243n12; universities in, 192, 194
Neckam, Alexander, 246n30
neoliberalism, 107–8
neologisms, 256, 267n9, 279–80, 282
New Deal, 8
New Orleans, La., 175
Newton, Isaac, 27n25; and "on the shoulders of giants" aphorism, 22, 136n3, 234, 236, 246n30

Nietzsche, Friedrich, 166, 178
Nisbet, Robert A., 27n19
Nixon, Richard, 245n27
nominalism, 129
norms: ambivalence in, 123; communalism as, 125, 146–47, 148, 154, 156, 234; and counter-norms, 96, 143; and democratic ethos, 193, 194–95, 198–99; and everyday life, 189; and rationality, 187–88; scientific, 23, 87, 96, 143, 149, 189, 191, 193, 195; social conflict over, 117; in social sciences, 187–88; time, 88; universalism as, 87
North, Douglass, 34
Norway, 200, 201, 206

Oakes, Guy, 171
obliteration by incorporation, 3, 10, 12–13, 90, 235, 285
Ockenden, R. E., 234
Office of Radio Research, 237
Ohlin, Lloyd, 66
On Christian Doctrine (Augustine), 220
Ong, Walter, 241n5
On Rhetoric (Aristotle), 216, 219
On the Connexion of the Physical Sciences (Somerville), 262
On the Shoulders of Giants (Merton), 21, 124–25, 202, 218, 233, 234, 246n31, 289; Coser and Crothers on, 278; history of book's writing, 233, 234, 278; as rhetorical and intellectual history, 22, 218, 233, 234, 281, 287; source of aphorism in title, 22, 233–38, 239, 246n30, 284, 289
opinion formation, 2, 191, 193, 198
opportunity hoarding, 58, 59–60
opportunity structure, 2, 63, 122, 187, 226, 287, 288; and cultural theory, 84; diffusion of theory, 13, 285, 286

option-pricing formula, Black-Scholes-Merton, 104–6, 109n9, 130
oral publication, 268n12, 285, 287
originality, 194, 195
orthodoxies: Merton avoidance of, 14, 38
Oxford English Dictionary, The, 255, 263, 267n4

Panofsky, Aaron, 11–12, 140–61, 298
paradigms: cost-benefit, 45–46, 187; and deviant social behavior, 27n23; for functional analysis, 115, 118, 119; functions and dysfunctions of, 15, 116–17; as historical invention, 120, 135; list of contents of, 115–16; means-end, 45–46; Merton's conception of, 2, 20, 27n23, 114, 207n2; plurality of, 117, 119, 136; self-fulfilling prophecy as, 114; in sociology, 15, 20; for sociology of knowledge, 110, 115, 117–18, 121, 179, 208n11; for sociology of science, 113–14, 116, 119, 120–22, 135–36; for structural analysis, 115, 118–19, 121, 135
Pareto, Vilfredo, 4, 96, 167, 179, 273
Parsons, Talcott, 10, 19, 25–26nn6–7, 289; European influence on, 1–2, 165; Merton's differences with, 4, 18, 27n22, 165; and Pareto cult, 4, 167; sociological approach of, 16–17; structural-functionalism of, 14, 18, 38, 119; on von Schelting's study of Weber, 169, 178; works: The American University, 204–5, 206; The Social System, 121–22; The Structure of Social Action, 10
Parsons's Sociological Group, 223, 243n11
particularism, 142, 143, 189, 193
Pasteur, Louis, 81

patient advocacy, 146–48, 155, 158, 159n4, 160n8

Perelman, Chaim, 221

performativity, 255–56; in economics, 103–6, 109n6, 109n9, 130

Pericles, 196

Permanence and Change (Burke), 223, 232, 241–42n6

Personal Influence (Katz and Lazarsfeld), 68

Peter of Blois, 246n30

Phaedrus (Plato), 216, 227

Philosophy of Rhetoric, The (Richards), 215

Philosophy of the Inductive Sciences (Whewell), 259

physicists, 261

"Physics and Finance" (MacKenzie), 105

Piazzi, Giuseppe, 274

Pierce, C. S., 257

Plato, 166, 207n3, 207n6, 237–38; *Gorgias,* 216, 219; *Phaedrus,* 216, 227; and rhetorical tradition, 216, 218–19, 220, 227, 229, 230

Platt, Gerald M., 204–5, 206

political correctness, 14

Portes, Alejandro, 15, 32–49, 94, 99, 106, 298; "The Hidden Abode: Sociology of the Unexpected," 100

positivism, 68, 73, 75n12

Posner, Richard, 88

postmodernism, 33–34

Poulain de la Barre, François, 268n15

Pound, Ezra, 166

poverty, 39, 43–44, 71

pragmatism, 205

Principles of Literary Criticism (Richards), 215

Project on Human Development in Chicago Neighborhoods, 73

propaganda: and ideology, 232–33; and language, 225–26; and mass communication, 218, 220–21, 226–27; Merton definition of, 228, 242n7; Merton study of, 222, 223–24, 230–31, 243n11; Nazi, 224; persuasion techniques in, 219, 220, 229; and rhetoric, 216, 221, 228–29; and social psychology, 225, 227–28; uses of, 231; during World War II, 69, 225–26, 228–29, 231

propensity accounts, 55–56

Protestant Ethic and the Spirit of Capitalism, The (Weber), 47, 80

Protestantism, 5, 47, 80

pseudofacts, 33, 282

pseudo-*Gemeinschaft,* 227, 232, 245n24

Public and Its Problems, The (Dewey), 205

public image, 227, 232

public opinion, 198, 222, 242n7, 244n15

punishment, sociology of, 74n4

Purchase of Intimacy, The (Zelizer), 102

Puritanism, 5, 80, 144, 222–23

PXE: advocacy group, 147–48, 152, 153, 155, 160n7; disease, 160n7

Quetelet, Adolphe, 274

Rabinow, Paul, 157

racial prejudice and discrimination: Merton work on, 6, 8, 20, 26n15, 114, 190–91, 232; and self-fulfilling prophecy, 57, 98–99, 190–91, 231, 245n23

Rahv, Philip, 83

rational choice theory, 45–47, 81, 187

rationality: as concept, 187–88, 191, 193; as cultural value, 99; and human fallibility, 192; SSK critique of, 150; and unanticipated consequences, 95

Raudenbush, Stephen, 72

Rawls, Anne Warfield, 187–88

Rayleigh, Lord, 258

realism, 129, 208n8; of Merton, 73, 75n9

reality: and construction, 128–29; cultural definitions of, 80; and illusory, 178; and self-fulfilling prophecy, 106, 107; social, 39, 47, 191; and theory, 41, 130–31, 172–73

reasons and reasoning: deductive and inductive, 38, 41; economic, 46, 130; in everyday life, 189–90; formation and testing of, 191; norm of universalism in, 193; and rationality, 191

reconstructive approach, 185–86, 207n3, 288, 292n8

Reed, Jonathan L., 200

reference group theory, 10–11, 82, 85

reification, 41, 160n11

religion, 87, 101–2, 132, 222; Protestantism, 5, 47, 80; and science, 2, 5, 80, 131, 132, 156, 194

research: as academic task, 199, 202–3; basic and applied, 8, 21, 64–66, 67, 73; community, 70–71, 72–73; and contradiction, 135; heroic amateurs in, 27–28n25; impact of private ownership on, 147; medical, 67, 144–48, 158; normative-empirical, 188; research groups, 17, 148, 155, 203; sociological, 5, 18, 65, 72, 116, 121, 133, 148; and theory, 2, 14, 16, 18, 19, 64–65, 67–68, 70, 73. See also empirical research

Reskin, Barbara, 60

Reuter, Edward, 175

rhetoric: Aristotle on, 216, 219, 227, 228, 229, 236; categories of, 220; contemporary studies of, 221; definition of in antiquity, 217, 218–19; and dialectic, 219, 225,

226, 243–44n15; digression in, 235; and epithets, 214, 215, 231, 245n23; imitation in, 235; intellectual tradition of, 219–20; Merton study of, 23, 215, 216, 222, 225, 240; and modern technology, 220–21; and persuasion, 227; and propaganda, 216, 221, 228–29; Puritan, 222–23; and science, 214, 216, 218, 240; and sociology, 217–18, 235; sociology of, 217, 221, 226, 227, 228, 230, 233–34. See also language; sociological semantics; words and expressions

Richards, I. A., 215, 218, 221

Rickert, Heinrich, 171

Riesman, David, 240

role model, 2, 3, 203

role sets, 13, 186; academic, 187, 199–204, 206; of scientists, 202–3; tensions and conflicts in, 85, 196–97

Rorty, Richard, 217

Rosenberg, Alexander, 133–34

Rossi, Alice, 19, 82

Rossi, Peter, 9, 68–69

Russell, Bertrand, 179

Rust, Bernhard, 243n12

Sampson, Robert, 11, 63–75, 298–99

Sarton, George, 4, 177, 234, 236, 246n30

Schegloff, Emanuel, 267n6

Scheler, Max, 166; and sociology of knowledge, 117, 164, 168, 177, 179

Schiappa, Edward, 219

Schiebinger, Londa, 268n15

Schneider, Louis, 95

Scholes, Myron S., 104

Schopenhauer, Arthur, 225

Schumpeter, Joseph, 4, 167

science: advancement of knowledge in, 11, 140, 141, 156, 157, 160n13;

as autonomous and embedded, 131–33; boundary-work in, 127–28, 151, 153, 154, 214; commercialization of, 133, 147, 148, 156, 158–59; conceptualizations in, 22–23; cooperation and competition in, 124–26, 152–53, 191–92; and culture, 5, 81, 123, 124, 126, 127, 189; and democracy, 183, 184–85, 192; economic science, 130; as embedded, 131, 132, 133; epistemic cultures in, 151, 160n11; generalization in, 15–16; governance and regulation, 131–32, 157, 158, 189, 191; hostility to, 73, 75n12, 142, 159n1; idea of progress in, 246n30; and ideology, 150, 151, 157; ignorance as function in, 42–43; innovation in, 2, 24, 27n25, 32, 35, 37, 108n4, 260–61; as institution, 2, 128, 131, 142, 160n13, 197; institutional imperatives in, 87, 141, 152, 155, 156, 189, 191–92, 197; "Jewish," 87, 224; and legitimacy, 123, 127, 131, 132, 133, 155; motivations of scientists, 20, 149–50, 223, 242–43n10; Nazi, 6, 142, 183, 192, 207–8n7, 224, 243n12; and nonscience, 150–51, 258; "normal," 73, 75n10; and politics, 20, 23, 126, 132, 152, 157, 183, 197, 207–8n7; "pure," 10, 142; and religion, 2, 5, 80, 131, 132, 156, 194; reward and recognition system in, 123, 124, 125, 131, 153, 156, 161n14; and rhetoric, 214, 216, 219, 240; role sets in, 202–3; scientific replication, 160n10; social character of, 2, 5, 23, 87, 123–24, 149, 154–55, 191, 206; and social conflict, 152, 156–57; specialization in, 17, 258, 269n21; and technology, 8, 184, 260–61; and totalitarianism, 183, 184, 207–8n7; unity of, 258, 268n16; and universalism, 133–35, 142, 189, 193, 194; women in, 258, 262–63. *See also* research; sociology of science

scientific autonomy: and advocacy groups, 147–48, 158; and behavior genetics, 146, 159; and commercialization, 158; and embeddedness, 131–33; and political advocacy, 20–21, 23, 158; from political and vested interests, 20, 23, 132, 183, 197, 207–8n7; and scientific ethos, 141–44, 150, 152–53, 154–55; SSK and, 150, 151, 154, 160n12

scientific discoveries: multiple, 152, 160n10, 285; and prediscoveries, 256, 267n7; priority claims of, 235; as public good, 32, 37; role of serendipity in, 22, 54, 81

scientific ethos: of communalism, 125, 146–47, 148, 154, 156, 234; and democratic ethos, 183, 184–85; as ideology, 150, 151; as incompatible with secrecy, 143, 197; Merton commitment to, 5, 11, 87, 140–41, 186, 224, 233; organized skepticism in, 80, 87, 146, 155, 186, 189, 191–92, 202; and scientific autonomy, 141–44, 150, 152–53, 154–55; and scientific misconduct, 188; and scientific norms, 23, 87, 96, 143, 149, 189, 191, 193, 195; and social conflict, 156–57; sociological debate over, 148–54; value-neutrality in, 118, 183, 190

scientist: as gender-free word, 91n4, 262–63, 268n15; origin of word, 257–63, 284

secrecy, 143, 197

Seductions of Crime (Katz), 64, 74n2

self-fulfilling prophecy, 10, 188, 227; becomes commonplace expression,

self-fulfilling prophecy (*Continued*)
2, 32, 36, 255; in economic
performativity, 104–6, 109n9; and
false definitions, 107, 190, 231; and
financial debacle of 2008, 107–8;
implications for social life, 203–4;
and institutional controls, 107;
as middle-range concept, 231; as
paradigm, 114; and racial and ethnic
prejudice, 57, 98–99, 190–91, 231,
245n23; suicidal, 108;and uncertainty, 97
Sen, Amartya, 187–88
Seneca, 273
serendipity: as causal mechanism, 54; and
culture, 99; definitions of word, 98,
266n2, 284, 289; elements of, 97, 99; in
scientific discoveries, 22, 54, 81; social
character of, 54–55. *See also Travels and
Adventures of Serendipity, The*
Shakespeare, William, 178
Shapin, Steven, 160n12
Shils, Edward, 171–72, 176–77
Shorett, Peter, 157
Short, J. F., 66
Sica, Alan, 5, 24, 164–80, 214, 299
Sills, David, 278
Simmel, Georg, 166
Simonson, Peter, 21, 23, 214–47, 299
Simpson, George, 25n5
Simpson, George E., 4, 25n5, 171, 225
Siu, Lucia, 109n6
skepticism, organized, 43, 80, 286; and
autonomy, 158; and democratic ethos,
194, 195, 202; and scientific ethos,
80, 87, 146, 155, 186, 189, 191–92,
202; socially organized, 285, 297;
undermining of, 145, 146, 152, 154,
156, 159
slogans, 253, 256, 263, 282; political, 286;
popular, 278, 283

Small, Albion, 164, 167–68, 178, 179
Smith, Adam, 96, 208n8, 273
Smith, Kate, 228–29, 232, 243n11, 245n24
Smith, R. S., 91
social anthropology, 27n22, 118
social capital, 3, 34, 44, 83
social causation, 73
social conflict, 13; and science, 152,
156–57
social control, 34, 72, 74n2, 144, 204,
244n17
Social Forces, 4
social groups: as factor in social life, 168;
in-groups and out-groups, 57, 98–99,
190–91; as transmitter of ideas, 80.
See also class; collectivity
socialization, 71, 81, 82
social mechanisms, 16; community-level,
65; and middle range theories, 13, 54–
55, 60; self-fulfilling prophecies and,
57; serendipity as, 54; social scientists
and, 55–56
social movements: in civil society, 198;
Merton involvement in, 203; during
1960s, 13, 21, 89; and science, 133, 158
social psychology, 12, 290; and
propaganda, 225, 227–28; and social
structure, 6, 26n14
social roles: ambivalence in, 84–85, 121,
132; depictive portraits of, 86; and
expectations, 121; hierarchies, 21; of
scientists, 131; and status, 65, 83–84,
127, 144, 242n9; and time norms, 88
social sciences: antipathy toward theory
in, 173; media-related studies in,
221; normative issues in, 187–88;
and opinion formation, 187, 188;
organized skepticism in, 80; social-
institutional analysis in, 12; and
social mechanisms, 55–56, 57, 60;

and social policy, 20, 106, 107;
specified ignorance in, 43. *See also*
science; sociology
Social System, The (Parsons), 121–22
Social Theory and Social Structure
(Merton), 10, 25n4, 36, 37–38, 96,
228, 274, 289; aim of, 9; editions
of, 27n17, 87, 184, 246n31, 275; on
Mannheim and *Wissenssoziologie*,
172–74, 175, 178
Sociological Imagination, The (Mills),
27n21, 238, 247n36
sociological semantics: bibliography of
Merton's works on, 257, 264–66,
268n11, 278; and conversational
analysis, 267n6; and "culturally
strategic words," 280; Merton
interest in, 21, 22–23, 217, 253–54,
255; Merton research program on,
218, 253–54, 263–64, 278–84, 286–87,
289–90; objectives of, 256–57; "on
the shoulder of giants" aphorism,
22, 233–38, 239, 246n30, 284, 289;
as sociology of rhetoric, 233–34; and
speech act theory, 207n4, 255; and
systematics of sociological theory,
289–91. *See also* rhetoric; word
definition and origin; words and
expressions
sociology: analytic, 65, 70, 74n6; angle
of vision in, 80, 81; antiscience critics
within, 73, 75n12; applied research
in, 8, 9, 10, 20, 21, 24, 65–66, 67,
167; assertions of "crisis" in, 118–19;
Chicago School of, 9, 10, 74n2, 164,
168; Columbia School of, 19–20, 67–
70, 75n7, 227; and constructivism,
69–70, 126, 141, 157, 158; cultural,
79, 81, 86, 90n1, 226; dominance of
structural-functionalist school in,

38–39; and grand theories, 14, 32–33,
38–39, 40, 41, 49; growth of as field,
7, 8; history of, 11, 275, 279–80,
289–90; integrative approach to,
21; Merton on sociological project,
14–15; Merton's influence on, 1, 2,
6, 7, 12–17, 21, 24, 165, 166; during
1960s, 7, 18, 20–21, 89; origin of
word, 261, 269n19; paradigms in, 15;
polemics and debates in, 10, 63–64,
80, 148–54, 238; professionalization
of, 7, 9, 21, 217; public, 20–21, 205;
of punishment, 74n4; on real and
rational, 95, 128–29; recognition
and legitimacy of, 7, 8, 19, 26n12;
reconstructive approach in, 185,
207n3; research techniques in, 17–18;
and rhetoric, 217–18, 235; right-wing
attacks on, 8; as science, 15, 134, 214;
self-evident concepts of, 35–36, 37,
94; of social roles, 86, 88; statistical
analysis in, 14, 55; structural, 72;
study of crime in, 65, 67; subfields,
3, 10, 11, 16, 17, 49; teaching of, 14;
theoretical, 14, 19, 95; theory-research
relationship in, 10, 16, 17–18, 19, 20,
67–68; and uncertainty, 96–97, 101;
urban, 70–71, 72–73. *See also* social
sciences
sociology of knowledge, 114, 141, 214;
paradigm for, 110, 115, 117–18, 121,
179, 208n11; and rhetoric, 244n15;
Wissenssoziologie transformed into,
175, 176, 180. *See also* knowledge;
Wissenssoziologie
sociology of rhetoric, 217, 221, 226,
227, 230; eight qualities of, 228;
sociological semantics as, 233–34
sociology of science, 12, 16, 23, 24,
28n27, 122, 129, 233; debate over

sociology of science (*Continued*)
direction of, 149–50; paradigm for,
113–14, 116, 119, 120–22, 135–36. *See
also* science
sociology of scientific knowledge (SSK),
122, 149–50, 153, 154, 160–61n13
Socrates, 219, 227
Solow, Robert M., 263
Somerville, Mary, 259, 262, 269n20
Sorokin, Pitirim, 96, 165, 179, 273;
attacks Marxism, 38; *Fads and Foibles
in Modern Sociology,* 247n36; and
Mannheim, 164, 176; and Merton,
4, 25–26nn5–6, 88, 166, 267n4; and
sociology of knowledge, 117, 164, 177
specified ignorance, 32, 41–45
speech act theory, 207n4, 255
Speier, Hans, 164, 169, 171
Spencer, Herbert, 38
Spengler, Oswald, 167
stage models, 55, 56
status conferral function, 227
Steele, Claude, 42
Stehr, Nico, 152, 184
stem cell research, 67
Stensen, Niels, 274
Stern, Fritz, 208n7
Sterne, Laurence, 3, 202, 235
Stinchcombe, Arthur L., 282
Storer, Norman, 28n27, 184
strain theory, 64, 67, 73
strategic research sites, 17, 28n26, 269n22
structural analysis, 114, 122; paradigm
for, 115, 118–19, 121, 135
structural-functionalism, 14, 27n22,
38–39, 125. *See also* functionalism
*Structural Transformation of the Public
Sphere* (Habermas), 239
Structure of Scientific Revolutions, The
(Kuhn), 27n23, 269n18

Structure of Social Action, The (Parsons), 10
student-mentor ambivalence, 285
Suicide (Durkheim), 65, 79
Sumner, William Graham, 38
Supreme Court, 20, 26n15, 201, 208n10
Sutherland, Edwin, 66
systematics of sociological theory, 275–77;
and sociological semantics, 289–91;
systematics and history, 275, 280
Sztompka, Piotr, 17, 27n24, 197, 278–79

Tabboni, Simonetta, 89
Temple College, 4, 167, 171
Terry, Sharon and Patrick, 147–48
theory: action-based, 74n6; American
antipathy toward, 173; grand systems
of, 32–33, 38–40, 41, 45–46, 49; and
method, 64–65, 70, 73; and reality,
41, 130–31, 172–73; and research, 2,
14, 16, 18, 19, 64–65, 67–68, 70, 73;
systematics of, 275; and "system of
thought," 17; and universal laws, 32,
39–40
Thomas, Dorothy Swaine, 91
Thomas, W. I., 10–11, 290; and
authorship of Thomas Theorem,
91n4; influence on Merton, 10, 80
Thomas Theorem, 10, 36, 80, 285, 286,
288; authorship of, 91n4
Tilly, Charles, 47–49, 54–60, 99–100,
299
time: cultural aspects of, 88–89; socially
expected durations, 284
Tocqueville, Alexis de, 207n3, 229
Tonnies, Ferdinand, 38
Torrents of Spring, The (Hemingway), 166
*Transactions of the New York Academy of
Sciences,* 172
Travels and Adventures of Serendipity, The
(Merton and Barber), 54, 79, 81, 95,

99, 256, 267n8, 286–87; history of, 253–54, 278; as intellectual-historical work, 21, 281

Tristram Shandy (Sterne), 3, 22, 202, 235

Tulane University, 6, 174–75, 225, 230, 232, 242n8

Tumin, Melville, 42

Tverski, Amos, 46

Twentieth Century Sociology (Gurvitch and Moore), 172

Über Declamation als Wissenschaft, 227

unanticipated consequences, 32, 33, 97; becomes commonplace expression, 2, 94, 255; in economics and market, 106–8; examples of, 47–49, 106–8; following in Merton's footsteps on, 23, 99–100, 108n4; intellectual precursors of, 96, 241n2, 273–74; and means-end paradigm, 46–47; of words, 261–62

uncertainty: and economics, 100–101; and immigrant remittances, 102–3; and intimate relations, 102; and life insurance, 101–2; sociology of, 96–97; structured, 99

Union Democracy (Lipset), 68

universalism: and democratic ethos, 186, 192, 194, 195; and discrimination, 188, 194; Merton concept of, 193; as norm, 87; and science, 133–35, 142, 189, 194

universities: functions of, 204–5, 206; growth of during 1950s and '60s, 7; and Humboldt tradition, 205–6; in Nazi Germany, 192, 194

Veblen, Thorstein, 241n6

Vico, Giambattista, 273

Vienna Circle, 255

Vives, Juan, 237, 238

von Schelting, Alexander, 169–70, 176, 178, 179, 273

Wallas, Graham, 273

Wallerstein, Immanuel, 21

Weaver, Richard, 221

Weber, Marianne, 171

Weber, Max, 1–2, 207n3; on "charisma of rhetoric," 229; on ethos of politics, 233; and grand theories, 32–33, 39–40, 41; influence on Merton, 5, 15, 32–33, 49, 80, 166; and Marxism, 41, 165; on Protestant ethic, 5, 47, 80; reputation in U.S., 170; sociological skepticism of, 43; and unexpected, 96, 273

Webster's Dictionary, 255, 260

Whewell, William, 257, 259–60, 262, 268n15

Whitehead, Alfred North, 10, 36, 178, 291n4

Whyte, William F., 167

Williams, Raymond, 239

Wilson, William Julius, 74n2

Wirth, Louis, 172, 175, 218

Wirtschaft und Gesellschaft (Weber), 170

Wissenssoziologie: American Sociological Review on, 168–69; initial reception in U.S., 164, 167–68; Merton attacks on, 164–65, 169–70, 172–74; Merton's initial views of, 164, 169; transformed into sociology of knowledge, 175, 176, 180. *See also* Sociology of knowledge

Wittgenstein, Ludwig, 150, 255

Wolff, Kurt, 176

women: and hierarchy, 59; in science, 258, 262–63

word definition and origin: *function*, 118; *gnome*, 234, 236, 237, 246n33; *paradigm*, 114; *physicist*, 261; *rational*, 191; *rhetoric*, 218–19; *scientist*, 91n4,

word definition and origin (*Continued*)
257–63, 268n15, 284; *sensate,* 267n4;
serendipity, 98, 266n2, 284, 289;
sociology, 261, 269n19

words and expressions: acquisition of
new meanings, 286–87; as arising
from need, 258, 259–61; contexts
of creation, 258, 261; diffusion of,
284, 285, 286, 288, 289; obliteration
by incorporation of, 3, 10, 12–13,
90, 235, 285; resistance to, 258, 261,
284; sociological study of, 254, 256,
263–64, 267n4, 268n10, 277–78,
282–84, 288, 289–90; unanticipated
consequences of, 258, 261–62

work-family balance, 85
World War I, 188, 208n7
World War II, 87, 225; propaganda
during, 69, 225–26, 228–29, 231;
sociology during, 8
Wundt, Wilhelm, 273

Zedekiah ben Abraham "Anav," 237
Zelizer, Viviana A., 19, 20, 86, 94–109,
299
Zerubavel, Eviatar, 79
Zuckerman, Harriet, 19, 21, 22–23,
136n1, 143, 149, 217, 253–69, 299–
300; as Merton collaborator, 89,
235, 253